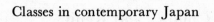

Classes in contemporary Japan

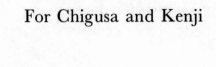

For Chigusa and Kenji

Classes in contemporary Japan

ROB STEVEN

*Senior Lecturer in Political Science
at the University of Canterbury
Christchurch, New Zealand*

CAMBRIDGE UNIVERSITY PRESS

CAMBRIDGE

LONDON   NEW YORK   NEW ROCHELLE
MELBOURNE   SYDNEY

Published by the Press Syndicate of the University of Cambridge
The Pitt Building, Trumpington Street, Cambridge CB2 1RP
32 East 57th Street, New York, NY 10022, USA
296 Beaconsfield Parade, Middle Park, Melbourne 3206, Australia

First published 1983

Printed in Great Britain at the
University Press, Cambridge

Library of Congress catalogue card number: 82-17766

British Library cataloguing in publication data
Steven, Rob
Classes in contemporary Japan.
1. Social class – Japan
I. Title
305.5'0952   HN723.5
ISBN 0 521 24779 9 hard covers

Contents

List of figures		*page*	vi
List of tables			vii
Preface and acknowledgements			xv
Introduction			1
1	The bourgeoisie		12
2	The petty bourgeoisie		62
3	The peasantry		91
4	The middle class		122
5	The working class		155
6	Crisis and the state: accumulation functions		215
7	Crisis and the state: functions of social control		266
8	Conclusion		317
	Notes		330
	Select bibliography		344
	Index		355

Figures

2.1 Annual net profits of unincorporated firms (averages for manu-   *page* 84
facturing, services, and wholesale and retail) and incomes of
employees, by age and by size of establishment (persons engaged),
1980

5.1 Monthly payment by sex, education, age, and firm size, 1980   161

Tables

1.1 Pattern of shareholding in companies quoted on the Stock   *page* 15
Exchange, 1975–80

1.2 Percentage of shares held, by type of shareholder, 1945–80   17

1.3 Numbers of shareholders, by type of shareholder, 1975–80   17

1.4 Amounts of surplus-value-earning savings (¥ million) per   18
household, by occupation of household head and annual
household income, 1979

1.5 Interests in capitalism of household heads, from ownership of   21
major surplus-value-earning assets, 1979 (1,000 persons)

1.6 Numbers of directors, by capitalisation of institutions (¥ million),   25
1980

1.7 Involvement in controlling labour power, by rank of employee   27

1.8 Percentages of persons involved in control over investment and   27
other tasks

1.9 Most important ability required of managers   28

1.10 Monthly pay of capital's functionaries: averages in June 1981   29

1.11 Estimated numbers of capital's functionaries, 1980   30

1.12 Persons engaged in unincorporated enterprises, by sex, occu-   32
pational status, and firm size, 1979 (1,000 persons)

1.13 Rates of profit by firm size (money value of capital) and industry   36
in the corporate sector, 1975 and 1980

1.14 Evidence of differential monopoly in the corporate sector: all   38
industries excepting finance, 1975 and 1980 (¥ million)

1.15 Shares of total sales in each industry of the different fractions of the   40
capitalist class (corporate sector only), 1975 and 1980

1.16 Proportions of females in small and large firms, by major industry,   42
1974–9

1.17 Dependence on sub-contracts of small manufacturing firms, 1971   43

1.18 Distribution of small manufacturing firms, by sales to three major   43
customers as a per cent of total sales, 1971

1.19 Extent of parent companies' use of sub-contracts, 1971   44

1.20 Proportions of child companies which receive 'guidance and   45
assistance' from parent companies, 1975

1.21 Proportions of small (under 300 operatives) manufacturing firms 45
which depend on their major customer for raw materials, 1971

1.22 Fractions of the economically active bourgeoisie, 1975–80 48

1.23 The financial reach of the six leading *keiretsu*, 1980 50

1.24 Corporate stockholdings of the six leading *keiretsu*: member 51
companies and ones quoted on the Stock Exchange, 1980
(includes top 20 shareholders only)

1.25 Interlocking directorships within *keiretsu* and from them to quoted 52
companies, 1980

1.26 Numbers of companies with close affiliations to the six *keiretsu* 54

1.27 The top twenty 'non-financial' *keiretsu*, 1980 56

1.28 Re-subcontracts by firm size (no. of operatives), 1975 57

1.29 The extent to which the company president/firm proprietor 60
engages in productive work in manufacturing, by firm size (no. of
operatives), 1971

2.1 Distribution of the economically active population, by industry 65
and size (no. of operatives) of enterprise, 1979

2.2 Distribution of persons in non-agricultural unincorporated en- 67
terprises with under 5 operatives, by major industry and occupational status, 1974–9 (1,000 persons and %)

2.3 Distribution of petty firms, involvement in sub-contracting, and 69
cost of entry, by minor industrial group in manufacturing

2.4 Proportions of university graduates in petty bourgeois manu- 70
facturing firms, by selected branches, 1971

2.5 Hours worked per week, by employment status, and annual 70
income, 1979 (among persons in all industries working over 200
days a year)

2.6 Profitability of unincorporated manufacturing firms, 1980 71

2.7 Distribution of self-employed persons in manufacturing, by 71
income and firm size, 1979 (1,000 persons and %)

2.8 Net profits per person in unincorporated manufacturing firms, by 73
minor industry, average number of persons engaged, and whether
or not involved in sub-contracting, 1980 (¥ million)

2.9 Distribution of persons engaged in services and manufacturing, by 74
firm size, in the private business sector, 1974–9

2.10 Distribution of unincorporated service enterprises with 1–4 75
operatives, by minor industry and the net value of total assets,
1980

2.11 Profit per person engaged in unincorporated service and whole- 76
sale and retail enterprises, 1980

2.12 Profitability of unincorporated service enterprises, 1980 76

2.13 Distribution of persons engaged in wholesale and retail, by firm 78
size, in the private business sector, 1974–9

2.14 Distribution of unincorporated wholesale and retail enterprises with 1–4 operatives, by minor industry and the net value of total assets, 1980   78

2.15 Value added per operative and profits per firm of unincorporated wholesale/retail establishments, 1980   79

2.16 Distribution of self-employed persons and family workers in food-related retail firms and personal service firms, by sex, 1979 (1,000 persons)   80

2.17 Number of unincorporated enterprises with 1–4 operatives, and average number of operatives per unincorporated enterprise   81

2.18 Distribution of small manufacturing firms in 1971, by date of establishment   82

2.19 Rates at which small firms disappeared and new ones were opened up, by major industry, in 1976–8   82

2.20 Previous occupational status of persons who entered the petty bourgeoisie in selected years, 1959–79   83

2.21 Composition of self-employed, home handicraft, and family workers, by age and sex, 1980   85

2.22 State-sponsored organisations in the manufacturing industry: proportions of firms which are members, 1971   88

2.23 Distribution of support for parliamentary parties, by major occupational groups, 1976–80 (%)   89

3.1 Home ownership and money value of homes, by type of household, 1970   94

3.2 Home ownership, by type of household and age of household head, 1970 (% with own homes)   95

3.3 Distribution of agricultural households by size of cultivated plots (hectares), 1975–80   96

3.4 Numbers of agricultural households which rent land and which lend land out, by per cent of cultivated and owned land, 1980   97

3.5 Agricultural households, by size of cultivated plot and value of annual agricultural sales, 1975 and 1980   98

3.6 Agricultural households, by size of cultivated plot and degree of dependence on agricultural production, 1975–80   100

3.7 Distribution of economically active members of agricultural households, by type of job and sex, 1975–80   101

3.8 Non-agricultural jobs of members of peasant households who are partly, mainly, or solely engaged in them, by sex, 1980   102

3.9 Changes in the status of agricultural households, 1960–80   103

3.10 Annual income (¥1,000) of agricultural households, by size of cultivated holdings (outside Hokkaido), 1974–9   104

3.11 Employment and sales of agricultural companies, 1975–80   107

3.12 Indices of agricultural production, 1969–79 (1970 = 100)   108

3.13 Numbers of households which raise dairy cattle and pigs, by the   109
numbers of head raised, 1970–5

3.14 Numbers of self-employed persons who declared taxable income   110
in 1974–9, by industry and amount of taxable income

3.15 Ratios of self-sufficiency for selected foodstuffs, 1960–77   111

3.16 Distribution of votes in the 1980 general election, by type of area   112

4.1 Technical and professional persons, by industry and sex, 1974–9   128
(1,000 persons)

4.2 Medical practitioners, by type and by employment status, 1977   129

4.3 Numbers of medical-related personnel, 1978   130

4.4 Numbers of teachers and pupils taught, by type of institution,   130
1980

4.5 Monthly earnings of teachers, by rank, August 1981 (¥1,000)   131

4.6 Monthly salaries by age and type of teacher (¥1,000), 1974   132

4.7 Distribution of teachers, by age, sex, and type of institution, 1974   133

4.8 Monthly earnings of nurses, by rank, August 1981 (¥1,000)   134

4.9 Monthly earnings of medical practitioners, by rank, August 1981   135
(¥1,000)

4.10 Pay differentials of members of managerial hierarchies, August   138
1981 (¥1,000)

4.11 Numbers of military and police personnel, 1980   139

4.12 Estimated numbers of persons in the Japanese middle class, 1980   140
(1,000 persons)

4.13 Occupational mobility and education of business leaders, 1960   142

4.14 Students' most common views on society and on the benefits of   146
university, 1976

4.15 Class consciousness in private companies, by education and by   147
rank, 1976

4.16 Class consciousness of *shunin*, by union membership, 1976   149

5.1 Monthly payment, by age, sex, education, and firm size, 1980   162
(¥1,000)

5.2 Annual bonuses and basic wages, by establishment size and sex,   164
1980 (¥1,000)

5.3 Availability of company welfare, by firm size, 1973   167

5.4 Numbers of employees, by firm size, education, and sex, 1979   170
(1,000 persons)

5.5 Summary of class membership of all employees, 1980   171

5.6 Persons who moved to new jobs the previous year in relation to   175
total employees in 1979, by size of firm left (1,000)

5.7 Total present value of pensions, by education, firm size, years of   176
service, and age when received, 1980 (¥ million)

5.8 Average number of working days and hours worked per month, by firm size, 1975–9   177

5.9 Rate of industrial accidents, by firm size (manufacturing), 1975–80   177

5.10 Strength of the ideology supporting the sexual division of labour, 1975   181

5.11 Women's wages as a percentage of men's, by age and by length of service, 1980 (and averages for 1975)   181

5.12 Average years of employment, by age and sex, 1975–80   183

5.13 Women employees, by age and marital status, 1979 (1,000 persons)   183

5.14 Persons 'wishing to work,' by age and sex, 1974 and 1979 (1,000 persons)   185

5.15 Persons 'wishing to work,' by sex, household income, and relationship to household head, 1979 (1,000 persons)   186

5.16 Movements of reserve army and mass workers, by age and sex, 1979 (1,000 persons)   187

5.17 Present place of employment and wage reductions (by size of firm employed by in 1975) of workers who retired in 1967–73 (% of total number of persons in each category)   188

5.18 Firms with uniform retirement systems, and the retirement ages in them, 1978–80   190

5.19 Employment and wages of workers who retired in 1972, 1975, and 1978   191

5.20 Summary of class membership of all employees and the working class, by main fractions and by sex, 1979 (1,000 persons)   193

5.21 Total employees, by industry (excluding directors), occupation, and sex, 1974–9 (1,000 persons)   194

5.22 Indices of labour productivity, employment, real wages, and working hours in manufacturing 1970–80 (1975 = 100)   199

5.23 Numbers of unionised workers and proportions of total employees unionised, by firm size, 1974–9   199

5.24 Trade union members, by industry and sex, 1975–80   200

5.25 Affiliations of trade unionists, by industry and major national federations, 1980   201

5.26 Class consciousness, by class position, 1976   203

5.27 Class consciousness, by class position and sex, 1976   204

5.28 Workers' class consciousness, by age and sex, 1976   206

5.29 Workers' class consciousness, by firm size, 1976   208

5.30 Forms of redundancy, by firm size, 1975 (% of firms)   210

6.1 Public investment by the Construction Ministry, 1962–73   222

6.2 Finance needed to secure energy supplies, 1966–75 and 1976–85 (¥ billion, at 1975 prices)   223

6.3   Planned diversification of total energy supplies (%)   224

6.4   Terms of trade of major capitalist powers, 1973–80 (period just   225
      before each major oil price rise = 100)

6.5   Capacity utilisation rates of nuclear reactors, 1973–80   226

6.6   Distribution of equipment investment in the electric power   228
      industry, 1977 (¥ billion and %)

6.7   Investment funds of major public corporations producing con-   230
      stant capital goods, 1977–8 (¥ 100 million)

6.8   Major economic indices during the postwar boom, 1955–71   232

6.9   Industrial origins of Net Domestic Product, 1961–75 (%)   234

6.10 Indices of land prices, 1955–77   234

6.11 Main indicators of the recession in manufacturing, 1973–8   236

6.12 Markets of Japanese overseas textile firms, 1974   238

6.13 Bankruptcies of textile firms, 1974–7   238

6.14 Employment indices in manufacturing, by firm size, 1962–74   239

6.15 Degree of dependence on imports for major raw materials,   241
      1967–77

6.16 Changing composition of Japanese trade, 1971–80 ($ million   242
      and %)

6.17 Changes in the use of computer equipment in iron and steel,   243
      1971–80

6.18 Use of capacity in major shipbuilding firms, 1974–7 and estimated   244
      use, 1978–9

6.19 Production indices of chemicals, 1965–77   245

6.20 Production and export of motor vehicles in Japan, 1960–80   246

6.21 Production of industrial robots, robot prices, and average wages,   247
      1968–79

6.22 Numbers of independent computerised systems in use, by industry,   247
      1973–9

6.23 Hourly labour productivity in manufacturing and average hourly   248
      wage costs in major capitalist countries, 1960–79 (annual per-
      centage increase)

6.24 Numbers of employees in manufacturing, by firm size, 1974–9   249
      (1,000 persons)

6.25 Bankruptcies in the construction industry, 1968–77   249

6.26 Employment and changes in building orders in construction,   250
      1973–9

6.27 The Seven Year Plan's vision of the industrial structure in 1985   252

6.28 Growth of real GNP, 1973–80   253

6.29 Changes in planned equipment investments by industry for   254
      1981–2

6.30 Main cuts in public servants planned for 1982–7   255

6.31 Direct overseas investments, 1951–79 (fiscal years, ending March 1980) — 256

6.32 The top 100 firms' rationalisation of employment at home and expansion of employment abroad, 1974–8 — 258

6.33 Breakdown of Japanese overseas investments, by area and main industries (shares of accumulated total as of March 1980) — 260

6.34 Japanese overseas investments, by area, workers in subsidiaries, and wage rates in subsidiaries, March 1980 — 260

6.35 Overview of fiscal and monetary policy, 1970–81 — 262

7.1 Taxation and social security contributions as shares of national income in major capitalist countries, 1977 (Japan also 1980) — 271

7.2 Estimates of the rising tax burden, by income group, 1977–84 (¥1,000 and %) — 272

7.3 Changes in the structure of monthly average household expenditure of employees, 1974–80 — 273

7.4 Social security expenditures, 1966–79 — 275

7.5 Housing finance, 1965–78 (¥ billion and %) — 277

7.6 Housing and national finances, 1960–80 — 278

7.7 Houses built during Five Year Plans, by type of company, 1966–80 (1,000) — 280

7.8 Housing, by type and degree of satisfaction, 1973–8 (1,000) — 280

7.9 Home ownership in metropolitan Japan, by age and income class, 1973–8 — 281

7.10 Annual education costs for households, by type of institution, 1979 — 288

7.11 Numbers of school textbook publishing companies and the range of texts published, 1959–80 — 291

7.12 Ratios of applicants to vacancies in academic universities, by type of department and type of university, 1969–74, and the total numbers of applicants to academic universities, 1974–80 — 293

7.13 *Rōnin* as proportions of applicants and entrants to academic universities, by type of department and type of university, 1969–74, and composition of university entrants in 1980, by sex and years spent as *rōnin* — 294

7.14 Distribution of persons at junior colleges, by sex, jobs after graduation, and regular courses, 1980–1 — 296

7.15 Voter turnout in Lower House elections, 1946–80 — 299

7.16 Election turnout in selected prefectures, 1979–80 — 300

7.17 Numbers of seats and share of vote of main parliamentary parties in Lower House elections, 1960–80 — 305

7.18 Liberal Democratic Party factional strength in the Lower House, 1979 and 1980 — 306

7.19 Leadership changes, leadership popularity, and LDP fortunes, 1960–80 — 307

7.20 Reported criminal offences, 1969–78 312

7.21 Persons arrested and illegal incidents accompanying labour 313
disputes, plus total working days lost through strikes, 1974–80

7.22 Budgetary allocations on military expenditure, 1970–82 315

8.1 Total population over the age of 15, by economically active class, 319
non-active class, and sex, 1979 (1,000 persons)

Preface and acknowledgements

Since my aims in writing this book are explained in the Introduction, I merely mention here a few matters which are not directly related to the themes or content of the work. I have placed almost all of the factual information in tables, partly because to me nothing is more boring than having to wade through prose which is cluttered with statistical details, partly so that I could make available in English data which might be of interest even to readers who do not share my interpretations of them. The text is therefore almost entirely interpretative. As far as the data are concerned, in many cases the numbers in the rows and columns do not add up to the totals indicated. However, rather than repeat in each case that the totals include unclassifiable or minor categories, or that numbers have been rounded, I simply mention it once here. Finally, throughout I have followed the Japanese convention of always placing people's family names before their given names, even when a work cited in translation appears with names the other way round.

My debts, on the other hand, are innumerable, since they were accumulated during the entire seven years that I spent working on this book. My most profound thanks must surely go to all the working people in Japan who spent so much time with me: talking, showing me around, taking me into their confidence and even along with them on demonstrations and during disputes, and above all being friends to me. I hesitate to mention names, because I literally would not know where to stop. But I still have in my mind's eye the picture of many good friends in Japan, through whose kindness I came to love their land and people very dearly and to whom I look when I feel pessimistic about the future. I will therefore mention only one name, that of Professor Ōhashi Ryūken, whose work on classes in Japan first interested me in the subject and who spent many hours of his precious time with me, guiding me through materials and avenues about which I knew next to nothing when I started.

My final acknowledgement is to the *Bulletin of Concerned Asian Scholars*, who published earlier versions of my chapters 1 and 5, and who agreed to the use here of sections from those earlier versions.

Christchurch   ROB STEVEN
February 1982

Introduction

The empirical research for this book began in 1975 soon after the first 'oil shock' had visibly revealed some of the fragile foundations on which Japanese capitalism rested.[1] Before this, it was unthinkable to suggest that the so-called 'Japanese miracle' was no more unusual than the unprecedented boom that had produced similar ideologies of optimism and progress in most advanced capitalist societies. However, after nearly a decade of gradually deepening recession in Japan and elsewhere, the 'oil shock' is increasingly being recognised as the first clear sign that the bubble had burst. Henceforth, scholars would have to focus their attention on the underlying forces that had plunged the capitalist world into what promises to be its deepest crisis this century.[2]

In Japan, that scholarly tradition which has always claimed to understand underlying forces has produced volumes of detailed critical analysis of the crisis and its various forms. The scope and depth of these Marxist studies are perhaps without parallel outside Japan, possibly because the Japanese have a stronger tradition of sophisticated theoretical Marxism even than do the French. However, apart from a few samples of this work in translation,[3] the achievement of that tradition in documenting and explaining what is really happening in Japan is almost entirely unknown to Westerners. The main reason for this is that Western scholars with substantial training in Japanese language and society are almost all products of the North American conservative establishment. Jon Halliday's *A Political History of Japanese Capitalism* (New York: Pantheon, 1975) stands out as the sole Marxist work on Japan by an English-speaking scholar.

Halliday's study has had a major influence on the themes I selected for detailed examination.[4] First, mine is a structural rather than an historical analysis, with the emphasis on the structure and composition of the various social classes in present-day Japan. Second, insofar as there is an historical dimension, this covers only the most recent period of recession beginning around the time Halliday's manuscript was completed. My exclusive preoccupation with the 1970s was therefore carefully chosen both to update a story whose interest lies very much in the current crisis and to make known to the English-speaking world some of the rich empirical detail which surrounds the people facing this crisis and which is available in Japan.

Since these people confront their situation, not as isolated atomised individuals, but as members of social classes, class analysis became the dominant purpose of my research, which was guided by two main influences. The first was the classic analysis of classes in Japan by Ōhashi Ryūken,[5] whose painstaking documentation of the structure and composition of classes in Japan became a model I sought to emulate. However, since our theoretical views differed on so many important issues, there was no question of any simple updating of his statistics or translation of his text. A distinctive theoretical perspective was therefore the other guiding influence on my research, and although it is developed implicitly as the text proceeds, some of the central tenets must be made explicit right at the outset.

No one can write on classes today and entirely disclaim the influence of Louis Althusser, no matter how radically one disagrees with his approach to the subject.[6] The very title of this book echoes that of the main theoretical treatise on classes by one of Althusser's followers, the late Nicos Poulantzas, who wrote *Classes in Contemporary Capitalism* way back in 1974.[7] However, two points of departure from the Althusserian orthodoxy need particular emphasis.

First, I have set aside the Althusserian interpretation of the 'base–superstructure' metaphor in favour of one which I initially encountered in the work of Maurice Godelier and then more rigorously in that of Derek Sayer.[8] Althusser had more or less consistently equated the base–superstructure distinction with two entirely different distinctions: between economics on the one hand and politics and ideology on the other, and between non-state institutions like corporations and state institutions like parliament and the army. The result was that the 'base' of a capitalist society was seen as its 'economic level,' which meant capitalist enterprises, while the 'superstructure' comprised the 'political and ideological levels,' or the institutions of the state.

It was hardly coincidental that this Althusserian schema bore such a close resemblance to the structural functionalism of contemporary bourgeois scholars like Gabriel Almond.[9] In both cases, we find the misleading fragmentation of social reality into economics, politics, and ideology as well as the view that these take place in separate and functionally specific institutions.

Once reality has been broken up in this way, the problem is of course to understand how the pieces fit together. And in an attempt to preserve something of the Marxian idea that the infrastructure 'determines' the superstructure, the Althusserians postulated a 'relative autonomy' of the political and ideological levels (and their corresponding institutions) from the predominant economic level (and its respective institutions).[10] However, this notion of relative autonomy was never satisfactory, because no one could give a specific meaning to either of its component parts. And when the schema was brought to the analysis of classes, serious problems of logical inconsistency emerged. It was never clear what role the relative autonomy of the political and ideological levels allowed them to play in shaping social classes. Poulantzas accorded them such prominence that the whole theory of determination by the base was lost, and although a more rigorous work by Erik Wright partly saved the schema from complete logical breakdown, the main difficulties remained.[11]

The central problem was that the base–superstructure distinction could simply not be equated with the other two distinctions. The original German words Marx chose to express it in fact fairly accurately captured the essence of the discovery he had made, which had nothing to do with 'levels' of society or its different institutions. These words were *Grundlage* (literally 'foundation') and *Überbau* (literally 'building').[12] The former referred to the (hidden) mechanisms which set the limits within which the latter, the (visible) forms of day-to-day life, could vary. There is here no reference at all to the distinction among economics, politics, and ideology, which is of dubious validity anyway, or to different types of social institution. Rather, the words formed a short-hand phrase for the method of doing social science which Marx discovered and which requires brief restatement here.

Of fundamental importance is the recognition that in observing the concrete visible world, the world as we directly experience it, we do not necessarily perceive the reality which determines our observations. For example, the atomic structure which lies behind the physical things we see does not present itself to the senses, but must be uncovered by scientific enquiry. So the social reality behind the experiences of daily life might be equally hidden from observation, in which case the job of social science is to find it, that is, to uncover the 'base' (or infrastructure) which lies behind the 'superstructural' forms as we experience them. The base–superstructure distinction therefore corresponds to the distinction between essence and form.

However, what exactly this essence of society consists in is a more controversial question on which there is little agreement, although it seems that to Marx the term 'infrastructure' (or base) connoted that mechanism in society which generates the most powerful tendential forces. They can be called the predominant forces, so long as this does not mean that they determine every detail of concrete daily life but only that they set limits within which variation is possible. According to Marx and the tradition to which he gave rise, the infrastructure of a society is its mode of material production, that is, the mechanism which regulates the activity of human beings in producing what they need to sustain life. How people produce what they live on establishes predominant tendential forces within which more subordinate forces operate. At this point we must make explicit what Marx actually did.[13]

So far we have not come across this notion of a subordinate force, which would seem to belong in an intermediate position between the infrastructure (which produces predominant forces) and the super-structure (the world as we experience it). It is not something Marx mentioned explicitly, but it is implicit in almost everything he wrote, particularly *Capital*. In that work he reconstructed the mechanism of the capitalist mode of production as the *basis* of capitalist society. However, this was a relatively complex mechanism comprising a number of simple mechanisms, namely production, exchange, and distribution. The most fundamental of these was production, while exchange and distribution were subordinate. Marx showed that even though the latter generated distinctive tendential forces (e.g. supply and demand), these operated within the limits of (although at times in opposition to) the laws of production, such as the general law of capital accumulation.

What the base–superstructure distinction therefore implies is the notion of a (hidden) infrastructure comprising an indefinite number of simple mechanisms, which produce forces of unequal strength and which jointly shape concrete reality as we experience it. The simple mechanisms, some of which are more basic than others, are bound together to form a more and more elaborate infrastructure (a more and more complex mechanism) by the dominant forces of the most basic one. For example, the capitalist mode of production, which is a relatively complex mechanism lying behind the visible forms of capitalist society, is held together by the predominant force generated by the simple mechanism of production, namely capital.

The details of day-to-day life are shaped by the most subordinate of the simple mechanisms which together make up society's infrastructure, for example, the structure of organisation adopted by workers (in their unions) and by capitalists (in the institutions of the state). Although Marx did not examine all the subordinate mechanisms which influence daily life (notably the state), one can include these as part of the infrastructure, in their appropriate subordinate position, without doing injustice to the main point of the distinction between base and superstructure. That the infrastructure lies behind the visible forms of daily life is retained, although the original suggestion that it comprised solely the mode of production is dropped.

Although the meaning of the concept of the infrastructure has been extended to include mechanisms other than the mode of production, this has not meant setting aside the Marxian theory of the predominance of this mechanism. On the contrary, it has helped us specify more precisely what this predominance consists in: the generation of the strongest tendential forces. Such forces do not determine the details of everyday practice, but only set the limits to what this practice can be. The details are shaped by the internal structure of the particular mechanism governing a particular practice. For example, production sets limits on what happens in circulation, but the latter mechanism is responsible for the forms in which the process of exchange takes place.

To see the basis of society as a series of mechanisms ranked according to the relative strengths of the forces they generate does, of course, contradict the Althusserian schema at almost every point. Whatever is apparent to the senses and is directly experienced is superstructure (or, better, 'building,' since behind the building resting on the foundation is the building's structure), whether this happens in a corporation or a government department, and whether it has to do with productive activity, power relations, or ideas. On the other hand, the unseen mechanisms, which in whatever degree influence the way concrete reality is experienced, are part of the infrastructure. They include the real mechanisms governing the schools, parliamentary elections, and other similar activities about which Marxists know next to nothing because they have seen them simply as part of the superstructure.

The infrastructure is therefore the complex reality that lies behind the visible world. To understand how it functions requires knowing how its component parts are ordered as well as connected to one another. The first task, ordering, was worked out by Marx through his method of abstraction, while the second, tracing interconnections, was more difficult because of the universality of contradictions which he discovered.

Marx's method of abstraction was one of his most ingenious scientific discoveries.[14] The simple mechanism which he hypothesised to be the most basic of all, namely production, was analysed in complete abstraction of all other mechanisms, so as not to confuse its tendential forces with those of subordinate mechanisms. Only when these forces had been clearly identified did he analyse the latter: exchange and distribution. However, each of them was reconstructed in abstraction from more subordinate mechanisms than itself, but not from more fundamental ones within whose limits it operated. Thus exchange was analysed in abstraction from distribution but not from production, while distribution was analysed in the context of production and exchange but not from the more subordinate mechanisms of the state. Even though Marx himself did not do so, the use of his method requires one to follow the same procedure until no new mechanisms are introduced. At that point abstraction ceases and one is left with a complex infrastructure to account for concrete reality.

Although working out in this way what the infrastructure of society might look like need not be too complicated (since the order in which the mechanisms are placed is a matter of hypothesis), it takes a long time adequately to confirm by means of empirical testing whether or not society's infrastructure is in fact as Marx reconstructed it. At this point I will accept that it is, although a crucial modification is suggested a bit later on. Before this is done, a few more methodological points must be made so that the concept of class can first of all be clarified.

Assuming that Marx did discover the order in which to place the various mechanisms of the infrastructure, it remains to be shown why tracing their interconnections is so difficult. Marx recognised that even the simplest mechanism produces opposing forces of unequal strength and that predominant forces of the different simple mechanisms often move in opposite directions. There are thus contradictions within and among the simple mechanisms of the infrastructure. For example, there are contradictions between capital and labour in production, buying and selling in exchange, and supply and demand in distribution, and also contradictions among production, exchange, and distribution (low wages, for instance, assist capitalist production but obstruct exchange). In each case, the stronger force is what binds the simple mechanism together, giving it its characteristic qualities, or a number of simple mechanisms into a complex one.

Since the functioning of a mechanism is shaped mainly by its predominant force, or what Mao called its principal aspect, a qualitative change in the mechanism occurs when the subordinate or secondary force becomes dominant. For example, capital and labour are the dominant and subordinate aspects of capitalist production, the main characteristics of which result from the position of capital, but should labour gain enough strength to become dominant a qualitatively different mechanism of production would come into existence. As the two aspects of a contradiction become more equal, a struggle normally ensues and ends only when one or the other establishes itself as dominant.

What makes tracing particular interconnections difficult in practice is that weaker forces, particularly in the more subordinate mechanisms, are continually coming together in combinations and both bringing about qualitative changes in these subordinate mechanisms and counteracting the influence of stronger forces. This is how historical change occurs, but the continually shifting infrastructure (which keeps society in a continual state of movement, not necessarily in the same direction) means that tracing actual interconnections among particular mechanisms requires careful investigation in each case. Most of the difficulties arise with the more subordinate mechanisms, since the momentous historical changes resulting from qualitative changes in the more fundamental mechanisms are extremely rare.

The massive task of reconstructing the entire infrastructure of Japanese society is far beyond the scope of this study, which focuses on classes in Japan. Yet, in order to understand what classes are, it has been necessary to present a broad outline of how social reality as we experience it is produced by a complex and continually changing infrastructure comprising a variety of mechanisms which generate

unequal and contradictory forces. Since such an interpretation of the
base–infrastructure metaphor is diametrically opposed to that of the
Althusserians, whose orthodoxy still holds sway in Marxist writing on
classes in the West, it has required considerable elaboration.
However, my second point of departure from this orthodoxy is
equally crucial to the theory of class which has guided my research. In
the context of the first point, it should not be too controversial, even
though it concerns the thorny problem of epistemology.

In spite of Althusser's strenuous attempts to break with idealism in
all its forms, his epistemology is essentially idealist.[15] This is because
he argues that our very observations of the concrete world are shaped
by the concepts we use to describe them. The result is that if
unscientific concepts are used, the world is observed through tainted
spectacles and there is no objective evidence against which to test
scientific theories. Only if one starts with the correct scientific
concepts can one observe the world at all, and so the starting point for
scientific enquiry must be concepts and theories.

This position is idealist in at least two senses. First, it throws back to
intellectuals and theorists the task of sorting out false ideas from
correct ones and assumes that historical change occurs when the
correct ideas are formulated and then embraced by the working class.
History is then after all, as Hegel had always said, propelled along by
the clash of ideas and the gradual emergence of the scientifically
correct ones. Apart from the disastrous style of communist politics
that follows from this form of idealism, it is an epistemology which
contradicts all the normal practices of science, which involve
continual testing of theory against some or other form of empirical
evidence.

The second sense in which Althusser's epistemology is idealist lies in
its implicit assumption that the world does not exist independently of
the person who perceives it. Although Althusser would deny this and
claim to preserve the scientific assumption that reality exists whether
or not it is perceived, he cannot consistently do that, since reality for
him emerges only when approached with the correct conceptual
apparatus. He does not accept that there are both a concrete real
world of experience and a real infrastructure behind it. His flawed
epistemology is therefore related to his inability to understand the
base–superstructure distinction.

To reverse the Althusserian starting and finishing points – start
with the concrete world of experience and end with a theoretical

reconstruction of the infrastructural reality behind it – does not mean one always has to begin from scratch. One can and does approach the experiential world with theories which have been tested and confirmed to be adequate reconstructions of aspects of the infrastructure behind it and still expose to experience for further testing refinements of those theories and even sometimes substantial modifications of them. However, no matter how broad or narrow the revisions to existing theory involved, the goal is always the same: to reconstruct the reality behind (that is, to account for) the concrete world as it is experienced. The latter is therefore always the final judge of the scientist's reconstructions.

To return to the question of social classes, the central problem is whether they belong to the concrete world of experience or the hidden world of the infrastructure. There is no question that they really exist; what is at stake is whether one can actually see classes or whether what one observes are the visible forms of a hidden infrastructure of classes. The position adopted in this book is consistently the latter, which must now be briefly explained.

Working within a materialist methodology, the purpose of class analysis is not to classify individuals as if individuals were the independent variables whose 'choices' to act out of class 'interest' shaped the course of history. Rather, since the way concrete individuals act is a result of the entire complex infrastructure, class analysis involves pin-pointing certain mechanisms in that infrastructure and mapping out the concrete forms in which their tendential forces manifest themselves. The relevant mechanisms are the various modes of production (in the narrow sense of mechanism of production alone, and not exchange etc.), which generate tendential forces called class forces: of capital and labour in the capitalist mode of production and of the petty bourgeoisie in the simple commodity mode of production.

Concrete individuals are of course subject to many social forces besides the class forces generated by mechanisms of production, ones which can either bring the individuals together when class forces divide them or vice versa. For example, when an employer and a shop-floor employee (the forms in which class forces are manifested) go shopping and talk to each other about the high price of butter, the forces which divide them (emanating from the mechanism of production, where positions are unequal) can be temporarily obscured by the forces which unite them (emanating from the mechanism of exchange, where positions are equal). But when the scientist classifies the individuals concerned as capitalist and worker, it is not being denied that they are also consumers, but that the class forces which manifest themselves in the form of occupational status are more powerful than the forces of exchange, which manifest themselves in the form of consumer status. Classifying individuals is therefore a way of saying something about the infrastructure and the relative importance of the simple mechanisms (particularly production) which compose it. It is also a way of drawing attention to the concrete forms (mainly occupational status) in which the infrastructural forces manifest themselves.[16]

The scientist is not bound always to focus solely on the most basic forces of the infrastructure and to trace their manifestations. On the contrary, to account for the details of certain activities, the forces of more subordinate mechanisms are normally of greater relevance. For example, if one is interested in the specifics of trade union meetings, the class forces of capital and labour are mainly relevant insofar as they explain why the structure of trade unions developed along the broad lines that it did. Beyond that, the specific trade union structure itself will be the most relevant mechanism to investigate. Viewed from such a Marxian standpoint, the value of a great deal of bourgeois social science can also be appreciated, since although bourgeois scholars rarely relate visible forms of the world to fundamental mechanisms, they often relate them to more subordinate ones. In fact, their understanding of details is typically far superior to that of Marxist scholars, who dislike descending from high-level theory to investigate mechanisms which shape immediate details.

The mechanism which a scientist makes the subject of further research is always at least in part a matter of choice, though not necessarily entirely free choice. Often, mechanisms which show some signs of developing the potential for qualitative change are selected, because they suggest the possibility of more or less fundamental (depending on the location of the mechanism) historical change. This is overwhelmingly where my motivation in focusing on classes in Japan lies: the current capitalist crisis holds some potential for a realignment of class forces which could lead to fairly important social changes in Japan. It is also an appropriate point to mention the crucial modification to Marxist theory that I believe is necessary and that was hinted at earlier on.

The feminist movement and the rigorous materialist analyses it has produced, particularly in Britain and America,[17] have convinced me that modes of production tell us little about the roots of women's oppression. It now seems quite clear that even more fundamental than mechanisms of production are mechanisms of species reproduction, and that patriarchy has its ultimate basis in the latter. This is not the place to argue for such a radical turning on its head of traditional Marxist theory – I have done that elsewhere[18] – although in chapter 8 I briefly outline this theory and bring together the most pertinent evidence from the study of Japanese classes in support of it. That chapter is also intended as a transition to my current research, 'Class, Gender, and Capitalist Patriarchy in Japan.'

However, whether or not that revisionist theoretical position is accepted does not greatly affect the argument of this book. Feminists who also see the basis of patriarchy in a mechanism more fundamental than the mode of production are asked to read this book as one which deals with middle-level theory, that is, the manifestations of patriarchy in the subordinate world of production. They might view the class forces which stem from production as providing important details on women's lives, and they might anticipate the possibility of qualitative change in this (subordinate to species reproduction but nonetheless quite basic) mechanism. This is how I myself understand the book. More orthodox Marxists, however, for whom there is not yet sufficient proof that anything more fundamental than the capitalist mode of production exists in Japan, can read the book as it stands without being asked to question their orthodoxy in that regard. The book is about classes and the capitalist mode of production in Japan. For some, that is all it should be about, whereas for others it will be incomplete until its sequel is placed by its side.

I
The bourgeoisie

The possibility of revolutionary social change in Japan, stemming from a qualitative change in the capitalist mode of production, depends directly on shifts in the balance of class forces in that country, in particular the combination that can come together against the bourgeoisie. Since the dominance of this class not simply binds together the entire system of production, giving it its characteristic forms, but as a result all the various subordinate elements in Japanese society, it is appropriate to begin with an analysis of the ruling class and the basis of its power.

To assess the strength of the Japanese bourgeoisie requires laying bare the infrastructural mechanisms through which that social force is generated. This is not an easy task, since the infrastructure is not amenable to direct observation and must be reconstructed from an examination of the various forms in which it is manifested. Yet it is not a task one has to begin entirely from scratch, since considerable scientific work on capitalist societies has already reconstructed in varying degrees of detail the different parts of a capitalist infrastructure. Because such an infrastructure has been shown to be broadly similar wherever it exists, analysis of any particular one can concentrate on what has been seen to contain variation. Most pertinent is the degree of capital's overall strength as well as the extent to which this strength is concentrated or fragmented. In each case, the underlying reality must be grasped through examination of the particular forms in which it is manifested.

The bourgeoisie is normally seen as the ruling class of a capitalist society, because it is the class that gets away with the social surplus. In all non-subsistence societies, in which people who work produce more than they consume, there is such a social surplus. It may be used in a variety of ways, but in pre-communist society it is appropriated by a non-producing ruling class. What is meant by the term 'ruling class' therefore is those positions in the system of production that somehow or other manage to get hold of the social surplus. It is important not to confuse the methods this class uses to extract the surplus with the fact that it does so, since there is no one method employed in common by all the different ruling classes in the many systems of production that have so far been discovered. The particular method used only helps one identify the type of ruling class involved.

In capitalist societies, particularly advanced ones such as Japan, the ways in which ruling classes get the surplus are much less visible than in almost all others. There are no legal slave owners, conspicuous military leaders, or manifestly idle feudal lords who can visibly be seen to compel the ruled classes to work for them. On the contrary, it is the near-invisibility of the transfer of the surplus from the working class to the capitalist class that forms the concrete support of the ideology that there are no ruling classes in capitalist societies. Two ways in which the surplus is transferred are particularly prone to concealment and correspond to two forms in which the ruling class is concretely manifested.

The first lies in the ownership of money capital, which yields unearned incomes in the form of dividends (or business profits), interest, or rent. What makes this possible are the infrastructural mechanisms through which money capital is transformed into productive capital, that is, used to purchase means of production (raw materials, fuels, machinery, buildings, etc.) and labour power (wage labourers), and then getting them to produce commodities that are worth more than what was originally laid out. This extra value, or surplus value, is produced by wage labourers under no compulsion from capital other than the threat of unemployment. How does this happen?

Wage labourers sell their capacity to work, or their labour power, for a full week (usually not less than forty hours) at a price that allows a conventionally and historically determined standard of living to be maintained. If all that the labourers could produce in a week was the equivalent of what they could buy with their wages, there would be no surplus to extract and the society would be a subsistence one. This possibility can never arise under capitalism, because producing for subsistence and producing a surplus for the ruling class take place simultaneously in one and the same operation. Production for surplus or not at all is one of the distinctive characteristics of the capitalist system. In feudal systems, where peasants would work about three days for their subsistence and about three more for their lord, they could always do one without the other. In particularly bad times, due, for example, to poor weather conditions, peasants might temporarily produce little or no surplus whatsoever, but spend all their time working to keep body and soul together. The one thing they would not do is stop working. However, under capitalism this is exactly what happens: workers either produce the equivalent of their subsistence plus a surplus, or they become unemployed and do nothing.

Why is this? The answer lies in the fact that the skills and capacities which workers sell in the commodity market, or their labour power, have two entirely different values. The first is called the exchange value, which broadly speaking is the value of the goods and services workers live on and which they must buy with their wages. The second is the use to the capitalist of the labour power purchased, or what might be called the value labour power creates, and this is equal to what the labourers can produce during the time they sell their skills and capacities. The owners of money capital only convert this into productive capital (buy means of production and hire workers) if the value labour power creates is well above the value it must be paid (its exchange value), that is, only if surplus value is produced.

What therefore compels the working class to produce a surplus for the capitalist class is that workers have no independent access to means of production. Having nothing to work on or to work with, they cannot even engage in subsistence production if no owner of machines and materials is able to extract a surplus out of hiring them. Hence the reason why ownership of money capital is a form in which the ruling class manifests itself is that such ownership allows the extraction of a surplus from people who have nothing to sell apart from their labour power and can never buy anything besides what is required to recreate that labour power.

In contemporary Japan, as in other capitalist countries, ownership of means of production takes at least two main forms. The first is where the owner of money capital is the same person who converts it into productive capital and receives the surplus in the form of business profits. I discuss these unincorporated enterprises in more detail later on.

The second form of ownership is where a number of persons use their money capital to buy 'shares' in firms, and many of them play no part in the job of converting the money into productive capital. Shareholders in such joint stock companies include people who do

Table 1.1. *Pattern of shareholding in companies quoted on the Stock Exchange, 1975–80*

No. of shares owned	Owners[a]		Total shares owned	
	No.	%	No. (1,000)	%
1975 (1,710 companies)				
Under 1,000	5,244,223	27.34	1,628,272	0.94
1,000–4,999	11,007,209	57.39	21,367,948	12.39
5,000–9,999	1,878,408	9.79	11,763,798	6.82
10,000–49,999	893,104	4.66	14,782,445	8.57
50,000–999,999	137,191	0.72	26,944,311	15.62
1 mil. and over	20,916	0.11	95,986,764	55.65
Total	19,181,051	100.00	172,473,538	100.00
1980 (1,734 companies)				
Under 1,000	5,398,197	27.28	1,529,192	0.71
1,000–4,999	11,117,929	56.19	21,481,804	9.95
5,000–9,999	1,949,342	9.85	12,215,311	5.66
10,000–49,000	1,122,501	5.67	18,608,524	8.62
50,000–999,999	170,801	0.86	33,097,068	15.32
1 mil. and over	26,686	0.13	129,041,389	59.75
Total	19,785,456	100.00	215,973,287	100.00

[a]Owners include individuals as well as firms.
Source: Zenkoku shōken torihikijo [Japan Stock Exchange], *Kabushiki bunpu jōkyō chōsa* [Survey on the Distribution of Shares], 1975 and 1980 (Tokyo: Zenkoku shōken torihikijo, 1976 and 1981), pp. 30, 32 and p. 20.

nothing at all as well as people who actively plan how to obtain the most surplus from the wage labourers they hire.

Of fundamental importance in identifying the form in which the ruling class in Japan manifests itself is thus the pattern of shareholding in joint stock companies. In 1967, Yamamura Kozo, an influential establishment economist, hailed what he called the 'Stockholding Revolution of Japan,' pointing out that in the years 1946–60 the number of individuals owning more than 100 shares in firms quoted on the Stock Exchange (the largest ones, in which capital is most concentrated and most centralised) grew from 1.7 million to 10.6 million.[1] Does the fact that by 1975 this number exceeded 17 million and by 1980 19 million mean that over a third of economically active people have become partakers of the social surplus, which is now so widely distributed that to talk of a ruling class is becoming more and more misleading?[2] It does not, since, as table 1.1 reveals, the concentration of large shareholdings in a small number of hands is extremely high.

By 1980, in the companies quoted on the Stock Exchange (that is, most of the 'giant' corporations capitalised at over ¥1,000 million), the bottom 99% of owners (19.59 million persons) held only 25% of shares, while the top 1% of owners (197,487 persons) held a full 75%. The great mass of individual shareholders among whom capital ownership is supposed to have been spread feature mainly among the holders of fewer than 5,000 shares: the 16.5 million individuals own less than 10% of the shares.

Although the absolute number of shareholders has grown since the war, the concentration of large holdings in a few hands has more than kept pace. In 1950, the bottom 81% of owners in quoted companies held 26.3% of shares, while the top 0.8% held 54%. Far from there being a 'Stockholding Revolution' which has spread the ownership of capital among growing numbers of Japanese people, shares were increasingly held by fewer and more wealthy individuals and firms. Table 1.2 shows how the proportion of shares in quoted companies held by individuals fell over the years, while the proportion held by corporations and financial institutions rose. The concentration of ownership revealed in table 1.1 is therefore partly accounted for by the large holdings of a small number of capitalist institutions. Table 1.3 shows what their numbers were in 1980.

This general view of high levels of corporate stockholding is confirmed when any typical giant corporation is examined. In Nissan Motor Company, for example, the top twenty shareholders are all banks, insurance companies, or other corporations. In 1980, among them they held 54.0% of the company's shares. The largest individual shareholders were all members of the board of directors, who together owned 3.46% of the shares and thereby collectively became the sixth largest shareholder.[3] Nissan is also fairly typical in this respect, since in quoted companies the average proportion of shares held by the directors of the issuing company was 1.8% in 1980. In 1975 it had been a bit higher: 2.2%.[4]

The largest individual shareholders in Japan are therefore corporation executives, while the holdings of wage labourers are in the vast majority of cases very small. Table 1.4 confirms this by presenting the amounts of savings in three major surplus-value-earning assets that more-than-one person households have: time deposits, loan trust and debenture, and stocks and investment trust. The importance in Japan

Table 1.2. *Percentage of shares held, by type of shareholder, 1945–80*

Type of shareholder	1945	1955	1960	1975	1980
Government	8.29	0.39	0.20	0.2	0.2
Financial institutions	11.17	23.61	39.62	36.0	38.8
Brokerage firms	2.82	7.94	3.72	1.4	1.7
Corporations	24.65	14.64	17.80	26.3	26.0
Individuals	53.07	53.15	46.19	33.5	29.2
Foreigners	—	0.27	0.27	0.1	0.1
Foreign firms	—	1.46	1.07	2.5	4.0

Sources: Yamamura, p. 125; *Kabushiki bunpu jōkyō chōsa*, 1975, p. 24; 1980, p. 11.

Table 1.3. *Numbers of shareholders, by type of shareholder, 1975–80*

Type of shareholder	1975		1980	
	No.	%	No.	%
Government	2,134	0.0	1,928	0.0
Financial institutions	47,269	0.2	58,922	0.3
Brokerage firms	39,671	0.2	49,798	0.3
Corporations	275,168	1.4	367,413	1.9
Individuals	18,775,700	97.9	19,252,854	97.3
Foreigners	18,053	0.1	17,661	0.1
Foreign firms	23,056	0.1	36,880	0.2
Total	19,181,051	100.0	19,785,456	100.0

Source: Kabushiki bunpu jōkyō chōsa, 1975, p. 22; 1980, p. 9.

of the first two in particular, which generate unearned incomes in the form of interest, cannot be overemphasised. This is not simply because banks and the other financial institutions which pay the interest are major shareholders in large corporations, but because these institutions lend corporations the money to buy over 80% of their working capital. The greater importance of time deposits and loan trust and debenture than shares is also revealed by the respective shares in household income from property typically commanded by interest (73.6% in 1979) and dividends (18.8%).[5] Banks and other financial institutions therefore end up with the bulk of the surplus value produced in Japan, and they distribute much of this to holders of financial assets. The 'Total' columns in table 1.4 are therefore

Table 1.4. *Amounts of surplus-value-earning savings (¥ million) per household, by occupation of household head and annual household income, 1979*

Occupation of household head (more-than-one-person households)	Annual income (¥ mil.)								
	Under 1.0	1.0–1.4	1.4–1.8	1.8–2.4	2.4–3.2	3.2–4.0	4.0–6.0	6.0–10.0	Over 10.0
Labourers[a]	*0.57*	*1.28*	*3.43*	*11.75*	*27.07*	*23.81*	*25.08*	*6.33*	*0.46*
Time deposits	0.43	0.60	0.65	0.88	1.11	1.42	2.10	3.16	6.20
Loan trust/debenture	0.00	0.13	0.04	0.08	0.15	0.18	0.39	0.63	0.41
Stocks/investment trust	0.00	0.01	0.01	0.01	0.04	0.07	0.18	0.36	1.34
Total	0.43	0.74	0.70	0.97	1.30	1.67	2.67	4.15	7.95
Salaried office employees	*0.14*	*0.24*	*0.67*	*3.99*	*14.76*	*20.00*	*39.01*	*18.92*	*2.02*
Time deposits	1.62	0.89	0.98	0.97	1.29	1.61	2.22	3.49	5.78
Loan trust/debenture	0.17	0.04	0.15	0.14	0.25	0.42	0.64	1.24	2.46
Stocks/investment trust	0.01	0.04	0.01	0.06	0.10	0.15	0.36	0.86	2.62
Total	1.80	0.97	1.14	1.17	1.64	2.18	3.22	5.59	10.86
Petty bourgeois[b]	*1.50*	*2.84*	*4.45*	*11.95*	*20.94*	*16.47*	*25.56*	*12.05*	*2.86*
Time deposits	1.15	0.97	1.07	1.33	1.87	2.17	3.34	5.16	10.43
Loan trust/debenture	0.15	0.03	0.05	0.05	0.20	0.16	0.33	0.76	2.86
Stocks/investment trust	0.12	0.08	0.12	0.14	0.16	0.15	0.41	0.60	1.92
Total	1.42	1.08	1.24	1.52	2.23	2.48	4.08	6.52	15.21
Individual proprietors[c]	*0.75*	*0.76*	*1.86*	*5.65*	*13.57*	*12.82*	*30.42*	*24.06*	*8.87*
Time deposits	0.95	1.10	1.46	1.45	1.88	2.08	4.19	5.25	12.07
Loan trust/debenture	0.00	0.22	0.59	0.45	0.14	0.21	0.37	0.47	1.67
Stocks/investment trust	0.00	0.11	0.81	0.10	0.16	0.08	0.39	0.74	3.44
Total	0.95	1.43	2.86	2.00	2.18	2.37	4.95	6.46	17.18

Corporation executives[d]	*0.35*	*0.24*	*0.23*	*0.69*	*5.23*	*7.52*	*27.18*	*36.28*	*21.82*
Time deposits	4.10	1.77	3.69	1.88	2.84	2.58	3.64	5.62	11.58
Loan trust/debenture	0.00	0.86	0.42	0.00	0.24	0.42	0.70	1.72	3.90
Stocks/investment trust	0.00	0.49	1.62	0.01	0.70	0.25	0.98	2.02	7.20
Total	4.10	3.12	5.73	1.89	3.78	3.25	5.32	9.36	22.68
Professional	*2.83*	*3.86*	*4.22*	*6.82*	*14.96*	*13.95*	*26.64*	*18.30*	*6.99*
Time deposits	0.87	1.19	0.93	2.13	2.17	2.05	3.32	5.49	13.41
Loan trust/debenture	0.03	0.11	0.21	0.58	0.67	0.80	0.74	1.48	3.56
Stocks/investment trust	0.00	0.01	0.89	0.20	0.30	0.25	0.52	1.56	4.29
Total	0.90	1.31	2.03	2.91	3.14	3.10	4.58	8.53	21.26
No occupation	*8.26*	*13.42*	*15.11*	*19.73*	*16.33*	*8.92*	*11.19*	*3.78*	*0.51*
Time deposits	1.20	1.96	2.17	3.05	3.43	4.40	5.05	7.42	6.25
Loan trust/debenture	0.16	0.32	0.97	1.38	1.62	2.57	3.40	5.14	2.27
Stocks/investment trust	0.06	0.21	0.23	0.38	0.71	0.91	1.10	3.43	1.17
Total	1.42	2.49	3.37	4.81	5.76	7.88	9.55	15.99	9.69

[a]The first row of figures for each occupational group indicates the percentages of the households in it which fall into each income group.

[b]Petty bourgeois are self-employed persons in unincorporated enterprises with 4 or fewer operatives as well as executives of similar-sized corporations.

[c]Individual proprietors are self-employed persons in firms with 5 or more operatives.

[d]Executives in corporations with 5 or more operatives.

Source: Compiled from Sōrifu tōkeikyoku [Bureau of Statistics, Office of the Prime Minister], *Zenkoku shōhi jittai chōsa hōkoku* [National Survey of Family Income and Expenditure], 1979, vol. 3, *Chochikuhen (Futari ijō no futsū setai)* [Savings (Two-or-More-Person Households)] (Tokyo: Nihon tōkei kyōkai, 1980), pp. 136–40. This survey is published every 5 years.

truer indicators of capital ownership as something which generates unearned incomes.

Although capital ownership is concentrated in the hands of large corporations and their directors (particularly of financial institutions), this does not mean that the power of the bourgeoisie is manifested through them alone. Even fairly moderate levels of ownership can be sufficient to steer people into political alliance with giant corporation executives. The power of the Japanese bourgeoisie must therefore be assessed in terms of the full 'reach' that capital in Japan has, and it is manifested in the numbers of people who can be brought into acting out the role of the capitalist. One is not here mechanically classifying individuals and counting heads, but numerically identifying forms in which the bourgeoisie manifests itself. Among these is that contradictory situation in which wage labourers own sizeable surplus-value-earning assets: here the same concrete individuals mediate opposite (infrastructural) class forces. To work out which level of capital ownership is sufficient for the influence of the bourgeoisie to predominate is a matter of judgement and experience, and I have estimated that capital ownership in excess of ¥5 million was about the critical amount in 1979. It would have generated an unearned income of over ¥350,000 ($1,400), while the ownership of capital of about ¥3–5 million would have yielded something like ¥210,000–350,000 ($840–1,400) in unearned income.[6] The latter category of person stands right in the middle of the opposing class forces, and therefore belongs to the middle class. Table 1.5 estimates the numbers of households in each grouping, but since their heads are usually males, the occupational breakdown is confined almost entirely to men.

About 0.5% of male labourers in 1979 owned enough capital to play mainly the role of the capitalist, but 6.33% were in that ambiguous situation of acting out the roles of both capitalist and worker. However, fairly large proportions of men from other occupational groupings owned enough capital to receive strong interests in bourgeois social relations, in all about 5.3 million of them. To them must be added two other categories of owners – of land and of unincorporated capitalist enterprises – in order to get a complete picture of those members of the bourgeoisie who receive surplus value from capital ownership. In the second category are the proprietors of unincorporated capitalist (that is, relying on mainly wage labour) enterprises who were not included because they owned less than ¥5

Table 1.5. *Interests in capitalism of household heads, from ownership of major surplus-value-earning assets, 1979 (1,000 persons)*

Occupation	Little or no interest		Contradictory interest		Predominant interest	
	Persons	%	Persons	%	Persons	%
Labourers	12,700	93.2	860	6.3	62	0.5
Salaried office employees	2,312	40.1	2,250	39.0	1,208	20.9
Petty bourgeois	2,971	59.5	1,275	25.6	744	14.9
Individual proprietors	175	36.7	144	30.4	156	32.9
Corporation executives	43	2.0	280	12.8	1,877	85.3
Professional services	77	19.2	222	55.6	101	25.3
No occupation	716	24.4	1,020	34.8	1,193	40.7
Total	18,994	62.5	6,051	19.9	5,341	17.6

Note: The estimates were made by taking the percentages of household heads in each occupational group with the stipulated assets (over ¥5 million for strong interests and ¥3–5 million for contradictory ones) as outlined in table 1.4, and multiplying them by the total estimated numbers of household heads in two-or-more-person households in each occupational grouping. Direct statistical information was not available, so that the numbers of married men were used for household heads in more-than-one-person households. For these, see Sōrifu tōkeikyoku [Bureau of Statistics, Office of the Prime Minister], *Shūgyō kōzō kihon chōsa hōkoku* [Employment Status Survey], 1979, *Zenkokuhen* [All Japan] (Tokyo: Nihon tōkei kyōkai, 1980), pp. 34–5, 50–1, 62–3.

million in the three surplus-value-earning assets: about 319,000 persons.

The details of non-agricultural land ownership, speculation, and deals, which is one of the biggest of all rackets in Japan, are almost impossible to obtain. What we do know is that about a half a million people tend to have rent as their major source of income, while another million receive taxable income from rent even though rent is not their major source of income.[7] It is a pity that no occupational breakdown of major rent earners is available, since rent typically makes up some 8% of household income from property.[8] However, since large owners of one form of capital are also in most cases large owners of other forms of capital, it is reasonable to assume that most landowners of substance have already been included.

Also important to note in tables 1.4 and 1.5 is that corporation executives are easily the largest owners of capital in Japan. We have already seen the proportions of shares owned by directors of large companies. In small ones, the tendency for the company president to own the overwhelming majority of shares increases as the size of the company decreases. The smaller the firm, therefore, the rarer it becomes for anyone other than a director to own any shares whatsoever.

Before we can show how the capitalist class in Japan is fractionalised according to the relative strengths of the different capitals, we must explain how the control of capital is also a method by which the social surplus is transferred and therefore a form in which the bourgeoisie is manifested. This can best be understood by contrasting the small firm, where the owner is himself responsible for converting money capital into productive capital, with the joint stock company. In the former, the same concrete person (what we might call the same *class agent*) acts out the functions of both the ownership and the control of capital, that is, supplies and decides the monies to be spent on machines, materials, and labour power, and also makes sure that the labourers work efficiently enough to produce a handsome surplus. Though these owners, unlike those shareholders in joint stock companies who merely supply money, might be very busy people, they are not productive workers. The time they spend trying to get the best prices for the commodities they buy and sell as well as the time spent overseeing the work of their labourers is not necessary for the production of useful articles, though it is crucial to the survival of capitalist production of them. Only where the whole purpose of the labour process is to extract a surplus from the sale of what is made is this time required, since the functions of buying machinery, materials, and labour power in proportions and at prices that yield the maximum surplus value are peculiar to capitalism. They are just as limited to capitalist production as is the function of ownership, that is, hoarding enough money to be able to purchase means of production and labour power. In a society where the whole purpose of work is to use what is made or to render work enjoyable, these functions would fall away, as would the task of seeing that labourers work at breakneck speed. However, it is for all the functions of capital that surplus value accrues – hoarding and supplying money, buying and selling in the right markets, and supervising labour power – and in the smaller capitalist enterprises one and the same person performs all these functions and receives the entire surplus in return (apart from rent, taxes, etc.).

In joint stock companies, however, there is an increasing separation, as firms become larger, between the agents who own and those who control capital. Relatively few shares are owned by the directors of large firms, whereas the great bulk of shares in small firms are in the hands of directors. The functions of controlling capital in the former are carried out by a variety of agents, only a few of whom are major owners. The larger the firm, the more complicated is the system of control, but this can generally be seen in terms of two hierarchies of control, which merge at the top. The first is the hierarchy of control over means of production, that is, machines, materials, fuels, and so on, which workers use when they produce commodities. The second is the hierarchy of control over labour power, or the capacity to work which hired labourers sell. These hierarchies merge towards the top, because anyone responsible for buying new machinery, or even someone in charge of an automated production line, thereby controls the way and speed at which labourers must work. At the level of the board of directors the two hierarchies become indistinguishable, since it is at this level that decisions are made on investment (converting money capital into productive capital) and therefore on everything that affects employment and its conditions.

Corporation directors mediate the bourgeois class force even if they own little or no capital, because the functions they perform belong to that class. The time they spend busily negotiating contracts and in long meetings to decide how many workers will be hired or laid off is not time productively spent, and owners of capital must surrender some of the surplus to pay directors for performing these tasks. Directors' fees consist of surplus value because they are in payment for the unproductive tasks – peculiar to capitalism – that the individual capitalist in his small firm does himself.

However, since not all persons in both hierarchies are exclusively engaged in performing capitalist functions, not all of them are paid entirely out of surplus value. Some mediate opposing class forces and receive incomes that have quite opposite origins. For example, the supervisor, who is at the bottom of the hierarchy which controls labour power, usually spends more time doing the same productive work as those supervised than is spent in telling them what to do. We might divide the payment of supervisors into two parts: that which comes out of (variable) capital, that is, wages for their productive work (the value of which they produce along with some surplus), and that which comes out of surplus value for doing the capitalist's job of supervision. What characterises all the class agents in the hierarchies of control is that their job security and prospects for promotion in the hierarchies do not depend on whether they produce more value than they receive (as they do with labourers). Since most of them get salaries far in excess of their productive contributions anyway, their job security and prospects depend on how successfully they perform the capitalist functions allocated to them. The higher up in the hierarchies they are, the more exclusively do they perform these functions and the greater is the proportion of surplus value in their salaries. Salaries above the value of labour power, that is, in excess of what is needed to maintain the conventional standard of living of someone who can do the relevant productive work, are a major method of transferring the social surplus from the ruled to the ruling class. They are a particularly 'invisible' method, because the unproductive tasks for which supervisors are paid can sometimes appear not dissimilar in kind to the productive tasks of wage labourers. Nevertheless, people who receive salaries which consist largely of surplus value have interests in common with the owners of capital and therefore act out the role of the bourgeoisie. We will call such agents *members* of the bourgeoisie, remembering that the word 'member' in this context connotes concrete mediation of a (hidden) infrastructural force.

Although it is difficult to calculate how many such members of the bourgeoisie there are in Japan, estimates can be made. There are at least four ranks in most Japanese companies which are engaged in one or both hierarchies of control. I have already mentioned directors, whose composition by the capitalisation of the institutions they control is given in table 1.6. Although there is no question of the interests in capitalism and membership in the bourgeoisie of these directors, there are, as we shall see below, differences in the strengths of these interests.

The particular class mediation of upper and middle managers is not quite as clear-cut and requires careful analysis, particularly because Ōhashi places them in the labour aristocracy.[9] In spite of certain variations, the hierarchies of control in Japanese companies are remarkably similar in broad outline, and can be summarised as follows: board of directors (*torishimariyaku*)→ department managers and factory managers (*buchō, kōjōchō*)→ section managers (*kachō*)→ division managers (*kakarichō*)→ supervisors and chargehands (*shunin and sagyōchō*)→ ordinary employees (*ippan shain*). By the time the department level is reached, control over means of production and

Table 1.6. *Numbers of directors, by capitalisation of institutions* (¥ *million*), *1980*

	Under 2	2–5	5–10	10–50	50–100	100–1,000	Over 1,000	Total
Finance and insurance[a]	15,301	18,147	8,102	9,515	1,090	2,330	2,304	56,789
All other industries[b]	1,146,500	1,140,255	621,767	763,648	87,543	85,136	27,061	3,871,910
Total	1,161,801	1,158,402	629,869	773,163	88,633	87,466	29,365	3,928,699
Minus directors of firms with under 5 persons[c]	550,000	—	—	—	—	—	—	550,000
Total	—	—	—	—	—	—	—	3,378,699

[a]Because information on the numbers of directors in finance and insurance companies is not available, estimates had to be made on the assumption that the numbers per company were the same as in other industries. For data on the numbers and size of financial institutions, see Shūkan Tōyō Keizai [The Oriental Economist], *Keizai tōkei nenkan* [Economic Statistics Yearbook], 1979, Rinji zōkan [Special issue], no. 4153 (Tokyo: Tōyō keizai shinpōsha, 1979), p. 347.

[b]See Ōkurashō [Ministry of Finance], *Zaisei kin'yū tōkei geppō* [Monthly Bulletin on Monetary and Financial Statistics], no. 355, Hōnin kigyō tōkei nenpō tokushū [Special Yearly Issue on Statistics in Incorporated Enterprises] (Tokyo: Ōkurashō insatsukyoku, 1981), pp. 46–7.

[c]Since such enterprises do not rely predominantly on wage labour, their directors are under the influence of the petty bourgeoisie rather than the bourgeoisie. There are an estimated 500,000–600,000 directors of small companies in this category.

control over labour power are hard to distinguish, but below this level particular sections and divisions are usually concerned more with one than the other. Only at the supervisory level is control purely over labour power, since supervisors play very limited roles in deciding what machinery to introduce or how it should be used.

In my survey of 459 employees in sixty-two companies conducted in the winter of 1976–77, I tried to ascertain how far members of the hierarchy were involved in the function of controlling labour power. They were asked to indicate the extent to which their jobs involved the following: supervising the work of other employees; hiring, firing, evaluating, and promoting other employees; dealing with disputes among other employees; and assigning tasks to other employees. They selected answers from the following: 'the major part of my job,' 'an important part of my job,' 'I sometimes do it,' and 'no part of my job.' These answers were weighted and an overall score of the extent to which respondents performed capital's function of controlling labour power was computed. High scores indicate high involvement in this function, while low scores indicate a low involvement. Table 1.7 presents the results. A sharp difference in involvement in controlling labour power is revealed between ordinary employees and those persons in the hierarchy. There is little doubt that ranks are given to Japanese employees in order to have them perform this, the most important, function of the capitalist.

But the hierarchy of control does more than simply keep workers in line. Department, section, and division managers are the main persons responsible for gathering the information on which long- and short-term decisions concerning plant and investment are made (by directors). These are the major decisions affecting the company's present and future profitability, and they concern such matters as developing new production processes and new products, establishing branches in some areas and closing down others, buying and selling in new markets, rationalising the labour force, and experimenting with new ways of raising productivity. Though final decisions on these matters are made at directors' meetings, the preparation and information gathering is made by middle and upper management, all tasks which the individual capitalist undertakes himself. In the survey I conducted, middle and upper managers (of sections and departments) described their jobs largely in these terms when asked to say in their own words what their jobs involved. Lower managers (of

Table 1.7. *Involvement in controlling labour power, by rank of employee*

	0%	1–2%	3–6%	7–10%	11–16%	Total no.
Directors	0.0	5.3	5.3	36.8	52.6	19
Department managers	0.0	0.0	20.8	41.7	37.5	24
Section managers	2.3	4.5	6.8	43.2	43.2	44
Division managers	7.4	11.1	44.4	31.5	5.6	54
Supervisors	1.4	11.4	27.1	40.0	20.0	70
Ordinary employees	48.0	27.9	18.3	3.9	1.7	229

Table 1.8. *Percentages of persons involved in control over investment and other tasks*

	MAP	MAP/TP	SO	P	U	Total no.
Directors	70.6	11.8	5.9	5.9	5.9	17
Department managers	71.4	4.8	0.0	0.0	23.8	21
Section managers	63.4	9.8	22.0	2.4	2.4	41
Division managers	28.0	0.0	24.0	12.0	36.0	50
Supervisors	3.1	4.7	67.2	12.5	12.5	64
Ordinary employees	0.9	0.5	2.7	23.7	72.1	219

divisions) were also significantly involved, although very few supervisors were. Replies were grouped into the following five categories;

(*a*) managerial, administrative, and planning, which refer to the above-mentioned tasks (abbreviated MAP);

(*b*) MAP plus technical or professional tasks which might be seen as productive (abbreviated MAP and TP);

(*c*) supervisory plus any one or more of MAP, TP, P, and U (abbreviated SO);

(*d*) productive non-supervisory work (abbreviated P);

(*e*) unproductive labouring tasks (abbreviated U).[10]

Table 1.8 shows that capital's function of control over investment and planning is carried out by all ranks above that of supervisor, and that the higher one goes the larger the proportion of persons involved in it.

In another survey, in which managers were asked to list the most important ability required of their rank, a similar predominance of

Table 1.9. *Most important ability required of managers*

	Department managers	Section managers	Division managers
Analytical judgement	18	15	7
Planning ability	13	15	5
Feeling of responsibility	9	6	13
Firm conviction	9	3	2
Leadership and supervision	20	26	19
Specialised knowledge	14	19	22
Social common sense	13	3	3
Improvement of one's work	3	8	11
Cooperation with decisions	0	1	4
Implementation of plans	1	4	14
Total	100	100	100
Total no.	131	441	317

Note: Numerical values represent the percentages of each group which mentioned each ability.
Source: Ueda Toshiaki, 'Kanrishoku yōin kanri o kangaeru' [Thoughts on the Management of Managers], in Rōmu gyōsei kenkyūjo [Research Institute of Labour Administration], *Gendai no kanrishoku mondai: sono tamenteki kentō to kaiketsu e no michi* [Problems of Contemporary Management: Towards a Thorough Investigation and Solution] (Tokyo: Rōmu gyōsei kenkyūjo, 1976), p. 258.

capitalist functions was mentioned, particularly by department and section managers. Table 1.9 provides the percentages of each managerial group which mentioned each ability. Division managers, who seem to perform capitalist and labouring functions more or less equally, and supervisors, who also perform both functions but have little control over means of production, are clearly on the boundary of the capitalist class, since neither can be said to have unambiguous interests. However, division managers seem on the whole to be much closer to the capitalist than to the working class, and they do not occupy a sufficiently ambiguous position to be placed in the middle class. Supervisors, however, do occupy such a position, and are in the middle class.

For their roles as capital's functionaries, managers receive part of the surplus in the form of large salaries. Department managers, who in some cases are also directors, generally get only a bit less than ordinary directors. Table 1.10 shows the pay differentials among members of the controlling hierarchy as well as between them and a typical woman worker. In addition to the basic pay indicated here,

Table 1.10. *Monthly pay of capital's functionaries: averages in June 1981*[a]

	Amount (¥)	Index
Directors	616,298	423
Department managers	485,696	333
Section managers	371,284	255
Division managers	292,517	201
Supervisors		
Office	263,042	180
Factory (skilled)	275,772	189
Workers		
General machine operator	216,484	149
Typist	145,731	100

[a]The amounts for supervisors and workers are for April 1981.
Source: Shūkan Tōyō Keizai [The Oriental Economist], *Dēta fuairu: chingin, nenkin, jinji kanri* [Data File: Wages, Pensions, and Personnel Management], 1982, Rinji zōkan [Special issue], no. 4342 (Tokyo: Tōyō keizai shinpōsha, 1981), pp. 267, 274.

bonuses and other allowances widen the differentials even further. For example, a director's bonuses add up to about the equivalent of 6.4 months' basic pay, while those of a productive worker equal only about 5.1 months' pay.[11] Neither do productive workers get the car and entertainment expenses thrown in which directors do.

The evidence so far considered suggests very strongly that department, section, and division managers are all members of the bourgeoisie in virtue of the functions they perform and the surpluses they receive in return. It is thus important to know just how large a group in the system of social relations they compose. Though comprehensive information in this regard is not available, reasonable estimates can be made on the basis of one study which calculated the proportions of the different types of managers in firms of different sizes. Table 1.11 sets out the results of these estimates.

A number of points explicit in this table require explanation. First, I have not made estimates of functionaries in firms capitalised at under ¥2 million or in ones with fewer than ten operatives, simply because in these firms most functions of capital are exercised by directors or individual proprietors themselves. In firms capitalised at ¥2–10 million and the unincorporated firms, no attempt was made to estimate the numbers of particular types of managers, partly because the survey on which I relied did not cover small firms, partly

Table 1.11. Estimated numbers of capital's functionaries, 1980[a]

Firm size and type	Department managers No.	%	Section managers No.	%	Division managers No.	%	Total No.	%
Corporations	*252,161*	—	*900,429*	—	*1,278,425*	—	*2,976,600[b]*	—
¥2–5 mil.	—	—	—	—	—	—	218,003	5.0[c]
¥5–10 mil.	—	—	—	—	—	—	327,582	10.0[c]
¥10–50 mil.	147,171	1.9	542,209	7.0	751,347	9.7	1,440,727	18.6
¥50–100 mil.	30,052	1.7	88,387	5.0	104,296	5.9	222,735	12.6
¥100–1,000 mil.	42,466	1.3	130,666	4.0	186,198	5.7	359,330	11.0
Over ¥1,000 mil.	32,472	0.7	139,167	3.0	236,584	5.1	408,223	8.8
Financial institutions	*3,311*	—	*11,824*	—	*16,787*	—	*40,095[b]*	—
Unincorporated enterprises	—	—	—	—	—	—	*277,000*	—
10–29 persons	—	—	—	—	—	—	220,400	20.0[c]
30–49 persons	—	—	—	—	—	—	32,000	20.0[c]
50 & more persons	—	—	—	—	—	—	24,600	20.0[c]
Government	*48,410*	*1.0[c]*	*193,640*	*4.0[c]*	*290,460*	*6.0[c]*	*532,510*	*11.0[c]*
Total	303,882	—	1,105,893	—	1,585,672	—	3,826,205	—

[a] The total numbers of persons in the different corporations, on the basis of which the estimates are made, come from the same sources as table 1.6, while the totals in unincorporated enterprises and government come from *Shūgyō kōzō kihon chōsa hōkoku*, 1979, pp. 50–2.

[b] This total includes the functionaries in firms capitalised at less than ¥10 million for which estimates of particular types of managers were not made.

[c] These are my estimated proportions; the others come from Rōmu gyōsei kenkyūjo [Research Institute of Labour Administration], 'Shūgyō kigyō ni okeru kanrishoku kōsei nado no jittai' [The Composition of Managers in Major Enterprises], in *Gendai no kanrishoku mondai*, p. 330.

because of the great variety of hierarchies in small firms. Second, my estimated proportions of functionaries in small firms (5% for those capitalised at ¥2–5 million and 10% for the ¥5–10-million ones) are based on the fact that their directors normally carry out many of capital's most important tasks. Third, although the functioning of the Japanese state is analysed only in chapters 6 and 7, I have included in the capitalist class the hierarchies of control in government enterprises and the civil service. This is because the state is part and parcel of capitalist production and a major form in which the ruling class is organised and its power manifested. Fourth, my estimated proportions of functionaries in unincorporated enterprises, which are generally small, may seem large (20%) in comparison with the proportions in small companies. But since unincorporated firms do not have boards of directors, individual proprietors require larger numbers of additional functionaries.

To estimate the numbers of functionaries in small firms is fraught with difficulties. There is no reliable information on their proportions, and my estimates are based solely on observations of a small sample. The variety of systems of control, ranging from that typical of large firms to ones in which a single owner monopolises this function, also makes precise calculations extremely hazardous. Another difficulty is that as the size of firm decreases, so does the ability of functionaries to avoid productive work, and in the smallest establishments even owners spend considerable time working alongside their employees. Though the impact of these problems has been reduced by not making detailed estimates of functionaries in smaller firms (which usually have only the equivalent of a supervisor), the ones that were made should be seen as no more than guidelines for grasping the overall 'reach' of the Japanese bourgeoisie. Some of these problems, which are related to divisions within the capitalist class, are discussed in more detail below.

To get an overall idea of the size of the Japanese bourgeoisie, we must add to the estimated 3.8 million functionaries and the 3.4 million directors the owners of unincorporated enterprises. Together these groups comprise the economically active members of their class, namely those persons who in one way or another are directly involved in the control of capital. The numbers of individual proprietors (who of course both own and control capital) in the bourgeoisie can be estimated from table 1.12.

Since interests in capitalism derive from an ability to extract

Table 1.12. *Persons engaged in unincorporated enterprises, by sex, occupational status, and firm size, 1979 (1,000 persons)*

Firm size (persons)	Proprietors		Family members		Employees		Total	Employees as % of total
	No.	% females	No.	% females	No.	% females		
1	3,999	54.8	15	80.0	45	71.1	4,059	1.1
2–4	4,926	11.9	5,100	82.2	1,937	43.7	11,962	16.2
5–9	464	8.0	504	70.8	1,591	43.7	2,559	62.2
10–49	140	8.6	113	76.1	1,262	50.1	1,515	83.3
50 and over	4	0.0	2	50.0	123	61.0	129	95.3
Total	9,537	29.6	5,733	81.1	4,963	46.0	20,234	24.5

Source: *Shūgyō kōzō kihon chōsa hōkoku,* 1979, pp. 50, 58.

surplus value from wage labourers, we can only include in the bourgeoisie those proprietors who rely predominantly on wage labour, that is, with five or more operatives. These 608,000 persons bring the total number of economically active members of the bourgeoisie to 7,812,904. On the basis of table 1.5, it is safe to assume that these people are also the major owners of capital, even though the two groups do not coincide exactly. Correspondence is particularly close in the case of salaried office employees, who include capital's functionaries and all the technical and professional persons who become functionaries once they receive their promotions into the hierarchies of control. Since corporation executives and individual proprietors of capitalist enterprises are also generally both owners and controllers of capital, the overlap here is also considerable. The main large owners of capital who exercise little control over it are a few labourers and those persons in the petty bourgeoisie, the group engaged in professional services, and the group without occupation who own over ¥5 million in surplus-value-earning assets. If we add them to the 7.8 million controlling group, we get a capitalist class of some 9.91 million. This indicates an enormous reach for a ruling class in a population of 88.3 million (over the age of 15). Over one in ten Japanese adult persons is therefore firmly in the grip of ruling-class forces.

The larger the ruling class in any society, the more important it is to know which divisions within its ranks can be exploited in order to weaken its hold. Since owners of capital in Japan largely coincide with its controllers, there would be little point in trying to drive a wedge between these two groups. Neither must we look to the different sectors of the economy for exploitable conflicts, since in Japan the most powerful interests operate in almost all industries simultaneously. For divisions which might temporarily swing sections of the capitalist class into alliances with the working class, we must look instead to the way in which the social surplus is distributed among members of the ruling class. The easiest way to illustrate how this happens is to take a hypothetical example.

Suppose in any industry there are only three firms with very different technologies, which correspond to different labour productivities. Firm A has the most backward technology, and produces a given output, say 110 units, in a total time of 130 hours, of which 70 is embodied in the materials and machines used up and 60 is put in by the labourers. The money spent on the machines and materials is called constant capital, because what they are worth and so what must normally be paid for them is exactly equivalent to the value they add to the final product. We are here reckoning value in terms of labour hours, but the labour hours of a worker of average skill, with average technology, and working at average speed. These are called socially necessary hours. To say therefore that the constant capital of firm A is worth 70 means simply that the machines, materials, and so on used up in producing 110 units themselves require a total of 70 hours to produce in average firms (that is, with average technology, skills, etc.) in those industries. The 70 are called constant capital because if the machines and materials are completely used up in producing the 110 units, of the total time needed 70 are as it were embodied in the means of production consumed. We might refer to the 70 as the indirect time, as opposed to the direct time put in by the workers. It is important to see that the source of the capitalist's profit cannot lie in this indirect time, for if he made his money by paying the equivalent of only 60 for what was worth 70, the capitalists who produce means of production would make a loss. The profit must somehow derive from the 60 hours of direct time, but since firm A has the most backward technology, we cannot call these 60 hours actually worked socially necessary hours. To find out how many socially necessary hours were worked, we must examine the other firms in the industry.

Suppose firm B uses average technology and produces 120 units in a total of 120 hours, of which 80 are indirect and 40 are direct. We let firm C, which has the most advanced and expensive technology, produce 130 units in only 110 hours (90 indirect and 20 direct). The *new value*, as opposed to the old value embodied in the machines and materials used up, produced by each firm will be equal to the difference between this old value and the total value of its output. The latter will be equal to the number of units produced multiplied by the average time per unit of the three. Since a total of 360 units were produced in a total of 360 hours, the socially necessary (or average) time per unit is 1. The total value of A's output is therefore 110 times 1, which is 110. Since its constant capital was worth 70, the new value is 40. Because it had below-average technology, 60 hours of actual direct time produce only 40 hours of socially necessary labour. The opposite applies to firm C, which we see in the illustration below produced 40 hours of new value in only 20 hours actually worked. If firms employ different technologies, similar actual direct hours produce different amounts of socially necessary labour. Since this new value is the source of the capitalist's profit, if each of the workers is paid the same for the same hours actually worked, the owners of the firms will get different rates of profit. Let us assume that for a 40-hour week actually worked all workers get wages which can buy commodities worth 20 socially necessary hours. The money spent on wages we call variable capital, since the new value that can be created by hiring workers varies from the value of the goods they buy with their wages. The new value is therefore divided into variable capital (V) and surplus value (S), and the rate of profit of each will be equal to its surplus value divided by its costs (constant capital plus variable capital, or $C+V$). The operations of the three firms can be represented as in the accompanying unnumbered table.

	Value of constant capital	+	Actual direct time	=	Actual total time	Units	Total value	New value	V	S	$\dfrac{S}{C+V}$
A	70	+	60	=	130	110	110	40	40	30	10%
B	80	+	40	=	120	120	120	40	20	20	20%
C	90	+	20	=	110	120	130	40	10	30	30%
	240	+	120	=	360	360	360	120	60	60	20%

The above-average profit rate of firm C results from the above-average technology it employs, which makes its workers more productive, that is, produce more new value in a given amount of actual direct time, than those of the other firms. Its extra profit is only possible so long as there are firms with a lower labour productivity than its own, so that the socially necessary time per unit of output is greater than its actual time. We refer to this extra profit as *differential monopoly profit*, because it results from different labour productivities within an industry.

Differential monopoly power, which is based on above-average technology (or employing workers with above-average skills), is the most important source of division among members of the Japanese bourgeoisie. But the differences do not typically reveal themselves in the balance sheets of firms as different rates of profit. This is because the greater a firm's labour productivity, the higher the wages it can afford and the more surplus value it can distribute to functionaries as

Table 1.13. *Rates of profit by firm size (money value of capital) and industry in the corporate sector, 1975 and 1980*

Industry	Firm size, by capital (¥ mil.)									
	Petty firms (under 2)		Small firms (2–50)		Medium firms (50–100)		Large firms (over 100)		Average	
	1975	1980	1975	1980	1975	1980	1975	1980	1975	1980
Agriculture	16.9	1.3	2.7	−0.9	−0.8	2.5	2.0	0.0	4.3	0.0
Forestry/hunting	3.7	6.2	2.2	5.5	1.6	0.3	2.4	2.5	2.2	3.6
Fisheries	16.4	−2.6	0.5	−0.9	−0.2	4.7	3.0	2.3	1.9	0.1
Mining	3.0	5.5	5.4	9.7	2.4	8.7	23.0	26.6	14.4	20.4
Construction	4.9	2.0	6.4	4.5	6.1	5.4	4.9	4.0	5.5	4.2
Manufacturing	1.9	7.0	6.1	7.5	3.2	8.0	3.9	7.1	4.3	7.2
Wholesale/retail	4.5	3.9	4.6	4.4	4.1	4.7	2.6	3.9	3.6	4.2
Transport/communications	4.4	0.2	4.2	5.3	5.0	4.8	3.5	4.8	3.8	4.8
Electricity/gas/water	—	—	8.2	8.0	7.0	7.3	6.6	10.0	6.6	10.0
Real estate	1.4	8.0	3.0	4.9	2.9	3.8	4.2	5.4	3.5	5.1
Services	7.2	−0.8	3.8	4.9	3.8	4.7	4.9	5.3	4.6	4.7
Average	4.1	4.3	5.0	5.3	3.8	5.7	4.0	6.2	4.3	5.8

Source: Zaisei kin'yū tōkei geppō, nos. 295 and 355 (1976 and 1981), pp. 46–87 and 46–119.

'salaries.' Table 1.13 reveals that the balance sheets of firms in the corporate sector in Japan show very similar rates of profit (money profit as a percentage of the money value of assets) for small firms (with their generally more backward technologies) and large ones (with their normally more advanced technologies) in almost all industries.

The largest variations from the 4.3% and 5.8% averages in 1975 and 1980 respectively were in agriculture (which is overwhelmingly a small-scale and somewhat unique industry, discussed in chapter 3), fisheries (certain branches of which share the pertinent characteristics of agriculture), electric power (which, as is pointed out in chapter 6, benefited from the 'oil shocks'), and mining. In each of these cases, but particularly the latter two, there is what might be called an *absolute monopoly power*, which is based on an ability to prevent entry into an industry through controlling vital non-reproducible factors of production. Part of their profit is therefore a concealed form of what is called the *rent* that ownership of natural resources can extract. Further discussion of this rent must await the analysis of the peasantry in chapter 3 and the energy 'crisis' in chapter 6.

If, apart from a few special cases involving rent, the profit rates of the different capitals are very similar, what evidence is there for differential monopoly power and divisions within the capitalist class? The best evidence is found in the bourgeois concept of value added (which equals money wages, salaries, profits, interest, rent, and taxes), which comes closest to representing the Marxist concept of new value, and in the different wages of workers and salaries of functionaries in firms of different sizes. Table 1.14 reveals that the value added per person engaged, the average wages, and the directors' salaries in large firms are all typically about twice what they are in small firms. It also shows that the value of fixed assets per person engaged, which is a good measure of the different technologies employed, is six or seven times as much in large firms as it is in small firms.

The variations among directors' fees suggest similar variations among the salaries of other functionaries. Both result primarily from differential monopoly power and separate the capitalist class into different fractions. Although the incomes of all derive from surplus value, those in small firms receive not simply less than half of what those in large firms get, but even less than many of the latter's workers.

Table 1.14. *Evidence of differential monopoly in the corporate sector: all industries excepting finance, 1975 and 1980 (¥ million)*

| | Firm size, by capital (¥ mil.) | | | | | | | | | |
| | Petty (under 2) | | Small (2–50) | | Medium (50–100) | | Large (over 100) | | Average | |
	1975	1980	1975	1980	1975	1980	1975	1980	1975	1980
Value added per operative	2.4	3.7	2.6	3.8	2.8	4.5	4.1	7.1	3.1	4.8
Fixed assets per operative	1.4	2.3	2.4	3.5	3.6	5.8	9.3	13.6	4.5	6.4
Average wages/salaries	1.4	2.0	1.7	2.3	2.0	2.9	2.7	4.0	2.0	2.8
Average directors' fees	1.9	2.5	2.6	3.4	3.2	4.9	4.5	6.2	2.4	3.3

Source: As table 1.13.

Apart from receiving smaller amounts of surplus value and paying their workers lower wages, the non-monopoly fractions of the capitalist class have one other way of dealing with their inability to afford the technological equipment of the monopoly fraction. They can try to get out of industries or branches and processes within industries in which a competitive advantage depends so heavily on the use of costly technology, and concentrate on small-scale labour-intensive industries. Table 1.15 shows that there is a tendency, which the recession accelerated, for non-monopoly capital to specialise in agriculture and other primary industries, construction, certain branches of light manufacturing industry, wholesale and retail, and services. Monopoly capital is concentrated in heavy industry: chemicals, petroleum, iron and steel, non-ferrous metals, electric/electronics, transport machines, shipbuilding, marine transportation, and electric power. The former are all more labour intensive than the latter, so that the new value small firms produce in the industries of their specialisation is not so much less than the actual time put in. In fact, in all these industries, excepting services (analysis of which belongs to a discussion of the petty bourgeoisie), the value added per person in small firms is not much less than ¥1 million of what it is in large firms.

One of the major reasons for the persistence of large numbers of small firms in Japan is this specialisation in labour-intensive industries and processes, which has reduced, but not eliminated, the differential monopoly power of large firms. Small firms still rely heavily on paying lower wages to their workers and lower salaries to their functionaries in order to compensate for their lower labour productivity. Although the smaller surpluses generate divisions among members of the capitalist class, these are not sufficient to make the Japan Communist Party's strategy of an anti-monopoly alliance between the working class and small capital a viable one. The sole expedient open to small capital of keeping wages well below average rates makes it more rather than less reactionary than monopoly capital.

Partly in response to increasing imports of light manufacturers from low-wage countries in Asia, small firms have either themselves been moving overseas or replacing male with low-paid female workers. Table 1.16 shows the changes in the proportions of women in large and small firms in major industries in 1974–9. There was an across-the-board increase in women workers in small firms, which

Table 1.15. Shares of total sales in each industry of the different fractions of the capitalist class (corporate sector only), 1975 and 1980

	Petty		Small		Medium		Large		Share of industry in total corporate sales	
	1975	1980	1975	1980	1975	1980	1975	1980	1975	1980
Agriculture	15.0	21.8	76.8	59.5	5.7	15.1	2.4	3.6	0.2	0.2
Forestry/hunting	12.0	10.6	45.3	39.9	13.5	19.4	29.3	30.1	0.0	0.0
Fisheries/aquatics	4.0	4.1	43.7	50.6	7.4	5.7	44.8	39.7	0.3	0.3
Mining	6.9	5.5	45.8	35.1	3.7	3.5	43.6	55.9	0.5	0.5
Construction	10.6	7.0	46.3	53.6	3.5	5.6	39.5	33.8	7.9	8.3
Manufacturing	4.4	3.7	30.1	28.7	4.7	6.0	60.9	61.6	32.5	32.0
Food/tobacco	4.9	4.1	35.5	34.6	4.7	7.0	54.8	54.3	3.7	3.2
Textiles/clothing	6.7	7.2	57.5	52.6	7.7	9.8	28.0	30.5	2.8	2.1
Lumber/wood	14.0	11.1	60.4	63.3	5.6	10.6	20.0	15.1	0.9	0.9
Paper/pulp	6.6	3.5	28.4	32.6	7.6	7.3	57.3	56.7	1.0	1.0
Printing/publishing	13.9	13.0	54.7	46.4	6.0	6.9	25.2	33.6	1.0	1.1
Chemicals	0.7	1.1	14.4	12.1	3.8	5.7	81.1	81.1	3.5	3.3
Petroleum	0.1	0.0	1.3	1.2	0.2	0.4	98.4	98.4	2.1	2.1
Ceramics	3.8	2.5	40.0	41.4	5.1	8.9	51.0	47.2	1.2	1.2
Iron/steel	2.3	1.2	8.3	13.9	3.0	4.1	86.3	80.9	2.4	2.2
Non-ferrous metals	0.8	0.6	10.5	12.5	5.5	3.9	83.1	82.9	0.9	1.2
Metallic products	7.9	8.5	61.8	54.8	6.4	8.1	23.9	28.6	2.1	1.8
Machines	5.2	3.2	33.2	35.8	8.2	6.9	53.5	54.1	2.2	2.1
Electric/electronics	2.6	1.0	14.8	22.9	3.3	4.7	79.1	71.4	2.9	3.6
Transport machines	0.7	0.9	11.8	9.8	2.4	5.1	85.2	84.2	2.3	2.9
Precision instruments	5.3	5.7	35.1	35.6	9.5	7.5	50.0	51.2	0.5	0.6
Shipbuilding	2.0	4.2	10.1	13.6	0.9	2.6	87.0	79.6	0.9	0.6
Other	7.9	9.3	56.5	50.2	5.4	6.5	29.9	34.1	2.0	2.1

Wholesale	4.6	3.4	37.6	39.5	6.2	7.5	51.6	49.5	40.0	39.5
Retail	21.6	14.3	46.8	49.2	3.1	4.8	28.6	31.7	8.7	8.2
Real estate	10.8	8.2	49.5	59.3	7.8	6.8	32.0	25.7	1.6	2.1
Land transportation	7.4	4.9	46.0	50.4	5.0	6.4	41.5	38.3	1.7	1.6
Marine transportation	1.8	1.1	19.6	19.9	5.9	4.2	72.7	74.8	1.0	0.8
Other transport/ communications	5.1	2.9	32.1	29.4	11.5	12.8	51.3	54.8	0.9	0.9
Electricity/gas/water	—		0.4	0.2	0.4	0.3	99.2	99.5	1.2	1.6
Services	17.6	11.2	50.2	56.3	6.7	6.7	25.5	25.9	3.4	4.0

Source: As table 1.13.

Table 1.16. *Proportions of females in small and large firms, by major industry, 1974–9*

	1974		1979	
	Small[a]	Large	Small[a]	Large
Manufacturing	40.2	24.4	44.3	21.8
Wholesale	29.5	27.9	30.3	26.7
Retail	51.6	47.1	53.1	46.8
Services	52.4	42.0	54.1	42.6
Total	37.9	29.3	40.1	30.2
Total no. (1,000)	10,092	3,762	12,146	4,087

[a]Small firms in most industries are ones with fewer than 300 persons engaged (100 in wholesale and 50 in retail).
Source: Chūshō kigyōchō [Small and Medium Enterprise Agency], *Chūshō kigyō hakusho* [White Paper on Small and Medium Enterprises], 1980 (Tokyo: Ōkurashō insatsukyoku, 1981), pp. 287–8.

paralleled the large numbers of women (and men) laid off by monopoly firms. As is pointed out in chapter 6, the latter carried out major staff rationalisations in the same period.

The anti-monopoly strategy, however, is defended for reasons besides the productivity differences between small and large firms. The most important is the widespread practice of sub-contracting. This can be linked to the putting-out system, under which those who receive orders from capitalist enterprises are no less exploited than wage labourers. However, as we shall see below, it makes a world of difference whether the recipients of sub-contracts are family firms which do not use wage labour or whether they are themselves capitalist enterprises.

There is little doubt that the practice of sub-contracting work out is more widespread in Japan than anywhere else. In manufacturing, for example, the overwhelming majority of small firms receive sub-contracts, and most of the smallest of them do nothing but work received in this way. Table 1.17 shows how dependence on parent companies increases as firms become smaller. It is based on a massive survey conducted in 1971 and published only in 1974, which provides the most detailed analysis of the system of sub-contracting that is available. Though it may appear dated, subsequent White Papers

Table 1.17. *Dependence on sub-contracts of small manufacturing firms,* *1971*

Firm size (no. of operatives)	Total no. of firms	% tied solely to one parent company	% tied to two or more parent companies	% partly engaged in sub-contracting	% not engaged at all
1–3	246,657	30.2	27.5	4.5	37.8
4–9	227,763	17.0	33.0	7.5	42.5
10–29	93,738	11.1	34.5	9.7	44.7
30–99	29,654	10.3	31.5	11.1	47.1
100–299	7,351	8.8	24.2	13.2	54.1

Source: Chūshō kigyōchō [Small and Medium Enterprise Agency], *Dai 4 kai kōgyō jittai kihon chōsa hōkokusho* [Report on the Fourth Basic Survey of Factory Conditions], *Sōkatsuhen* [Summary volume] (Tokyo: Tsūshō sangyō chōsakai, 1974), p. 126.

Table 1.18. *Distribution of small manufacturing firms, by sales to three major customers as a per cent of total sales, 1971*

Firm size (operatives)	Under 20%	20–40%	40–60%	60–80%	80–100%
1–3	5.9	3.2	3.9	5.5	81.5
4–9	6.1	5.8	7.5	9.0	71.6
10–29	5.6	8.6	10.4	11.6	63.9
30–99	7.0	11.9	11.4	12.9	56.8
100–299	8.7	13.6	13.4	13.0	51.4

Source: Dai 4 kai kōgyō jittai kihon chōsa hōkokusho, p. 126.

have relied on it and noted that most of the tendencies which it brought to light have if anything been strengthened.

An important measure of the degree to which small firms are at the mercy of large ones is the share in their total sales occupied by their sales to their three main customers. In manufacturing this dependence is enormous, as is revealed by table 1.18. Upwards of three-quarters of the smallest firms sell between 80 and 100% of their output to no more than three customers.

From the point of view of the parent companies, sub-contracts are extremely useful, since in many cases the parent only assembles parts

Table 1.19. *Extent of parent companies' use of sub-contracts, 1971*

Industry	Value of sub-contracts ———————————— % Total shipment value		Average no. of child companies per parent company
Iron/steel	9.3		30.9
Nonferrous metals	8.9		18.9
Metal goods (hardware)	14.2		30.6
General machines	22.6		104.1
Electrical machines	23.7		106.5
Transportation machines	26.8		108.4
Precision instruments	40.9		123.8

Source: Chūshō kigyō hakusho, 1975, p. 133.

made by small firms. The 1980 White Paper on Small and Medium Enterprises noted that in manufacturing, apart from the principal process, sub-contracted work had surpassed the halfway mark.[12] Table 1.19 indicates the proportions in 1971 in various manufacturing lines of the value of sub-contracted work in the total shipment value of the output of those parent companies which had over 300 employees and which were quoted on the Stock Exchange.

The power of parent over child companies is not limited to the ability to expand and cut orders with impunity or to dictate contract prices. It penetrates the very methods of production the child companies employ. Table 1.20 shows, for 1975, the proportions of child companies (according to the shares of their total sales taken by their single major customer) which depended on their parent companies for various forms of what are referred to as 'guidance and assistance.' An even greater degree of power is wielded over the sources from which child companies obtain raw materials. This increases greatly with the extent to which they are involved in sub-contracting, as is revealed by table 1.21.

The sole freedom child companies which are heavily engaged in sub-contracting seem to have is to absorb losses and be highly vulnerable to bankruptcy. The only independent countermeasures they can take are against the wages and jobs of their own employees. By 1977 close to 2,000 small firms were going bankrupt each month, forcing more than three times this number of workers to look for new

Table 1.20. *Proportions of child companies which receive 'guidance and assistance' from parent companies, 1975*

Type of 'guidance and assistance'	Proportion of child companies by degree of dependence on single major customer				
	Average	Under 30%	30–50%	50–75%	Over 75%
Management techniques	22.9	9.6	18.5	26.8	32.6
Skills	53.9	33.5	50.5	58.4	68.2
Loan and sale of machinery	29.1	15.8	23.7	27.1	43.4
Finance	15.0	7.1	12.3	16.0	22.8

Source: As table 1.19, p. 144.

Table 1.21. *Proportions of small (under 300 operatives) manufacturing firms which depend on their major customer for raw materials, 1971*

Degree of engagement in sub-contracting	Source of raw materials			
	Free from major customer	Bought from major customer	Bought on authority of major customer	Other
Tied to one parent	73.5	8.2	6.9	11.4
Tied to more than one parent	32.5	8.2	18.9	40.4
Partly engaged in sub-contracting	17.8	8.6	21.2	52.5
Not engaged in sub-contracting	8.4	7.4	17.7	66.5

Source: Dai 4 kai kōgyō jittai kihon chōsa hōkokusho, p. 127.

jobs.[13] For reasons to be discussed in the next chapter, new small establishments sprang up almost as rapidly, but they faced the same problems and were threatened by the same fate. By 1980, when large firms seemed to have emerged from the worst of the recession, small ones in almost every industry were planning to reduce their equipment investments.[14]

It would be tedious to discuss in detail all the difficulties small firms face because of fluctuating sales, shortages of finance, rising costs, low output prices, and shortages of raw materials, all of which are largely under the control of large firms.[15] There is no question of the control of parent companies, or that the former derive the greater benefit. What is questionable, however, is whether sub-contracting and other relationships between small and large firms can be described as antagonistic and the cause of contradictory interests between them. The present strategy of the Japan Communist Party assumes that they can, and the party has spared little effort in its campaign to win small capitalists into the anti-monopoly alliance.

This strategy is fraught with difficulties, and it can at worst do irreparable harm to the socialist movement. This is because it plays down the most basic mechanism by which the surplus is created and extracted in the process of production in favour of an emphasis on the struggle among capitalists over relative shares of the surplus in the process of circulation. It is a particularly misleading strategy for the bulk of the Japanese working class, which is employed in small firms, since these workers are asked to see their interests in terms of their bosses' efforts to capture as large a share of the surplus as they can. They are asked to help their bosses get back from the monopolies some of the surplus which their bosses extract from them. The anti-monopoly strategy therefore tends to divide the working class according to the different abilities of the various fractions of the bourgeoisie to appropriate shares of the surplus. It confuses their understanding of the dynamics of capitalist exploitation and under-mines their ability to develop united organisations against it.

However, to reject an alliance of small capital and workers against monopoly capital does not mean that the working class cannot weaken the bourgeoisie by exploiting differences within its ranks. To know at which point this becomes collaboration with some members of the capitalist class requires a more detailed analysis of that class's various fractions: their size, interests, and organisational and other strengths and weaknesses.

At least four fractions of the ruling class can be identified in the corporate sector: (*a*) monopoly capital in large firms (capitalised at over ¥100 million) to which surpluses are transferred from smaller firms; (*b*) medium capital which surrenders very little surplus and which itself sub-contracts work out; (*c*) small capital in firms (¥2–50 million) which surrender massive surpluses to monopoly capital, on which they are dependent for much of their finance, sub-contracts, and so on; (*d*) petty capital in the smallest corporations (under ¥2 million), which employ little wage labour and which are therefore almost part of the petty bourgeoisie. Table 1.22 shows the size of each fraction and its importance to the corporate sector over the period 1975–80 as well as the numbers of persons in other sectors who mediate similar fractional interests.

One of the most remarkable developments during the recession of the 1970s was an enormous expansion of small capital (into sectors already noted in table 1.15) and a considerable extension of the overall grip the bourgeoisie has on Japanese society. The predominance of monopoly capital in the corporate sector remained overwhelming, though as a result of its rationalisations of plant and personnel the impression was left that it lost ground. Its share of total corporate assets (excluding finance) fell from 61% to 57%, but its share of total corporate turnover fell only from 51% to 50%. However, the power of monopoly capital does not lie only in the amount of economic activity it directly and indirectly (through subcontracting) controls, but also in the methods by which it is organised into a cohesive and highly coordinated force. The ability of its members to work together is unparalleled in the capitalist world and is greatest among those in the giant firms capitalised at over ¥ 1,000 million.

Although each of the forms in which large Japanese corporations come together to coordinate their operations has parallels elsewhere, the combination which binds them into what are known as *keiretsu* (linked groups) is quite unique. The result has been the formation of over two dozen groups of cooperating companies, each of which includes the leading competitors in most major industries. Since members work very closely with one another, the group can be likened to a single company of unequalled power and size. The largest of the groups, Mitsubishi, has an annual turnover which is twice that of General Motors and twenty times that of British Steel. Each therefore has more financial and industrial clout than the entire capitalist classes of many countries. There are five main ways in which group members are bound together. Each requires brief discussion.

The first applies mainly to the big six *kin'yū keiretsu* (financial linked groups) which stand at the apex of the organised corporate power structure in Japan. Each has among its core members a major bank and from one to three leading finance or insurance companies, on which group members rely for the largest proportion of their borrowings. Because of the unusually high levels of debt financing in

Table 1.22. *Fractions of the economically active bourgeoisie, 1975–80*

	Year	Petty (under ¥2 mil.)	Small (¥2–50 mil.)	Medium (¥50–100 mil.)	Monopoly (over ¥100 mil.)	Total
Corporations						
No. of corporations	1975	581,443	605,300	10,472	11,486	1,208,701
	1980	588,484	946,662	17,593	15,065	1,567,764
Value of assets (¥ bil.)	1975	14,371	95,503	14,877	195,140	319,890
	1980	19,662	166,517	30,996	282,231	499,406
Value of turnover (¥ bil.)	1975	31,887	168,150	23,877	232,648	456,562
	1980	41,912	315,256	53,195	409,456	819,819
No. of employees	1975	3,432,866	12,733,968	1,306,533	7,807,734	25,281,101
	1980	2,907,462	15,381,728	1,767,736	7,905,537	27,962,463
No. of directors	1975	544,253	1,691,137	58,949	94,200	2,388,539
	1980	596,500	2,525,670	87,543	112,197	3,321,910
No. of functionaries	1975	—	1,608,940	164,623	754,979	2,528,542
	1980	—	1,986,312	222,735	767,553	2,976,600
Total capitalists	1975	544,253	3,300,077	223,572	849,179	4,917,081
	1980	596,500	4,511,982	310,278	879,750	6,298,510
Finance						
Total capitalists	1977	26,104	61,014	1,860	7,906	96,884
Unincorporated sector						
No. of proprietors	1975	490,000	161,000	—	—	651,000
	1980	464,000	144,000	—	—	608,000
No. of functionaries	1975	—	247,000	—	—	247,000
	1980	—	277,000	—	—	277,000
Total capitalists	1975	490,000	408,000	—	—	898,000
	1980	464,000	421,000	—	—	885,000

Public sector No. of functionaries				
1975 —	—	—	427,190	427,190
1980 —	—	—	532,510	532,510
Total 1975 1,060,357	3,769,091	225,432	1,284,275	6,339,155
1980 1,086,604	4,993,996	312,138	1,420,166	7,812,904

Sources: Tables 1.6, 1.11, and 1.12 above; Rob Steven, 'The Japanese Bourgeoisie', *Bulletin of Concerned Asian Scholars*, 11, 2 (April–June 1979), p. 11.

Table 1.23. *The financial reach of the six leading* keiretsu, *1980*

Group name and major lending members	Mutual dependence		External dependence[b]	
	No. of group members involved	% borrowed[a] internally	No. of companies	% borrowed from group
Mitsui (total)	*20*	*19.1*	*865*	*6.32*
Mitsui Bank		9.0	635	2.48
Mitsui Trust and Banking			551	3.20
Mitsubishi (total)	*23*	*24.9*	*1,009*	*7.92*
Mitsubishi Bank		12.1	799	3.09
Mitsubishi Trust and Banking			603	3.38
Sumitomo (total)	*17*	*27.8*	*927*	*7.50*
Sumitomo Bank		13.3	670	3.25
Sumitomo Trust and Banking			634	3.29
Fuyo (total)	*25*	*18.8*	*921*	*6.11*
Fuji Bank		10.0	747	3.15
Yasuda Trust and Banking			589	2.47
Sanwa (total)	*36*	*21.0*	*1,033*	*7.57*
Sanwa Bank		12.5	773	3.32
Toyo Trust and Banking			499	1.98
Dai-ichi Kangyo Bank (total)	*39*	*13.2*	*931*	*4.98*
DKB		10.8	848	3.93
Total	160			40.38

[a]This refers to the percentage of funds the core group members borrow from member banks, etc.
[b]This provides the numbers of quoted companies which borrow from *keiretsu* financial institutions and the percentage of funds borrowed from them.
Source: Shūkan Tōyō Keizai [The Oriental Economist], *Kigyō keiretsu sōran* [A General View of Linked Companies], 1982, Rinji zōkan [Special issue], no. 4333 (Tokyo: Tōyō keizai shinpōsha, 1981), pp. 23, 25.

Japan (for more than 80% of working capital), the financial institutions which lend the money have considerable influence, particularly when the borrower is in difficulties. Members of the core group are thus bound together through their dependence on leading member banks and finance companies, while the group as a whole exercises a power outside itself through the dependence of non-members on it for finance. Table 1.23 shows the level of financial dependence of group members on their own lending companies as

Table 1.24. *Corporate stockholdings of the six leading* keiretsu*: member companies and ones quoted on the Stock Exchange, 1980 (includes top 20 shareholders only)*

	No. of members	Share of stock in member companies	Share of stock in all quoted companies
Mitsui	*23*	*15.8*	*3.14*
Banks etc.		11.5	1.76 (top 3)[a]
Mitsubishi	*23*	*23.7*	*4.77*
Banks etc.		15.8	3.79 (top 4)[a]
Sumitomo	*19*	*26.9*	*3.64*
Banks etc.		15.6	2.52 (top 3)[a]
Fuyo	*28*	*14.2*	*3.75*
Banks etc.		10.7	1.95 (top 3)[a]
Sanwa	*38*	*13.8*	*5.31*
Banks etc.		8.7	4.35 (top 3)[a]
DKB	*41*	*11.9*	*4.07*
Banks etc.		8.2	2.33 (top 2)[a]
Total			23.74

[a]The shares listed here are not the ones of all the finance companies in the group, but only of its 2, 3, or 4 leading ones.
Source: As table 1.23.

well as the financial dependence on the six leading *keiretsu* of all companies which are quoted on the Stock Exchange.

The second way in which group members are tied together and through which they wield power over non-members is by corporate stockholding. Effective control of a modern Japanese corporation, to the extent that this rests with shareholders, is normally confined to the top twenty of them. *Keiretsu* members are therefore widely represented among the top twenty shareholders of their own group members and of many other companies which are quoted on the Stock Exchange. Normally, the group's core financial institutions are the major stockholders. Table 1.24 indicates their levels of mutual stockholding as well as their holdings in all quoted companies.

A typical example of corporate stockholding within a group can be seen in Mitsubishi Steel Manufacturing Company, whose first five and seventh largest shareholders are all group members: Mitsubishi

Table 1.25. *Interlocking directorships within* keiretsu *and from them to quoted companies, 1980*

	No. of companies	No. of directors			
		Total	Dispatched within groups	Dispatched from them to quoted companies	Of which company presidents
Mitsui	24	577	22	545	52
Mitsubishi	28	764	100	555	43
Sumitomo	21	463	62	525	49
Fuyo	29	733	31	743	80
Sanwa	39	891	52	664	67
DKB	43	1,088	89	896	79
Keiretsu total	179	4,322	356	3,522	318
Total of quoted companies	1,734	28,269	—	7,562	1,658

Source: As table 1.23, p. 23.

Heavy Industries (which owns 6.94% of the shares), Meiji Mutual Life Insurance Company (5.47%), Mitsubishi Bank (5.00%), Mitsubishi Trust and Banking Corporation (4.26%), Mitsubishi Corporation (3.88%), and Tokio Marine and Fire Insurance (3.13%). Insofar as real power is concentrated in the top ten shareholders, which own 38.01% of the company's shares, the influence of group members is indisputable, since they own three-quarters of the 38.01%.[16]

Interlocking directorships is the third method by which member companies are linked and through which the group wields power. By dispatching directors to one another and to companies over which they require influence, they can make sure that their day-to-day decisions are actually coordinated. To take another typical example, the President of Mitsui Construction Company had been a director of a major Mitsui group member and shareholder, Mitsui Real Estate (18.88% of shares). Its board included one other director who was still also a member of Mitsui Real Estate's board, two from Mitsui Mining (13.59% of shares), one of whom was still on that board, and one from Mitsui and Company (3.78% of shares). To ensure that it was well primed with government contracts, it also had one director from the National Railways, one from the Hokkaido Development Agency, one from Aichi prefecture, and one from the Japan Public Highways Corporation.[17] Table 1.25 provides a general picture of interlocking directorships and shows that out of 7,526 directors in quoted companies who came from outside, 46.6% came from companies in the six *keiretsu*.

A fourth method by which these linked groups coordinate their interests is through members' reliance on the group's general trading companies to market their goods. These *sōgō shōsha*, as they are called, are not only major shareholders in and suppliers of directors to member firms, they possess marketing facilities which have made them one of the most influential types of corporation in Japan. Originally engaged in marketing alone, they gradually became involved in almost everything. The Mitsubishi group's *sōgō shōsha*, Mitsubishi Corporation, apart from owning significant proportions of shares in most group members, also has an average of about 80% of shares in anything up to a hundred affiliated companies. Most are too small to be quoted on the Stock Exchange, and the numbers have varied as the parent company rationalised its operations during the recession of the 1970s. Mitsubishi Corporation is typical in this regard.

The top nine *sōgō shōsha* (there had been ten until C. Itoh absorbed Ataka in 1977) are all affiliated to one or other of the big six *keiretsu*, although the affiliation is not equally close in all cases. Mitsubishi Corporation, Mitsui and Company, and Sumitomo Shoji are all core members of their respective groups, whereas relations are not as intimate between the other six trading companies and their affiliated group: Marubeni Corporation with Fuyo, C. Itoh and Company and Kanemitsu Gosho with DKB, Nissho-Iwai Company and Nichimen Company with Sanwa, and Toyo Menka with Mitsui. Although the proportion has declined slightly in recent years, these nine general trading companies continue to handle half of Japan's entire exports and imports. Their combined total turnover was equal to 34.3% of GNP in 1974, but this fell to 29.5% in 1976 as a result of the recession.[18]

The pre-eminent position of the *sōgō shōsha* in Japan is indisputable, and together with the *keiretsu* banks they form one of the two most influential group members which bind the groups together. Although the power that results from the function of marketing goods is not as important as the power deriving from lending money or from corporate stockholding and interlocking directorships, it can directly

Table 1.26. *Numbers of
companies with close affiliations
to the six* keiretsu

	1974	1976
Mitsubishi	131	136
Mitsui	96	101
Sumitomo	104	109
Fuyo	95	103
DKB	69	66
Sanwa	79	78

Source: Dodwell Marketing
Consultants, *Industrial Groupings in
Japan*, rev. ed. (Tokyo: Dodwell
Marketing Consultants, 1978), p.
10.

affect policy and appointments, particularly when a group member is
in difficulties. It can be of much greater importance when exercised
outside the group.

The final method by which the *keiretsu* are linked is through
councils comprising the core members, which formulate general
policy and ensure coordination of interests. The Nimokkai, a twenty-
four-member council, formulates policy for the Mitsui group, while
the Kinyōkai (twenty-eight members) does so for the Mitsubishi
group, the Hakusuikai (twenty-one members) for Sumitomo, the
Fuyōkai (twenty-nine members) for Fuyo, the Sansuikai (thirty-nine
members) for Sanwa, and the Sankinkai (forty-five members) for
DKB.[19] Strictly speaking, group membership is confined to these core
members of the *keiretsu* councils: the data on finance, corporate
stockholding, and interlocking directorships already provided are
limited to them. However, sometimes the control of the core group
members over 'non-members' through one or more of the first four
methods of forging linkages is so great that the company in question is
a group member in all but name.

In the early 1970s, an American firm, Dodwell Marketing
Consultants, began tracing in this way the affiliations of all companies quoted on the Stock Exchange and worked out their degrees of
affiliation to the *keiretsu*.[20] Table 1.26 indicates the numbers of
companies Dodwell considered *de facto* members of the big six *keiretsu*

in the 1970s. The earlier claim that the Mitsubishi group's turnover is twenty times that of British Steel refers to the turnover of this larger *de facto* group.

Powerful as the big six *kin'yū keiretsu* are, they are not the only important groups of linked corporations in Japan. In 1980, there were at least another twenty major *keiretsu*, which brought together companies mainly through corporate stockholding, interlocking directorships, and marketing, but also to some extent through finance, and which were in varying degrees affiliated to the big six.[21] For example, the group around Mitsubishi Electric, which is a member of the Kinyōkai, is much closer to the Mitsubishi group than is, say, the Nippon Steel group to Mitsubishi or any other *kin'yū keiretsu* which has important ties with Nippon Steel Corporation.[22] The numbers of quoted companies in these twenty *keiretsu* are listed in table 1.27. In some cases there are overlapping memberships between groups, and affiliations which are fairly loose and which change over time. The single most important method through which members are linked are the corporate stockholdings of the core company.

Although these *keiretsu* do not match the big six in terms of either production of turnover – the largest, Nippon Steel, possesses only about one-third of the clout of the smallest *kin'yū keiretsu*, Sanwa – they are nonetheless important forms of organisation and cooperation for monopoly capital. However, although the quoted companies which are linked to one or other *keiretsu* comprise the strongest capitals in their respective industries, there are some which are not part of any particular grouping. Sony Corporation, for example, is 23% owned by Moxley and Company, but even among its top ten shareholders we find familiar names: Mitsui Bank (4.59%), Mitsui Trust and Banking (2.68%), Mitsubishi Trust and Banking (1.62%), etc.[23]

The institution through which non-*keiretsu* monopoly firms achieve their required coordination with one another and with more organised large firms is the one which brings most large corporations in Japan together, chiefly to provide a united monopoly capitalist front in their dealings with the state. Keidanren (the Federation of Economic Organisations) is a unique institution, since, unlike the Confederation of British Industries, it includes and speaks for monopoly capital alone. Its ability to direct government policy on wages, prices, investment, interest rates, employment, economic growth, regional development, trade, foreign policy, taxation, education, police powers, and almost every facet of the nation's life is

Table 1.27. *The top twenty 'non-financial' keiretsu, 1980*

Core company	% of its shares in linked companies[a]	No. of linked companies		
		Total[b]	Quoted	Leaning[c]
Nippon Steel	36.6	151	40	Independent
Mitsui and Co.	67.7	464	32	Mitsui
Mitsubishi Corp.	51.4	368	24	Mitsui
Toyota Motor Co.	53.1	64	37	Mitsui
C. Itoh and Co.	52.4	308	19	DKB
Kawasaki Steel	38.4	59	8	DKB
Nissan Motor Co.	61.1	231	27	Fuyo
Hitachi Ltd	66.7	190	28	Fuyo, DKB, Sanwa
Marubeni	69.4	323	19	Fuyo
Mitsubishi Heavy Industries	45.0	118	6	Mitsubishi
Nippon Kokan	35.7	96	10	Fuyo
Sumitomo Metal Industries	34.8	88	14	Sumitomo
Matsushita Electric Industrial	81.5	611	15	Independent
Nissho Iwai	34.1	181	13	Sanwa
Tokyo Shibaura Electric	62.7	172	14	Mitsui
Sumitomo Shoji	32.9	191	4	Sumitomo
Kobe Steel	26.5	63	12	Sanwa, DKB
Tokyu Corporation	72.1	103	9	Independent
Mitsubishi Electric	55.2	139	10	Mitsubishi
Asahi Chemical Industry	67.9	145	14	DKB

[a]This refers to the proportion of the total numbers of shares held by the company which it holds in linked companies.
[b]Since the totals include large and small and domestic and overseas companies, they are quite large, particularly in the case of the *sōgō shōsha*.
[c]This lists membership of the councils of the big six *keiretsu*.
Source: *Kigyō keiretsu sōran*, 1982, pp. 54ff.

widely documented even in the conservative Japanese press. Apart from their membership in Keidanren, non-*keiretsu* large firms also coordinate their activities with one another and with the *keiretsu* firms through the over one hundred trade associations that work closely with government departments. They include the National Federation of Bankers' Associations, the Iron and Steel Federation, the Shipbuilding Industry Association, and the Japan Foreign Trade Association. In addition, there are many other less formal organis-

Table 1.28. *Re-subcontracts, by firm size (no. of operatives), 1975*

	Total (%)	Under 19 (%)	20–49 (%)	50–99 (%)	100–99 (%)	200–99 (%)	300 and over (%)
Re-subcontract work to others	100	25.5	30.8	20.7	14.1	5.5	3.4
Receive re-subcontracts	100	61.0	23.2	9.6	4.3	1.9	—

Source: *Chūshō kigyō hakusho*, 1975, p. 136.

ations of businessmen which deal with government officials and through which monopoly capital pursues its interests.[24] However, since the state is in fact the highest form of organisation of the entire capitalist class, discussion of how it works must wait until chapters 6 and 7.

An important distinctive contribution to the power of monopoly capital in Japan is the high degree of mutual cooperation and coordination of interests achieved by large firms even without the assistance of the state. The bourgeoisie is highly organised, or at least its leading fraction is, even without considering the role of the state in this regard. The *keiretsu* have no real equivalents outside Japan, and, while trade associations are common elsewhere, Keidanren is a more distinctive and powerful form of bourgeois organisation than its closest counterparts in other capitalist countries.

The second fraction of the Japanese bourgeoisie controls firms capitalised at ¥ 50–100 million, and it comprises about 4.9% (1980) of directors and functionaries in the corporate sector (see table 1.14). The firms handle a similar share of total corporate turnover (6.5%) and possess a similar proportion of total corporate assets (6.2%). Directors' salaries averaged about ¥ 4.9 million in 1980 (table 1.14), which was moderate for firms which are widely regarded as being 'medium sized' (usually employing over 50 but fewer than 300 workers). Although medium-sized firms are victims of the sub-contracting system, they can more often than not avoid its worst effects by re-subcontracting work out to even smaller firms. Table 1.28 shows how involvement in re-subcontracting increases as firms become smaller.

To the extent that medium capital can keep its head above water, this results more from the industrial power of its individual members than from their ability to organise and coordinate their interests. Although some 80% of medium-sized enterprises do belong to some or other business organisation, the type of assistance they receive is largely confined to such matters as raising finance and paying minimal taxes. The organisations do not help them coordinate their operations in ways that might check the power of monopoly capital or enable them to wield a united power vis-à-vis the working class. Even their attempts to obtain legislation to prevent monopoly encroachment into their preferred spheres of activity have been quite ineffective.

Since the recession has forced increasing numbers of medium-sized firms into bankruptcy or near-bankruptcy, hostility to the power of monopoly capital (which loads problems off onto firms further down the line) has on occasion been fairly intense. These feelings can, and to some extent have been, successfully exploited by the working class and its allied organisations. However, when the role of medium capital in working-class exploitation is overlooked, as the Japan Communist Party tends to do when it uses this strategy, the results can be very confusing. One of the main difficulties in organising workers in small and medium shops stems from non-monopoly capital's intense hostility to working-class organisation.

Small capital, which embraces over half the total number of directors, proprietors, and functionaries in Japan, forms the most reactionary fraction of the bourgeoisie. As the size of the firm in Japan decreases, relationships between workers and employers become more personal and more intimate. Bourgeois ideology and control is therefore enormously personalised, as bosses almost force-feed their workers each day with the moralisms that make demands for industrial action look like shameless disloyalty and ingratitude. The critical importance of small capital in the Japanese class struggle does not lie in its industrial or financial power (of which it has little), but in the fact that it is directly responsible for the domination of the majority of Japanese workers. Small capitalists are the visible forms through which most workers experience the power of capital. Hence, since small firms are themselves scattered all over the country with little ability to coordinate their activities, they are at one and the same time the weakest vis-à-vis monopoly capital and, through their dispersion of and direct contact with the bulk of the working class, the most crucial to the hegemony of monopoly capital and the forms of class struggle required to dislodge it.

Because small capital depends so heavily on markets and contracts under the control of monopoly capital, when the times compel the latter into such practices – e.g. cutting contract prices or cancelling orders – as occurred during the latter half of the 1970s, it is easy to understand the bitterness small capitalists feel towards big business. Interviews with the owners of some of these small concerns convinced me that their antipathy towards big business is only matched by their even greater hatred of unions and any form of worker organisation. The reason why they are more rather than less reactionary than monopoly capitalists is that the only economic factors over which they have any control are the wages and conditions of their workers. Small capital would not survive if it paid even average wages and provided average conditions. In not a single one of the small firms randomly selected did I encounter the slightest sympathy for working-class organisation by the company president or his (they were all men) functionary. Almost all said unions were at best unnecessary because they themselves took personal care of all their workers' needs.

The final fraction in the bourgeoisie might be referred to as petty capital, since its ability to load off onto wage labourers the effects of monopoly exploitation is limited by the small numbers of labourers employed. Petty capitalist enterprises usually have between five and nine operatives, large proportions of whom are owners' relatives. According to table 1.12, in 1979 only 62.2% of persons engaged in unincorporated enterprises with five to nine operatives were wage labourers. This means that if petty capitalists must make adjustments to meet demands from monopoly capital, over one-third of these will fall on the owner and the members of his family.

It might therefore be more correct to see petty capitalists as occupying a contradictory position between the bourgeoisie and the petty bourgeoisie, with both of which it shares some common interests. Of all the fractions of the capitalist class, only petty capital can be more or less safely entertained as a possible ally of the working class. This is not only because it is much less able than other fractions to make its workers the sole victims of monopoly exploitation, but because petty capitalists tend to engage in productive work to a much greater extent than do other capitalists. The smaller the firm, the more do the same individuals mediate the class forces of both the bourgeoisie and the working class. Table 1.29 shows how far this has occurred in manufacturing.

Although the Japan Communist Party has tried to win all non-

Table 1.29. *The extent to which the company president/firm proprietor engages in productive work in manufacturing, by firm size (no. of operatives), 1971*

	1–3 (%)	4–9 (%)	10–19 (%)	20–9 (%)	30–49 (%)
Does mainly office work	1.4	7.0	19.3	29.9	33.4
Does both office and labouring work	94.9	88.8	72.8	57.9	50.5
Does neither	3.6	4.2	7.9	12.1	16.1

Source: Dai 4 kai kōgyō jittai kihon chōsa hōkokusho, p. 444.

monopoly capitalists into its anti-monopoly alliance, its greatest success has undoubtedly been among petty capitalists. The reasons for and the extent of this relative success cannot be discussed here, since they are more pertinent to the examination of the petty bourgeoisie in the next chapter. What gives petty capital some common interest with workers is what unites it with the petty bourgeoisie.

The composition, structure, and organisation of the Japanese capitalist class have been analysed in sufficient detail to allow some tentative conclusions on the possibilities of successful revolutionary struggle against it. These can only be tentative at this stage and somewhat limited, since many relevant considerations fall beyond the scope of what applies solely to the bourgeoisie. Nevertheless, what has been said about the structure and composition of this class has some definite implications for revolutionary struggle.

The most important is that since the Japanese bourgeoisie is by no means an insignificant minority that can be easily isolated from the masses, it is not a class that can be easily overthrown. With over one person in ten possessing a strong interest in capitalism, the problems of overthrowing the bourgeoisie are similar to those of removing the white regime in South Africa. Nothing short of full mobilisation of the entire masses can have the slightest chance of success, while premature armed struggle can, as it has been in Japan, easily be eliminated.

Because the relative size of the bourgeoisie in Japan will require a revolutionary party in that country to win more explicit mass support than was necessary in a country like Russia, it is easy to see how the

JCP could become revisionist and try to win support through parliamentary politics. It is also easy to understand why the party has isolated monopoly capital as the chief target of popular discontent. Both strategies represent attempts to build a party with the power to tackle the massive and highly organised Japanese bourgeoisie, the one by uniting the opponents of this class, the other by dividing and weakening it.

Our analysis of the interests of monopoly and non-monopoly capital suggests that if the bourgeoisie is to be weakened by playing on differences among its fractions, this will probably be at the price of obscuring the real exploitative processes in Japanese society. The JCP might be able to win mass support, but not for the revolutionary overthrow of the bourgeoisie. A large ruling class can only be matched, not simply by a large revolutionary movement, but by one with a thorough understanding of what is at stake. The less united in purpose the members of the revolutionary movement, the less will even a very large one be able to wage revolutionary struggle. Neither parliamentarism nor the policy of class collaboration in the anti-monopoly alliance is likely to forge the masses into a force with the required level of organisation and understanding.

The other main conclusion that emerges from the analysis of the bourgeoisie is that this is an unevenly organised class. Only monopoly capitalists have any real ability to act in common, whereas the overwhelming majority of agents that support bourgeois social relations must rely on the state to help them work out differences among them and to present them with a set of policies around which they can unite. Because the capitalist class cannot initiate common action without the assistance of the state, class struggles will, if qualitative changes in Japanese society are to result from them, need to be directed against the highest form in which the capitalist class organises: the state.

2

The petty bourgeoisie

In most capitalist societies, accompanying the development of monopoly capitalism and the division of the bourgeoisie into fractions based on the exploitation of labour with different productivities has been the conversion of many members of the petty bourgeoisie into proletarians. It is part of the normal process of capital accumulation that small firms, when faced with vastly superior technologies, either go bankrupt or get absorbed by larger ones. However, it is not so common for new ones to spring up at a rate which, even in depression times, more than keeps pace with the numbers that disappear, or for proletarians to be converted into members of the petty bourgeoisie.

Yet just such a process has been a distinctive feature of capital accumulation in Japan and a major support of the widespread petty bourgeois ideology that everyone in capitalist society is free to enter the world of business and, through thrift and hard work, to reach the ranks of the bourgeoisie itself. The real basis of that ideology in Japan is not manipulation of ideas in schools and by the media, but the real petty bourgeois experience of owning property, not simply means of consumption, but means of production apparently just like capitalists, and in many cases doing so after having been mere wage labourers. It need never be known that the actual route which leads to membership of the capitalist class is quite different, since the experience of being free from direct supervision in a capitalist labour process is normally enough for the Japanese petty bourgeoisie to cling to the hope that the break lies just round the next corner. What must be explained therefore are the realities that both drive vast sections of the petty bourgeoisie into bankruptcy and simultaneously create replacements for them. This will lay the basis for an analysis of the concrete forms of organisation, ideology, and political activity of this powerful and in many ways key social force of some nine and a half million people.

I will show that even though the petty bourgeoisie owns and

operates its means of production, it is an impoverished class because the technical backwardness of these means of production reduces the value that its labour power can create. Unlike the petty capitalist, who can extract some surplus value from a low-paid worker to compensate for this, the person who does not hire wage labour has no way of dealing with differential monopoly power other than working extra hours. Although under certain conditions this might form the basis for an alliance with the working class, the Japanese petty bourgeoisie has so far provided one of the most secure sources of popular support for the bourgeoisie. It has not simply been thoroughly incorporated into state-sponsored organisations of the bourgeoisie, but its hostility to monopoly capital has spilt over into a hostility towards the working class, particularly workers in monopoly firms who enjoy a standard of living which is much higher than its own. The analysis of these phenomena will be divided into three main sections: the productive activity of the petty bourgeoisie and its impoverishment; its reproduction out of proletarians; and its forms of organisation, ideology, and political activity.

As neither wage labourers nor employers of wage labour, the petty bourgeoisie might seem to be a class which works entirely for itself, neither exploited nor exploiter. Since it sells the product of its labour power rather than this labour power itself, the petty bourgeoisie has the appearance of a class which is entirely independent of the capitalist mode of production. There is a real basis to this appearance: the mechanism of production in which the petty bourgeoisie works, the simple commodity mode of production, is in fact quite distinct from the capitalist mode of production, though in capitalist society it is not independent of it. The simple commodity mode of production, in which only the products of labour but not labour power itself are bought and sold on the market, functions as a real but subordinate mechanism in capitalist society. It regulates the details of daily life, just like any other subordinate mechanism, and it similarly does so within the limits of the more fundamental mechanism of capitalist production. But because it does in fact regulate details, longer working hours do in fact provide an opportunity to earn more and therefore (hopefully) to save enough to be able to enter the bourgeoisie. That how long or how hard one works does actually affect one's income is the real basis of the petty bourgeois ideological commitment to free enterprise.

However, since the *value* of what is made by simple commodity producers is determined, not by conditions internal to that mode of production, but by the socially necessary time required for their production in mainly capitalist enterprises, the market prices members of the petty bourgeoisie receive for what they do are totally beyond their control. The more their techniques lag behind those of the predominant capitalist enterprises, the less new value do they produce in any given amount of time actually worked. The more therefore do they have to compensate by relying on a variable which does lie within their control, namely the numbers of hours they put in.

However, no matter how long they work, the development of monopoly capitalism has so widened the technological gap between themselves and capitalist enterprises (and therefore the differences in labour productivity) that it has become a rare exception for anyone to accumulate enough savings and enter the bourgeoisie through sheer hard work. Whenever it does happen, this is almost invariably in industries which have remained more labour intensive and so in which the technological discrepancies between petty bourgeois and capitalist production are lowest. That some industries are more labour intensive than others is a natural result of the uneven development of productive forces (the techniques employed in production) under capitalism.

The motive force of technical change and the development of productive forces in any industry derives from the potential profitability of introducing new techniques and raising the rate of accumulation. It is greatest in those industries in which capital can make extra profits by large reductions in time per unit output through introducing labour-saving technologies, and least in industries where a competitive advantage over rival capitals depends more on paying lower wages or intensifying the speed of work than on replacing workers with machinery embodying new techniques. The former industries tend to become increasingly capital intensive, while the latter tend to remain labour intensive. The range of possible technical differences among producers in capital-intensive industries is therefore much greater than the possible range in labour-intensive industries. One would therefore expect the petty bourgeoisie, with its limited resources, to move more and more into industries where the technical disadvantages it suffers are lowest, that is, the labour-intensive industries in which competitive power depends heavily on wage levels and intensity of work.

This is exactly what has happened in Japan. Table 2.1, which

Table 2.1. *Distribution of the economically active population, by industry and size (no. of operatives) of enterprise, 1979*

Industry	1–4	5–29	30–299	300 and over	Government service	Total[a]
All industries	31.5	21.0	18.8	19.7	8.8	100
Agriculture	94.1	3.7	0.8	0.2	1.2	10.1
Fisheries/aquaculture	58.7	23.7	13.0	4.3	0.4	0.8
Mining	6.1	27.8	27.0	39.1	0.0	0.2
Construction	28.3	40.8	20.2	10.3	0.2	9.6
Manufacturing	17.2	22.6	27.7	32.5	0.1	24.8
Wholesale/retail	40.0	26.9	18.2	14.5	0.2	22.1
Finance/insurance/real estate	14.7	9.4	13.8	60.8	1.2	3.6
Transport/ communications	5.5	13.3	23.9	45.9	11.4	6.3
Electricity/gas/water	0.0	0.8	4.2	60.0	34.7	0.7
Services	26.3	20.3	20.1	10.1	23.1	18.1
Government	—	—	—	—	100.0	3.5

[a]The percentages in this column refer to the proportions of the economically active population in the different industries.
Source: Shūgyō kōzō kihon chōsa hōkoku, 1979, pp. 50–1.

indicates the proportions of the economically active population in each major industry by the size of enterprise worked in, confirms that labour-intensive light industries tend to be the preserve of small-scale production and capital-intensive heavy industries tend to be dominated by large-scale production.

The most labour-intensive industries are agriculture and forestry, fisheries and aquaculture, construction, wholesale and retail, and services: at least a quarter of the persons engaged in them are in petty bourgeois enterprises. The most capital-intensive industries are mining, manufacturing, finance/insurance/real estate, transport and communications, and electricity, gas, and water. However, within each major industry there are some branches or processes which are more labour intensive than others. This applies particularly to the manufacturing and service industries, in which certain areas are almost entirely the preserve of petty bourgeois production. Also not apparent from table 2.1 are the reasons why the two entirely unproductive sectors, wholesale and retail and finance, insurance, and real estate, are mainly occupied by small and large concerns respectively. There are no technical reasons why this should be the case. Rather, the reasons lie in the fact that money capital tends to merge with industrial capital in the period of monopolies, so that the former is increasingly centralised and held in large banks, from which it is made available to giant industrial concerns for large-scale investments. But the sale of commodities, as opposed to the function of accumulating a hoard, is often aided by the multiplication of small outlets all over the country, where the major customers are not other capitalists but workers and members of other classes with not much money to spend.

To explore these questions more fully requires a detailed breakdown by minor industry of the petty bourgeois firms with under five operatives. Although one should not exaggerate the difference between petty capital in enterprises with five to nine operatives (over half of whom are wage labourers) and the petty bourgeoisie in enterprises which use mainly family labour, the distinction is a real one. I shall therefore ignore the contradictions at the boundary between these two class forces, and concentrate purely on firms with one to four operatives. Moreover, since the overwhelming majority of these firms are unincorporated (the exceptions being the ones run by the 550,000 directors who were excluded from the bourgeoisie), most of the data used to analyse their operations are confined to the unincorporated sector. And since agricultural establishments are analysed in the next chapter, on the peasantry, we are limited to non-agricultural industries. Table 2.2 thus presents a breakdown by occupational status (and by major industry) of all the persons engaged in unincorporated enterprises with under five operatives in 1974–9.

Some extremely interesting points emerge from this table. Most unexpected perhaps is that, far from comprising a falling proportion of the economically active population, as one might think would occur in times of recession, the petty bourgeoisie grew in both absolute numbers and relative to other classes. While the increase in the total economically active population in 1974–9 was 6.6% (from 51,341,000 to 54,737,000),[1] petty proprietors expanded by 20.5% and family workers for them by 26.6%. Explanation of this remarkable phenomenon as a form of concealed unemployment is attempted towards the end of the chapter. A more pertinent and equally interesting development to note at this point is that the tendency for the petty bourgeoisie to be concentrated in labour-

Table 2.2. *Distribution of persons in non-agricultural unincorporated enterprises with under 5 operatives, by major industry and occupational status, 1974–9 (1,000 persons and %)*

	Year	Proprietors		Family workers		Total petty bourgeoisie		Employees as % of total engaged
		No.	%	No.	%	No.	%	
Forestry/hunting	1974	22	0.4	4	0.2	26	0.3	40.1
	1979	23	0.4	9	0.3	32	0.4	31.9
Fisheries	1974	165	2.9	100	4.5	265	3.4	5.4
	1979	157	2.5	99	3.8	266	3.0	4.9
Mining	1974	3	0.1	1	0.0	4	0.1	42.8
	1979	4	0.1	2	0.1	6	0.1	14.2
Construction	1974	622	11.1	105	4.8	727	9.3	37.0
	1979	722	11.4	163	6.3	885	9.9	34.3
Manufacturing	1974	1,177	21.0	459	20.9	1,636	21.0	15.9
	1979	1,383	21.9	467	18.0	1,850	20.8	12.4
Wholesale/retail	1974	2,095	37.4	1,180	53.6	3,275	42.0	15.9
	1979	2,231	35.3	1,397	53.9	3,628	40.7	16.3
Finance/insurance/real estate	1974	128	2.3	14	0.6	142	1.8	13.5
	1979	153	2.4	31	1.2	184	2.1	11.9
Transport/communications	1974	135	2.4	18	0.8	153	2.0	15.5
	1979	132	2.1	19	0.7	151	1.7	12.2
Services	1974	1,253	22.4	319	14.5	1,572	20.1	20.6
	1979	1,510	23.9	404	15.6	1,914	21.5	18.4
Total	1974	5,606	100	2,200	100	7,806	100	19.2
	1979	6,315	100	2,591	100	8,906	100	17.9
Total petty bourgeois (plus 550,000 directors)	1974					8,356		
	1979					9,456		
Petty bourgeoisie as % of total economically active population	1974					16.3		
	1979					17.3		

Source: Shūgyō kōzō kihon chōsa hōkoku, 1974, pp. 36–7; 1979, pp. 50–1.

intensive industries, particularly services, was accelerated during 1974–9. I examine these industries – services, wholesale and retail, and manufacturing – in some detail. Although almost 10% of the class is in construction, I exclude it from the same scrutiny, partly because of the much greater importance of the other industries, partly because of the relatively high proportion of employees in petty construction firms, which makes the industry more suited to capitalist than simple commodity production.

In manufacturing, petty enterprises are concentrated in a limited number of the most labour-intensive light industries into which entry is relatively easy because of the cheapness of the required means of production: food and tobacco, textiles, clothing, lumber and wood products, publishing and printing, and fabricated metal products. Table 2.3 shows the distribution of petty manufacturing firms by minor industrial groups. It also provides an indication of the degree to which sub-contracting occurs in each and of the cost of entering it. The industries in which petty firms are most concentrated, textiles and fabricated metal products, are also the ones whose means of production are the cheapest.

However, these small manufacturing firms are less productive than large ones, not only because they use the cheapest possible technical equipment, but also because their operatives are typically of below-average technical skill. They have a relatively low proportion of university graduates in all branches of manufacturing, though this is partly offset by the fact that average skills are lowest in those branches in which petty firms are concentrated. Table 2.4 indicates the proportions of university graduates in petty firms and in the total number of firms in each of a number of selected branches of manufacturing.

There is therefore good reason to believe that the *new value* (the socially necessary labour which depends on the use of average techniques and average skills) produced in petty bourgeois firms is much less per person than it is in capitalist firms. In view of the almost round-the-clock hours that many of these people spend making, in a lot of cases beautifully crafting, their products with often quite primitive implements, the *new value produced per hour* is certainly much less than occurs in capitalist enterprises. The work is also often much more dangerous, since the old lathes, printing presses, and so on that are used were not designed, even in their heyday, for all the jobs to which petty producers often ingeniously put them. To the hours that

Table 2.3. *Distribution of petty firms, involvement in sub-contracting, and cost of entry, by minor industrial group in manufacturing*

	Distribution[a] (1980)	Do sub-contracts[b] (1980)	% with capital under ¥2 mil.[c] (1971)	Value of inventory assets[d] (¥ mil.) (1980)
Food/tobacco	9.6	0.5	86.4	0.88
Textiles	21.4	77.2	95.5	0.64
Apparel	8.4	80.5	81.5	0.62
Lumber/wood products	7.1	29.5	92.3	1.50
Furniture/fixtures	5.4	21.3	70.5	1.03
Pulp and paper	1.7	37.4	84.8	0.66
Publishing/printing	8.6	24.2	93.9	0.26
Chemicals	0.4	42.4	79.5	0.96
Rubber products	0.9	61.5	93.4	1.90
Skins/hides	2.8	72.9	65.4	2.39
Ceramics	3.0	32.4	72.8	0.84
Iron/steel	0.6	61.9	—	0.80
Non-ferrous metals	0.7	10.9	82.0	—
Metallic products	14.5	60.6	94.8	0.48
General machines	5.3	63.5	74.1	0.50
Electrical machines	0.9	66.4	86.2	0.44
Transport machines	0.6	85.4	91.9	0.21
Precision instruments	1.2	78.8	92.6	0.53
Others	7.1	41.7	82.0	1.02

[a]Firms with 1–4 operatives.
[b]All unincorporated firms; nevertheless a good indication of the degree of sub-contracting done by petty firms.
[c]Of firms with 1–3 operatives, incorporated and unincorporated.
[d]All unincorporated firms. The amount would be less for the petty firms.
Sources: Sōrifu tōkeikyoku, *Kojin kigyō keizai chōsa nenpō* [Annual Report on the Unincorporated Enterprise Survey], 1980 (Tokyo: Nihon tōkei kyōkai, 1981), pp. 96, 101–2; *Dai 4 kai kōgyō jittai kihon chōsa hōkokusho*, pp. 2–13.

the proprietors and their more or less full-time family members put in must also be added the hours of many family members who are not listed as working in the firm, but who, as a visit to any one of these backyard manufactories will confirm, put in a large number of invisible hours doing a thousand and one little jobs. Table 2.5 shows the extent to which the employment status survey has picked up the much longer hours of petty producers than wage labourers in both small and large firms, as well as the lower median incomes of the former.

Table 2.4. *Proportions of university graduates in petty bourgeois manufacturing firms, by selected branches, 1971*

	% graduates in petty firms (1–3 operatives)	% graduates in all firms
Total	7.4	26.9
Food	6.5	19.4
Textiles	3.6	18.9
Clothes/other textiles	2.7	9.9
Lumber/wood	3.1	12.6
Furniture	5.2	14.2
Printing/publishing	11.0	19.3
Iron/steel	7.3	36.5
Metallic products	7.8	19.2
General machines	10.9	29.1

Source: *Dai 4 kai kōgyō jittai kihon chōsa hōkokusho*, pp. 14–19.

Table 2.5. *Hours worked per week, by employment status, and annual income, 1979 (among persons in all industries working over 200 days a year)*

Employment status	Firm size	Hours per week		Median annual income (¥ mil.)
		Under 48 (%)	48 and over (%)	
Self-employed	1 person	56.6	43.2	1.0–1.5
	2–4 persons	33.5	66.5	2.0–2.5[a]
	Home handicraft	85.3	14.4	Under 0.5
Family workers	2–4	45.6	54.4	—
Employees	1–9	52.7	47.2	1.5–2.0
	Over 1,000	71.6	28.4	2.5–3.0

Source: *Shūgyō kōzō kihon chōsa hōkoku*, 1979, pp. 160, 200, 208.
[a] Since the petty bourgeoisie relies heavily on family labour, the income per person in this class is considerably less.

The longer hours, the technical backwardness, the below-average skills, and the low incomes of petty bourgeois firms all confirm that the value they produce in a given period of time is far less than what large firms produce. So even in spite of their concentration in labour-intensive industries, or in the labour-intensive branches and processes

Table 2.6. *Profitability of unincorporated manufacturing firms, 1980*

Persons engaged	Annual sales (¥ mil.)	Value added per person (¥ mil.)	Net profit (¥ mil.)	Average no. of persons engaged	Net value of total assets (¥ mil.)
Petty bourgeois					
1	3.54	1.66	1.68	1.01	0.68
2	6.92	1.42	2.73	2.01	1.89
3	13.41	1.78	4.26	2.99	3.18
4	17.72	1.75	4.89	4.00	3.81
Petty capitalist					
5–9	33.92	2.11	7.30	6.18	5.83
Small capitalist					
10–19	67.75	2.11	12.33	12.22	8.70

Source: Kojin kigyō keizai chōsa nenpō, 1980, pp. 38–9, 72–3.

Table 2.7. *Distribution of self-employed persons in manufacturing, by income and firm size, 1979 (1,000 persons and %)*

Persons engaged	Under ¥1 mil. No.	%	¥1–3 mil. No.	%	Over ¥3 mil. No.	%	Total no.
1	761	83.1	136	14.8	18	2.0	916
2–4	25	5.4	269	57.6	174	37.3	467
5–9	3	3.0	38	37.6	61	60.4	101
10–19	0	0.0	6	23.1	19	73.1	26
Home handicraft	700	96.7	22	3.0	0	0.0	724

Source: Shūgyō kōzō kihon chōsa hōkoku, 1979, pp. 160, 200, 208.

of these and other industries, they must continually compete against more productive capitalist enterprises. Their low incomes per person engaged reveal that even long hours are insufficient to compensate for their lower labour productivity. The best available measure of this productivity is the bourgeois concept of value added (net profit plus wages in unincorporated firms). Table 2.6 shows that value added per operative in petty bourgeois manufacturing firms is about 30% below that of small capitalist and petty capitalist firms.

However, although value added per operative does rise as firms become larger, the higher profits (table 2.6) and incomes (table 2.7) of petty and small capitalists than members of the petty bourgeoisie clearly originate more from the surpluses extracted from their wage labourers than from higher labour productivity owing to superior technology. Indeed, because of rising overheads (particularly in manufacturing firms) as the scale of operations increases, the profits per person engaged in small capitalist enterprises are lower than in petty bourgeois enterprises. From table 2.6 one can work out that in 1980 the sums were ¥1.42 million in a three-person petty enterprise and only ¥1 million in a small capitalist firm with ten to nineteen operatives. Capitalist profits clearly derive from the surpluses of wage labourers.

Income differences within the petty bourgeoisie therefore also result primarily from the same source. Those with employees obtain surplus value from their workers, while those who use family labour are in effect reporting a family income that should be compared to that of households with more than one wage earner. Family workers are recorded as unpaid (hardly surprising, since most are women), and so the incomes of self-employed persons who rely on family labour do not really report their own individual earnings. The actual income earned per person in those petty bourgeois firms which use only family labour is thus rarely more than what one-person firms can make. Small wonder that in a survey of small firms conducted by the Small and Medium Enterprise Agency in December 1980, the largest proportion of respondents in manufacturing (17.3%) listed vigorous use of family labour as a special characteristic of good management! When asked why dependence on family workers was so high, the most frequently mentioned reason in the sample as a whole (40%) was that there was no money left to hire wage labourers.[2]

The combination of low levels of skill, backward techniques, and the long hours needed just to keep the household functioning all prevent the bulk of the petty bourgeoisie from being able to hire wage labourers. Moreover, even when a few do manage to get into this happy situation, they must cross yet another hurdle lest they lose with one hand to monopoly capital what the other took from their workers. The widespread system of sub-contracting which most small manu-facturing firms are involved in means an even greater vulnerability to prices determined by monopoly capital than would otherwise be the case. Table 2.8 confirms that involvement in sub-contracting reduces profitability in all manufacturing industries: although firms which do sub-contracts are in all cases, excepting food and tobacco, smaller on

Table 2.8. *Net profits per person in unincorporated manufacturing firms, by minor industry, average number of persons engaged, and whether or not involved in sub-contracting, 1980 (¥ million)*

	Independent		Do sub-contracting	
	Profit/person	Persons	Profit/person	Persons
Food/tobacco	1.14	3.6	1.04	5.3
Textiles/clothing	1.16	3.9	0.96	2.6
Lumber/wood products	1.44	3.3	1.45	2.6
Pulp/paper/printing etc.	1.38	3.6	1.24	3.3
Chemicals/petroleum/ rubber etc.	1.45	5.9	0.70	4.4
Ceramics and related	1.40	3.7	1.37	2.8
Iron/steel/non-ferrous metals	1.85	3.8	1.11	3.5
Machinery/metallic products	1.43	3.5	1.29	3.1
Other	1.33	4.0	1.23	2.9
Total	1.32	3.6	1.14	2.8

Source: Kojin kigyō keizai chōsa nenpō, 1980, pp. 46–7.

average than the ones which do not, their profits per person are invariably less. Since we have just noted (from table 2.6) that profits per person in unincorporated firms actually fall as firms get larger, the effect of the sub-contracting system is indisputable.

However, most petty producers tied into the sub-contracting system are not free to leave it. In order to survive in the industry, they must specialise in certain labour-intensive processes, such as the manufacture of parts, of an overall production process which is firmly in the hands of monopoly capital. The status of these persons is more than superficially similar to that of workers in the old putting-out system. However, the modern version, which is a unique combination of the best worlds of advanced and early capitalism, has some extraordinary advantages for monopoly capital. It permits the exploitation of whole families without the disadvantages of provoking working-class antagonism, since the workers are kept divided in their various households, the females nicely dominated by the males, and are compensated with an illusion of independence. Though their productivity could be raised by freeing them of their backward means of production, this is made unnecessary by the fact that they can be

Table 2.9. *Distribution of persons engaged in services and manufacturing, by firm size, in the private business sector, 1974–9*

Firm size	Manufacturing				Services			
	No.		%		No.		%	
	1974	1979	1974	1979	1974	1979	1974	1979
1	702	918	5.1	6.8	835	996	19.0	18.1
2–4	1,406	1,406	10.3	10.5	1,238	1,466	28.2	26.6
5–9	1,092	1,151	8.0	8.6	601	740	13.7	13.4
10–29	1,700	1,886	12.4	14.0	564	794	12.8	14.4
30 and over	8,761	8,079	64.1	60.1	1,153	1,512	26.3	27.4
Total	13,661	13,440	100.0	100.0	4,390	5,509	100.0	100.0

Source: Shūgyō kōzō kihon chōsa hōkoku, 1974, p. 37; 1979, pp. 50–2.

forced into labour-intensive work where differences in technique are not too great and into putting in very long hours for little remuneration per person because 'the whole family' is engaged. Marx recognised that a surplus population of low-paid workers made it unnecessary to develop productive forces in the industries or branches they worked in. Capital could therefore be used elsewhere, in heavy industry in Japan and to exploit even cheaper and less-organised workers in Asia. The impoverishment of the Japanese petty bourgeoisie is therefore not unrelated to the expansion of imperialism abroad, a theme we pick up in chapter 6. Accompanying the destruction of jobs in large manufacturing firms during the recession was thus an expansion of operations overseas and a growth of employment in small manufactories (see table 2.9).

The growth of petty bourgeois firms in the service industry was even more rapid (see table 2.2), although overall employment in them did not increase to the same degree that it did in petty manufacturing, simply because in the latter there are on average not only more employees but also more persons engaged per firm. Table 2.9 compares the distribution of the total numbers of persons engaged in private businesses in these industries. Services are no doubt a much safer long-term bet for a class of small-scale labour-intensive producers than is manufacturing, something which has not been lost on members of the class. In the previously mentioned survey by the Small and Medium Enterprise Agency, a full 30% of those involved

Table 2.10. *Distribution of unincorporated service enterprises with 1–4 operatives, by minor industry and the net value of total assets, 1980*

	Distribution (%)	Net value of assets[a] (¥ mil.)
Lodgings/hotels	7.5	1.96
Cleaning/hygiene	63.4	1.30
Laundry	11.5	0.88
Barbershops	27.1	1.23
Beauty parlours	20.1	2.90
Other personal services	9.5	0.90
Automobile services	9.5	1.10
Other repair services	4.6	2.39
Miscellaneous business services	3.5	1.48
Services average	—	1.35
Manufacturing average	—	2.75
Wholesale/retail average	—	3.08

[a]All unincorporated firms. The amounts would be less for the petty firms.
Source: *Kojin kigyō keizai chōsa nenpō*, 1980, pp. 96–7, 100–1.

in commerce, though only 11.1% of those in manufacturing, saw moving in part into the service industry as a way of coping with the recession.[3]

Within this industry, petty bourgeois enterprises are concentrated in lodgings, cleaning and hygiene, certain personal services, and automobile maintenance and parking.[4] These are not just labour-intensive branches, but by their very nature are more suited to small than to large-scale business, although not uniformly so. Monopoly capital's main interests are in rental, movies, and entertainment services. Since all but 115,000 of the total of 2,462,000 persons[5] engaged in petty bourgeois firms in the service industry are in unincorporated firms, the data that follow are confined to this sector. Table 2.10 shows the distribution of the firms by minor industry.

The relative ease of entering the cleaning and hygiene services, both in terms of the means of production to be purchased and the necessary skills, has meant that these branches comprise almost entirely petty bourgeois firms. The average number of persons per establishment (not firm) in them is the lowest of all sections of the industry in Japan, namely 2.5, the next smallest average scale of operation being in other personal services, with 3.5 persons to the establishment. The largest, incidentally, is horse racing, a service

Table 2.11. *Profit per person engaged in unincorporated service and wholesale and retail enterprises, 1980*

	Profit/person (¥ mil.)	Persons/enterprise
Service	*1.09*	*2.35*
Lodgings/hotels	0.81	3.25
Cleaning/hygiene	1.12	2.35
Rentals/other personal services	1.05	2.06
Automobile and other repairs	1.25	2.15
Wholesale/retail	*1.30*	*2.75*
Wholesale	2.07	3.48
Retail	1.35	2.64
Food/beverages	1.38	2.53
Eating and drinking places	0.86	2.96

Source: Kojin kigyō keizai chōsa nenpō, 1980, p. 89.

Table 2.12. *Profitability of unincorporated service enterprises, 1980*

Persons engaged	Annual sales (¥ mil.)	Value added per person (¥ mil.)	Net profit (¥ mil.)	Average no. of persons engaged	Net value of total assets (¥ mil.)
Petty bourgeois					
1	2.22	1.28	1.23	1.02	0.78
2	5.11	1.40	2.58	2.01	1.51
3	8.21	1.43	3.27	2.99	1.64
4	11.65	1.54	4.07	3.99	2.50
Petty capitalist					
5–9	19.96	1.68	5.09	6.04	2.35
Small capitalist					
10–19	46.03	1.77	9.80	12.59	1.82

Source: Kojin kigyō keizai chōsa nenpō, 1980, pp. 40–1, 74–5.

which apparently cannot be provided with fewer than an average of 112.6 persons.[6] However, in the industry as a whole and particularly in the branches of cleaning and hygiene, the low profits and value added per person are only comparable to what was found in that manufacturing industry into which equally easy access had drawn the largest numbers of petty firms: textiles and clothing (see tables 2.3, 2.8, 2.11, and 2.12). Although considerable training in the relevant skills in both of these is necessary, the fact that women acquire them almost imperceptibly through their socialisation makes the jobs look unskilled. The relatively low profitability of the small-scale service industries is thus not hard to understand.

Unlike manufacturing, in which productive forces are highly developed even in sectors where the petty bourgeoisie is concentrated (though less so in the particular processes specialised in), productive forces in the service industry are not advanced. This is especially true of the branches into which the petty bourgeoisie has moved in large numbers, so that the skills and techniques it applies are not so much below the average. However, even though the time its members pour into services is much closer to being socially necessary time, the industry as a whole loses value to the monopoly-dominated industries because of the much greater ease with which it can be entered. The causes of petty bourgeois poverty in services thus take on the visible form of excessive competition among members of their own class. The impression that monopoly capital has nothing to do with it is reinforced by the almost entire absence of sub-contracting in small-scale services. And since the petty bourgeoisie in services is also less dependent on monopoly capital because of its reduced need to borrow money for investment in costly plant and equipment, it has still less reason to see the capitalist system as the cause of its difficulties.

Manufacturing and services account for over two-fifths of the petty bourgeoisie, that is, about the same proportion as is occupied by wholesale and retail alone. The great majority of these are small shopkeepers, who run retail stores of one type or another or small eating and drinking places, mostly from part of the family home. Table 2.13 indicates that upwards of 40% of all persons engaged in wholesale and retail work in petty bourgeois enterprises, confirming the attractiveness of the industry to small-scale interests. Table 2.14 shows that food and beverage retail outlets and eating and drinking places together comprise over half the targets of these petty firms and that although the value of their net assets is higher than in services, there are no great financial barriers to entering them.

To a visitor, it seems that petty bourgeois retail firms are open literally all the time, an impression that is well supported by survey data. An average firm with two persons operates no fewer than 321 days a year, while similar firms in manufacturing and services operate only 295 and 306 days respectively.[7] These extraordinary hours are possible in retailing only because more unpaid family members can

Table 2.13. *Distribution of persons engaged in wholesale and retail, by firm size, in the private business sector, 1974–9*

	No.		%	
Firm size	1974	1979	1974	1979
1	835	799	8.2	6.7
2–4	3,454	4,034	34.0	33.9
5–9	1,391	1,613	13.7	13.5
10–29	1,280	1,605	12.6	13.5
30 and over	3,205	3,862	31.5	32.4
Total	10,165	11,913	100.0	100.0

Source: Shūgyō kōzō kihon chōsa hōkoku, 1974, p. 37; 1979, pp. 50–2.

Table 2.14. *Distribution of unincorporated wholesale and retail enterprises with 1–4 operatives, by minor industry and the net value of total assets, 1980*

	Distribution (%)	Net value of assets[a] (¥ mil.)
Wholesale	5.6	5.55
Retail	75.0	3.38
Dry goods/apparel	13.2	4.22
Food/beverages	31.3	2.23
Motor vehicles/bicycles	2.1	2.66
Furniture/household goods	8.6	4.54
Others	19.8	4.12
Eating and drinking places	19.5	1.29
Total	100.0	3.08

[a]All unincorporated firms. The amounts would be less for the petty firms.
Source: Kojin kigyō keizai chōsa nenpō, 1980, pp. 96–7, 100–1.

assist in a retail business than in those manufacturing and service firms which require special skills. This is why over half the total unpaid family workers outside agriculture are in wholesale and retail, which employs fewer wage labourers per firm than either manufacturing or services. Table 2.15 outlines the resulting profitability of petty bourgeois firms in wholesale and retail. Comparison of the data with those in tables 2.6, 2.11, and 2.12 suggests that this is the most remunerative of all petty bourgeois industries.

Table 2.15. *Value added per operative and profits per firm of unincorporated wholesale/retail establishments, 1980*

Persons engaged	Annual sales (¥ mil.)	Value added per person (¥ mil.)	Net profit (¥ mil.)	Average no. of persons engaged	Net value of total assets (¥ mil.)
Petty bourgeois					
1	5.38	1.15	1.16	1.01	1.57
2	13.97	1.53	2.96	2.01	2.81
3	22.21	1.69	4.31	3.00	3.66
4	31.85	1.71	5.30	4.00	7.51
Petty capitalist					
5–9	54.35	2.17	8.56	5.98	10.24
Small capitalist					
10–19	94.59	1.70	9.06	12.27	21.53

Source: Kojin kigyō keizai chōsa nenpō, 1980, pp. 38–9, 74–5.

However, the higher profits are in part only apparent, since more unpaid family workers are engaged in this industry. Nevertheless, since the higher profits are associated with a higher value added per person engaged (wages plus profits per person), it seems that the petty bourgeoisie in this sector is better off than in other sectors. One reason for this is the longer hours put in by people in small retail outlets than by their counterparts in services and manufacturing. For example, 60% of persons engaged in food and beverage retail stores and eating and drinking places work over forty-eight hours a week, while only 35% of those in the textile industry do, although in personal services the proportion rises to 56%.[8] Another reason for the higher earnings of petty bourgeois firms in retail is that entry into the industry is not in fact as easy as it is in the case of many services. One generally needs more spacious premises and a higher level of net assets, but then selling is not a skill requiring the training that personal services require. Perhaps the real answer lies somewhere in the data presented in table 2.16.

If one was to summarise the working conditions of the Japanese petty bourgeoisie, the most important things to emphasise would be the involvement of whole families (unevenly to be sure) in very long hours of work for lower incomes than most wage labourers, all compensated for by illusions of independence and gratitude for having jobs to do. In manufacturing, this illusion wears thin under

Table 2.16. *Distribution of self-employed persons and family workers in food-related retail firms and personal service firms, by sex, 1979 (1,000 persons)*

| | Food-related[a] | | | | Personal services[b] | | | |
| | Males | | Females | | Males | | Females | |
	No.	%	No.	%	No.	%	No.	%
Self-employed	757	84.4	447	35.5	257	87.7	467	69.3
Family workers	140	15.6	813	64.5	36	12.3	217	32.2
Total	897	100	1,260	100	293	100	674	100

[a]This includes food and beverage retail outlets as well as eating and drinking places.
[b]This includes lodging, cleaning and hygiene, and other personal services.
Source: Shūgyō kōzō kihon chōsa hōkoku, 1979, pp. 46, 48.

the pressure of extensive sub-contracting, though in the service and retail sectors the law of value regulates petty bourgeois operations without this necessarily being recognised. In services, the class surrenders value to other sectors because of the relative ease with which it can be entered. In wholesale and retail, monopoly capital can minimise the loss of value in the process of circulation by bringing in the labour power of masses of entire families at very little cost. So if monopoly capital benefits from petty bourgeois production in manufacturing through getting cheap parts, it is equally happy to see this class provide cheap wage goods in the services specialised in as well as a speeding up and cheapening of commodity circulation in the wholesale and retail sector by a breed of dedicated shopkeepers.

Reproduction of the petty bourgeoisie

The concentration of the petty bourgeoisie in labour-intensive sectors means that the labour it performs is not as far from the socially necessary average as might at first be expected. This is particularly true of the services it specialises in, and although no value is created in the retail industry, the petty bourgeoisie is not at an insuperable technological disadvantage in retailing. Only in the manufacturing industry does the petty bourgeoisie face vastly more efficient producers, and this has compelled it to specialise in labour-intensive processes under contracts from monopoly capital.

Table 2.17. *Number of unincorporated enterprises with 1–4 operatives, and average number of operatives per unincorporated enterprise*

	No. of enterprises with 1–4 operatives		Average no. of operatives per unincorporated enterprise		
	1960	1972^a	1967	1974	1979
Total	2,452,129	3,194,871	—	—	—
Manufacturing	263,218	368,460	4.28	3.93	3.33
Wholesale/retail	1,441,641	1,762,812	2.71	2.64	2.55
Services	531,343	663,517	2.72	2.28	2.24

^{a}The government has a great many data on the numbers of establishments (main offices, branch offices, etc.) with 1–4 operatives after this date, but not enterprises, that is, firms. Nevertheless, table 2.2 provides a fair indication of the growth of petty bourgeois firms in 1975–80.
Sources: Kojin kigyō keizai chōsa nenpō, 1974, pp. 3, 7, 11, 108; 1980, pp. 22, 26, 34.

These conditions have allowed the petty bourgeoisie to be reproduced on a gradually expanding scale. Far from disappearing with the development of monopoly capital, firms with fewer than five operatives have risen steadily over the years and, as noted earlier on, the pace only quickened during the recession in the 1970s. However, the average number of operatives per unincorporated enterprise has been falling, revealing not simply a growing impoverishment of the petty bourgeoisie and its inability to enter the capitalist class, but a consolidation of the division of labour by which the petty bourgeoisie specialises in labour-intensive processes. Table 2.17 reveals the extent to which these developments have taken place.

The persistence of the petty bourgeoisie should not, however, be seen as evidence for the stability or security of its working conditions and livelihood. On the contrary, small firms go bankrupt at a phenomenal rate in Japan, and, as table 2.18 reveals, only half the manufacturing firms with under four operatives in 1971 were in existence before 1955. Table 2.19 shows the rates at which small firms disappeared and new ones opened up in 1976–8.

If petty bourgeois firms are therefore being continually reproduced, it is important to know where the agents who fill the different positions in them come from. This will help explain why the class has not decreased in either absolute or relative size during the period of

Table 2.18. *Distribution of small manufacturing firms in 1971, by date of establishment*

Firm size (operatives)	Total	Prewar	Date of establishment (% in each period) End of war to 1955	1956–60	1961–5	1966–71
1–3	100	20.4	30.7	13.9	18.6	16.4
4–9	100	20.6	32.4	15.8	17.6	13.6
200–99	100	38.9	37.5	10.5	8.5	4.5

Source: Dai 4 kai kōgyō jittai kihon chōsa hōkokusho, p. 274.

Table 2.19. *Rates at which small firms disappeared and new ones were opened up, by major industry, in 1976–8*

	Rate of closure (%)	Rate of opening (%)
Manufacturing (1–20 persons)	2.4	3.6
Wholesale (1–4 persons)	4.8	7.8
Retail (1–4 persons)	3.6	4.7
All secondary and tertiary	3.8	6.2

Source: Chūshō kigyō hakusho, 1980, p. 107.

monopoly capitalist hegemony and particularly during the more recent period of crisis. Table 2.20 reveals that by 1968 a full 82% (although this fell slightly thereafter) of persons entering the petty bourgeoisie had previously been in the working class, which was a massive increase from the 62% in 1959. The proportion who had previously been self-employed fell from 21.2% to 10.9% in the same period, but this rose again to 16.9% as a result of the recession. The proportion who had been peasants fell steadily from 11% in 1959 to a mere 1% in 1979. Of the ex-workers who each year enter the petty bourgeoisie, an overwhelming proportion come from small firms with under 300 operatives. Although the reasons why they enter the petty bourgeoisie in such large numbers will become clearer when we discuss the working class, fig. 2.1 shows that it has a great deal to do with the system of payment by length of service. Since workers must

Table 2.20. *Previous occupational status of persons who entered the petty bourgeoisie in selected years, 1959–79*

Year	Total entrants into petty bourgeoisie (self-employed plus family workers)	Occupational status the previous year					
		Self-employed	Family workers	Peasants	Workers (total)	Workers in firms of 1–299 persons	Workers in govt or in firms of 300 or more persons
1959	118,000	25,000 (21.2%)	7,000 (5.9%)	13,000 (11.0%)	73,000 (61.9%)	60,000 (50.8%)	12,000 (10.2%)
1968	211,000	23,000 (10.9%)	10,000 (4.7%)	5,000 (2.4%)	173,000 (82.0%)	136,000 (64.5%)	37,000 (17.5%)
1974	217,000	29,000 (13.4%)	13,000 (6.0%)	3,000 (1.4%)	170,000 (78.3%)	128,000 (59.0%)	41,000 (18.9%)
1979	207,000	35,000 (16.9%)	7,000 (3.4%)	2,000 (1.0%)	160,000 (77.3%)	127,000 (61.4%)	34,000 (16.4%)

Sources: Ōhashi, p. 123; *Shūgyō kōzō kihon chōsa hōkoku,* 1974, pp. 256–7; 1979, pp. 342–3.

ML: males in large firms (1,000–5,000)   P1: profit of firm with 1 person
MM: males in medium firms (30–100)   P2: profit of firm with 2 persons
MS: males in small firms (under 10)   P3: profit of firm with 3 persons
FL: females in large firms
FM: females in medium firms
FS: females in small firms

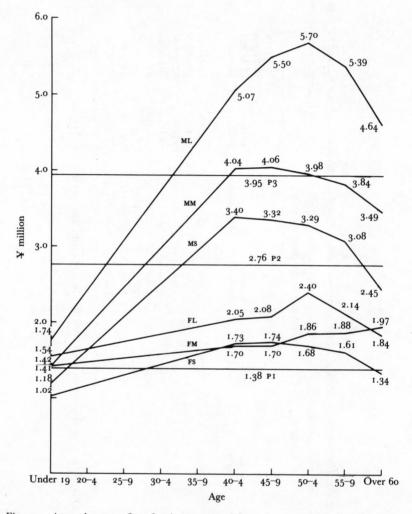

Fig. 2.1. Annual net profits of unincorporated firms (averages for manufacturing, services, and wholesale and retail) and incomes of employees, by age and by size of establishment (persons engaged), 1980. (*Sources: Kojin kigyō keizai chōsa nenpō*, 1980, pp. 38–41; Kokuzeichō chōkan kanbō sōmuka [Administrative Division of the Secretariat of the Director of the National Taxation Agency], *Zeimu tōkei kara mita minkan kyūyo no jittai* [The Real Situation of Private Incomes from the View of Taxation Statistics], 1980 (Tokyo: Ōkurashō insatsukyoku, 1981), p. 86.)

Table 2.21. *Composition of self-employed, home handicraft, and family workers, by age and sex, 1980*

Age	Self-employed No.	Self-employed %	Home handicraft No.	Home handicraft %	Family workers No.	Family workers %	Regular employees No.	Regular employees %
15–29	387	6.5	108	11.5	613	19.6	10,914	31.3
30–39	1,505	25.3	382	40.8	973	29.9	9,773	28.0
40–54	2,457	41.3	302	32.3	1,005	32.1	10,774	30.9
55 and over	1,594	26.8	144	15.4	541	17.3	3,384	9.7
Total	5,944	100	936	100	3,134	100	34,845	100
Females as % of total		24.5		97.8		81.0		30.5

Source: *Shūgyō kōzō kihon chōsa hōkoku*, 1979, p. 113.

retire at around the age of 55 and can generally only continue as temporary employees with vastly reduced wages, the temptation to set up a business increases with age among members of the working class.

Male workers in large firms have an interest in joining the petty bourgeoisie only on retirement as an alternative to having no job at all, an option which many have to take. However, to make anything like what they had received as employees, they would have to run an enterprise with three or four persons. Sometimes even this is not too difficult when a number of family members would otherwise be out of work. For male workers in smaller firms, a petty enterprise with three persons is always an attraction, though after the age of 55 a firm with only two operatives would raise the income of a worker retired from a small firm. Women workers, on the other hand, no matter how large the establishment they are employed in, could always do better in a two-person petty enterprise, and when they retire, even a firm in which they work alone would raise the income of some of them. The problem that women normally face, however, is that their wages are so low that what are comparatively easy industries to enter for males with lump-sum retirement payments are closed to most of them. They must therefore be content with the role of unpaid family workers if they wish to better their lot by entering the petty bourgeoisie. Table

2.21 shows how the forces at work in fig. 2.1 affect the age and sex composition of the agents in the petty bourgeoisie.

There are significant differences by sex in the reproduction of these groups of agents. The age composition of the self-employed, who are mainly men, reflects the influence of the age and retirement structure of male workers: over two-thirds are above the age of 40. But the two groups which consist mostly of women reveal interesting differences. Home handicrafts seem to be undertaken more by married women, for whom the retirement age from employee status is in practice about 30. But the large group of family workers under the age of 30 suggests that many young women work in their fathers' petty firms until they get married. The age composition of unpaid family workers is more similar to that of ordinary employees, who are considerably younger than the self-employed.

The expanded reproduction of the Japanese petty bourgeoisie has therefore depended on the fulfilment of two general conditions. The first is that it had actually to be possible to make a living out of simple commodity production, and we saw how specialisation in certain sectors and branches which were more labour intensive allowed this, even if it only barely did so in one-person firms. The second general condition is that certain sections of the working class had to receive overriding incentives to set up petty bourgeois firms. These, we saw, originated in the system of increasing wages until retirement, but then reducing them to levels lower than what can be made in a petty firm, particularly one which can bring in unemployed family members.

The petty bourgeoisie therefore functions simultaneously as a source of cheap labour to meet a number of capital's needs (cheap parts, wage goods, and circulation costs) and a way of both concealing unemployment and ensuring that the unemployed do not become a financial burden or a political danger. It has thus replaced the peasantry as the haven to which persons without jobs can return in times of recession or when for whichever reasons capital no longer needs them. The rural areas are now too remote for the peasantry to fulfil that function as adequately as it used to. By moving into the petty bourgeoisie, the unemployed are kept working and so contribute both to their own subsistence and capital's enrichment even though capital could find no way of directly exploiting them. Moreover, safely in the ranks of a reactionary class, the discarded workers cease even to be a political threat.

Organisation and ideology

It is not necessary to demonstrate in detail that the petty bourgeoisie in Japan is largely unorganised by progressive forces and continues, in spite of attempts by the Communists to reverse this long-standing situation, to serve as one of the main sources of popular support for bourgeois rule. Since what shape people's views of themselves and the world are their day-to-day experiences and activities in the world as it presents itself to them, we must look for an explanation of petty bourgeois conservatism not in what is said to them by all the competitors for their support but what they do each day. We have already seen what they do: they produce and sell commodities in small isolated work places which are part of the family home and from which the main forms of capitalist exploitation are not immediately visible. It is inevitable that this class should champion above all else the principles of hard work, thrift, and freedom of choice and enterprise. If it is to break with illusions like these, this will happen only when it engages in daily activities which help lay bare some of the realities behind its impoverishment and which can point to solutions. Until then, it would be quite fruitless to expect the deteriorating material circumstances of petty producers to mould them into a progressive force. The only thing that can do that is practical involvement in progressive forms of political organisation.

However, to the extent that petty bourgeois firms do belong to organisations, these are mainly ones set up by the state for the use of small and medium capitalists. Their purposes are almost entirely to help these capitalists maintain profitability, by getting smaller firms to cooperate wherever possible to reduce costs, modernise facilities, obtain finance, engage in joint purchasings, share warehousing facilities, and solve 'labour problems.' They also act as pressure groups to obtain state assistance in such matters as protecting certain sectors of industry from monopoly penetration.

The Small and Medium Enterprise Agency of the Ministry of International Trade and Industry has a number of departments which are concerned with small and medium capital. The 'Organisation Division' of the 'Guidance Department' promotes the above-mentioned organisations in accordance with a number of laws, such as the 'Cooperative Union Laws.' The integration of somewhere round one-quarter of petty bourgeois firms into one or other of these state-sponsored organisations of small and medium capital doubly

Table 2.22. *State-sponsored organisations in the manufacturing industry: proportions of firms which are members, 1971*

Firm size (operatives)	Shōkōkai, Shōkōkaigisho[a]	Shōkō Kumiai[b]	Jigyō Kyōdō Kumiai[c]
1–3	29.1	7.2	27.6
4–9	46.1	10.9	39.9
10–19	63.4	13.2	48.5
20–9	61.5	15.4	52.8
30–49	77.4	16.5	54.7
50–99	82.1	16.8	56.3
100–99	85.3	17.8	54.2
200–99	87.3	19.1	52.3

[a]The Association of Merchants and Industrialists is a thoroughly bourgeois organisation, which focuses primarily on communication and negotiation among businessmen and between them and the state. Its head office is in Tokyo, but it has branches all over the country.
[b]Unions of Merchants and Industrialists are sponsored under the law to promote organisations of small and medium enterprises.
[c]Cooperative Unions are sponsored under the law to encourage combinations among small and medium enterprises as a means of strengthening their weak positions.
Source: *Dai 4 kai kōgyō jittai kihon chōsa hōkokusho*, p. 116.

ensures their functioning as adjuncts of the capitalist class. Table 2.22 shows the proportions of manufacturing firms of different sizes which belong to the three main types of organisation.

The Japan Communist Party has organised similar activities for small and medium capital under the umbrella of what it calls Minshū Shōkōkai or Minshō (The Association of Democratic Merchants and Industrialists). Many of its approximately 200,000 members are petty bourgeois, and its activities centre mainly on the problems of raising finance and paying the minimum of taxes. But members are also exposed to other party activities which gradually loom larger the more they themselves get involved in them. However, this has so far not led much beyond bringing certain sections of the petty bourgeoisie together with similar elements of small and medium capital into the welfare capitalist alliance which even the ruling class claims to support. There is little evidence that Minshō has generated among its members any great sense of common interests between the working class and the petty bourgeoisie. By focusing mainly on contradictions between monopoly and non-monopoly capital, it actually helps

Table 2.23. *Distribution of support for parliamentary parties, by major occupational groups, 1976–80 (%)*

	LDP[a]		JSP[b]		JCP[c]		CGP[d]		DSP[e]		NLC[f]		No party		No answer	
	1980	1976	1980	1976	1980	1976	1980	1976	1980	1976	1980	1976	1980	1976	1980	1976
Clerical/managerial	31	25	16	19	5	5	3	3	7	5	1	3	23	24	14	16
Factory workers	28	21	18	23	4	5	5	6	7	5	1	2	21	20	16	18
Sales workers	32	27	13	17	4	4	7	7	4	3	1	2	22	21	17	19
Self-employed	49	42	6	8	4	4	4	4	5	4	1	3	17	19	14	16
Farmers/primary industry	55	50	7	9	1	1	2	2	2	2	1	1	13	13	19	22
Others	36	31	10	11	3	3	5	5	5	3	1	2	17	18	23	27

[a] Liberal Democratic Party.
[b] Japan Socialist Party.
[c] Japan Communist Party.
[d] Clean Government Party (Kōmeitō).
[e] Democratic Socialist Party.
[f] New Liberal Club.
Source: Asahi Shinbun, 3 December 1976, p. 2; 20 June 1980, p. 2.

preserve the alliance between the petty bourgeoisie and the bourgeoisie. Minshō parallels the state-sponsored organisations which
lump all small businesses together, regardless of their relations of
production, and thereby delay the development of specifically petty
bourgeois organisations.

What is needed is not an anti-monopoly alliance, but an anti-
capitalist alliance, which leads to understanding capitalist production – the source of inequalities – rather than simply capitalist
exchange where everyone is more or less equal anyway. If the petty
bourgeoisie cannot be brought directly into working-class organisations, surely the best way to detach it from the bourgeoisie is to
encourage the development of purely petty bourgeois organisations
rather than to integrate it even further into the most reactionary
fractions of the bourgeoisie. Although time and patience would still
be needed to bring it to the point of supporting working-class
demands, this would be easier once it became an anti-capitalist force.

As the crisis deepens, both tasks should if anything become easier,
since the petty bourgeoisie is increasingly a class not out of which one
rises into the bourgeoisie but into which one sinks from the working
class. As growing numbers of workers fail to get even temporary
employment on retirement and have no source of livelihood other
than setting up petty firms, the possibilities of detaching this class
from the bourgeoisie will increase. Since it functions increasingly as a
reserve army of labour, it will share growing interests with those class
agents who more visibly perform the same role and who are less shy of
working-class organisations.

A sobering way to conclude this chapter might be to reflect on the
results of a poll the *Asahi* daily took just before the last election. The
support of self-employed persons for the ruling Liberal Democratic
Party was exceeded only by that of farmers. The only glimmer of light
to be found in the findings was that these people shared in the
widespread disillusionment with parliamentary politics that grew up
in the 1960s and 1970s. However, that is a subject that must wait until
chapter 7.

3

The peasantry

It may seem that what I call peasants in Japan are no more than petty bourgeois producers who happen to be engaged in agriculture.[1] In a crucial sense this is what they are: like members of the petty bourgeoisie, they own and operate their means of production without the use of wage labour and sell what they do or make, not their skills and capacities, on the market. Also like the petty bourgeoisie, the peasantry has been steadily impoverished through its inability to match the efficiency of capitalist production. However, relevant similarities between the two classes end here: the peasantry is not a class into which one sinks from the working class; neither is it being reproduced in increasing numbers. Rather, impoverished peasants disappear altogether, and their members re-emerge as either workers or petty bourgeois.

The most important material condition which separates the peasantry from the petty bourgeoisie is the extent of the former's ownership of a unique factor of production, land. Unlike labour power, tools, machinery, and other reproducible factors of production, land can neither be produced nor reproduced. Yet it is an equally vital condition of production and of human existence. Because land cannot be produced, it has no *value*, that is, it embodies no socially necessary time apart from the human effort put into its improvement. However, although unimproved land has no value, it can and does command a price because of its crucial role in production. The price of unimproved land, unlike that of anything which can be produced, depends purely on its demand and supply. It has nothing to do with socially necessary labour time, because it embodies none. This price is referred to as *rent*, because the money one gets from selling or hiring out land comes out of the social surplus, that is, what the working class produces over and above what it consumes.[2] Rent accrues to owners of land simply in virtue of this ownership, while the amount of rent depends on the supply and demand of the type of land concerned: the greater the scarcity of the land and the more it is sought after, the greater will be the rent it can command.

Land is of course a vital factor of production for both the peasantry and the petty bourgeoisie. The differences in their material conditions lie in the size, location, and use of their land, both by themselves and by potential buyers. Most members of the petty bourgeoisie operate from their homes in towns and cities, and the demand for this land increased so rapidly as a result of the high rate of accumulation in the 1960s that land prices skyrocketed all over the country in the 1970s. Prime Minister Tanaka in the early 1970s promised to assist the relocation into rural areas of major industrial projects, thereby helping even rural land prices to keep pace somewhat with those in urban areas. However, throughout the 1970s there was no let-up in the rising prices of metropolitan land, so that the people who had not been home owners before then could only buy homes on the minutest pieces of land (for example, apartments in ten-storey buildings) and then with mortgages that their children would inherit (see chapter 7). In other words, people are today probably as well off renting homes in metropolitan areas. What all this means is that entry into the petty bourgeoisie has never, neither before nor after the land boom, been barred by an inability to own or rent a home from which to run the family business. Before the land boom of the 1970s, retired workers could acquire homes with their retirement cheques without excessive mortgages, whereas now they do so simply by mortgaging future generations as well as themselves. Anyone in urban and metropolitan Japan with a roof over his head, regardless of land prices, can find some petty bourgeois occupation into which he can sink.

Very little of the same can be said of agricultural land. Although the holdings are small in comparison with plots in other countries, they are large and expensive enough to be well beyond the means of retired workers with or without mortgages which bind future generations. But the demand which has forced up agricultural land prices has not come from budding young farmers or people looking for a home in the countryside. It has come from the requirements of capital both to relocate factories and for large-scale agricultural production. The reason why retired workers do not buy themselves jobs in the peasantry (as they do in the petty bourgeoisie) lies in the absence of one of the two conditions in agriculture which ensured the expanded reproduction of the petty bourgeoisie in other industries. It is simply not possible for a family to survive on the size of farm which could even remotely be bought with the credit that a retired worker could raise. The reason why existing farmers are taking side jobs and moving off the land is precisely because the family farm, unlike the family firm in the cities, is no longer a source of subsistence.

Since peasants cannot themselves use their holdings productively, they are unable to take advantage of the rising rents the land can extract, unless of course they sell it. But they are very reluctant to do so, largely because of the way they come to acquire land in the first place. This separates them significantly from the petty bourgeoisie. Ever since the postwar land reform of 1946, by which tenant farmers were given legal ownership of the small holdings they had previously cultivated under the control of landlords, peasants have acquired land almost exclusively through inheritance within peasant families. However, from the outset the holdings were too small for profitable agricultural production, and the almost exclusive buyers of agricultural land became large-scale capitalist interests: in agriculture, industry, housing development, and state-sponsored infrastructural undertakings such as roads and railways. The only people who actually work on small family farms in Japan are persons whose families inherited agricultural land. The low productivity of this scale of agriculture and rising land prices have made it impossible for new families to enter the peasant class.

This, almost paradoxically, is the reason why existing peasant families are so reluctant to part with their land. Although they are partly proletarianised by having to send more and more of their household members into wage-labouring jobs, they cling to their land as a final security against total impoverishment and unemployment. The potential rent they could realise from the sale of their land ties them to it and prevents their complete proletarianisation. Thus the traditional ideology of passing on the family property from one generation to the next, which was born in an earlier period when land was more fully the peasant household's sole source of subsistence, is reproduced. The petty bourgeoisie, on the other hand, since it increasingly has to pay rent through either buying or renting homes which are used as places of production, is not as disposed as is the peasantry to see the home as a form of protection and security, but rather as a necessary outlay to maintain a job and earn a living. The home must be bought or hired both as a place of residence and as a

Table 3.1. *Home ownership and money value of homes, by type of household, 1970*

Type of household	% with own homes	Average value of homes (¥ mil.)
One-person households	7.6	0.2
Two-or-more-person households		
Agricultural households	98.4	3.3
Wage/salary households	44.1	1.1
Individual proprietors	70.6	1.9
Capitalist	78.0	2.8
Petty bourgeois	70.1	1.8
Corporation executives	78.3	3.2

Source: Sōrifu tōkeikyoku [Bureau of Statistics, Office of the Prime Minister], *Kokufu chōsa* [National Wealth Survey], 1970, vol. 6, *Kakei shisan chōsa hōkoku* [Report on the Survey of Household Assets] (Tokyo: Ōkurashō insatsukyoku, 1973), pp. 60–1, 98–9.

location for the family enterprise. There is thus not so much room in petty bourgeois ideology for such notions as the family line and the sacredness of family property.

My identification of the peasantry as a distinctive social force in Japan requires emphasising three important differences in its material circumstances from those of the petty bourgeoisie: the proportion of peasants who own land and homes is much higher; the value in money terms of their property is much higher; and they are more reluctant to sell their land (just as potential farmers are reluctant to buy it). Table 3.1 indicates the differences in home ownership and the money value of homes in 1970, that is, before the real boom in land prices, among different classes. The data come from the 1970 National Wealth Survey, which has not been repeated since then.

Table 3.2 relies on the same source and shows, by the age of the household head, the proportions of the different types of household which owned their homes in 1970. Although more recent data (see chapter 7) have shown that home ownership among non-agricultural households has increased since then, the main patterns have not. In 1979, for example, 30% of wage and salary earners' households under the age of 30 had their own homes, as did 82.3% of those over the age of 60.[3] Clearly, with almost 100% home ownership among peasants, agricultural property changes hands mainly through inheritance, while working-class families buy homes in later life. The same applies

Table 3.2. *Home ownership, by type of household and age of household head, 1970 (% with own homes)*

Age of household head	Type of household (all over 2 persons)		
	Agricultural households	Wage and salary households	All non-agricultural households
Under 25	100.0	17.0	17.8
25–9	100.0	22.7	23.8
30–4	91.8	25.2	28.8
35–9	96.4	38.9	43.6
40–4	100.0	51.2	55.1
45–9	98.9	53.5	58.5
50–4	98.4	63.2	67.1
55–9	99.2	63.1	68.7
60–4	100.0	68.5	73.6
65 and over	97.7	64.1	72.8

Source: As table 3.1, pp. 227, 232, 237.

to members of the petty bourgeoisie, who, although not shown separately in table 3.2, fall into the category of 'all non-agricultural households' together with wage and salary earners.

The Japanese peasantry: working and living conditions

The Japanese peasantry is a class which has been steadily pro-letarianised ever since it acquired its land in the 1946 reform, so that impoverished peasants leave the land altogether (in stages, as will be shown) for jobs in the petty bourgeoisie or the working class. There is increasingly no branch of agricultural production in which peasants can specialise to compensate for the growing power of agribusiness, as yet manifested mainly through cheap imports but beginning to take hold of certain sectors in Japan too.

Productive forces in agriculture have advanced rapidly in countries where land holdings, whether publicly or privately owned, are large, because only large-scale farming permits the efficient use of the most advanced agricultural technology. In Japan, however, the bulk of agricultural land is divided into minute holdings, which are owned and operated by peasant families. These property relations have 'fettered' (to use some Marxist jargon) the development of efficient agriculture in Japan, much as they did even in a country like New

Table 3.3. *Distribution of agricultural households by size of cultivated plots (hectares), 1975–80*

	1980		1975	
Plot size	No.	%	No.	%
Hokkaido				
Under 1	22,756	19.0	27,382	20.4
1.0–3.0	18,466	15.4	22,351	16.6
3.0–7.5	38,738	32.4	46,947	35.0
7.5–15	20,895	17.5	21,251	15.8
Over 15	18,789	15.7	16,332	12.2
Total	119,644	100.0	134,263	100.0
Rest of Japan				
Under 0.5	1,921,563	42.3	1,995,046	41.4
0.5–1.0	1,304,243	28.7	1,436,111	29.8
1.0–2.0	980,627	21.6	1,076,340	22.3
2.0–3.0	240,047	5.3	235,612	4.9
Over 3.0	95,260	2.1	75,699	1.6
Total	4,541,740	100.0	4,818,808	100.0

Source: Nōrinsuisanshō keizaikyoku tōkei jōhōbu [Statistics and Information Department of the Ministry of Agriculture, Forestry, and Fisheries], *Nōrinsuisanshō tōkeihyō* [Statistical Yearbook of the Ministry of Agriculture, Forestry, and Fisheries], 1979–80 (Tokyo: Nōrin tōkei kyōkai, 1981), pp. 6–7.

Zealand, where land holdings were from the beginning infinitely larger. Table 3.3 shows that over 70% of farmers outside Hokkaido (where the larger and more prosperous dairy farms are situated) cultivate plots of less than one hectare. These are substantially the plots they also own, since, as table 3.4 shows, the renting of agricultural land is rare in Japan.

The close correspondence between the size of the plots owned and the land actually cultivated strongly suggests that the fundamental reason for the technical backwardness of Japanese agriculture is the structure of land ownership, the legal form of which dates from the postwar land reform, but which has its real origins in the tenancy system of feudal property. The smallest holdings therefore hardly manage to market anything at all, and many produce no more than part of their own subsistence. Table 3.5 shows how only the cultivators of larger holdings sell substantial amounts of produce on the market.[4]

Table 3.4. *Numbers of agricultural households which rent land and which lend land out, by per cent of cultivated and owned land, 1980*

	Under 10%	10–30%	30–50%	50–80%	Over 80%	Total
Households renting land[a]	165,554	323,786	149,265	86,188	62,368	787,161
Households lending land[b]	106,773	190,044	113,354	102,260	30,873	543,304

[a]The proportions refer to the shares of total cultivated land which is rented.
[b]The proportions refer to the shares of total owned land which is lent out.
Source: As table 3.3, pp. 8–9.

These differences in the value of agricultural sales do not correspond to a difference between production for subsistence and production for the market, a distinction which ceases under monopoloy capitalism to be relevant to the forms in which class forces manifest themselves. This is because the agricultural products that peasants produce have come to constitute only a very small proportion of the many goods they require for their subsistence. In this respect, they are not unlike certain groups in the petty bourgeoisie, who also directly consume some of what they produce. Far from being able to subsist on the land, peasant households are increasingly having to send members into part- and full-time wage-labouring jobs outside agriculture in order to obtain the necessities of life. Not all the persons in the 4.7 million agricultural households in Japan mediate the social force of the peasantry, let alone unambiguously so. The households on the smallest plots not only produce least, but have more members in working-class jobs than they have doing farm work, and are peasant households in not much more than name only.

Farm households are as a result even officially classified into three groupings according to their dependence on wages for their total incomes. In the first, referred to as 'full-time agricultural households,' all economically active members are engaged on the farm. The second group comprises households with some members engaged in non-agricultural industries but whose main income derives from agriculture. They are known as 'part-time farming households, type one,' while the third group ('part-time farming households, type

Table 3.5. *Agricultural households, by size of cultivated plot and value of annual agricultural sales, 1975 and 1980*

Cultivated plots (ha)	No sale	Value of sales (¥ mil.)					Total
		0.0–1.0	1.0–3.0	3.0–5.0	5.0–10.0	Over 10	
Hokkaidō (1975)							
Under 1	14,642	11,139	1,023	187	200	191	27,382
1.0–3.0	1,976	8,847	10,145	945	315	123	22,351
3.0–7.5	1,264	5,502	16,793	15,162	7,879	347	46,947
7.5–15.0	129	830	4,100	6,559	8,623	1,010	21,251
Over 15	20	147	982	2,849	9,370	2,964	16,332
Total 1975	18,031	26,465	33,043	25,702	26,387	4,635	134,263
Total 1980	14,067	16,531	17,485	16,711	31,003	23,847	119,644
Rest of Japan (1975)							
Under 0.5	824,238	1,127,941	28,843	4,588	4,569	4,867	1,995,046
0.5–1.0	55,084	1,197,525	160,075	13,378	6,505	3,544	1,436,111
1.0–2.0	7,581	441,698	559,623	46,627	15,622	5,189	1,076,340
2.0–3.0	877	17,059	171,424	34,950	9,295	2,007	235,612
Over 3	317	3,306	28,645	30,482	10,646	2,303	75,699
Total 1975	888,097	2,787,529	948,610	130,125	46,637	17,910	4,818,808
Total 1980	831,135	2,169,542	1,072,524	270,951	150,866	46,722	4,541,740

Sources: Nōrinshō nōrin keizaikyoku tōkei jōhōbu [Statistics and Information Department of the Ministry of Agriculture and Forestry], *Nōka chōsa hōkokusho* [Report on the Census of Agricultural Households], 1975; *Nōka jinkō hen* [Volume on Agricultural Households and Population] (Tokyo: Nōrin tōkei kyōkai, 1977), pp. 112–13; *Nōrinsuisanshō tōkeityō*, 1979–80, pp. 14–15.

two') consists of those households whose main income is earned in other industries. Table 3.6 shows the numbers and proportions of farming households, by the size of their cultivated plots, which fell into each category in 1975 and the total numbers in each in 1980. Already from table 3.3 it might have been noticed that the numbers of large farms had increased in the years 1975–80, while the numbers of small ones had declined sharply. The same forces can be seen at work in table 3.6: a rise in the numbers of full-time farming households (for the first time in many years, reflecting the consolidation of small farms into larger ones) and a jump in each stage of peasant proletarianis-ation, from full-time to part-time type one, from that to part-time type two, and finally disappearance from the statistics altogether.

If one considered households as the main concrete institutions which mediated class forces, the bulk of agricultural households on small holdings would obviously be in the working class rather than the peasantry. However, in capitalist society, households are mainly units of consumption, and individual members need not necessarily share the same production relations (unlike feudal society). Since class forces stem from relations of production, and members of peasant households mediate different ones, it would be a mistake to take the household as the unit of class analysis. To be sure, relations of consumption might often affect the actions of class agents (they often work in the opposite direction and make unequals look equal), but they are not their fundamental determinants. In the final analysis, it is people's roles in mechanisms of production which produce the class forces that are so basic to the movement of history. Precisely to identify the concrete forms in which the peasantry is manifested, therefore, we must analyse the production relations of individual members of peasant households. When we look at the organisation, ideology, and political activity of peasants, we will see how far the household as the common unit of consumption has affected peasant struggles. Table 3.7 breaks down the economically active persons in agricultural households by their production relations.

If one sees the core of the peasantry (the persons who mainly mediate this force) as those household members who are engaged solely or mainly in agriculture, then in 1975–80 the strength of this class declined from 7.9 million to 6.97 million, that is, by 13.4%. However, persons partly engaged in agriculture (but mainly in other jobs), and to some extent even those who are solely engaged in other jobs, play the roles of both peasants and other classes simultaneously.

Table 3.6. Agricultural households, by size of cultivated plot and degree of dependence on agricultural production, 1975–80

Cultivated plots (ha)	Full-time No.	%	Part-time (1) No.	%	Part-time (2) No.	%	Total No.	%
Hokkaido (1975)								
Under 1	2,849	10.4	1,173	4.3	23,360	85.3	27,382	100
1.0–3.0	5,903	26.4	7,889	35.3	8,559	38.3	22,351	100
3.0–7.5	20,983	44.7	20,786	44.3	5,178	11.0	46,947	100
7.5–15.0	14,413	67.8	6,010	28.3	828	3.9	21,251	100
Over 15	13,343	81.7	2,776	17.0	213	1.3	16,332	100
Total 1975	57,491	42.8	38,634	28.8	38,138	28.4	134,263	100
Total 1980	50,287	42.0	38,419	32.1	30,938	25.9	119,644	100
Rest of Japan (1975)								
Under 0.5	154,926	7.8	98,704	4.9	1,741,416	87.3	1,995,046	100
0.5–1.0	137,332	9.6	346,709	24.1	952,070	66.3	1,436,111	100
1.0–2.0	186,887	17.4	565,491	52.5	323,962	30.1	1,076,340	100
2.0–3.0	57,085	24.2	159,467	67.7	19,060	8.1	235,612	100
Over 3.0	22,711	30.0	49,714	65.7	3,274	4.3	75,699	100
Total 1975	558,941	11.6	1,220,085	25.3	3,039,782	63.1	4,818,868	100
Total 1980	572,846	12.6	963,843	21.2	3,005,051	66.2	4,541,740	100

Sources: Nōka chōsa hōkokusho, 1975, Nōka jinkō hen, pp. 20–1; Nōrinsuisanshō tōkeihyō, 1979–80, pp. 10–11.

Table 3.7. *Distribution of economically active members of agricultural households, by type of job and sex, 1975–80*

		Males		Females		Total	
	Year	No.	%	No.	%	No.	%
Engaged only in own farm	1980	2,068,134	34.3	3,967,570	65.7	6,035,704	100
	1975	2,147,182	32.7	4,418,389	67.3	6,565,571	100
Engaged mainly in own farm	1980	605,443	64.6	331,938	35.4	937,381	100
	1975	827,881	61.7	514,035	38.3	1,341,916	100
Engaged mainly in other jobs	1980	3,748,579	67.3	1,817,533	32.7	5,566,112	100
	1975	3,901,732	67.0	1,922,996	33.0	5,824,728	100
Engaged only in other jobs	1980	866,155	51.9	804,322	48.1	1,670,477	100
	1975	815,484	54.2	687,734	45.8	1,503,218	100
Total economically active	1980	7,288,311	51.3	6,921,363	48.7	14,209,674	100
	1975	7,692,279	50.5	7,543,154	49.5	15,235,433	100

Source: Nōrinsuisanshō tōkeihyō, 1979–80, pp. 24–5.

Table 3.8. *Non-agricultural jobs of members of peasant households who are partly, mainly, or solely engaged in them, by sex, 1980*

	Males		Females	
	No.	%	No.	%
Regular employees	3,242,865	62.1	1,763,996	59.7
Seasonal workers	133,980	2.6	16,048	0.5
Day labourers and temporary workers	1,096,810	21.0	719,433	24.4
Subtotal	4,473,655	85.7	2,499,477	84.6
Self-employed	878,526	16.8	487,192	16.5
Total	5,220,177	102.5	2,953,793	101.1

Source: Nōrinsuisanshō tōkeihyō, 1979–80, pp. 34–5. Attempts were made to avoid double counting of people who had more than one side job, but these were apparently not entirely successful.

(Table 3.8 shows what these classes were in 1980.)[5] They do so not simply or even mainly because the peasant household is their unit of consumption, but because they at the very least share in the family's ownership of the farm and in the ultimate security this provides.

The proletarianisation of the peasantry is therefore an historical process that begins with the conversion of full-time farming households into part-time farming households and only ends when the family is forced to leave the land altogether. During the process it is difficult to draw a precise boundary between the working class and the peasantry in the countryside, since vast numbers of agents mediate contradictory forces which are constantly changing. Table 3.9 summarises the process during the years 1960–80 and shows how the different stages followed one another, although sometimes with considerable lags. The first stage, which involved reducing the numbers of full-time farming households to the ones which could survive comfortably, took place most rapidly of all and was more or less complete by 1975. After a lag of a few years, the second stage, that is, converting part-time type one into part-time type two farming households, took off and has proceeded quite rapidly since about 1970. Finally, the removal from the land of peasant families has taken place more slowly, but also more steadily, at a rate of 6–8% each five years.

The immediate forms in which peasants experience the forces

Table 3.9. *Changes in the status of agricultural households, 1960–80*

	Full-time		Part-time (1)		Part-time (2)		Total	
	No.	% change	No.	% change	No.	% change	No.	% change
1960	2,078,124	—	2,036,330	—	1,942,176	—	6,056,630	—
1965	1,218,723	−70.5	2,080,663	2.2	2,365,377	21.8	5,664,763	−6.9
1970	831,350	−46.6	1,801,814	−15.5	2,708,680	14.5	5,341,844	−6.0
1975	616,432	−34.9	1,258,719	−43.1	3,077,920	12.0	4,953,071	−7.8
1980	623,133	1.1	1,002,262	−25.6	3,935,989	−1.4	4,661,384	−6.3

Sources: Nōrinshō tōkeihyō, 1974–5, pp. 6–7; Nōrinsuisanshō tōkeihyo, 1979–80, pp. 10–11.

Table 3.10. *Annual income (¥ 1,000) of agricultural households, by size of cultivated holdings (outside Hokkaido), 1974–9*

Cultivated plots (ha)	Agricultural income		Non-agricultural income		Total income	
	1974	1979	1974	1979	1974	1979
Under 0.5	226.4	193.3	2,636.8	4,089.1	2,863.2	4,282.4
0.5–1.0	722.9	715.9	2,136.0	3,648.1	2,858.9	4,364.0
1.0–1.5	1,317.9	1,509.9	1,571.6	2,836.5	2,889.5	4,346.4
1.5–2.0	1,741.2	2,180.6	1,288.0	2,349.1	3,029.2	4,529.7
Over 2.0	2,436.2	3,343.8	955.4	1,631.3	3,391.6	4,975.1

Sources: *Nōrinshō tōkeihyō*, 1974–5, p. 230; *Nōrinsuisanshō tōkeihyō*, 1979–80, p. 248.

behind their proletarianisation are simply incomes on which it is impossible to live. The pittances that those on small holdings received in 1975 had by 1979 fallen even further, not simply in real terms, but even in nominal terms. The share of their total household income from agriculture thus fell from 8.6% to a mere 4.5% (see table 3.10).[6] If the declining share of agricultural in total household income is one measure of peasant proletarianisation, another is the growing inability of farming to provide incomes which keep up even with those of workers in small firms. One study showed that in 1960 peasants who worked their land could earn about 97% of what they could get as wage labourers in small manufacturing firms, provided of course they were males. However, by 1971 they could make only 71.5% of that wage, and even peasants on holdings of over two hectares could make only 91% of it. Very few peasants therefore could escape from the forces which lay behind the decline of Japanese agriculture as a whole.[7]

The decline of Japanese agriculture

The fundamental reason for the proletarianisation of the Japanese peasantry has been the uneven development of productive forces in that country. While secondary and tertiary industries have boomed (themselves unevenly), agriculture has not kept pace, and its contribution to net national product fell from 10.2% in 1960 to 4.2% in 1973. The share of agriculture, forestry, and fisheries in the latter

year was only 6.3%, but by 1979 this had fallen to 4.7%.[8]
Productivity in Japanese agriculture has fallen further and further
behind agricultural productivity in other countries, chiefly the
United States and Australia, from where the largest shares of
agricultural imports come (35.3% and 10.5% respectively in 1980).[9]
The result was that in 1979 Japan became the third largest importer
of food in the world, lagging only just behind the United States and
West Germany.[10] Among the world's net importers of food, Japan
occupies the top position.

The development of productive forces under capitalism results
from competition among capitals to increase profits through the use
of more efficient production techniques. A capital which can gain a
competitive advantage over its rivals gets an extra profit for as long as
it maintains that advantage. Its competitors are therefore compelled
either to match its efficiency or leave that branch of production, and
the result is an overall increase in the efficiency of the industry as a
whole. This process does not, however, take place at the same rate in
all industries, for two main reasons.

The first is the prevailing system of property relations in the
different industries. If these are not capitalist relations, productive
forces will lag behind industries in which capitalist relations are
dominant. Since the purpose of production under simple commodity
relations (as in Japanese agriculture) is not to achieve the average
rate of profit or be threatened with bankruptcy, but to maintain the
family's consumption, producers are not under the same compulsion
to improve production techniques. They can continue in ways they
know and simply send family members into wage labour to supplement their falling agricultural incomes. And so long as capital does
not totally invade the agricultural sector and the state offers peasants
some protection, the rate of their proletarianisation will be retarded,
and along with it the development of productive forces in agriculture.

The second reason for the relative backwardness of agriculture in
Japan results from a combination of property relations and technical
factors. Since land is owned and cultivated in small plots, there is little
scope for one producer to keep stealing a march on rivals by
introducing the most efficient available techniques, since their
greater efficiency depends on them being used on a larger scale than is
possible on the small plots. The incentive for capital to enter
agriculture on a large scale and develop productive forces depends on
whether the optimum size and type of land can be easily obtained. So

far, not much capital (though the amount is increasing) has found it worth while to buy this land, since investing the money in other industries has produced much greater advantages over competitors and thus higher rates of return.

Although there are productivity differences among peasant producers and between peasant and capitalist producers in Japan, these are nothing like the differences to be found between American and Japanese agriculture. The cost of producing meat and wheat in Japan is three times its cost in the United States, while Japanese rice can be four times as costly as American rice. Compared to these differences, those in the Japanese livestock industry, where most capitalist agriculture is concentrated, are relatively small. However, they have increased in recent years, and capital has shown a correspondingly greater interest in moving into agriculture. In the years 1974–9, the differences in production costs incurred by small-scale peasants and large-scale capitalists grew from 28% to 32% in cow milk, 13% to 25% in fattening hogs, and 18% to 37% in hen eggs.[11] In the same period, the output of the capitalist agricultural sector increased by 2.3 times, so that its share of gross agricultural output increased from 8% to about 15%.[12] Table 3.11 summarises the growth of agribusiness in Japan during that period. In addition to these 11,148 corporations in 1980, only 28 of which were large ones, there were another 20,000-odd agricultural households which operated petty capitalist enterprises with five to nine persons.[13] In general, therefore, in spite of the growth of capitalist agriculture in Japan, the scale is still very small by American standards.

In view of the peasantry's rapid proletarianisation and the comparatively small capitalist agricultural sector in Japan, it is remarkable that production in the postwar period increased at all. That it did had a lot to do with the ways the state protected it from foreign imports, gave it subsidies to improve mechanisation, and provided various price-support schemes. The state also encouraged the expansion of the dairy industry as well as the use of chemical fertilisers and agricultural chemicals. The use of the latter has been phenomenal, but perhaps not unexpected on holdings which are too small for the application of agricultural technologies beyond those which allow more and more intensive farming of the same small area. In fact one of the great unsolved problems of Japanese agriculture is how to produce foods without carcinogenic chemicals. There is little future in a capitalist society for organic farming, since it is hopelessly

Table 3.11. *Employment and sales of agricultural companies, 1975–80*

		Company size (by capital, ¥ mil.)				
	Year	Under 2	2–50	50–100	Over 100	Total
No. of companies	1975	4,543	4,350	57	16	8,966
	1980	4,367	6,645	108	28	11,148
Sales (¥ mil.)	1975	106,343	544,082	40,584	17,212	708,221
	1980	353,624	965,238	245,419	57,699	1,621,980
Employees	1975	12,266	34,582	2,354	1,556	50,758
	1980	19,766	55,864	3,985	3,267	82,882
Employees per company	1975	2.7	7.9	41.3	97.3	5.7
	1980	4.5	8.4	36.9	116.7	7.4
Value added (¥ mil.)	1975	28,855	74,659	3,592	3,158	110,264
	1980	64,806	137,807	16,124	8,563	227,300

Source: Zaisei kin'yū tōkei geppō, no. 295, 1976, p. 51; no. 355, 1981, pp. 50–1.

Table 3.12. *Indices of agricultural production, 1969–79 (1970 = 100)*

	Index of production			Share of total value		
	1969	1974	1979	1969	1974	1979
Total agriculture	*102.3*	*101.7*	*111.3*	*100.0*	*100.0*	*100.0*
Field crops	*106.5*	*99.4*	*103.2*	76.4	72.9	72.1
Rice	110.3	96.8	94.9	45.6	37.6	33.7
Wheat/barley	147.2	44.7	93.4	2.2	0.5	1.5
Miscellaneous cereals	118.9	95.9	72.0	1.3	1.1	1.0
Pulses	94.4	89.6	74.2			
Potatoes	103.6	69.0	81.6	1.8[a]	1.9	1.6
Vegetables	100.3	102.2	112.3	12.3	17.0	19.4
Fruit/nuts	91.3	118.2	128.9	6.1	7.8	7.5
Flowering plants	—	178.3	235.8	0.6	1.0	1.2
Industrial crops	109.4	99.8	107.0	4.7	4.2	4.9
Others	116.1	81.4	61.6	1.8	1.7	1.3
Sericulture	*102.1*	*91.3*	*68.6*	*3.0*	*1.8*	*1.6*
Livestock	*90.9*	*110.6*	*138.9*	*20.0*	*24.5*	*25.6*
Milk cattle	97.0	86.1	97.7	5.0	6.4	7.6
Cow milk	94.7	102.1	135.4	4.0	5.4	6.3
Beef cattle	93.6	100.8	137.6	1.7	2.0	3.2
Swine	81.7	127.8	165.2	4.5	6.1	6.9
Layers	93.2	87.4	95.0	8.2[b]	9.5[b]	7.4[b]
Hen eggs	93.1	102.9	112.3	6.6	6.5	4.4
Broilers	91.7	137.5	187.6	—	—	—
Others	119.8	111.6	109.6	0.6	0.5	0.6

[a] Includes sweet potatoes.
[b] Includes broilers.
Sources: Nōrinshō tōkeihyō, 1974–5, pp. 420–1, 425; *Nōrinsuisanshō tōkeihyō*, 1979–80, pp. 422, 429.

'inefficient' and unprofitable. Yet in Japan it has become very much more than the middle-class luxury it is often seen as by workers in the West – rather a matter of sheer survival.

However, what has kept Japanese peasants solvent has not been the way of 'muesli and candles,' but concrete government assistance and protection. From 1961 to 1969, the index of agricultural production rose from 100 to 130.7,[14] but it declined after that in response to the removal of many forms of protection under pressure from the United States. By 1971, forty-five out of the sixty-three restricted agricultural items had been liberalised, and others have been trickling through

Table 3.13. *Numbers of households which raise dairy cattle and pigs, by the numbers of head raised, 1970–5*

	1970		1975	
	No.	%	No.	%
Dairy cattle				
Calves only	65,580	21.3	20,540	12.8
1–4 head	148,610	48.3	56,830	35.5
5–14 head	78,784	25.6	52,854	33.1
15–49 head	14,206	4.6	28,716	18.0
50 head and over	378	0.1	957	0.6
Total households	307,558	100.0	159,897	100.0
Total dairy cattle	1,804,000	—	1,787,000	—
Pigs				
Breeding only	130,400	29.3	100,600	45.0
1–29 head	283,870	63.9	88,980	39.9
30–39 head	22,603	5.1	20,046	9.0
100–499 head	7,078	1.6	12,451	5.8
500 head and over	553	0.1	1,356	0.6
Total households	444,504	100.0	223,433	100.0
Total pigs	6,335,000	—	7,684,000	—

Source: *Nōrinshō tōkeihyō*, 1974–5, pp. 144–5, 148, 150–1.

since then. Meats and fruits, however, which are among the few expanding branches of Japanese agriculture, have remained under heavy protection. Table 3.12 shows that since 1969 production in most other branches has either fallen heavily or remained fairly constant.

Where production did increase during the 1970s was among large-scale capitalist producers, who often merely consolidated the operations of the small interests they displaced. Table 3.13 shows that although the numbers of households involved in the production of dairy cattle fell by almost 100% in 1970–5, the numbers of dairy cattle fell by only 1%. Pig production, however, increased by 20% even though the households producing them were also halved. Similar developments occurred in 1975–80, but the results of the census which gathers this information each five years are not yet published.

Accompanying the proletarianisation of most small peasant

Table 3.14. *Numbers of self-employed persons who declared taxable income in 1974–9, by industry and amount of taxable income*

Declared taxable income (¥ mil.)	Agriculture		Other businesses		Lawyers, doctors, artists, etc.	
	Persons	%	Persons	%	Persons	%
1974						
Under 1	155,976	44.7	617,842	33.0	124,364	37.0
1–2	159,343	45.6	865,138	46.3	98,140	29.2
2–4	32,652	9.3	307,158	16.4	34,656	10.3
4–10	1,253	0.4	72,930	3.9	48,815	14.5
Over 10	52	0.0	7,493	0.4	29,839	8.9
Total	349,276	100.0	1,870,561	100.0	335,814	100.0
1979						
Under 1	61,190	28.7	394,225	19.0	109,674	24.2
1–2	96,989	45.5	934,339	45.1	163,818	36.1
2–4	48,592	22.8	599,833	29.0	68,189	15.0
4–10	6,050	2.8	130,983	6.3	45,734	10.1
Over 10	146	0.1	12,179	0.6	66,157	14.6
Total	212,967	100.0	2,071,559	100.0	453,572	100.0

Source: *Kokuzeichō tōkei nenpōsho*, 1974, p. 26; 1979, p. 25.

households is thus a movement of the largest of them into the capitalist sector. Almost all the data examined so far have confirmed the emergence of an agricultural bourgeoisie out of the peasantry itself, although it is still not much more above the petty capitalist in its scale of operations. If the amount of taxable income declared is any guide to the numbers of households in this category, it comprises only a minute proportion of the total agricultural households, and certainly no more than 0.5%. Table 3.14 shows that only a few thousand persons could possibly be included: far too few to require any addition to the estimates of the size of the bourgeoisie.

The overwhelming mass of peasants thus face a vicious circle of growing competition from imports due to both international pressure and the stagnation of small-scale Japanese agriculture which has led to a declining self-sufficiency in food. Products they have traditionally specialised in can be imported much more cheaply, while the ones which are still protected are being taken over by an emerging agribusiness sector in Japan. Table 3.15 shows how low are the self-

Table 3.15. *Ratios of self-sufficiency for selected foodstuffs, 1960–77*

	1960	1970	1974	1977
Aggregate ratio of all foods	*93*	*81*	77	*78*
Cereals	83	48	40	40
Rice	102	106	102	114
Wheat	39	9	4	4
Pulses	44	13	11	8
Vegetables	100	99	98	98
Fruits/nuts	100	84	83	84
Meat	93	89	85	77
Milk/milk products	89	89	83	87
Fish	110	108	103	106
Sugar	13	15	15	20
Fats/oils	42	22	24	26

Source: Shūkan Tōyō Keizai, *Keizai tōkei nenkan*, 1979, p. 260.

sufficiency ratios in many branches of production and therefore where peasants face the greatest competition from imports.

Although the impoverishment of both the petty bourgeoisie and the peasantry in Japan has stemmed from the technical backwardness of their means of production and their inability to exploit wage labour, there is an important difference between the capitalist competitors that these two classes face. In comparison to the petty bourgeoisie's capitalist rivals, those of the peasantry are still much more outside the country than in it. Productive forces in Japanese agriculture as a whole, and not just in a few limited branches into which peasants have been herded, are underdeveloped. Peasants are therefore much more susceptible to manipulation by a reactionary nationalist movement than is the petty bourgeoisie, since its problems can, like those of American car workers, be made to appear foreign in origin. However, this is only one of the many influences which shape peasant ideology, organisation, and political activity in Japan, a subject which must now be examined in some detail.

Organisation, ideology, and class struggle

The Japanese peasantry presents the socialist movement in that country with a paradox which it has so far been quite unable to resolve. In spite of its rapid proletarianisation and lowest incomes of

Table 3.16. *Distribution of votes in the 1980 general election, by type of area*

	Metropolitan	Urban	Semi-rural	Rural
LDP	23.0	33.4	42.0	49.7
Conservative Independent	1.0	2.5	3.1	1.4
NLC	4.0	1.0	1.4	1.1
JSP	12.8	13.3	14.4	15.4
CGP	10.5	7.5	5.2	1.8
DSP	5.4	5.1	4.9	2.6
JCP	10.0	8.0	4.7	4.9
SDF[a]	0.6	1.4	0.2	0.2
Did not vote/other	32.4	27.7	23.1	22.8

[a]The Social Democratic Federation. For an explanation of the other abbreviations, see table 2.23.
Source: Asahi Shinbun, 25 June 1980, p. 6.

all classes, the peasantry has remained firmly in the alliance of forces which sustain bourgeois rule. However one chooses to interpret election results and peasant voting behaviour, the conclusion that peasants have been an even more solid basis of legitimacy for the ruling Liberal Democratic Party than the petty bourgeoisie is inescapable. The *Asahi* poll taken just before the 1980 general election revealed that their commitment to the ruling party was even greater than it had been four years previously, although all classes that year moved the same way. Equally significant is that peasants revealed the lowest inclination to say that they supported no party, that is, they seemed least disenchanted with parliamentary politics. Table 3.16 shows that when it comes to election time, people in rural areas turn out in mass to support the ruling party. Although many of these people are workers and petty bourgeois operators in the areas concerned, the influence of the peasantry extends well beyond their own ranks, particularly in rural areas.

This rural conservatism cannot be accounted for in terms of any variant of the 'false consciousness' hypothesis, which is a frequent *deus ex machina* summoned by Marxists to fill the gaps in their analysis. Although schools and the media might put out ideas which account for some of the specific forms assumed by bourgeois ideology, none of this can explain why people find the ideas acceptable or why different classes do so in different degrees. At the risk of sounding repetitive, if one is to understand why people embrace ideologies one must analyse the day-to-day activities they engage in. People cannot consistently hold views which contradict what they do each day, or at least what they might consider it possible for them to do. To account for rural conservatism in Japan therefore requires an analysis of everyday social activities in the countryside.

The most important social activity is of course production, but since agricultural households include members with widely different roles in the various production mechanisms, they form different combinations of frequently contradictory social forces. In such cases, production relations do not shape the same range of household activities as where household members share similar production relations. So whether the peasant members of mixed households think and act more like their wage labouring members, or vice versa, might depend more on how and where the family consumes its income than on how its individual members earn it, or on the forms of political organisation of the different classes involved. This is because whenever social forces stemming from mechanisms of production confront one another more or less equally within an institution (in this case the family), the balance of power may rest with forces produced by less fundamental mechanisms, such as the capitalist circulation process or forms of class organisation. There are reasons to believe that both of these have been important in inclining working-class members of agricultural households to act in and see the world more from the point of view of their peasant members than the other way round.

One of the distinctive characteristics of the capitalist mode of production is that the detailed functioning of subordinate mechanisms, such as the circulation process in which the necessities of life are consumed, is not as rigidly determined as is the case, for example, under feudalism. Inequalities in the latter or in slave society take very similar forms in the processes of production and consumption, whereas the contrast between the more manifest inequality of the factory and the apparent equality of the shopping mall is distinctive of capitalism. Production does not determine as large a range of consumption activities under capitalism as it does under feudalism or slavery because, excepting during the period in which the labourers sell their skills and capacities, they are entirely free from the control of the capitalist and can, within the limits of their wages, live where they like and consume what they like. Peasants in feudal Japan were not free to choose where they would live, nor did they have anything like the range of social activities open to the modern proletariat after working hours.

In cases where class forces are more or less in the balance within modern peasant families, so that mechanisms of consumption can carry the balance of influence, the working-class members are more likely to be swayed by the consumption activities of peasants than vice versa. The peasants are less free than workers to adapt in this way, since their immediate working conditions are shaped by the simple commodity mode of production in which production and consumption are more closely integrated. What are the adjustments that workers might be asked to make to peasant life, and to what extent is it possible to make them? To answer questions like these requires a brief discussion of some of the changes in the social circumstances of the peasantry that have taken place since the war.

Until the 1946–7 Land Reform, the *ie* system (loosely translated 'household' or 'family' system) functioned simultaneously as the visible form in which both production relations in the countryside were manifested and in which village folk were politically organised. Two quite different mechanisms, the one right at the heart of the infrastructure and the other shaping only the details of concrete life, functioned through the identical institution. What were in reality therefore quite different social activities appeared indistinguishable. In fact, the *ie*'s functions were not even confined to those of production and political organisation, since they included others which were at least as close to the heart of the infrastructure as is production, namely, species reproduction. However, since I have chosen to leave this controversial argument to the final chapter, I will not introduce the debate on whether the most fundamental function of the *ie* was production or species reproduction. All that needs to be accepted at this point is that one and the same visible institution mediated infrastructural forces of vastly different strengths and importances. The realities that they produced were therefore bound to get mixed up in people's day-to-day lives, since the realities were experienced in identical forms.

The household head, for example, was simultaneously the representative of the family in its dealings with other families (and the state) and the person who authorised the roles members played in social production as well as in species reproduction. Everything that people did therefore seemed to be determined by the position they occupied in the hierarchical structure of the *ie*. Its ideologies and practices were therefore superimposed on the whole range of social activities: political organisation, productive work, and childbearing and rearing. It seemed to individual family members that their roles in day-to-day activities were determined by their sex and their age, because the visible forms that the real basis of control over roles (namely class and gender) took in the *ie* were the age and sex of its individual members. Family relationships based on age and sex were therefore dominant, that is, they were seen and experienced as the source of all other relationships – in other words, as if they were determinant. It seemed that the different social roles played by elder and younger sons, by sons and daughters, and by husbands and wives stemmed from their biological ages and sexes rather than their social classes and genders. Determination by class and gender (stemming from the mechanisms of production and species reproduction) was obscured by the domination of age and sex, because the *ie* institution which simultaneously mediated so many different infrastructural forces was organised on the basis of age and sex. Class and gender relations in the village therefore took on the same ideological forms of *loyalty to superiors, benevolence to inferiors*, and *harmony between unequals* as characterised relations among members of the *ie*.

The institution of the *ie* was very similar to the Roman institution of the *familia*, since it embraced the household's entire property as well as its individual members, including the servants. However, in Japan fictive kinship ties between servants and the rest of the family were created, so that the specific tasks carried out by servants might become the tasks appropriate to certain family members. The overriding duty of each member was to preserve the continuity of the *ie* and to raise its status vis-à-vis other *ie*. The role of each member represented a functional division of labour in the achievement of that goal.

Loyalty to the *ie* took the form of loyalty and obedience to the household head, who controlled the family property and who represented the family in law and in its dealings with the authorities. The head's primary relationship was not with his wife, whose role was to bear a male heir and to be a good worker, but with the eldest son, who would one day take his place. Second sons were important in case the first should not survive, while daughters were a liability, since it was necessary to give them a dowry when they married.

In return for the loyalty and obedience shown to the household head by the other members of the family, he was to treat them with benevolence and strictly according to their position. Primary relationships were therefore vertical, between him and the rest, rather than horizontal, between him and his wife, between brothers, or least of all between sisters. These core relations were referred to as *oyabun–kobun* (parent–child) relations, and they were characterised not only by the mutual obligations of benevolence and obedience but also by harmony, all for the sake of preserving the *ie*.

The productive (as opposed to species reproductive) material basis of the *ie* system was that the family constituted the unit of production for its subsistence, and, as we shall see below, for the landlord's surplus. However, when this began to change after the land reform and younger children got permanent wage or salary jobs, it became unrealistic for the household head to claim complete control over the money individual members earned outside agriculture.

Nevertheless, the *ie* system showed remarkable resilience even in part-time farming households, partly because many of their members could get jobs only as day or temporary labourers, partly because the more the very existence of the family farm was threatened, the greater was the need for even absent younger children to send money to maintain it. The importance of doing so increased in times of recession, because the *ie* then served as a place to which unemployed members could return until economic conditions improved. Throughout modern Japanese history and until very recently, when this function was taken over mainly by the petty bourgeoisie, the countryside has served as a source of subsistence for the reserve army. Working-class members of agricultural households have therefore had a material interest in preserving the *ie* system, since they shared in the protection and security it provided. Although their independent source of subsistence weakened the ideology of loyalty and obedience to the household head, it did not eliminate it. Fukutake Tadashi, who is one of the most acute rural sociologists in Japan, explains why:

> Until the farm as a business enterprise becomes fully disentangled from the farm family as a consuming social unit, and until agriculture becomes a profession freely chosen, rather than a 'family occupation' inevitably inherited, the *ie* will not disappear. Until there is an assurance of a decent livelihood in some other occupation, and a guarantee of security in old age, the 'family property', however small it may be, represents the staff of life. Here too is a factor preserving the *ie*. Hence, despite the tendencies for the *ie* system to disappear in the post-war period, Japanese farm families have still not reached the point at which the final dissolution of the *ie* is in sight.[15]

Working-class members of agricultural households are therefore not immune from the influences on the *ie* which emanate from rural settlements.

Before the land reform, rural settlements were bound together by both technical and social relationships. The main social relationship was between the landlord and the individual farming households, which lived in concentrated settlements rather than scattered farmsteads and over two-thirds of which had become tenants. The latter were tied to the landowner as children were to their parents, the landlord showing benevolence, especially when harvests were poor, the tenants loyalty and obedience.

Technical factors behind the development of the village into a close-knit community were the need to cooperate in such labour-intensive tasks as planting rice and thatching roofs, and in constructing irrigation schemes. As the only units of self-sufficiency, village communities regulated almost every aspect of the social, political, and religious life of their member households.

However, the village as a self-sufficient and all-embracing unit of social life was greatly undermined by the abolition of the landlord system, the development of modern methods of irrigation, and above all by the growth of part-time farming. Non-agricultural households predominate now even in village communities, which no longer live purely by means of agriculture, but which include many wage labourers as well as growing numbers of small and unstable enterprises. According to Fukutake, 'The era when the members of a village, regardless of occupation, formed a single community and cooperated in all aspects of life, when the village itself controlled and regulated its inhabitants – that era is a thing of the past.'[16]

In spite of recent developments, however, the ideology of village solidarity and obedience to authority has not disappeared, but has been reproduced through the substitution of the local political boss for the landlord as the source of benevolent dispensation, in this case of state assistance to decaying villages. Roads, bridges, schools, rural industries to create jobs close to home, and agricultural subsidies and price-support schemes are all 'favours' which the state can grant to those rural communities that provide loyal support to the governing party. A hierarchy of mutual obligations of loyalty and 'favours' extends from the major factions of the governing party through prefectural politicians right down to village leaders, who can deliver the votes of their communities to the politician who has seemed to

provide the most benefits to the area. Local government functions as a
channel of capital investment, factory location, and other village
requirements, all of which are seen as favours demanding the loyalty
and obedience of rural communities to the authorities which
'provided' them.

Although the basis of rural conservatism in present-day Japan is
not as secure as it used to be, it does extend beyond full-time farming
households to include both mixed and even non-agricultural households in rural areas. Fukutake concludes,

> The process is perpetuated by its [the LDP's] ability, through its individual
> Diet members, to keep the local interests of the farmers primed with the
> benefits of petition politics, while in the field of government activity proper,
> they requite these financial contributions by promoting policies attuned to the
> interests of monopoly capital. As long as the farmers are kept happy with the
> lollipops of local benefits, they fail to perceive the richer fare which is served up
> to the capitalists. Nor do they become conscious of the fact that these benefits,
> provided under the neutral guise of services to the whole community, by no
> means in fact benefit every member of the community.[17]

The uneven benefits to different members of the village community
include not only the assistance to local capital to exploit wage earners,
but the different advantages farming households receive from
assistance to agriculture. The latter is conferred through, and the
inequalities are obscured by, the organisations which allegedly
represent all farmers, the Agricultural Cooperatives (Nōgyō Kyōdō
Kumiai, or Nōkyō). Although all farmers belong to Nōkyō, they by
no means benefit equally from the activities of Nōkyō's main national
organs. For example, most farmers derive almost no benefit at all
from the annual campaign by Nōkyō to raise the producer's price of
rice: of those who have any interest in that campaign, the great
majority do not produce sufficient rice for the price increase to add
meaningfully to family income. Nōkyō also has a business arm, a
bank, and an insurance company which compare with the largest
corporations in Japan. Together they handle the bulk of farmers'
purchases of fertilisers and feeds, their sales of agricultural products,
and their financial requirements. They have come to form a *keiretsu* in
their own right, with vast assets accumulating in the organisations and
in the approximately 300 companies they have created. The small
minority of members who control the organisations receive substantial annual allowances (about ¥7 million in 1974), and in addition
draw handsome salaries as executives on the boards of Nōkyō

companies.[18] Yet because all households are members, Nōkyō functions as an organisation which controls the peasantry and ties it to the bourgeoisie. It is a major part of the network of political organisations which reproduce bourgeois ideology among peasants and working people in rural areas. Because all the organisations in this network – the local and national political groups allied to or part of the Liberal Democratic Party, all the personal networks that function through it, Nōkyō with all its tentacles, and indeed the *ie* itself – take on the identical form of the traditional household, exploitation is made to look like *benevolence*, contradictory interests appear *harmonious*, and the submission of the exploited takes on the form of *obedience* and *loyalty*.

Unless one recognises that the *ie* institution is the form through which far more fundamental infrastructural forces (of production and species reproduction) function than mere electoral and pork-barrel machines, one cannot grasp its power to structure other practices, such as electioneering, in ways which conceal reality so effectively.

It is therefore almost as difficult for the peasantry to develop effective strategies for class struggle as it is for the petty bourgeoisie. Both classes are locked into bourgeois organisations and confront capital in the realm of consumption rather than at the point of production, because both work under simple commodity relations. However, while growing proportions of the petty bourgeoisie have had past experiences of directly confronting capital at the point of production (when they were wage labourers), peasants have no comparable experience. They can only become part of working-class organisation through their family members who are engaged in wage labour or through sharing with workers (and members of other classes) some of capital's onslaughts in the realm of consumption.

Although peasants do have a considerable history of class struggles, these were largely against landlords in the prewar and immediate postwar periods. After the land reform, farmers' unions which had been built up in tenant struggles functioned more as electoral machines for the Japan Socialist Party than as organisations of class struggle against capital. They have done little more than try to outbid LDP politicians in promising higher agricultural prices and subsidies as well as the other 'benefits' dished out by conservative politicians.

Since 1958, when the various farmers' unions amalgamated to form Zen Nihon Nōmin Kumiai, or Zen Nichinō (the National Japan Farmers' Union), experience has demonstrated that this type of organisation and struggle has failed to detach peasants from the ruling-class alliance of forces. Nōkyō campaigns for higher rice prices and LDP petition politics are far more effective at this sort of game than Zen Nichinō, and the latter's membership fell from 250,000 in 1958 to a mere 45,000 in 1972.[19] Though attempts were made to bring in part-time farmers, the issues the union concentrated on were too narrow, and few part-time farmers joined it. For the same reason, it failed to attract working-class members of rural communities.

Organisations which have centred on workers in rural areas, on the other hand, have had little success in attracting peasants. Nōson Rōkumi Zenkoku Rengōkai, or Nōson Rōren (the National Association of Agricultural Workers' Unions) has managed on only a few occasions to form links between peasants and workers, for example, the joint struggles in Nagano prefecture against Nōkyō and the local government in order to raise wages and rice prices. These successes have been rare, because union members are typically casual employees on peasant farms, and their organisation directly confronts the peasantry. The weakness of Nōson Rōren also stems from the small membership of its individual unions, typically fewer than twenty. The organisation's total membership therefore fell from its peak of 20,000 in 1967 (eighteen months after its foundation) to only about 10,000 in 1971.[20]

The most successful struggles in rural areas in terms of organising both workers and peasants have been over specific issues, such as opposition to the nuclear ship *Mutsu*, the use of agricultural land for military purposes, anti-pollution struggles, and above all the protracted struggle since 1966 against the construction and opening of Narita Airport on land from which peasants had to be forcibly evicted.[21] It is pertinent to analysing the possibilities of socialist change in Japan briefly to analyse why these struggles have been so much more successful than the others.

The most important reason for the support they received was that they centred not on those specific interests of peasants and workers which are generated by their particular production relations (rice prices and wages), which are divisive, but on their common interests, which are manifested in the realm of consumption, namely, protection of their homes and living environments. It is precisely because people are equal in the world of consumption that this is always such a good place to build mass movements. Moreover, since the ultimate threat to rural communities is removal from their homes, the struggle against the construction of Narita Airport was the most determined and far-reaching Japan has seen in many years.

Second, these struggles have been on issues that make capital's domination of both workers and peasants, as well as its control of the state, much more visible than issues that stem directly out of day-to-day work experiences. It is particularly difficult for peasants, who depend heavily on state assistance and protection against foreign agriculture, to see capital and the state as totally hostile forces. Only experience can convince peasants otherwise, and the sort of experience that does so is when capital has to use the repressive apparatuses of the state to remove peasants from their homes or to protect the interests that threaten life in the community, such as nuclear power.

Finally, the intensity of these struggles has resulted very much from the fact that the participants were largely free from involvement in established organisations, either of peasants or of bureaucratic labour, which function to maintain bourgeois rule in Japan. Organisations that develop in boom periods tend to become economistic and hierarchical, since their members' basic material demands can generally be met without much grass-roots involvement or disruption to established ways of doing things. They are therefore quite ill equipped to handle the unexpected forms in which a crisis manifests itself, and they soon tend to give way to new organisations that grow directly out of the masses' experiences of how and where the crisis affects them. What agricultural households have increasingly had to face is not simply proletarianisation, but the destruction of their land and their ancestral homes. To protect these – from developers, nuclear power, and pollution – they have had to organise themselves in new ways, in the first place to fight the form that the attack on them took, and then to wage more protracted struggles with other oppressed classes. Such organisations and links among the oppressed masses have already begun, and much has been learnt from the fifteen-year struggle over Narita.

4
The middle class

If the foundation on which the legitimacy of bourgeois rule in Japan rests is the petty bourgeoisie and the peasantry, the pillar that supports it is undoubtedly the middle class. The middle class has not done so consciously, but more through its duplicities and ambiguities. As Henry Lefebvre has insightfully observed of middle classes in capitalist societies,

> The power structure undoubtedly rests on the middle class, i.e. it rests on their ambiguities. They are attributed with both an economic reality (in production as well as in consumption) and an illusion of political power. The middle classes – technicians, intellectuals, etc. – shore up the essential relations [of production] by believing that they are free of them. The individuals as such lead or try to lead an elitist life. Their escape route is 'culture,' although their cultural knowledge serves capitalism . . . The middle classes thus live on two levels, in a permanent duality or duplicity. At one level the individuals judge, criticise, sometimes argue and may even refuse. At another level they serve (and receive) the opposite: an illusory delegation of power, which gives them the impression that they are doing something different from what they actually are doing. They live a double life . . . part of 'the system' but supplied with alibis, engaged in thankless duties with an enjoyment that is half real and half tissued with illusions.[1]

Theory of the middle class

The duplicities of the middle class originate in what some writers have called the contradictory positions its members occupy in capitalist production.[2] Once it is recognised that classes are infrastructural forces which act on people, the notion of contradictory or ambiguous positions should present little difficulty. We have already seen how one and the same person can perform quite diverse social roles and therefore mediate quite different social forces, for example, as a worker and as a consumer. The contradictions which confront people in the middle class are broadly of the same kind, excepting that the ambiguities stem almost entirely from the types of positions occupied in the process of production. There are certain jobs which require their occupants to play the role of both the capitalist and the worker, so that the people who fill these jobs stand right in the middle of the two and are drawn towards each of them. They therefore have ambiguous class interests: in capitalism insofar as they perform functions of capital and receive special privileges, and in socialism insofar as they are exploited and contribute to capital accumulation. They are part of capital's hierarchies of control over means of production and labour power, but they are also subject to them. Since they do not predominantly perform the function of either the worker or the capitalist, they do not have overriding class interests, and are easily influenced by relationships outside the realm of production.

If we were to be consistent and include as classes only distinctive social forces, there would be no such thing as a middle class, since there is no such distinctive infrastructural force. However, because there is a distinctive combination of contradictory infrastructural forces, we need the concept of the middle class in order to account for the many duplicities in the daily lives of the people Lefebvre so graphically describes. Once the infrastructural contradictions which lie behind their 'double lives' are identified and reconstructed, it becomes easy to see why the agents who mediate contradictory class forces can never act as a 'class for itself,' that is, as a self-conscious group of persons bound together by common interests and in- dependent of both the bourgeoisie and the proletariat. In this sense, too, the middle class is not really a separate class, because the production relations concerned do not bring class agents together in large numbers, but scatter them here and there among groups belonging to other classes. The agents of the contradictory forces that constitute the middle class are thus united only by their common feelings that they belong nowhere.

To identify those contradictory positions in Japan which are characteristic of the middle class requires examining both of the forms in which the bourgeoisie was found to be manifested: the ownership of capital and the performance of capital's functions. As far as ownership is concerned, thoroughly contradictory interests are produced when wage and salary earners who are themselves exploited receive moderate amounts of unearned income from owning surplus-value-earning assets. Table 1.5 showed that there were about two million such people in 1979. They have sufficient stake in capitalism from the earnings of their assets to be unreliable, to say the least, allies of a socialist movement. But they do not have such a stake in the system that the ruling class can always presume even on their neutrality in class struggles.

Analysis of hierarchies of control is more complex, mainly because the form which control of means of production takes when productive forces are advanced obscures a very important distinction. The distinction is between controlling the means of production which other workers operate and controlling the means of production which one operates oneself. For example, carpenters or electricians control only the tools which they themselves use, whereas technicians who set in motion an automated production line control the machinery used by other workers. The former therefore have some control over the manner and intensity of their own labour process alone, whereas the latter in fact determine the manner in which and intensity at which other people work. Carpenters therefore do not perform functions of capital, while those who operate automated production lines do. The more advanced the productive forces are, the more the distinction between these two types of worker disappears, and anyone who can control his or her own labour process at the same time partly controls that of other workers.

The main reason why this happens with the development of productive forces is that the technologies incorporated in modern machinery, which require labourers to work at breakneck speed, cannot be separated from the technical knowledge of those who design, maintain, and operate the machinery. Advanced productive forces are not embodied in machinery alone, but also in those individuals without whose advanced technical skills the machinery could neither exist nor be set in motion. Once persons (living labour) rather than simply tools (dead labour) become an inseparable part of productive forces, capital has no alternative but to surrender to these persons extensive control over their own labour processes. But since what these people do is design and operate means of production which rob other workers of all vestiges of control over their labour processes, they in fact perform capital's function of regulating the overall production process. The form that control over means of production takes is therefore the possession of above-average technical skills, which allow one first to control one's own work situation and then that of other workers. It is only because certain production techniques require particular skills to develop and operate that persons with these skills have to be conceded control over their means of production and escape from the gruel of the production line. The higher than average the required skill, or the more the skill is itself part of the productive forces, the greater the power capital must surrender to its possessor.

If the technocrats' ability to load certain productive tasks onto workers is the source of their affinity with capital, then the requirements to engage in a different type of productive labour, from which capital also extracts surplus value, is the basis of their commonality with workers. That many of them receive very high salaries does not necessarily mean they are paid out of surplus value. It could be that, because of their above-average skills, in a normal working day they produce so many hours of 'average-skilled labour' that their employers can afford the extra wages and still extract a surplus from them. Value, or socially necessary labour, is reckoned in terms of time worked by labourers of average skill. So if, for example, some workers spend twice as long as others in training themselves to twice the others' level of skill, they produce twice the value in the same amount of time actually worked. Capital's ability to pay them more, as well as to exploit them more, is therefore much greater, as the accompanying illustration shows (A has twice B's skill, but is paid only one and a half times as much). Although, as we shall see, the high levels of consumption of technocrats divide them from the working class, as does their control over means of production, they share with workers a common exploitation by capital. They are Lefebvre's persons 'engaged in thankless tasks with an enjoyment that is half real and half tissued with illusions.'

	Time actually worked	Value created	Equivalent of wage	Surplus
A	40	80	30	50
B	40	40	20	20

Apart from technocrats, who perform functions of capital in the production process, there are two other types of middle-class position which perform functions of capital in a similar way, though at different 'moments' in the reproduction of the capitalist relationship. The first includes teachers and university lecturers, whose control over their own means of production also allows them to control other people, but at a stage in the turnover of the total social capital before these people enter the production process. Since teachers and lecturers provide labour power with skills for use in capitalist production, they simultaneously become the vehicles of reproducing bourgeois ideology among new generations. They help perform capital's function of winning consent for bourgeois social relations, a point which is developed more fully in chapter 7.

The second type of position comprises what we might call clerical technocrats, such as lawyers, economists, and accountants. They play a role in the circulation process comparable to what the other group plays in the production process and to what teachers play in training labour power. Capital requires an advanced technical knowledge of law, mathematics, economics, accounting, computer technology, etc. in order to minimise circulation costs, and those who possess these skills can significantly control not only their own labour processes but also those of less-skilled clerical workers. Although this control gives them an interest in capitalism, neither they nor teachers are any less exploited than productive technocrats, since they all perform unpaid labour. I will refer to both the productive and the clerical groups simply as technocrats, because both possess the advanced technical knowledge necessary for the production and realisation of surplus value. However, not all technocrats (or teachers) are equally exploited, since in spite of their similar levels of skill they apply these skills to very different ends – some performing more exclusively functions of workers and others more exclusively functions of capital – and they receive, in return, vastly different salaries. These will be discussed in more detail below when an attempt is made to analyse the class membership of a related group, namely doctors and nurses.

However, contradictory interests which stem from the direct control of labour power are less complex and typically belong to chargehands or supervisors, who occupy the lowest formal position in the Japanese managerial hierarchy. To become a supervisor (*shunin*) involves a substantial promotion from the shop floor, and if the position is received before the age of 35, it singles one out for possible promotion into the bourgeoisie itself. Since it also confers authority over workmates, it is sufficient to draw one towards the capitalist camp. But this is an ambiguous pressure, because the majority of chargehands not only do the same work as those they supervise but remain in this position for the rest of their lives.

Although it should now be possible to identify the Japanese middle class on the basis of the contradictory forces generated by control of means of production and labour power on the one hand, and the performance of unpaid labour on the other, there are certain features of the Japanese employment system which make this almost impossible to do precisely. The system is just riddled with contradictions, and it is hard to find jobs which unambiguously and exclusively mediate only one infrastructural class force.

Identification of the Japanese middle class

The easiest middle-class positions to identify are those demanding above-average technical and professional skills, which allow some control over means of production. In 1979, out of a total of 4.5 million persons in jobs requiring these skills, 3.8 million (2.1 million men and 1.7 million women) were employees and, to the extent that they were both exploited by capital and used to exploit other workers, they could be considered middle class. The remaining 607,000 self-employed professional and technical persons were in either the bourgeoisie or the petty bourgeoisie.[3] Table 4.1 provides a breakdown by industry and sex of all technical and professional persons, since this information was not available for employees alone. If the proportions of employees in the different industries and sexes coincide with the proportions who are self-employed, it is clear that technical and professional members of the Japanese middle class are overwhelmingly teachers, nurses, technocrats in the manufacturing industry, and medical practitioners. About 65% of women are nurses or teachers, while about 30% of men are teachers and another 13% are medical practitioners and related persons.

The central function of technical and professional people in the middle class is therefore the reproduction of labour power, which is an important productive activity. Among the increasing costs of reproducing labour power in modern Japan have been the costs of training it and maintaining it in good health. What were well-above-average levels of skill fifty years ago – nine years of schooling – are now simply the average minimum required, and what were regarded as bourgeois standards of health have become socially necessary even for the working class. These developments have taken place partly because of capital's need for a higher quality of labour power, partly in response to working-class struggles.

There is therefore great potential for capital to exploit those engaged in the reproduction of labour power, but this potential has

Table 4.1. *Technical and professional persons, by industry and sex, 1974–9 (1,000 persons)*

	Males				Females			
	1974		1979		1974		1979	
	No.	%	No.	%	No.	%	No.	%
Primary	12	0.5	12	0.5	1	0.1	2	0.1
Mining	2	0.1	2	0.1	0	0.0	0	0.0
Construction	125	5.5	106	4.1	2	0.1	2	0.1
Manufacturing	335	14.8	311	12.2	33	2.3	39	2.0
Wholesale/retail	57	2.5	72	2.8	35	2.5	54	2.7
Finance/insurance/real estate	19	0.8	21	0.8	2	0.1	3	0.2
Transport/communications	37	1.6	39	1.5	2	0.1	1	0.1
Electricity/gas/water	24	1.1	26	1.0	0	0.0	0	0.0
Services	1,543	68.2	1,864	72.9	1,316	93.3	1,860	93.5
Personal	25	1.1	29	1.1	8	0.6	7	0.4
Business	97	4.3	136	5.3	9	0.6	15	0.8
Repair	3	0.1	3	0.1	0	0.0	0	0.0
Medical	245	10.8	322	12.6	508	36.0	707	35.5
Education	684	30.2	745	29.1	461	32.7	581	29.2
Other	490	21.7	628	24.6	329	23.3	549	27.6
Government	108	4.8	105	4.1	19	1.3	28	1.4
Total	2,262	100.0	2,558	100.0	1,410	100.0	1,989	100.0

Source: *Shūgyō kōzō kihon chōsa hōkoku*, 1974, pp. 46, 48, 50; 1979, pp. 68, 72.

Table 4.2. *Medical practitioners, by type and by employment status, 1977*

	Physicians		Dentists		Pharmacists		Total	
	No.	%	No.	%	No.	%	No.	%
Medical								
Employers	63,065	45.6	31,330	68.5	14,518	14.4	108,913	38.2
Hospitals	3,225	2.3	2	0.0	—	—	3,227	1.1
Clinics	59,840	43.3	31,328	68.5	—	—	91,168	40.0
Pharmacies	—	—	—	—	14,518	14.4	14,518	5.1
Employees	68,563	49.6	12,576	27.5	39,467	39.1	120,606	42.3
Hospitals	60,189	43.5	3,282	7.2 }	21,584	21.4	102,723	36.1
Clinics	8,374	6.1	9,294	20.3 }				
Pharmacies	—	—	—	—	17,883	17.7	17,883	6.3
Other[a]	*6,688*	*4.8*	*1,809*	*4.0*	*46,912*	*46.5*	*55,409*	*19.4*
Total	138,316	100.0	45,715	100.0	100,897	100.0	284,928	100.0

[a]Working in universities, corporations, insurance companies, etc. and unemployed.
Source: Kōsei tōkei kyōkai [Health and Welfare Statistics Association], *Kokumin eisei no dōkō: kōsei no shihyō* [The Direction of the People's Health: Indices of Welfare], Tokushū [Special issue], 26, 9 (1979) (Tokyo: Kōsei tōkei kyōkai, 1979), 189, 191.

been unevenly achieved. Capital's greatest success has been among teachers and nurses, while medical practitioners have been able either to become capitalists themselves or to avoid the high rates of exploitation of teachers and nurses. Table 4.2 reveals that almost half of the doctors and over two-thirds of the dentists in Japan are actually employers in either hospitals or clinics. They can thus both avoid being exploited and also receive, in addition to the full value their labour power creates, surpluses from their employees. On the other hand, over 80% of pharmacists are employees of one type or another, so that in all an average of about 62% of the three most highly skilled and highly paid people in the health service are in the middle class. Apart from acupuncturists, almost all of the other 687,471 technical and professional health personnel are in the same category (see table 4.3). In general, employers are mainly males while employees are mainly females, and the most highly paid employees are males (in 1977 only 9.4% of physicians, for example, were females) while the lowest paid (nurses, for example) are females.

The overall picture in the teaching profession is, apart from a few exceptions relating mainly to the lower proportions of employers in education than in medicine, very similar. Like nurses, teachers are not generally able to establish private practices or hire employees: in

Table 4.3. *Numbers of medical-related personnel, 1978*

Health nurses	17,106
Midwives	26,493
Nurses	431,911
Dental technicians	18,075
Dental welfare personnel	16,964
Massagists and physiotherapists	89,520
Acupuncturists	87,402
Total	687,471

Source: As table 4.2, p. 189.

Table 4.4. *Numbers of teachers and pupils taught, by type of institution, 1980*

	No. of institutions	% private	No. of teachers	No. of pupils
Kindergartens	14,893	59.0	100,960	2,407,113
Elementary schools	24,945	0.7	467,931	11,826,574
Middle schools	10,779	5.1	251,274	5,094,402
High schools	5,208	23.4	243,627	4,621,936
Junior colleges	517	83.6	16,372	371,125
Universities	446	71.5	102,985	1,835,304
Other	6,225	83.6	83,907	1,295,458
Total	63,013		1,267,056	27,451,912

Source: Monbushō [Ministry of Education], *Wagakuni no kyōiku suijun* [The Level of Our Country's Education], 1980 (Tokyo, Ōkurashō insatsukyoku, 1981), fuzoku shiryō [appended materials], pp. 36–7, 51–69, 74–5, 96–9.

1979, for example, about 7,000 of the total of 1.8 million people gainfully occupied in education were self-employed, of whom only about 5,000 had employees.[4] Table 4.4 shows the total numbers of teachers and university lecturers in Japan in 1980, the types of institutions they worked in, and the numbers of pupils and students they taught.

Clearly, education has become an important business in Japan, since apart from elementary and middle schools, which provide compulsory education, most institutions are private: 878 kindergartens, 1,240 high schools, 432 junior colleges, and 319 universities in

Table 4.5. *Monthly earnings of teachers, by rank, August 1981*
(¥ *1,000*)

	Average age	Monthly earnings	Index (typist = 100)
University president	65.8	734.6	504
Professor	54.5	478.7	329
Assistant professor	43.1	360.3	247
Lecturer	38.4	300.7	206
Assistant lecturer	33.5	236.5	162
High school principal	59.1	490.2	336
Teacher	40.2	295.8	203
General machine operator	36.8	216.5	149
Japanese typist	29.4	145.7	100

Source: Jinjiin kyūyokyoku [Salaries Bureau of the National Personnel Authority],
Minkan kyūyo no jittai [The Realities of Private Salaries], 1981 (Tokyo: Ōkurashō
insatsukyoku, 1981), pp. 26, 29.

1980.[5] However, teachers are exploited in both the private and the
public sector, since in both they provide unpaid labour, although the
degree of exploitation varies considerably. A few might even be
placed in the bourgeoisie, while a large proportion, mainly women,
are close to the working class. Table 4.5 shows that the average
monthly earnings of teachers vary enormously with the rank they
occupy, university presidents and high school principals receiving
large payments and extra allowances for their unproductive functions
of wielding overall control.

The unequal rates of exploitation among teachers are even greater
when seen in the light of Japan's system of payment by age or length
of service. This system is one of the main sources of contradictory
interests among wage and salary earners, since the large increases in
earnings received in later life bear little relation to increases in levels
of skill or performance. Although these contradictions are discussed
more fully when we examine middle-class ideology, table 4.6 shows
their origins in the pay differentials by age of the different types of
teachers. It also shows that up to about 1974 the rate of exploitation
was higher in the private than in the public sector, particularly in the
case of kindergarten teachers, but that after 1977 the situation
changed for all educationists excepting kindergarten teachers.

It can now be seen why a very large proportion of teachers, in spite

Table 4.6. *Monthly salaries by age and type of teacher (¥ 1,000), 1974*

		Age				
	Status	25–9	35–9[a]	45–9	55–9[a]	Over 65
Kindergarten	Public	79.6	113.5 (166.0)	139.8	150.8	68.2
	Private	61.6	72.8 (120.7)	88.3	94.3	97.2
Elementary	Public	89.4	135.1 (183.1)	170.8	192.8	190.3
Middle School	Public	89.7	134.6 (183.9)	171.5	193.3	190.5
High school	Public	89.9	133.3 (178.8)	174.8	200.0	196.4
	Private	86.2	125.3 (188.3)	157.6	155.4	110.2
University	National	88.2	130.8	183.4	237.0 (306.7)	283.1
	Private	93.9	136.8	184.3	211.9 (321.7)	178.0

[a]The amounts in brackets are the 1977 earnings of university graduates in the age groups 35–9 (for school teachers) and 54–9 (for university staff). These figures were provided by the 1981 issue of the source listed below, and add the interesting point that salaries in private institutions in the few years 1974–7 came to surpass those in public institutions (except at the kindergarten level). This applies both to teachers who were and who were not university graduates.
Source: *Wagakuni no kyōiku suijun*, 1975, pp. 270–1; 1981, fuzoku shiryō, p. 94.

of their role in the process of reproducing labour power, are so heavily exploited that they are almost as close to the working class as are nurses. These are women teachers, who for various reasons are the victims of enormous pressures to 'retire' before they move into the higher salary ranges. Even in kindergartens and junior colleges (attended mainly by women students) few women teachers achieve senior positions. Table 4.7 shows that the proportions of women teachers are lowest in the upper age groups and in the highest-ranking institutions, and vice versa. Although the data refer to the situation in 1974, developments thereafter only reinforced the pattern they present: by 1980, for example, the proportion of women teachers in elementary schools had risen to 56.6%.[6]

The position of women in the teaching profession on the boundary between the middle class and the working class is paralleled by their similar position in the medical profession. In 1978 there were (according to table 4.3) altogether 475,510 different kinds of nurses, almost all women, and their earnings compared poorly even with those of teachers. Table 4.8 outlines the main pay scales of nurses in 1981, which can be compared with those of teachers by examining table 4.5.

Although it is clear that both teachers and nurses are heavily (but not evenly) exploited and that teachers perform ideological functions

Table 4.7. *Distribution of teachers, by age, sex, and type of institution, 1974*

	Total		29 and under		30–50 years		Over 50 years	
	No.	% women	No.	% women	No.	% women	No.	% women
Kindergarten	80,440	93.8	54,099	99.5	18,802	91.4	7,539	59.1
Elementary	393,517	53.8	45,960	72.7	234,665	50.0	62,892	39.4
Middle school	211,896	28.2	42,827	49.6	151,048	24.1	28,021	17.5
High school	216,774	16.7	42,489	27.9	135,095	13.8	39,180	14.3
Junior college	15,318	33.9	2,055	67.8	6,847	36.2	6,416	20.5
University	79,776	8.2	10,145	22.9	49,496	6.7	21,135	4.7

Source: Wagakuni no kyōiku suijun, 1975, p. 266.

Table 4.8. *Monthly earnings of nurses, by rank, August 1981 (¥ 1,000)*

	Average age	Monthly earnings	Index (typist = 100)
Matron[a]	53.9	336.7	231
Staff nurse[b]	47.3	281.6	193
Clinical nurse	35.2	207.2	142
Assistant clinical nurse	29.8	180.4	124
Japanese typist	29.4	145.7	100

[a]With 5 or more staff nurses under her authority.
[b]With 5 or more clinical nurses under her authority.
Source: Minkan kyūyo no jittai, 1981, p. 25.

for capital, nurses without rank seem to have few material interests in capitalism and might more properly be placed in the working class. However, a number of factors tend them towards the ambivalence characteristic of the middle class, the bottom layer of which they occupy with women teachers. The first is that the above-average skills required in their work allow them to earn more and to be more in control of what they do than less-skilled women workers. The second is that since their job is to look after ill people, it is psychologically very difficult for them to engage in revolutionary politics. Their job makes them uniquely vulnerable to ideological manipulation by the bourgeoisie, because they cannot avoid feeling that even strike action involves a gross neglect of their duty.

This latter, of course, is far less important in explaining the ambivalence of salaried doctors, since they have fairly strong interests in capitalism. These stem from their ability to command salaries that are very close to what self-employed doctors can earn; that is, they can receive close to the full value that their labour power creates and can almost avoid being exploited. The reason why this is possible for doctors but not for teachers or nurses is that the former can, but the latter cannot, set up private practices if their employers do not pay them fully for what they do. The means of production required to set up a private medical practice are comparatively easy to obtain, as evidenced by the fact that nearly half Japan's physicians have managed to do so, whereas no one without considerable independent means could possibly establish his or her own school. Nurses are tied to wage labour through their dependence on doctors,

Table 4.9. *Monthly earnings of medical practitioners, by rank, August 1981 (¥1,000)*

	Average age	Monthly earnings	Index (typist = 100)
Head of hospital[a]	57.8	1,277.0	876
Chief physician[b]	44.6	755.4	518
Physician	37.1	606.3	416
Dentist	34.8	470.0	323
Head of pharmacy[c]	46.6	341.8	235
Pharmacist	31.6	200.0	137
Radiotherapist	34.0	238.5	164
Radiographer	38.3	262.2	180
Clinical examiner	31.2	202.5	139
Dietician	29.5	166.8	114
Japanese typist	29.4	145.7	100

[a]With 5 or more physicians under his or her authority.
[b]With 1 or more physicians under his or her authority.
[c]With 2 or more pharmacists under his or her authority.
Source: As table 4.8.

and are therefore in a situation similar to (though worse than) teachers. The fact that medical training involves an extended period of study has little to do with the pay differentials between teachers and doctors, since university teachers must study as long but receive far less than doctors. Table 4.9, which can be compared with tables 4.5 and 4.8, shows the monthly earnings of selected medical practitioners in 1981.

A chief physician received 2.7 times the earnings of a staff nurse almost three years older than he and 1.6 times more than a university professor ten years his senior. The interests in capitalism of salaried medical practitioners are beyond question, and many of them move into the bourgeoisie when they start investing their salaries, either in a medical practice or in income-earning assets.

The final category of technical and professional person in the middle class comprises what we have called technocrats, but they are in practice difficult to identify as a distinct group. This is because most of the highly qualified university graduates who perform technocratic functions in both production and circulation become supervisors by the age of 30, and many proceed to higher ranks after that. My survey research in Japan in 1976/7, which focused largely on the university-educated technocrats in the factories and head offices of Japan's larger corporations, revealed that it was almost impossible to separate technocratic control over means of production from the managerial hierarchy. Eighty-six out of 459 respondents referred to themselves as technical or professional employees, and when they were asked to describe in their own words what their jobs involved, very few did not mention some sort of supervision over other employees. Of those who did not, almost all were either under 30 or were only high school graduates and had not yet received a major promotion. They were also more involved in learning the ropes than in controlling their own labour processes, let alone anyone else's.

An analysis of the interests and composition of technocrats is therefore inseparable from an analysis of supervisors (*shunin*). Technocrats above this rank belong to the bourgeoisie, while those below it generally wield too little control to receive interests in capitalism from that quarter, although the lure of promotion partly compensates for this.

However, rather than focus purely on the rank of *shunin*, a clearer picture of contradictory interests stemming from control over labour power emerges if we first examine the complex system of supervision that exists in most Japanese corporations. Large firms generally recruit workers in three main groups: university graduates, high school graduates, and those with only compulsory education. Each group is on its own pay scale, but the level and gradient of each scale rises with the level of the group's education. Movement up a scale occurs automatically with length of service, but each scale has what might be called a tangent for persons who receive higher ranks than other workers of the same age. Since the possibility of promotion to managerial rank is most unlikely for middle school graduates, who are recruited as blue collar workers, their 'tangential scale' is almost parallel to their normal scale. High school graduates, who are recruited for clerical work, stand a slightly better chance of receiving substantial promotions, but university graduates are recruited both as technocrats and as prospective managers, and their 'tangential scale' for rank is the steepest.

The illustration of the managerial and supervisory hierarchies by means of tangential lines which depart from the basic (length of service) pay scales is instructive, because it draws attention to the almost infinite number and variety of largely petty distinctions of rank among all three groups of employees. Most of the lower ranks, such as first-, second-, or third-grade clerical worker or machinist, might seem to be quite meaningless, but they play crucial roles in the system of supervision and in generating contradictory interests. Although it would be an exaggeration to say that no two members of any work group ever have the same rank, it is not far from the truth. Even when *shunin* or their deputies are not present to supervise, there is always 'someone in charge,' and this only ceases to be the case when only one worker is left. The reason why the system works so efficiently is that everyone sooner or later has some rank, some authority to tell another person what to do, on however trivial a matter.

Because ranks on each of the three main pay scales are conferred mainly for length of service, infrastructural class forces in Japan take the visible form of generational distinctions among people. And because women are forced into retirement before they reach the top age groups, generational differences take the form of relations between the sexes. Bosses are not therefore seen as bosses, neither is it noticed that they own and control capital. All that is apparent is that the highest-paid employees, who are also the ones in authority, are older men, and the capitalist enterprise is experienced as a happy family of the traditional type at work. The significance of this for the reproduction of bourgeois ideology among the agents of the middle class will be discussed towards the end of the chapter.

What concerns us here is to identify those sufficiently contradictory positions in the hierarchy of supervision which place their occupants in the middle class, that is, positions which generate equally strong interests in capitalism and socialism. From this point of view, ranks below that of *shunin* are purely mechanisms by which workers are made to control one another. They certainly do not confer sufficient authority to produce a managerial perspective or an interest in capitalism comparable with workers' interests in socialism, since they are illusory compensations for the absence of control rather than actual delegations of it.

It is because the rank of *shunin* (or its equivalents) involves a substantial promotion which sets those workers who receive it apart from their workmates and promises further substantial promotions that this position characterises the ambiguities of middle-class membership. Supervisors do not work in groups of persons with essentially the same production relations as themselves, but are dispersed into groups whose members are overwhelmingly and unambiguously working class.

Table 4.10. *Pay differentials of members of managerial hierarchies,
August 1981 (¥ 1,000)*

	Average age	Monthly earnings	Index (typist = 100)
Circulation process			
General manager[a]	48.8	503.8	346
Department manager	49.1	461.5	317
Section manager	43.9	370.3	254
Division manager	39.3	306.0	210
Supervisor	36.3	263.0	181
Clerk in charge	28.0	178.9	123
Japanese typist	29.4	145.7	100
Production process			
General manager[a]	49.8	423.6	291
Department manager	49.0	437.0	300
Section manager	43.9	352.6	242
Division manager	40.0	308.0	211
Supervisor	36.8	275.8	189
Skilled worker in charge	31.3	221.9	152

[a]Excludes persons who are also directors.
Source: As table 4.8, p. 24.

The remuneration of *shunin* is also considerably higher than that received by ordinary employees, in both the production and the circulation process, and the extra payment they receive for performing capital's function of supervision considerably narrows the difference between the new value they create (if in the production process, or the labour they put in if not) and the value they receive in the form of salaries and bonuses. They produce surplus value with one hand, as it were, and get it back with the other. Table 4.10 shows the extent to which this is so.

Of all the positions in the complex system of ranking and supervision, the *shunin* (supervisor) is the one at which the contradictory forces of the capitalist infrastructure most evenly converge. This is the position where interests in capitalism and interests in socialism seem more or less to balance one another and to produce the duplicity characteristic of the middle class. It is not therefore arbitrary to draw the line at the rank of *shunin* to separate the middle class from the working class, though to estimate their numbers is more difficult. The proportion of supervisors in the different types and sizes

Table 4.11. *Numbers of military and police personnel, 1980*

Military personnel	*241,000*
Ground forces	155,000
Air forces	44,000
Maritime forces	42,000
Police personnel	*248,400*
National officers	7,600
Local officers	240,800
Women police officers	*17,800*
Local officers	3,600
Traffic officers	2,600
Guides	800
General staff	10,800

Sources: Keisatsuchō [Police Agency], *Keisatsu hakusho* [White Paper on the Police], 1981 (Tokyo: Ōkurashō insatsukyoku, 1981), p. 257; Bōeichō [Defence Agency], *Bōei hakusho* [White Paper on Defence], 1981 (Tokyo: Ōkurashō insatsukyoku, 1981), p. 243; 1976, p. 93. There were even in 1981 a full 25,000 positions in the army which had not been filled.

of firms varies enormously. However, if we assumed that overall there were about as many *shunin* as there are *kakarichō* (division managers), we would not be very far wrong.[7] In small firms there are fewer than this number while in large firms there are more.

Before we attempt to estimate the total number of middle-class positions in Japan, one final category must be added, namely those low-ranking jobs in the police and military forces which pay no more than average working-class wages. There is little doubt that the ordinary members of these forces put in more time than they receive in the form of material goods, either in cash or in kind, so that all perform unpaid labour. Moreover, since most of the working lives of the nearly half a million people in this category are spent performing very ordinary and mainly useful public services, just like other civil servants, they clearly have much in common with the working class. Yet, as is argued in chapter 7, in spite of this useful role which they

Table 4.12. *Estimated numbers of persons in the Japanese middle class,
1980 (1,000 persons)*

	Total		Males		Females	
	No.	%	No.	%	No.	%
University lecturers and teachers[a]	1,000	100	600	60.0	400	40.0
Employees in medical and health services[b]	700	100	200	28.6	500	71.4
Technocrats[c]	100	100	68	68.0	32	32.0
Supervisors[d]	1,500	100	1,200	80.0	300	20.0
Military and police[e]	489	100	459	93.9	30	6.1
Total	3,789	100.0	2,527	66.7	1,262	33.3

[a]I have excluded from the total number of teachers (1,267,058) the 63,013 university presidents and school principals of the same number of educational institutions. The figure was rounded off to about 1 million because of the close proximity to the bourgeoisie of certain other persons, such as vice-presidents, vice-principals, and heads of departments. The sex composition is taken from table 4.7 above.
[b]These are rounded estimates based on the data in the text and tables above.
[c]This is a very rough estimate of the technical and professional employees not elsewhere included, that is, the numbers outside health and education who are neither supervisors nor bourgeois members of the managerial hierarchy. The proportions of men and women are taken from their proportions in the total number of technical and professional persons outside health and education, for which see *Shūgyō kōzō kihon chōsa hōkoku*, 1979, pp. 64, 68.
[d]The sex composition of the estimated 1.5 million supervisors not elsewhere included is taken from the sex composition of persons aged 35–44 who were mainly working and whose annual incomes in 1979 were ¥2.5–3.0 million. See *ibid.*, p. 37. Although women are concentrated in certain industries and by the age of 35 might be expected to produce *shunin*, large numbers of them are only temporary workers and would not receive this rank. The 300,000 persons thus probably represent a high estimate.
[e]The Self Defence Forces originally limited women to the role of nurses, and only in 1968 were women admitted to the army and in 1974 to the air force and navy. However, apart from nurses, the total numbers of women in December 1975 were 1,470, 74, and 21 respectively. See *Bōei hakusho*, 1976, pp. 130–1. The 1981 White Paper did not address itself to this question.

play (indeed very much because of it), when called upon by the dominant agents of the ruling class to apply force if this is needed to break up working-class organisations and struggles, either within Japan or in its neo-colonies, they seem to play this role with little sense of unease. Perhaps it is because they have not yet been used too frequently or conspicuously in this capacity in the postwar period that the ruling class assumes that they will under all circumstances remain loyal to the system and perform the crucial function for capital of compelling the working class into submission when all the other ways of achieving it break down. Yet history has taught us again and again that this loyalty cannot be counted on and that should it falter, as it did in Russia in 1917, entire regimes and even systems of social relations can collapse. Table 4.11 shows the numbers of military and police personnel in Japan in 1980, all but the top-ranking members of whom fell into the ambiguous category of the middle class. Table 4.12 then provides estimates of the total number of persons who mediated more or less equal contradictory class forces that year.

In view of press reports in Japan that some 90% of people are now middle class,[8] it may seem strange to find that the economically active membership of this class is less than half that of the bourgeoisie. The picture is not altered if one includes owners of moderate amounts of capital (see p. 21 above), since most of the clerical workers and labourers in this category would be part of the managerial hierarchy and be either bourgeois or middle class anyway. However, the comparatively small size of the middle class is to be expected, since the capitalist mode of production, with its two distinctive class forces, continually drives people into two opposite camps rather than into one whose common interests with each are more or less equal. As we noted earlier, far from being a source of independent political action, the middle class represents a combination of contradictory forces which come together to produce mainly transitional groupings through which some mobility from the working class to the bourgeoisie can occur. The importance of the middle class is not therefore its absolute size, but its role in the reproduction of the capitalist relationship. Its largest stable group,[9] teachers and university lecturers, controls the process by which class agents are reproduced.

Reproduction of the middle class

The reproduction of middle-class agents, that is, the persons who fill the contradictory positions requiring above-average skills, takes place in the very institutions in which the largest stable group in the middle class works. These institutions control the process of training labour power and channelling agents into the working class, as well as the process by which some class mobility is possible.

Table 4.13. *Occupational mobility and education of business leaders, 1960*

Occupation of father	Less than primary school (%)	Middle school (%)	Specialist school (%)	College or university (%)	Total (%)	No. in sample
Labourer	15	15	39	31	100	13
Farmer	14	11	29	46	100	65
Landlord	4	8	27	61	100	168
Small businessman	3	6	28	63	100	297
Large businessman	1	5	16	78	100	218
Professional man	0	2	20	78	100	206
All occupations	3	6	23	68	100	967

Source: Mannari, *The Japanese Business Leaders*, p. 68.

An educational background that has long since guaranteed access to managerial positions in large corporations has been attendance at one of the prestige national universities (Tokyo, Kyoto, or Hitotsubashi) or top private universities (Keio or Waseda). Of a sample in 1960 of 902 business leaders who had higher education, 36% were graduates of Tokyo University, 11% of Kyoto, 10% of Hitotsubashi, 7% of Keio, and 5% of Waseda.[10] Since the fees at national universities have not been beyond the means of working-class families, some mobility into the bourgeoisie has been possible. For example, in 1961, 39.9% of all students enrolled at national universities, but only 15.6% of those at private universities, came from the bottom 40% of households in terms of annual income.[11] Table 4.13 reveals the importance a university background has had for membership of the bourgeoisie as well as for the trickle of labourers' sons that have managed to 'make it.' Only 13 out of the 967 business leaders, who admittedly represented the top echelons of the bourgeoisie, were sons of labourers, of whom only 4 had attended a college or a university. Business leaders from all other backgrounds greatly exceeded those from working-class backgrounds, and much higher proportions of the former attended a college or a university. Higher education has clearly been an important prerequisite to becoming a business leader (so long as one is a male), but access to higher education has not been easy for sons of labourers. It has become even more difficult over the years, because the very opportunity for a degree of class mobility created the conditions for a massive increase in the number of students who went on to high school (from about 50% in 1955 to over 90% in 1976) and then on to university (from 19% in 1955 to 35% in 1976, where it has remained).[12] The numbers of agents seeking to fill middle-class and, via promotion, bourgeois positions greatly exceeded the available supply of these positions, and the education system adapted accordingly. It had to become more competitive so that just the right numbers of agents could be funnelled through.

The result was that while the top universities continued to provide their former guarantees – attendance at a top university exempts one from writing company entrance examinations – the number of universities in this category had to be limited and entry into them had to become more difficult. The system of entry into all educational institutions by competitive examination alone become more rigid and was extended right down to kindergartens. Experience had taught that certain high schools (increasingly the private ones) more successfully equipped their pupils to pass prestige-university entrance examinations, and that certain middle schools helped most in gaining access to the chosen high schools. There are now even highly competitive entrance examinations to prestige kindergartens.

Normal study hours have become insufficient to cross all the necessary hurdles (known as 'test hell'), and children require extra classes from private tutors, the escalating costs of which are putting working-class children out of the running. Where residential requirements are conditions of entering prestige state schools, bourgeois parents move into the areas or sometimes even pay someone to have their children registered as domiciled in those areas. Already in 1957, only twenty-seven out of a class of sixty-two in a better Tokyo high school were legal residents in that school district.[13] It is also becoming increasingly difficult to pass prestige-university entrance examinations without spending an additional year after high school in a top cram school which specialises in training students in examination techniques. Normally about one-half of the freshmen at Tokyo University had spent from one to three years after high school studying privately or in cram schools.

It is hardly surprising that working-class children have been finding it more difficult to get into first-class universities. By 1974 the proportion of students at national universities who came from the bottom 40% (in terms of annual income) of families had fallen to 25.6%, while the proportion in private universities had fallen to

12.6% (a decline since 1961 of 14.3 and 3.0 percentage points respectively).[14] In his study of the growing competitiveness of the Japanese education system, Thomas Rohlen concluded that 'the role of family background may have been altered to a greater emphasis on wealth, for the costs of private sector competition, especially private high schooling, must be prohibitive for many families regardless of their children's talents.'[15]

Educational institutions, as is argued in chapter 7, are thus a major form of social and ideological control over the working class. They govern the reproduction of all class agents and ensure that neither too much nor too little mobility takes place. They thereby legitimise class divisions as divisions based on merit, as well as make the knowledge and skills needed under capitalist relations of production appear to be requirements of engaging in productive activity itself.

To understand the role of the education system in the reproduction of the middle class one must distinguish very carefully between middle-class positions and the agents who occupy those positions. The reproduction of middle-class agents is just part of the reproduction of all class agents. However, since the number of middle-class positions is comparatively small, a large proportion of people who manage to acquire above-average skills through university education cannot find jobs which utilise these skills or which correspond to the positions they had hoped for. Of my sample of 459 respondents in 1976/7, 202 had attended university or college, but a full 77 said that their skills and abilities were either only slightly or not at all used in their jobs.

The cause of this problem has been a growing excess in the numbers of middle-class agents (university graduates) each year over the numbers of new or vacated middle-class positions. In other words, while the growth in the numbers of persons who attend university has resulted in the reproduction of middle-class agents on an expanded scale, the growth of capital accumulation has resulted in the reproduction of middle-class positions on a more simple scale, the main expansion taking place in the proliferation of educational institutions. By 1977, only 60% of college graduates were able to get white collar jobs, the rest having to settle for blue collar jobs. As the *Japan Times Weekly* explained, 'The obvious reason for this is that there are simply too many college graduates for a highly limited number of posts in a corporation.'[16] Since in 1980 it took some 17% of a family's monthly expenditures to keep one college student at university,[17] this fact has profound implications for the Japanese class struggle in general, and for the potential for revolutionary struggle by the agents of the middle class in particular. It marks the beginning of a process by which one of the main supports of bourgeois ideology, a realistic aspiration for upward mobility, is breaking down.

Ideology, organisation, and political activity

Although the particular positions occupied by members of the Japanese middle class are what ultimately shape their daily life activities and ideologies, there is a much greater influence on them of mechanisms other than production than is typical of other classes. This is because the distinctive characteristic of their production relations is that the opposing forces are in balance and do not create definite political dispositions. The most important of the more subordinate mechanisms which tend to carry the balance of influence on middle-class activity are the organisations to which the different groups belong.

Before we examine these organisations, at least three important common influences on middle-class ideology must be discussed. The first is that the endurance of many years of 'test hell,' when finally rewarded with a secure middle-class position, produces the central axiom of the middle class's rationalisation of its characteristic duplicity: independence and self-sufficiency. Since an enormous amount of effort is required to obtain higher education, those who graduate from the top universities and obtain middle-class positions tend to see their good fortune almost entirely in terms of their own merits, and they attribute the fewer privileges of ordinary workers to their lack of initiative in obtaining a good education. The route to middle-class membership via education is a major support of the ideology of independence. It is not surprising that one of the main slogans of even left-wing students has been a call on the Japanese people to become independent (*jiritsu*) of all oppressive social and family ties. The assumption is that people can somehow just choose to be independent, as if social relationships were voluntarily entered into.

This ideology was expressed in various forms in a survey of university students carried out in 1976, the year when the degree of competition to enter the top universities peaked. Large proportions saw their society as free but competitive and hierarchical, and their

Table 4.14. *Students' most common views on society and on the benefits of university, 1976*

	% which held the view
Views on Japanese society	
Free society	58.7
Competitive society	88.8
Many distinctions between members	70.9
Motives for going to university	
To get professional and technical qualifications	52.1
To educate myself	47.7
To lead a free life for four years	46.5
To improve my job prospects	42.1
Reasons for selecting preferred university	
The department is most suitable in my subject	67.2
It is closely related to my future job	51.6
Fees are low	42.0
To improve my job prospects	35.9
About right for my abilities	35.0
I like the university life there	31.7

Source: Nihon rikurūto sentā [Japan Recruit Centre], *Rikurūto chōsa geppō* [Monthly Report on Recruit Surveys], April 1976, pp. 29, 31.

main reasons for going to university related to getting better jobs and enjoying the freedom of university life. Table 4.14 summarises their main views on these questions.

Once middle-class jobs have been secured, two additional factors reinforce this ideology of independence through university education. The first is that these jobs are relatively autonomous of the two main social forces in capitalist society, because they are in the middle of and are drawn towards both. However, rather than see themselves as caught between the working class and the bourgeoisie, the agents of the middle class imagine they are independent of both of them, and they attribute this to their own achievements. The second reinforcement this view receives is the promotion into the bourgeoisie of many of their number. This too is a powerful influence on all of them, excepting perhaps women in health and education and to a lesser extent also men in education. So long as the bourgeoisie is reproduced in part from members of the middle class, the latter will have no material basis for any other ideology. Although (for reasons that will be discussed in the next chapter) class consciousness is low in Japan,

Table 4.15. *Class consciousness in private companies, by education and by rank, 1976*

| | Degree of awareness among those who attempted the set of questions | | | |
	None/ little (%)	Fair/ strong (%)	No answer (%)	Total no.
A. *Existence of classes*				
Persons outside managerial hierarchy				
Elementary/middle school	54.5	45.5	—	22
High school	62.9	37.1	—	105
Junior college (mainly women)	64.3	35.7	—	28
University	79.4	20.6	—	68
Total	67.3	32.7	—	223
Shunin				
Elementary/middle school	53.3	46.7	—	15
High school	80.0	20.0	—	40
Junior college	66.6	0.0	33.3	3
University	80.0	20.0	—	10
Total	73.5	25.0	1.5	68
B. *Antagonism of class interests*				
Persons outside managerial hierarchy				
Elementary/middle school	36.4	54.6	9.1	22
High school	52.4	42.9	4.8	105
Junior college (mainly women)	50.0	42.9	7.1	28
University	64.7	30.9	4.4	68
Total	54.3	40.4	5.4	223
Shunin				
Elementary/middle school	60.0	33.3	6.7	15
High school	57.5	40.0	2.5	40
Junior college	66.6	33.3	—	3
University	70.0	30.0	—	10
Total	60.3	36.8	2.9	68
C. *Existence of class struggles*				
Persons outside managerial hierarchy				
Elementary/middle school	45.4	36.4	18.2	22
High school	40.9	46.7	12.4	105
Junior college (mainly women)	25.0	71.4	3.6	28
University	51.5	42.6	5.9	68
Total	42.6	47.5	9.9	223

Table 4.15 *(cont.)*

| | Degree of awareness among those who attempted the set of questions | | | |
	None/ little (%)	Fair/ strong (%)	No answer (%)	Total no.
Shunin				
Elementary/middle school	46.7	46.7	6.6	15
High school	42.5	55.0	2.5	40
Junior college	33.3	66.7	—	3
University	40.0	60.0	—	10
Total	42.6	54.4	2.9	68

my research in 1976/7 revealed that university graduates were the most strongly disposed to deny the very existence of classes, and that *shunin* were significantly more inclined to do so than employees without any rank. Since the numbers in the sample in table 4.15, which presents the data, are small, the findings are only suggestive.

The survey also revealed that only 22.2% of university graduates, but almost 40% of middle and high school graduates, expected no promotion even if they did their jobs well. There is therefore some evidence for the conclusion that basic middle-class ideology results from enduring the 'test hell,' from the contradictory locations agents occupy, and from the fact that at least one such location, that of *shunin*, is a stepping stone to membership in the bourgeoisie.

The basic ideology is, however, subject to considerable modification by membership in political and ideological organisations. The position of *shunin* illustrates this fairly well, because *shunin* in large firms tend to belong to the company unions, which, as we shall see in the next chapter, actually function as organisations for the political and ideological control of workers. It is not therefore surprising that on all three dimensions of class consciousness I used, union membership actually seemed to reduce the class awareness of the *shunin* in my sample, as is revealed by table 4.16.

However, since very few small firms, but most large ones, have company unions, one cannot separate being a member of a union

Table 4.16. *Class consciousness of* shunin, *by union membership, 1976*

	Degree of awareness			
	None/ little (%)	Fair/ strong (%)	No answer (%)	Total no.
Existence of classes				
Never a union member	66.6	33.3	—	18
Was once, but not now	80.0	20.0	—	10
Currently a member	75.0	25.0	—	40
Antagonism of class interests				
Never a union member	50.0	50.0	—	18
Was once, but not now	30.0	60.0	10.0	10
Currently a member	72.5	25.0	2.5	40
Existence of class struggles				
Never a union member	27.8	72.2	—	18
Was once, but not now	20.0	80.0	—	10
Currently a member	55.0	37.5	7.5	40

from being an employee in a large firm, where promotion into managerial positions by education and skill is tempered by length of service. Company unions, which are integrated into the functioning of large firms, therefore modify the basic middle-class ideology to produce what Nakane Chie calls 'frame' consciousness, that is, loyalty to the company above loyalty to one's class or to oneself.[18] Middle-class members of large corporations thereby become victims of the same ideological and political domination of the company that affects workers. But so long as substantial promotions are possible for university graduates, *shunin* and technocrats have a more overriding material interest in remaining loyal to capital. Some 'independence' can be sacrificed if the reward is access into the ruling class.

Other examples of the importance of organisations in modifying middle-class ideology are the different ways in which Nikkyōso (Nihon Kyōshokuin Kumiai, or the Japan Teachers' Union)[19] and Nihon Ishikai (the Japan Medical Association) have influenced their members. We have noted the different material interests of teachers and doctors, but these cannot fully account for the far greater radicalism of the JTU than the JMA.

The material basis for substantial Marxist influence on the JTU was laid in the prewar years, when teachers suffered various forms of intense exploitation and domination, as well as in the immediate postwar years, when for the first time they could legitimately organise and struggle for improvements. However, in spite of teachers' growing interests in postwar capitalism (at least until the end of the long boom), the organisation managed to preserve a tradition of radical struggle, which it passed on to new members.

This has not been easy, because rank-and-file members have been torn between repeated attacks on teachers by the state and the attempt of the union to resist these attacks. While they continue to support it for its efforts (two-thirds in the early 1970s still regarded it as necessary), their material interests shy them away from the radical solutions proposed by left-wing leaders (two-thirds believed the leadership did not consider their views).[20]

The most important attacks by the state on teachers include removal of the right to collective bargaining and to strike, increasing control of textbooks and curricula (such as the reintroduction of courses on traditional ethics), the introduction of systems of efficiency rating for teachers and achievement tests for pupils, and the introduction into educational institutions of the *shunin* system. Struggles on all of these issues which directly affected teachers have had widespread support and resulted in a very high level of participation by the rank and file in union activities. Wage struggles, on the other hand, have been more divisive, and a moderate faction has gradually gained control of the union by appealing to teachers' sense of professionalism and flattery at the traditional deference shown by Japanese towards their *Sensei* (an honorific used for teachers and doctors). Demands for wage rises on these grounds have been unsuccessfully opposed by the radical minority faction, which saw that they divided teachers from workers and contradicted the union's Code of Ethics:

> Teachers are labourers whose workshops are the schools. Teachers, in the knowledge that labour is the foundation of everything in society, shall be proud of the fact that they themselves are labourers. At the present stage of history, the realization of a new society of mankind that respects fundamental human rights, not only in words but in deed as well, and that utilizes resources, technology, and science for the welfare of all men is possible only through the power of the working masses, whose nucleus is the labouring class. Teachers shall be aware of their position as labourers, shall live forcefully believing in the historical progress of man, and shall consider all stagnation and reaction as their enemies.[21]

Other struggles which have divided the union through failure to win sufficient support have been unrelated to working conditions, such as anti-Security Treaty struggles and those against Japanese involvement in the Vietnam war.

However, what is remarkable is not the JTU's growing conservatism during the boom years, when the material basis of its earlier radicalism was being eroded, but that in spite of the boom and the growth all around it of large reformist unions in the private sector, the organisation managed to preserve more of its tradition of struggle than almost any other union. A majority of members still support illegal strikes when these are necessary, even though they mean anything from imprisonment to heavy fines or suspension. Nikkyōso has remained the major teachers' organisation notwithstanding state attacks and attempts to organise rivals. In 1981, its membership stood at 672,393, while the total membership of its four rivals was only 142,549, less than half of what had been expected.[22]

In sharp contrast to the JTU, the Japan Medical Association has been a thoroughly bourgeois organisation which has drawn the bulk of middle-class doctors into an alliance with the ruling class.[23] It is almost futile to attempt to detach the JMA from the bourgeoisie, since its leadership has been consistently and vigorously anti-communist as well as dominated by private practitioners, although a few communist doctors are influential in some local branches. The JMA has firmly institutionalised even what had been a very secure material basis for the alliance between almost all doctors and the bourgeoisie.

A similar though more limited ability of student organisations in this case to preserve radical traditions in spite of the postwar boom need not be discussed here. The lessons of the rise and fall of Zengakuren (Zen Nihon Gakusei Jichikai Sōrengō, or the All-Japan Students' Self-Governing Associations)[24] are more pertinent to the final chapter on the possibilities in Japan of revolutionary change. For the same reason, we need not pause to explain how the thoroughly reactionary traditions of the Japanese police and military preclude any immediate possibility of their playing anything other than their traditional role. However, some tentative conclusions on the theme of possible social change do emerge from the analysis of the middle class.

The crisis and revolutionary change

The most important of these conclusions is that the middle class occupies a key position in the capitalist social relationship, not because of its absolute size, but because of its role in the reproduction of class agents and of the ideas and activities that legitimise class relations. We have also seen that Japanese teachers have been more prepared to resist this role than have teachers in most other capitalist societies, but that the long boom created a disjunction between what the advanced section of the teachers' movement tried to do and what the bulk of the working class expected from education. So long as capital accumulation was rapid and some class mobility was possible, teachers could not resist their sausage-machine role and win widespread working-class support, since individual workers saw education as a possible means of rising out of their class rather than as a means of rising with their class. A revolutionary movement under the leadership of teachers was bound to fail, although in fairness this was not what the JTU saw as its task, since it tried to integrate itself into the trade union movement as a whole. Students could more justifiably be accused of this kind of adventurism, which stemmed directly out of their middle-class ideology of voluntarism and independence.

The end of the boom has, however, once again created conditions for unity between teachers and the working class. To discover how this can be forged in practice requires understanding the various forms the crisis takes which most directly affect them both. Since the crisis is above all one of social relations, the breakdown of these relations can take unexpected forms, of which at least three are particularly relevant.

The first of these is what has been called 'the phenomenon of superfluous managers' (*kanrishoku kata genshō*), which was bound to occur in a system of promotion and payment by length of service as soon as accumulation began to falter.[25] A rapidly expanding company could recruit and promote large numbers of university graduates without adversely affecting personnel costs, because it also absorbed growing numbers of low-paid young workers. Since the crisis has put the brakes on both forms of recruitment, corporations are facing the problem of becoming top-heavy as larger proportions of employees get promoted to managerial positions or to the higher wage brackets of older workers. Mobility into the bourgeoisie therefore had to be drastically reduced, even if it was not reversed, since faltering accumulation could not sustain, let alone rapidly add new members to, a ruling class as large as the Japanese bourgeoisie. A recent government study in fact revealed that only 25% of a sample of managerial employees could retain jobs of this status after they 'retired.'[26]

This type of development means that a major support of bourgeois ideology, class mobility through education, will be increasingly eroded, with profound effects on both workers and teachers. For the first time in eleven years, in 1977, the percentage of high school students who went on to university fell, reflecting the realisation that a college degree no longer provided the guarantee it used to.[27] In 1976 a survey of university students revealed enormous pessimism about job prospects: only 23% thought they would be able to earn high incomes, 14.4% that they would obtain high-ranking positions, and 15.2% that they would get jobs in top-ranking firms.[28]

If the first form that the crisis took was reduced expectations of the advantages of higher education, a weakening of the loyalty to the bourgeoisie of technocrats and *shunin* might well be the next if large numbers of people in the managerial hierarchies are actually proletarianised. Although during the boom it would have been futile to consider them possible allies of the working class, they can now become a potential, even if unreliable, revolutionary force, because to emerge from the 'test hell' with no more guarantees of a secure livelihood than an average worker can shatter more illusions than if one's sights were lower to begin with.

The second form that the crisis has actually taken is cuts in the living standards and in the numbers of jobs available to the only fraction of the middle class which is capable of constituting itself into a united social force. Of all the members of the middle class, only teachers are brought together in large numbers in the same institutions, and attacks on them can, and often have been, firmly resisted. But when these attacks take place in the context of more widespread attacks on the labouring masses, as the bourgeoisie substitutes the stick for the carrot that worked so well during the boom, left-wing forces in the teachers' movement might find that conditions favour their strategy of alliance with the working class. It might even be possible to detach nurses from the ideological domination of doctors.

Finally, for some years now there have been symptoms of a breakdown of the process by which class agents in Japan are reproduced. Having to endure almost two decades of 'test hell' showed growing signs of being financially, psychologically, and physically unbearable, not only for those most directly affected, but for all the members of the families concerned. By 1974 even the government White Paper on School Children and Youth expressed grave concern over the extent to which the nation's youth was being crippled by excessive pressure to study. Associated with the pressure to cram, the White Paper noted, were sharp increases in juvenile crime and suicides, even among minors aged 10.[29] Once an established method which simultaneously reproduced class agents and legitimises class society breaks down, far-reaching opportunities for mass revolutionary struggles are opened up. However, whether these opportunities are seized and result in socialist revolution or whether they are lost and the society degenerates into fascism depends largely on the forms of organisation the working class manages to develop, a question which is picked up again towards the end of the next chapter.

5
The working class

The Japanese working class has the reputation, largely in the Western bourgeois press, of being notoriously hard-working, loyal to its employers, and lacking in class consciousness. Western managers envy their Japanese counterparts for the *harmony* and *cooperation* that are supposed to characterise industrial relations in Japan, but very few of them have any idea to what extent or why this supposed harmony exists. Even the Japanese bourgeoisie tends to attribute it to cultural values which are unique to Japan and which cannot be exported. Scholars are always writing about it, one even to the extent of hailing it as a sort of wonder of the capitalist world.[1]

However, to the extent that *harmony* and *cooperation* are peculiarly Japanese cultural values, and that industrial relations in Japan are freer from conflict than they are in the West, the explanation lies in a complex process by which people are channelled into jobs according to the traditional attributes of the members of the *ie*. The result is once again that the infrastructural forces of class and gender are mediated and obscured by the visible forms of the age, sex, and education of concrete individuals. The greater visibility of the company group than the class forces it conceals is the type of phenomenon we have come across many times already, and it is also one with a very firm material basis. The loyalty of Japanese workers to their employers, the benevolence they receive in return, and the harmony that characterises relations between them are all dependent on a rapidly growing capitalist infrastructure and a slotting of individuals into the growing numbers of jobs according to their traditionally valued personal characteristics. The harmony in the functioning of the infrastructure could thus make it seem that the 'Japanese way' of doing things was once again the source of industrial success.

We thus have two general tasks in this chapter: to reconstruct the relevant infrastructural forces and to show how they were mediated by certain traditional practices which as a result of their easy visibility looked like fundamental causes. The infrastructural forces concern the effects of the general laws of capital accumulation on the working class, for example, the fractionalisation of this social force, while the relevant attributes of the traditional family which mediate the fractional forces are the age, sex, and educational standing of individuals.

Theory of the structure of the working class

A capitalist infrastructure does not simply produce the two opposing class forces of the bourgeoisie and the working class, because uneven capital accumulation fractionalises these forces in fairly predictable ways. The bourgeoisie, we have already seen, always comprises at least two such fractions, monopoly and non-monopoly capital, simply because capital accumulation is always uneven within industries: larger, stronger capitals always coexist with smaller, weaker ones. The three main fractional forces of the working class which we will examine in some detail are the labour aristocracy, the mass worker, and the reserve army.

From the outset it cannot be emphasised too strongly that all three fractions of the working class are in the same fundamental relationship to the capitalist class as a whole. Together they function to produce the social surplus and promote the circulation of the total social capital under the direct control of the capitalist class. The distinctions between them are not based on different degrees of proximity to the ruling class or on different levels of income. Rather the different levels of income of the persons who mediate these forces result from the different roles capital requires the working class as a whole to play in order to ensure the uninterrupted reproduction, on an ever increasing scale, of capitalist social relationships. The fundamental laws of capital accumulation, with all the ups and downs and irregularities that they bring to this process, separate working-class agents into three groups corresponding to the three main (contradictory) functions the working class must fulfil if capitalist development is to proceed at all. In fact bourgeois class relations would not survive if exactly the same class agents (individuals) were required to fulfil all three functions, let alone simultaneously. What are these three functions?

To answer this question we examine the three main effects the dominant force in capitalist production has on the working class in the process of accumulation. The first is the development of the collective worker as a result of the concentration and centralisation of capital in large units, a process which is manifested in the growth of monopolies through the reinvestment of profits and through mergers and takeovers. Since the division of labour is greatest in large enterprises where each worker performs only one small task in the overall production process, the function of producing the whole commodity belongs to the workers as a whole, or to the collective worker. Once this happens, the contradiction between social production (the fact of a cooperative labour process) and private appropriation of the product becomes sharper and can threaten the capitalist relation. Moreover, since workers are brought together in large numbers in giant corporations, they can be more threatening because of the greater ease with which they can organise and act collectively. To minimise the growing threat of revolutionary working-class action, capital must at the very least ensure that workers' jobs are secure and that their standard of living remains stable, or preferably rises slowly. The growing danger from collective workers, who are a product of the concentration and centralisation of capital, must be countered by providing a material basis for their loyalty to capital, one which no nineteenth-century worker could possibly have dreamed of.

If the first thing capital accumulation demands of the working class is a willingness to accept a relationship whose contradictions become sharper at each stage, the second results from the effects of uneven accumulation within industries. Since this process is one of constant attempts by capitalists in each industry either to gain a productivity advantage over rivals or to make up for a productivity disadvantage, more concentrated and centralised capitals will continually coexist with smaller, less-productive capitals. We saw in chapter 1 how the survival of the latter depended on their paying lower wages than the former. From the point of view of capital in general, this wage difference is essential, since the more threatening workers in monopoly firms are more likely to remain loyal if they have some material basis for seeing themselves as privileged. Uneven accumulation within industries, therefore, both creates some of the conditions for working-class loyalty to capital, by giving the most advanced workers the greatest material stake in the system, and requires sizeable wage differentials among the members of the working class as a whole, that is, a mass of low-paid people in the large number of non-monopoly firms that necessarily exist side by side with the development of monopolies.

Finally, the working class must adapt to uneven accumulation of capital in general, that is, the periodic depressions in which the tendency for the rate of profit to fall and other systemic contradictions manifest themselves. At various times, masses of workers must become unemployed for considerable periods, but they must also remain available for re-employment when accumulation begins to pick up again. Marx referred to this as the function of the reserve army, and we will discuss it in more detail when we examine the Japanese reserve army.

Clearly, it is in practice impossible for the same persons to be able to fulfil all of these functions simultaneously, and in Japan, as in other capitalist countries, working-class agents have been divided into three corresponding fractions. They are products of the dynamic laws of development of the fundamental relationship between the capitalist class and the working class. However, they can only take the visible form of natural or traditional divisions of rank, based primarily on sex and age, to the extent that agents are channelled into the different fractions of the working class according to their sex and their age. In our analysis of the peasantry and the middle class, we saw how roles belonging to different members of the traditional family functioned as the visible forms in which infrastructural relations between classes were manifested and how this concealed class forces in the countryside and in large corporations by making them look like natural and cultural phenomena. For the same reason, the functioning of traditional family roles to channel agents into groups which manifest the fractional divisions of the working class make the visible distinctions among workers seem to be equally natural to Japanese society. In both cases, infrastructural mechanisms function through elements of the traditional family and thereby make them dominate day-to-day experience. I shall show that since the same familial relations serve both as relations of production (which generate opposing class forces) and as fractional divisions within the working class resulting from capital accumulation, differences between classes in Japan take on the identical form as differences within them, particularly within the working class.

Fractions of the Japanese working class

The labour aristocracy

Rapid accumulation and the consolidation of Japanese monopoly capital around the time of the First World War were the most important developments which produced a distinctive labour aristocracy in Japan. Productive forces were unleashed to an unprecedented extent and led to two forms of class struggle which stood in the way of further accumulation. The first was the opportunity seized by the limited supply of skilled workers (with the qualifications and experience needed to operate the new technologies) to bid up wages by frequently changing jobs. In some cases, capital had to face an annual rate of labour turnover of 100% and even used gangsters either to compel workers to return or to kidnap workers from rivals. Although the situation had been serious well before the war, it became intolerable afterwards. Carefully worked-out agreements by employers to prevent 'piracy' of one another's workers were not adhered to, and some permanent solution was desperately awaited. The second form of class struggle which intensified after the war was an escalation of strikes by the now unionised collective worker, strikes which reached tidal proportions in 1919.

It was as a result of the intensification of these forms of class struggle, which had existed on a more limited scale before the war, that the agents of capital consciously introduced an employment system which gave the Japanese labour aristocracy its characteristic form. Rather than discuss the various components of this system historically, I only outline its central present-day features, many of which were consolidated during the post-Second World War period of rapid accumulation.[2] The problem it was designed to solve was how to retain a stable supply of trained workers who would not resist accumulation in the monopoly sector. Workers in this sector had to be made loyal to capital and prevented from withdrawing their labour power through strike action or through switching employers. The solution to the problem was gradually worked out in class struggles after many years of trial and error. The reason for the present system's relative success, at least during boom periods, lies in how it combines a material basis for workers' loyalty with elements of the traditional family which demand the loyalty of inferiors to superiors.

The most important material components of the system are various methods of deferring wage payments, so that workers are compelled to demonstrate their loyalty to capital before they receive living wages. The most effective of these methods is the system of payment by length of service, since few workers will risk the promise of a secure living wage after some fifteen years of service by engaging in industrial action that might result in a loss of their jobs and of such seniority as they have acquired. To make these deferred wages ideologically acceptable, capital confines new recruits to school leavers and university graduates, so that payment for length of service takes the form of payment by age. The capitalist enterprise thereby takes the form of a traditional family, which in return for loyal service and obedience to authority provides a secure position in the family hierarchy.

The reality of the deferred wage and the function this fulfils are concealed not simply by the familial system of ranking by age, but also by the traditional roles assigned to the sexes. Since women who have children leave their jobs for at least a long enough time to lose their seniority, they are separated from the labour aristocracy, and, as we shall see when we discuss the reserve army, their 'deferred wages' are never paid. Since with very few exceptions only men are ultimately paid living wages, traditional ideology is reproduced through its present function of channelling workers into different fractions of their class.

What separates the labour aristocracy from the mass worker is the former's employment by monopoly capital, which because of its more advanced productive forces is both required to and can afford to provide a much more solid material basis for workers' loyalty than can non-monopoly capital. Table 5.1 shows how far this is true of wages.

It is remarkable how divisions between classes take on the same appearance as divisions within the working class, namely different strata based on age, sex, and the 'standing' of the firm employed in. The salaries of middle-aged male university graduates, who by this time tend to enter the middle class or the bourgeoisie, are lower than the wages ultimately received (after many years of deferment) by elderly male workers. Both seem to be paid on the same basis of rank in the familial hierarchy, whereas in fact the former is increasingly paid out of surplus value for performing the function of capital. Also important to note is that with the exception of women workers, whose position in the reserve army reduces the relevance of the type of firm they are employed in, deferred wages in monopoly firms are much greater than those in non-monopoly firms. Though men in both might have similar starting wages, the difference increases with length of employment and with education. Fig. 5.1 illustrates this graphically, using the information in table 5.1.

Education therefore serves not merely to reproduce class agents and to legitimise class society but to legitimise the allocation of

A: male, university, monopoly firms
B: male, high school, monopoly firms
C: male, university, non-monopoly firms
D: male, high school, non-monopoly firms
E: male, middle school, monopoly firms
F: male, middle school, non-monopoly firms
G: female, high school, monopoly firms
H: female, high school, non-monopoly firms
I: female, middle school, monopoly firms
J: female, middle school, non-monopoly firms

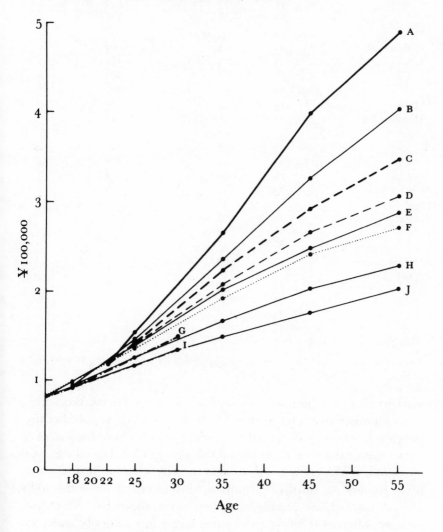

Fig. 5.1. Monthly payment by sex, education, age, and firm size, 1980.

Table 5.1. *Monthly payment, by age, sex, education, and firm size, 1980* *(¥ 1,000)*

Sex and education	Age	Non-monopoly (30–299 persons)	Monopoly (over 1,000 persons)
Male	22	119	120
University	25	145	156
	35	224	266
	45	293	400
	55	348	491
Male	18	99	96
High school	25	144	149
	35	209	237
	45	267	328
	55	308	406
Male	15	84	83
Middle school	25	138	140
	35	193	202
	45	242	249
	55	273	290
Female	18	96	95
High school	25	127	126
	30	148	151
	35	167	—
	45	203	—
	55	232	—
Female	15	83	82
Middle school	25	119	118
	30	136	136
	35	150	—
	45	178	—
	55	204	—

Source: Furukawa ed., *Chingin kentō shiryō* [Materials for Investigating Wages], 1982 (Tokyo: Nihon hōrei, 1981), p. 136.

workers into the labour aristocracy and the general mass. Workers in non-monopoly firms are assumed to be less productive, not because they work with less advanced technology, but because they went to the wrong schools or did not obtain the right grades. The educational background of a company's workers thereby seems to justify it as a first-, second-, or third-rate company, just as education seems to lie behind distinctions among members of a company. Moreover, because different levels of productive forces in monopoly and non-monopoly firms result in different pay scales between them for all employees, the fundamental basis of one's livelihood appears to be the type of company one works in rather than one's relationship to the means of production. Workers' loyalty to their employers therefore becomes not simply loyalty to their company, but a sense of rivalry with workers in other companies. Because of the reproduction of so many elements of the *ie* system, the company assumes the form of a traditional family, and class conflict is smothered beneath the form of rivalry among companies. Just as in feudal Japan, where the standing of one's family, which seemed to derive from kinship rather than from land ownership, was the most important mark of one's social position, in present-day Japan one's worth is socially assessed by the standing of one's company.

The deferment of wages by age is the single most important material condition which ties workers to their companies, but it is by no means the sole condition. Another form of deferred wages is the system of twice-yearly bonuses which represent the withholding of wages for periods of up to six months. However, because the amounts increase with each of the traditional forms assumed by the functioning of Japanese capitalism, bonuses serve three functions in addition to securing workers' loyalty. The most important is that they are a convenient means of cutting the value of labour power without reducing regular wages. Since in monopoly firms they compose an average of about 28% (the proportion rising sharply with length of service until the age of 25 and then levelling off) of workers' total annual income and are presented as a type of profit-sharing for high productivity, they offer considerable scope for manipulation by capital. For example, bonuses were cut by an average of 5% in 1976.[3] The second additional function of bonuses is that workers tend to save out of them for old age and for the education of their children, and they thereby release cheap money to capital through the banking system. Finally, since bonuses in non-monopoly firms compose a smaller proportion of annual income than in monopoly firms, they allow pay differentials between the two to look narrower than they actually are, as is revealed by table 5.2. The table also shows how the system of payment by length of service conceals the functioning of the sex–gender infrastructure, since women's low wages are obscured by their work records, which except in the lowest-paying small firms are less than half those of men.

Table 5.2. *Annual bonuses and basic wages, by establishment size and sex, 1980 (¥ 1,000)*

Firm size (persons)	Wages A	Bonuses B	A + B	B/A%	Indices (5,000 and over = 100) A	B	Average age	Average years of service
1–9								
Males	2,550	305	2,885	12.0	78	23	42.3	10.5
Females	1,356	218	1,574	16.1	82	31	43.1	10.2
10–29								
Males	2,784	525	3,309	18.9	85	40	41.1	9.9
Females	1,458	324	1,782	22.2	88	45	40.5	7.4
30–99								
Males	2,699	750	3,449	27.8	82	57	40.3	9.9
Females	1,390	393	1,783	28.3	84	55	38.4	6.5
100–499								
Males	2,701	923	3,624	34.2	83	70	38.5	11.1
Females	1,394	470	1,864	33.7	84	66	35.7	6.2

500–999								
Males	2,852	1,072	3,924	37.6	87	81	37.8	12.5
Females	1,428	525	1,953	36.8	86	74	33.1	6.0
1,000–4,999								
Males	3,080	1,234	4,314	40.1	94	93	37.8	14.0
Females	1,509	605	2,114	40.1	91	85	31.2	6.3
5,000 and over								
Males	3,273	1,324	4,597	40.5	100	100	37.8	15.0
Females	1,653	714	2,367	43.2	100	100	30.7	6.9
Total								
Males	2,764	760	3,524	27.5	84	57	40.0	11.1
Females	1,409	362	1,771	25.7	85	51	39.0	7.8

Source: Kokuzeichō chōkan kanbō sōmuka [Administrative Division of the Secretariat of the Director of the National Taxation Agency], *Zeimu tōkei kara mita minkan kyūyo no jittai* [The Real Situation of Private Incomes from the View of Taxation Statistics], 1980 (Tokyo: Ōkurashō insatsukyoku, 1981), p. 15.

Apart from deferring wages, capital employs one other main material incentive to secure workers' loyalty, namely the system of company welfare, which is most highly developed in monopoly firms. The discrepancy between what they and what small firms can offer is particularly significant in the provision of cheap company housing and medical facilities, since housing and medical care are among the most costly as well as most essential wage goods workers require. The historical origins of company welfare and recreation facilities reveal unambiguously that their major purpose was to bind the skilled male worker to his company. Capital has consistently opposed state intervention in this area, and so long as state welfare continues to lag behind company welfare – a theme pursued in chapter 7 – workers who choose or are forced to leave large companies lose very much more than their seniority wages. A lifetime's savings for old age and emergencies can be ruined in a few years should inflation get out of step with interest rates, as it did in the mid-1970s, and employment in non-monopoly firms secures at most only about half the welfare benefits provided by monopoly firms. In 1980, welfare expenditure per employee in firms with over ¥1,000 million capital was ¥689,044, while small firms (¥2–5 million capital) spent only ¥209,500.[4] Table 5.3 provides a general picture of the facilities that had been built up in the two sectors by the time of the first 'oil shock.'

The material conditions which have shaped the Japanese labour aristocracy have not, however, excluded certain contradictions. Although the employment system in monopoly firms is frequently seen as one of guaranteed lifelong employment and social welfare, even in boom periods the guarantees had definite limits. These derive from the fact that capital's total wage bill depends more on the average age and sex composition of its entire workforce than on the absolute numbers employed. As is revealed by fig. 5.1, in giant firms four female workers under 25 can cost less than one male over 50. This is why new recruits are almost entirely confined to young graduates and school leavers, why in times of crisis females replace males, and why total wage costs can actually fall even at times when the workforce expands rapidly so long as its age and sex composition changes in the appropriate ways. However, the reproduction of this happy state of affairs has required placing a relatively low upper limit on the age, soon after 55, by which workers in the labour aristocracy have to retire. To continue the seniority payments and job security beyond that age would cause two main problems: a possibly rising

Table 5.3. *Availability of company welfare, by firm size, 1973*

	Total of all firms (%)	Large firms (5,000 or more employees) (%)	Small firms (30–99 employees) (%)
Housing			
Family	47.0	93.9	42.2
Unmarried	34.9	89.9	28.8
House-buying incentive	34.8	96.5	28.2
Homeowner layaway	4.5	74.9	1.0
Housing loan	18.8	93.9	10.8
Medical and health care			
Hospitals	3.2	31.3	2.2
Clinics	8.3	74.3	3.8
Medical offices	24.9	85.4	18.2
Preventive medicine	58.2	95.6	52.1
Family medical check-ups	2.4	37.4	1.1
Living support			
Barber shops/beauty salons	3.8	50.3	1.3
Purchasing facilities	9.6	70.2	4.1
Nurseries	1.8	12.0	0.8
Employee canteens	33.3	79.2	27.4
Food provision	27.7	62.2	22.9
Mutual-aid credit			
Marriage	94.7	98.0	93.2
Birth	87.4	90.6	85.2
Death	94.0	98.2	92.2
Disease	86.2	88.9	83.6
Accident	77.2	96.2	72.0
Private insurance system (premiums borne by employer)	46.6	48.8	48.2
Culture/sport/recreation			
Libraries	22.1	75.1	14.2
Gymnasiums	3.4	54.1	2.0
Athletic grounds	10.9	84.5	5.0
Seaside/mountain lodges/ski resorts	15.1	73.3	9.8
Rehabilitation facilities	16.0	95.6	9.4
Tennis courts	11.4	86.5	4.0
Swimming pools	2.8	48.8	1.3
Cultural clubs	31.5	94.7	19.5
Athletic clubs	56.5	95.3	·46.5
Athletic meets	15.3	71.9	9.1
Pleasure trips	88.4	64.3	91.5

Table 5.3 *(cont.)*

	Total of all firms (%)	Large firms (5,000 or more employees) (%)	Small firms (30–99 employees) (%)
Others			
Employee shareholding	7.8	55.3	5.8
Supplemental labour compensation insurance	31.1	93.6	23.8
Supplemental health insurance (extra payment above legal minimums)	21.3	98.8	14.8

Source: Yakabe Katsumi, *Labour Relations in Japan : Fundamental Characteristics* (Tokyo: International Society for Educational Information, Inc. Japan, 1974), p. 64.

average age of the workforce and therefore rising wage costs on the one hand, and insufficient flexibility in being able to adjust the absolute numbers of workers to any unevenness in the rate of accumulation on the other.

Monopoly capital has therefore made a rigid distinction between so-called 'regular employees' (unmarried females and males under the age of about 55), and various types of 'temporaries,' among whom are the over-55 retired ex-regulars. Though we discuss the latter more fully under the reserve army, it is pertinent to note that the reproduction of a sizeable proportion of reserve army workers is out of the labour aristocracy, and that this process generates powerful forces in opposition to those which secure the loyalty of the latter to capital. When the same working-class agents are made to fulfil two contradictory functions required by capital accumulation, albeit at different times in their lives, the performance of both roles might be threatened. What has held the contradictory demands on the loyalty of the labour aristocracy in balance have been the postwar boom, which has allowed capital to provide job security until, and a living wage towards the time of, retirement and the comparative ease with which temporary jobs have been obtained after this, even if at lower wages than before. We will see below how the present crisis is altering the balance of forces in a way that might seriously undermine the loyalty of the labour aristocracy. How far capital can respond to restore the balance is an open question, since the forces that have shaped this fraction of the working class are themselves products of previous barriers to accumulation and are integral to the functioning of Japanese capitalism as a whole.

I have outlined how traditional familial relations function to channel workers into the labour aristocracy in a way that simultaneously conceals the real basis of both the difference between workers and employers and the differences that normally exist among members of the working class. Since the agents who occupy bourgeois, middle-class, and labour-aristocracy positions are all reproduced almost entirely out of men according to their educational background and length of employment, Japan takes the form of a stratified rather than a class society: there is no visible difference between inter-class and intra-class forces. This is of the utmost importance, since as we shall see when we examine the ideology and organisation of the working class as a whole, consciousness in Japan (as elsewhere) is determined more by the form than by the substance of Japanese capitalism. I conclude this section with a brief analysis of the composition of those persons who mediate the role of the labour aristocracy.

Since the employment system in monopoly firms was originally modelled on and has remained broadly the same as that in public corporations and in the civil service, to analyse the composition of the labour aristocracy requires identifying those working-class members of all three types of institution who receive the material benefits I have outlined. This requires the exclusion of two main groups of workers: (*a*) all the different types of temporary, part-time, and day labourers who have no seniority and therefore no overriding reason to knuckle down in order one day to receive deferred wage payments; (*b*) almost all women workers, since most of those whom the company regards as 'permanent' are under 35 and unmarried. They will 'retire' when they marry and will never receive their deferred wages. Most married women are over 35, and they are normally only hired in one or other temporary capacity. Almost the only women in the labour aristocracy are the small number in monopoly firms who never marry and a slightly larger number in government.

If we break down the total economically active population according to the main familial characteristics that channel the Japanese into classes and class fractions, we can get a general picture of the size of the labour aristocracy. Table 5.4 does this by firm size, age, education, and sex for all employees in Japan, although for firms

Table 5.4. *Numbers of employees, by firm size, education, and sex, 1979 (1,000 persons)*

Firm size (persons)	Education	Age 15–34	35–54	55–9	60 and over	Total
1–9	School/other	2,569	2,840	367	549	6,325
	University	552	304	41	57	955
10–99	School/other	3,863	5,014	689	765	10,331
	University	1,136	583	72	95	1,886
100–299	School/other	1,444	1,556	190	166	3,357
	University	566	276	32	35	909
300–999	School/other	1,102	1,057	110	78	2,346
	University	540	280	27	24	873
1,000 and over	School/other	2,665	2,659	225	112	5,661
	University	1,077	757	50	29	1,913
Government	School/other	944	1,502	201	154	2,801
	University	1,064	856	87	33	2,040
Total[a]	School/other	12,608	14,646	1,785	1,826	30,864
	University	4,935	3,059	309	275	8,578
Of which male						
100–299	School/other	888	976	125	128	2,119
	University	410	246	30	35	720
300–999	School/other	674	755	79	63	1,570
	University	423	261	27	23	735
1,000 and over	School/other	1,667	2,078	170	71	3,988
	University	781	722	47	27	1,576
Government	School/other	645	1,033	131	98	1,907
	University	575	653	72	29	1,329

[a]Includes unclassified.
Source: *Shūgyō kōzō kihon chōsa hōkoku*, 1979, pp. 88–93.

with fewer than 100 employees the breakdown by sex (in the combination presented) was not available. Although some firms with fewer than 1,000 workers are in the monopoly sector, the clearest cut-off point for this sector is firms larger than this and government. In order to get a rough estimate of the size of the labour aristocracy we must subtract the members of the bourgeoisie, the middle class, and the reserve army. If the first two largely coincide with university graduates, and the third with men over 55 and most women, then the core agents of the labour aristocracy are those males under the age of 55 in firms with over 1,000 employees and in government, that is, some 5,423,000 persons.

Table 5.5. *Summary of class membership of all employees, 1980*

	Non-monopoly[a]	Monopoly	Total
Corporate sector/total	22,051,000	7,574,000	29,625,000
– Bourgeoisie	5,507,738	887,656	6,395,394
– Middle class[b]	1,890,355	304,645	2,195,000
Teachers[c]	206,690	33,310	240,000
Medical/health[d]	512,420	82,580	595,000
Technocrats[d]	73,203	11,797	85,000
Shunin[d]	1,098,042	176,958	1,275,000
= Working class	14,652,907	6,381,699	21,034,606
Government/total	—	4,841,000	4,841,000
– Bourgeoisie	—	532,510	532,510
– Middle class	—	1,594,000	1,594,000
Teachers	—	760,000	760,000
Police/military	—	489,000	489,000
Technocrats/shunin/medical	—	345,000	345,000
= Working class	—	2,714,490	2,714,490
Unincorporated sector/total	4,963,000	—	4,963,000
– Bourgeoisie (functionaries)	277,000	—	277,000
= Working class	4,686,000	—	4,686,000
Total working class	19,338,907	9,096,189	28,435,096

[a]Although firms with over ¥100 million capital do not coincide exactly with those having over 1,000 employees, monopoly firms are assumed to be either. Errors on either side probably cancel out.
[b]The distribution of the middle class into the monopoly and non-monopoly sectors is assumed to be the same as that of the bourgeoisie.
[c]Only about 24% of teachers are in the private sector. See *Wagakuni no kyōiku suijun*, 1980, pp. 80–1, 89.
[d]Although these groups in the middle class are dispersed between the private and the state sectors, they are concentrated in the former, and 85% were assumed to be there.
Sources: Table 1.22; table 4.12; *Shūgyō kōzō kihon chōsa hōkoku*, 1979, pp. 50, 52.

However, a few adjustments need to be made to this number. First, not all university-educated males in monopoly firms, particularly those under the age of 35, would be in the bourgeoisie or the middle class, so that some 300,000 of them should be added to the labour aristocracy. So should a similar number of women in the 35–54 age group, particularly in government, where the exclusion of such women from regular status is not as widely practised as it is in the private sector. However, members of the bourgeoisie and middle class would account for a considerable proportion of government employees, some of whom should therefore be subtracted. A more precise estimate might be made if the class membership of all employees in the public and private sector is summarised, so that those who are in the bourgeoisie and the middle class might be subtracted. Table 5.5 presents the results of these calculations.

If from the 6.4 million working-class people in the corporate monopoly sector and the 2.7 million in government we subtracted at least all the women under 35 and all the women and men without university education over 55 (that is, about 1.34 million and 0.65 million respectively), we would have an upper limit on the labour aristocracy of some 7.1 million. If 5.5 million were to be the lower limit, a realistic estimate would be somewhere in between. However, until we know how many temporary and other types of casual labourers there are in the monopoly and government sectors, that is, until we have examined the other fractions of the working class, we cannot be more precise than this. It is thus time to look at the conditions of the mass worker in the massive number of non-monopoly firms scattered throughout the country.

The mass worker

If the labour aristocracy is a product of advanced productive forces, what determines and characterises the mass worker is employment by less concentrated and centralised capitals. Though all workers are in identical relationships to capital in general, the fact of uneven development among the many capitals that constitute it requires a division of the working class according to the types of material conditions the different capitals are able to provide. Differences in these conditions – wages, bonuses, welfare, and so on – are not the cause of the divisions within the working class, but the visible effects of the fundamental cause: uneven accumulation and the continual coexistence of backward with more advanced capitals. Wages and conditions are not determined independently of the rate of accumulation, but by that rate, and differences in wages and conditions are the effects of the different levels of productive forces resulting from different rates of accumulation. The more backward capitals with below-average technology can only continue to exist so long as they provide below-average working conditions to compensate for their technical disadvantages. Although uneven rates of accumulation among industries have also required some compensating differences in working conditions, the major differences are between monopoly and non-monopoly capitals in all industries.

Tables 5.2 and 5.3 have already shown the extent of the variations in wages, bonuses, and welfare conditions. These do not, however, correspond to a need for monopoly capital but not for non-monopoly capital to provide a material basis to secure their workers' loyalty, since the deferment of wages is practised by both. Rather the differences correspond largely to unequal abilities to employ these methods. In order to attract young workers in the first place, non-monopoly capital must offer starting wages which are comparable to starting wages in the monopoly sector. By doing so, the proportion of the total wage which it can defer is reduced, and with it the ability to use deferred wages as a means of securing workers' loyalty. Fig. 5.1 shows that the starting wages of all workers are not very different in large and small firms, but that the differentials widen with length of service.

However, non-monopoly capital's reduced ability to secure workers' loyalty by means of material incentives does not mean that it has had significantly greater problems of industrial conflict. This is partly because in most cases the more backward productive forces in small firms have not yet created a division of labour and a collective worker with the power to make larger wage deferments necessary. The greatest problems of worker indiscipline have been in medium-sized firms, which cannot compete with monopoly capital's wages, but which have considerably socialised the labour process in factories that bring together fairly large numbers of workers.[5] Elsewhere, and increasingly as firms become smaller, the familial form assumed by class relations in Japan is reproduced as much by actual personal contact between workers and bosses as through the structure of material incentives, which are more crucial in large firms where direct personal relations between workers and top-level management are rare.

What employers in small firms cannot provide in material conditions they provide in genuine personal concern. Although they are typically more authoritarian and reactionary than the global capitalist (the hierarchy which performs their function in the monopoly sector), they are also more respected, since the loyalty they cultivate is to themselves personally. Since they are personally seen as the provider of their workers' livelihood, the familial form of the capitalist relation in Japan is reproduced more purely than in the monopoly sector. Even most incorporated non-monopoly firms are largely owned by single families, and the head (normally a male) of this household appears as the head of an extended family which includes all his workers. Class relations therefore more thoroughly assume the form of familial relations, particularly since some of the workers will be actual relatives, either younger sons and daughters or more distant kin. The material basis of the employer's use of extra-economic coercion (the traditional ideology demanding loyalty and obedience to him personally) is therefore a much closer correspondence between family relations and production relations than exists in monopoly firms. The boss is both employer and head of the household which owns the firm. He does not need to provide his workers with the same material incentives for compliance as does monopoly capital.

The form of class action assumed by the mass workers' difficulty in reproducing their labour power on non-monopoly wages and conditions is not typically strike action, which is seen and treated as a mark of gross ingratitude to their employers, but a greater propensity to change jobs in search of better conditions. Rates of labour turnover in the non-monopoly sector vary widely and have been known to reach enormous proportions. A 1972 study of small firms in Tokyo revealed that almost 60% of employees in commerce and services, and 42% in manufacturing, had changed jobs twice.[6] A more general comparative view of the phenomenon is provided in table 5.6.

In spite of the reduced number of job opportunities in large firms after 1974 (see chapter 6), the rates of turnover in small firms remained twice those of large firms, as people still looked for better pay and conditions in firms larger than their own. However, more and more of these job changes had to be from one small firm to another, whereas before 1974 it was easier to move upwards in the hierarchy of firms. Those most eager to move have always been the under-35-year-olds, of whom 10–12% in firms with fewer than 100 employees moved in 1974.[7]

One form of deferred wages which has not been mentioned yet and which reinforces the pressure on mass workers to 'vote with their feet' is their retirement pay. Some firms provide only lump sums, while others separate the total amount into a lump sum and a division of the remainder into annual payments stretched over a number of years. In either case, monopoly firms can withhold larger amounts from ordinary wages to pay for what appear to be very generous handouts. Table 5.7 shows the discrepancies by firm size, education, and years of service. It also indicates the relatively small amounts women receive,

Table 5.6. *Persons who moved to new jobs the previous year in relation to total employees in 1979, by size of firm left* (*1,000*)

	1–9	10–99	100–299	300–999	1,000 and over	Government	Total
Total engaged	7,276	12,250	4,231	3,218	7,574	4,841	34,549
No. who left the previous year	379	590	176	131	227	80	1,585
% who left	5.2	4.8	4.2	4.1	2.9	1.7	4.6

Source: Shūgyō kōzō kihon chōsa hōkoku, 1979, pp. 50–2, 342–3.

Table 5.7. *Total present value[a] of pensions, by education, firm size, years of service, and age when received, 1980 (¥ million)*

Education and firm size (persons)	Average age when received							
	25	28	32	45	48	53	55	Retirement
	10 years' service			30 years' service				
University								
1,000 and over	—	—	1.7	—	—	15.2	16.7	18.0
300–999	—	—	1.6	—	—	12.3	12.5	13.9
Under 300	—	—	1.3	—	—	10.1	11.3	12.0
High school								
1,000 and over	—	1.3	—	—	12.0	—	15.9	16.8
300–999	—	1.3	—	—	10.1	—	13.4	13.6
Under 300	—	1.2	—	—	8.4	—	11.8	12.4
Middle school								
1,000 and over	1.0	—	—	8.6	—	—	13.3	14.3
300–999	1.0	—	—	8.5	—	—	11.6	12.1
Under 300	0.9	—	—	6.8	—	—	9.9	10.3

[a]Includes lump-sum payments as well as present value of later instalments.
Source: Furukawa ed., *Chingin kentō shiryō*, pp. 378, 380, 382.

since it is mainly they who 'retire' after some ten years of service and men who can maintain uninterrupted work records of thirty or more years. The discrepancies caused by the sex–gender system are once again beautifully concealed.

Apart from these and other types of withheld wages, which together result in much wider real differentials between the monopoly and non-monopoly sectors, workers in the latter must endure at least two additional disadvantages: longer working hours and higher risks of industrial accidents. Table 5.8 indicates the extent of the difference in hours as well as the difference in the number of working days per month. Although the recession resulted in a greater increase in hours for workers in large firms than small ones, the differences have remained substantial.

Longer working hours in small firms form a major means by which non-monopoly capital compensates for its technical backwardness, almost the entire burden of which it places on the working class. Although functionaries must put up with lower salaries than their counterparts in the monopoly sector, they are nonetheless responsible

Table 5.8. *Average number of working days and hours worked per month, by firm size, 1975–9*

Firm size (operatives)	Days		Hours			
			Total		Of which fixed	
	1979	1975	1979	1975	1979	1975
500 and over	21.1	20.9	173.8	166.6	157.6	155.8
100–499	21.9	21.7	175.1	171.9	161.9	160.6
30–99	22.6	22.3	178.7	175.5	167.0	165.8
5–29	23.6	23.4	183.8	182.7	N.A.	N.A.

Source: Rōdōshō tōkei jōhōbu [Information Department of the Ministry of Labour], *Maitsuki kinrō tōkei yōran* [Summary Tables of Monthly Employment Statistics] (Tokyo: Rōdō hōrei kyōkai, 1980), pp. 68–9, 88.

Table 5.9. *Rate of industrial accidents, by firm size (manufacturing), 1975–80*

	Year	Firm size					
		1,000 and over	500–999	300–499	100–299	50–99	30–49
Accident rate[a]	1975	1.64	3.23	5.14	8.27	11.91	15.81
	1980	0.82	1.77	2.76	4.90	—	—
Rate of intensity[b]	1975	0.29	0.34	0.43	0.48	0.74	0.91
	1980	0.14	0.23	0.26	0.43	—	—

[a]Number of persons laid off more than 1 day per million working hours.
[b]Number of days lost per thousand working hours.
Source: Rodōshō [Ministry of Labour], *Rōdō hakusho* [White Paper on Labour] (Tokyo: Nihon rōdō kyōkai, 1976 and 1981), 1976, p. 286; 1981, fuzoku shiryō, p. 77.

for ensuring that workers accept the conditions capital can afford, not least greater exposure to industrial hazards. Table 5.9 shows how these hazards increase as firms become smaller. In 1975, in a small firm with about 40 workers, one would have an accident each year, which means that at some stage during their working lives most workers would be affected. However, in firms with over 1,000 employees the rate was only about one worker every three or four years, and few would be affected.[8] By 1980, both the rate and intensity of accidents had fallen even further in large firms and to some extent in medium-sized firms. Unfortunately, the Labour Ministry's survey did not cover small firms that year, although the tendency had been for the rate of accidents to fall, but not their intensity.

Since in all respects, therefore, the conditions of the mass worker are vastly inferior to those of the labour aristocracy, strategies for class struggle depend greatly on the relative size of each fraction. However, because there is some mobility between small and large firms as well as from regular to temporary jobs, these estimates must await analysis of the reserve army.

The reserve army

The function of the reserve army is to allow the usual forms of uneven development, which require reducing the value of the working class's labour power and shunting workers in and out of the labour process, to occur without serious threats to the overall functioning of the system. In Japan, this role has been played more effectively than in most advanced capitalist societies, which is a major reason for the relatively smooth reproduction of bourgeois social relations in that country. To clarify why this is so requires a detailed examination of what a reserve army is and how it works.

Since uneven development takes three main forms, the reserve army must play three corresponding roles. The first is related to the widespread increases in accumulation that (under appropriate conditions) can follow such cases of scientific or technical progress as the invention of the steam engine, the motor car, and even the silicon chip. Accumulation in a variety of industries can be favourably affected by such momentous advances in any one of them.[9] However, a crucial condition on which this depends is whether capital has at its disposal sufficient workers to carry out the expansion. To avoid drawing them from other capitalist enterprises and either bidding up wages intolerably or provoking social unrest through the rapid destruction of backward firms, a large pool of *latent* workers must be available. So that the capitalist relationship is not threatened at its existing and increasingly weakest points, the bulk of the workers needed for the new developments must come from outside capitalist production. Their departure from their previous productive activities can only avoid a serious threat to capital in general if these activities are under pre- or non-capitalist relations.

However, the coexistence of rapid accumulation in some industries with modest and often declining accumulation in others will sooner or later lead to a social crisis unless the differences are somehow gradually reduced. Industries, or capitals within industries, that remain backward in the long term will need to disappear. To smooth over the transition, some workers will have to *float* to and fro for a while, though it might be possible for most to spend their working lives where they are. Since capital will not require the reproduction of their jobs, the new generations of workers can move straight into the expanding sectors and help smooth over the transition.

Apart from these epochal stages in capitalist development, it is normal in any period for all capitals to make regular, even if relatively small, adjustments to their workforces. Never sure of what lies ahead, no capital can be certain that the exact number of workers required one year will still be needed the next. For this reason as well, a pool of workers who are prepared to float from one employer to another, regardless of wages or working conditions, is necessary to the normal functioning of capitalist production.

In addition to latent and floating workers, about once each generation capital requires large numbers of workers to be shifted out of employment for extended periods corresponding to the length of these extended depressions. They will become *stagnant*, and because they have no alternative form of subsistence, they can be the most dangerous from capital's point of view. Even outside conditions of general depression, some workers for whom no capital can find a use will be laid off and form a stagnant reserve. Wherever possible, they must be somehow recycled into the latent pool, so that they have some form of subsistence to prevent their growth into a revolutionary force.

Each of the latent, floating, and stagnant groups of workers is both a product and a condition of the normal process of uneven development. Their main functions are to allow capital to adjust the numbers of workers needed at any time to the requirements of profitability, adjustments which involve continual movements of workers in and out of employment. However, profitability is also served by these shifts through their effects on the *value of the labour power* of the working class as a whole. The continual possibility of bringing in new workers enables capital to prevent existing ones from bidding up wages, and the reserve army as a whole ensures that the value of labour power does not rise above what profitability can tolerate.

As a cushion for uneven development in Japan, the reserve army has so far functioned close to the ideal. No large stagnant reserve has built up, and workers who have not been needed have usually been converted into some or other latent reserve with a relatively independent subsistence. Floating workers have been available in sufficient numbers to permit fairly smooth adjustments to uneven development. Furthermore, the working-class agents in the reserve army have on the whole been different from those in the other two fractions of their class, so that the danger of united working-class action has been averted.

This last condition is important, because if all workers stand a more or less equal chance of sinking into the reserve, there is a danger that other fractions of the working class will make common cause with it. Fortunately for the Japanese bourgeoisie, traditional familial relations have once again come to the rescue and channelled workers into the reserve army primarily according to age and sex. The insecurity of these positions thereby takes the form of the insecurity of particular persons in the family hierarchy, namely women and the very old.

Although because of their relative predominance in certain jobs and industries (for example, typing and the service industry) women cannot fulfil all functions of the reserve army on their own, they do so to a degree far in excess of their sisters in other capitalist societies. They are particularly useful in the ease with which they can be converted from a stagnant to a latent reserve, since even when they are laid off and cannot find jobs they secure through their husbands a subsistence independent of their own wages. Their role in the sexual division of labour in the family also predisposes them to accept the status of latent worker. A survey conducted in 1975 by the Office of the Prime Minister confirmed that they were both prepared and expected to sink into the latent reserve when they married or had children. Table 5.10 presents their answers to the question 'What do you think of using marriage or having children as an opportunity [*sic*] to retire?'

Far from being an opportunity for working women, early retirement allows capital to replace older and more highly paid workers with cheap new recruits. The widespread practice of retiring women when they marry and have children therefore simultaneously reproduces the latent reserve and uses it to keep wage costs down. The young women who retire so willingly are never paid their deferred wages, since when capital draws on this latent reserve they

Table 5.10. *Strength of the ideology supporting the sexual division of labour, 1975*

	Should women retire on marriage or having children?			
	Naturally	Inevitably	No	Don't know
Males	22%	58%	12%	8%
Females	17%	61%	13%	9%

Source: Rōdōshō fujin–shōnen kyoku [The Women and Young People's Bureau of the Ministry of Labour], Fujin rōdō no jitsujō [The Real Situation of Women Workers] (Tokyo: Ōkurashō insatsukyoku, 1976), p. 75.

Table 5.11. *Women's wages as a percentage of men's, by age and by length of service, 1980 (and averages for 1975)*

	Average		Length of service (years)			
Age	1975	1980	0	3–4	10–14	20–9
17	92.7	89.2	86.2	—	—	—
18–19	91.1	92.4	92.3	86.6	—	—
20–4	85.3	87.6	85.1	90.4	—	—
25–9	75.5	78.1	67.9	77.6	80.1	—
30–4	63.9	65.1	56.5	62.6	74.9	—
35–9	55.9	55.9	52.9	55.6	61.7	70.7
40–4	54.1	50.4	52.8	54.7	59.0	68.5
45–9	56.1	50.9	53.8	55.3	59.6	67.2
50–4	53.5	54.3	57.7	59.0	63.3	64.8
55–9	58.2	59.3	59.3	56.1	64.9	71.7
60–4	66.4	68.5	60.7	64.8	67.1	72.1
65 and over	66.4	73.2	69.8	73.4	68.7	76.8
Average, 1980	—	59.4	69.0	68.3	65.9	67.1
Average, 1975	61.4	—	86.6	68.3	68.1	73.8

Source: Fujin rōdō no jitsujō, 1976, p. 58; 1981, p. 89.

re-enter the workforce without seniority. Neither do middle-aged mothers who have lost a few years', or even months', 'experience' ever acquire any real seniority, since even if they work a full week, they receive the ambiguous status of 'non-regulars' or 'permanent temporaries.' In fact, the average number of days taken off by working women in 1978 was only 36.6 days before childbirth and 48.3

after childbirth.[10] Nevertheless, this has been sufficient to rob them of their work records. Table 5.11 shows that middle-aged men and women who enter new jobs are treated quite differently: some of the men's previous experience is recognised, but the women are treated like young girls. It also shows how women's wages fell relative to men's during the recession years, particularly for those aged 40–9 and those without any years of previous service.

Because men who switch jobs before they reach retirement age do not lose their seniority entirely, some can often get better wages by doing so, particularly when they move from smaller to larger firms. This type of labour turnover does not concern the floating reserve, because capital cannot with impunity take the initiative when it involves men under 55. What legitimises capital's initiative in the case of the floating reserve is that the workers have all 'retired.' They can then be kept on or not, but only at reduced wages and with the ambiguous status of 'non-regular employee.' Since men and women 'retire' at different times in their lives, the ages at which they enter the floating reserve are correspondingly different. Only between the ages of 15 and 29 and again after 60, when both men and women are of pre- and post-retirement age respectively, is there any comparability in their membership of different fractions of the working class. Table 5.11 shows that wage differentials are narrowest during these years, and Table 5.12 that this is because only then are their average years of service almost the same.

If length of service is one of the ways in which women's inferior pay and conditions are concealed, then education is another, since women not only have shorter work records but on average lower levels of education than men. Only 12.3% of female high school graduates proceeded to university in 1980, in comparison with 39.3% of males in the same category.[11] If one therefore controls for both length of service and education, the differences in payment between the sexes are reduced to levels comparable in other capitalist societies, though in 1980 middle-aged women without a university education still got only about 70% of what their male counterparts got.[12]

However, since the overwhelming majority of women under 30 are never paid their deferred wages and in practice 'retire' as soon as they marry, often only for very brief periods, they spend almost their whole lives performing one or other function of the reserve army. Until retirement they form a reserve of cheap floating workers; they then sink into the latent reserve for varying lengths of time; and finally

Table 5.12. *Average years of employment, by age and sex, 1975–80*

Age	Males		Females	
	1980	1975	1980	1975
17 and under	1.0	1.2	1.3	1.4
18–19	1.0	1.4	1.1	1.4
20–4	3.0	3.2	2.9	2.9
25–9	6.0	5.7	5.5	4.8
30–4	9.3	9.1	6.8	6.5
35–9	12.8	11.6	7.3	7.0
40–4	15.1	14.3	7.8	8.3
45–9	17.3	17.6	9.4	10.2
50–4	19.9	18.8	11.2	10.4
55–9	14.8	14.5	10.8	10.1
60–4	10.3	10.3	10.8	9.8
65 and over	11.4		12.9	
Average	11.3	10.1	6.3	5.8

Source: Fujin rōdō no jitsujō, 1981, p. 68.

Table 5.13. *Women employees, by age and marital status, 1979 (1,000 persons)*

	Total		Age			
	No.	%	15–24	25–34	35–54	55 and over
Total	13,238	100.0	3,119	3,120	5,727	1,273
Married	7,462	56.4	272	1,948	4,564	677
Never married	4,366	33.0	2,841	1,046	428	50
Widowed/divorced	1,410	10.7	6	126	735	546

Source: Shūgyō kōzō kihon chōsa hōkoku, 1979, pp. 112, 114.

many re-enter the floating reserve. Out of a total of 13.2 million women employees in 1979, less than half a million were in the 30–54 age group and had never married. They were unambiguously outside the reserve army. The rest were either in that fraction of the working class or never very far from it. Table 5.13 presents the breakdown of women employees in 1979 by their marital status and their age. One of the most important developments in the years since 1974 was that the proportion of married women increased from 49.6% to 56.4% of the total, indicating mainly the need for working-class households to send extra wage earners out to supplement their declining real incomes.[13] Supplements were all that they could get, since even in 1980 a wife's earnings comprised on average no more than 7.0% of household income.[14]

To estimate the size of the female latent reserve, we must first subtract from the total number of employees those who are in the bourgeoisie, the middle class, and the labour aristocracy. In 1979, only 5.2% of persons listed in the Employment Status Survey as managers and officials were women.[15] If we regard this as the rough proportion of women in the bourgeoisie as a whole, then of the 7,204,904 employees in the bourgeoisie in 1979, 374,655 were women. If we also subtract the 1,262,000 women in the middle class (see p. 140 above) and the 300,000 in the labour aristocracy (see p. 171 above), and if we ignore the 428,000 in the 30–55 age group who had never married (most of whom were bourgeois, middle class, or in the labour aristocracy), the remaining 11.3 million would be divided between the mass and the reserve army. However, since mass workers have a level of job security and payment in non-monopoly firms which few women workers enjoy, about the same proportion of women in small firms would belong to this fraction of the working class as belong to the labour aristocracy in monopoly firms, that is, 8.3%. Since there were 9,618,000 women employees in the non-monopoly sector in 1979, about 800,000 would have been in the mass fraction rather than the reserve army. The remaining 10.5 million were thus the active members of the reserve army, whose function it has been to keep the average level of wages within the limits that capital accumulation requires as well as to float from job to job in response to unevennesses in this process.

It is possibly even more difficult to make precise estimates of the females in the latent and stagnant reserves, though some survey data can provide general indications of the numbers of women capital can draw on. According to the government's 1979 Employment Status Survey, a full 8.5 million women, of whom 7.7 million were doing unpaid housework,[16] were 'wishing to work,' presumably in paid jobs. Table 5.14 shows the total numbers of people in this category, by sex and by age, in 1974 and 1979.

A rough division of these people into latent and stagnant reserves can be made according to the extent of their alternative sources of

Table 5.14. *Persons 'wishing to work,' by age and sex, 1974 and 1979* *(1,000 persons)*

	Males		Females		Total	
Age	1974	1979	1974	1979	1974	1979
15–24	696	623	1,218	926	1,914	1,549
25–34	147	213	2,998	3,207	3,144	3,420
35–54	199	295	2,776	3,408	2,975	3,703
55–64	205	368	534	702	738	1,069
65 and over	213	330	232	281	445	612
Total	1,459	1,829	7,757	8,524	9,217	10,353

Source: Shūgyō kōzō kihon chōsa hōkoku, 1974, pp. 229, 233; 1979, p. 294.

subsistence. We make the division by examining the incomes of the households they were in as well as their status in these households, since the family would have been the main source of an alternative subsistence. Table 5.15 suggests that most persons wishing to work in 1979 were latent rather than stagnant workers, since most were in households with incomes of more than ¥2 million, which was probably the minimum a family of two or more persons needed to live on that year. However, anyone not earning in a two-or-more-person household with less than ¥2 million or on his or her own with less than ¥1 million in 1979 could not really be said to have an alternative subsistence. The 1,819,000 women and the 823,000 men in this category were thus the most obvious agents of the stagnant reserve. Another 350,000 women who were themselves household heads, or who were in households where household heads had no jobs, and total household income was less than ¥5 million, were perhaps bordering on the stagnant reserve. So were some 370,000 men in the same category. But if they are excluded, the latent reserve would have come to some 6,705,000 women and 1,006,000 men in 1979. It seems therefore that Japanese capitalism has been able to recycle un-employed married women, through the sexual division of labour in the family, into the less threatening of the two unemployed groups in the reserve army. We shall see below how the current crisis is beginning to interfere with this process and how the working class as a whole is affected by the changes.

Although women are overwhelmingly concentrated in and form

Table 5.15. *Persons 'wishing to work,' by sex, household income, and relationship to household head, 1979 (1,000 persons)*

Relationship to household head and household head's employment	Annual household income (¥ mil.)				
	Under 1	1–2	2–5	Over 5	Total
Females, total	*501*	*1,380*	*5,352*	*1,264*	*8,524*
Household head	62	77	88	11	243
Spouse of household head					
Who has a job	71	968	4,289	823	6,153
Who has no job	71	106	119	23	320
Family member of household head					
Who has a job	19	118	698	365	1,200
Who has no job	25	49	146	41	261
One-person households	252	62	10	1	333
Males, total	*416*	*435*	*729*	*226*	*1,829*
Household head	143	272	330	67	817
Spouse of household head	2	2	2	0	6
Family member of household head					
Who has a job	17	74	347	149	586
Who has no job	19	28	40	10	97

Source: *Shūgyō kōzō kihon chōsa hōkoku*, 1979, pp. 304–7.

the bulk of the reserve army, they are clearly not the only members of it. They are joined by at least four categories of men: 'non-regulars' who are rehired after retirement (*shokutaku*), 'part-timers' (*rinjikō*), and 'day labourers' (*hiyatoi*) in the floating reserve and the 'wishing to work' in the latent and stagnant reserves.

What distinguishes the rapid turnover of mass workers in the non-monopoly sector from the floating of reserve workers in and out of both sectors are the different reasons the two groups have for changing jobs. The former leave largely at their own initiative in search of improved conditions, while the latter typically move out of regular jobs to less-secure and less-remunerative ones because they are of post-retirement age. This is confirmed by the reasons given by persons who changed jobs or gave up work in 1979. The overwhelming majority of the total over the age of 55 as well as women under 35 gave reasons which had little or nothing to do with any initiative of their own. In the case of men under 35, the proportions were reversed. Table 5.16 reveals that, if we regard reasons for movements of workers as indicators of the class fraction to which they belong, there

Table 5.16. *Movements of reserve army and mass workers, by age and sex, 1979 (1,000 persons)*

	Age					
	Under 35		35–54		55 and over	
	No.	%	No.	%	No.	%
Persons who changed jobs[a]	*1,096*	*100.0*	*532*	*100.0*	*147*	*100.0*
Mass workers[b]	499	45.5	207	38.9	17	11.6
Floating workers[c]	319	29.1	199	37.4	109	74.1
Of which males[a]	671	100.0	312	100.0	122	100.0
Mass workers	350	52.2	123	39.4	15	12.3
Floating workers	165	24.6	121	38.8	94	77.0
Of which females[a]	424	100.0	220	100.0	25	100.0
Mass workers	151	35.6	84	38.2	3	12.0
Floating workers	153	36.1	87	39.5	13	52.0
Persons who stopped work[a]	*1,073*	*100.0*	*518*	*100.0*	*557*	*100.0*
Mass workers	204	19.0	93	18.0	25	4.5
Latent/stagnant reserve[d]	674	62.8	299	57.7	476	85.5
Of which males[a]	202	100.0	119	100.0	344	100.0
Mass workers	81	40.1	20	16.8	14	4.1
Latent/stagnant reserve	60	29.7	78	65.5	307	89.2
Of which females[a]	871	100.0	399	100.0	212	100.0
Mass workers	105	12.1	71	17.8	8	3.8
Latent/stagnant reserve	612	70.3	223	55.9	166	78.3

[a]Totals include persons who gave reasons other than the ones included in the classification.
[b]Mass workers were regarded as those who either changed jobs or gave up work because of the wages or conditions in their former jobs.
[c]Floating workers were seen as those who changed jobs for any of the following reasons: lay-off, bankruptcy, temporary job, transfer of a family member, marriage or child care, retirement, illness, and old age.
[d]Stagnant or latent workers are those who gave up work for any of the reasons in note c. They are not distinguished, because whether or not they have an alternative subsistence is not relevant here.
Source: *Shūgyō kōzō kihon chōsa hōkoku*, 1979, pp. 346–7.

is a very clear distinction between the mass worker and the reserve army.

Seventy-seven per cent of men over the age of 55 who changed jobs and 89% of those who gave up work seem to be in one or other group in the reserve army. Since the male members of this fraction of the

Table 5.17. *Present place of employment and wage reductions (by size of firm employed by in 1975) of workers who retired in 1967–73 (% of total number of persons in each category)*

Place at time of retirement	Total	Present place of employment				
		5,000 and over	1,000– 4,999	500–999	100–499	Under 100
Total	100.0	3.1	10.1	8.7	31.6	46.8
5,000 and over	58.6	2.2	6.2	5.2	20.7	24.3
1,000–4,999	29.2	0.8	3.2	1.7	7.0	16.5
500–999	7.9	0.1	0.7	1.6	1.6	3.9
100–499	4.3	0.0	0.0	0.2	2.3	1.8

	% wage reduction			
	Over 100%	25–100%	0–25%	No reduction
5,000 and over	18.9	43.4	21.3	16.4
1,000–4,999	14.1	42.1	24.2	19.6
500–999	16.1	34.3	22.5	27.1
300–499	12.8	31.2	22.9	33.1
100–299	20.6	24.1	14.9	40.4
Average	16.9	41.2	22.2	19.7

Source: Rōdōshō rōdō kijunkyoku [Labour Standards Bureau of the Ministry of Labour], *Teinen tōtatsusha chōsa no kekka* [Results of the Survey of People Who Reach Retirement Age] (Tokyo: Rōdōshō, July 1975), pp. 4, 28.

working class are overwhelmingly elderly workers, we need to examine what happens to workers after retirement. In general, they must change their places of employment as well as the type of work they do, they receive some form of temporary status, and they face large reductions in wages. According to a government survey of the persons (mainly men) who reached retirement age in 1967–73, 63.3% had to move to jobs in different establishments, mainly smaller ones than they had been in before. Table 5.17 shows that there was almost no movement in the other direction. The survey also shows that only 34.5% of these people did the same type of work they had done previously, revealing that they were used as mainly unskilled workers. Moreover, almost 76% of them received some or other form of temporary status: 66.7% became 'non-regulars' and 9.2% 'part-timers' or 'day labourers.' A full 33.7% had spent some time unemployed. Although among those who remained on in the same establishments as they had worked in before the proportions who had to do different jobs and accept temporary status were lower, this applied to only 36.7% of the people who retired during the period.[17] Finally, over 80% of the workers had to accept wage reductions on retirement.

Even this not so happy state of affairs for retired workers has worsened considerably under the impact of the recession, particularly for workers in large manufacturing firms where the greatest staff reductions were made. Caught between the contradictory demands both to get rid of older workers and to extend their retirement ages – made by the requirements of profitability and by trade unions respectively – large firms and government have so far done little beyond flaunting all kinds of promises. The state keeps demanding a general extension of the retirement age until at least 60 but preferably until 65, while individual capitals continue to replace high-paid older workers with new recruits. There is now even a White Paper on Retirement (*Teinen hakusho*), and the most recent issue included an analysis of surveys by the Labour Ministry in 1978 and 1980 on retirement. The results were not encouraging. As is revealed by table 5.18, still only 73% of firms had uniform retirement systems, and still almost 60% of those retired their employees by the age of 58. Of the 22.4% of surveyed firms with systems which were not uniform for men and women, 46% required women to retire by the age of 50 and another 46.7% by the age of 55.[18] Moreover, in the preceding two years only 8.1% of all surveyed firms said they had reformed their retirement systems, though another 18.2% said the matter was 'under investigation.' A full 70.9% indicated neither an intention to reform their systems nor even to 'investigate' the matter. Why was this? Nearly 82% of giant firms with over 5,000 employees said the wages of older workers were too high.[19]

On reaching retirement age, therefore, most workers have to look for new jobs, hopefully in the same firms under either re-employment or extension of employment schemes, or, for the second time in their lives, in the open labour market (*saishūshoku*). Table 5.19 shows that, even more so than in the past, recently retired workers must scratch around for jobs and tolerate substantial reductions in their income. Almost 30% of those who retired in 1978 were unemployed at the time of the survey.

Since the labour aristocracy which retires out of monopoly firms

Table 5.18. *Firms with uniform retirement systems, and the retirement ages in them, 1978–80*

	% of total with uniform retirement systems		Retirement age in firms with uniform systems (% of firms in each)							
			55		56–8		60		Over 60	
	Jan. 1978	Jan. 1980	1978	1980	1978	1980	1978	1980	1978	1980
5,000 and over	76.5	79.4	38.1	35.3	39.2	36.5	21.2	27.6	—	—
1,000–4,999	69.0	70.6	41.8	38.9	35.7	36.3	19.7	22.8	1.3	1.7
300–999	66.1	70.5	47.6	45.1	26.0	28.2	23.1	25.1	2.5	1.0
100–299	68.0	70.3	42.0	44.4	24.4	21.9	30.1	30.8	3.1	2.4
30–99	73.4	74.5	40.3	37.1	15.8	17.6	36.9	40.4	5.9	3.7
Average	71.3	73.0	41.3	39.5	19.3	19.9	33.7	36.5	4.8	3.2

Source: Teinen hakusho, 1980, p. 7.

Table 5.19. *Employment and wages of workers who retired in 1972, 1975, and 1978*

	1972	1975	1978
Total %	*100*	*100*	*100*
With jobs, total	83.8	80.7	70.1
Route to new job			
Employment extension and re-employment	25.0	28.5	31.2
Mediation by old company, e.g. in subsidiaries	28.1	25.2	23.1
Public works	6.0	7.2	4.7
Other	24.7	19.9	11.1
Unemployed	16.2	19.3	29.9
Present wage as % of previous wage	*100*	*100*	*100*
Under 50%	20.0	21.9	21.2
50–70%	33.1	37.6	39.6
70–80%	14.3	15.0	14.4
80–90%	13.2	11.4	10.4
90–100%	5.7	5.1	5.1
Over 100%	13.7	9.0	9.5

Source: Teinen hakusho, 1980, pp. 115–16.

must face either unemployment or massive wage reductions when it enters the reserve army, there is here an important material basis for working-class unity, which, as we see below, is becoming firmer as the crisis of Japanese capitalism deepens. However, so far most male members of the reserve army have managed to remain in the floating category, which in addition to 'non-regulars' includes what are known as 'part-timers' and 'day labourers.' The last two are closest to sinking into the latent (insofar as they have some form of subsistence) or, worse still, the stagnant reserve. Day labourers in particular are extremely insecure, since they must somehow find work each day. They tend to congregate in urban slums, such as the Sanya district in Tokyo or Kamagasaki in Osaka, and are herded onto buses employers send into the areas.

Large proportions of day labourers are middle-aged men or *burakumin* who have been excluded from the normal process by which workers are channelled into the 'familial' hierarchy.[20] One study of day labourers in the Sanya district revealed that even during the boom, in an average three-day period only 23.3% found work the full three days, 36.1% worked two days, and 13.4% remained on the streets. Being used for mainly heavy work, such as concreting or miscellaneous factory jobs, they would be lucky to have got ¥ 500 an hour in 1980, or even one-third of the monthly income of regular workers. Their conditions are generally similar to those of 'temporary part-timers' (*rinji pāto taimu*), which means they also get few of the welfare and other benefits of more regular workers, though not many fewer than 'regular part-timers' (*jōyō pāto taimu*).[21]

The use of part-time and temporary labourers as a means of reducing wages and asserting discipline has reached almost epidemic proportions in Japan.[22] Among women employees, their proportion increased from 12.2% in 1970 to 19.3% in 1980, the numbers almost doubling from 1.3 million to 2.56 million.[23] The numbers of men in this category grew from 0.86 million to 1.34 million in the same period. Part-timers are particularly numerous among school teachers (41.8% in 1979), shop assistants (33.4%), cash register operators (30.9%), debt collectors (42.0%), delivery persons (68.4%), wrappers (53.4%), cleaners (40.6%), ironers (38.9%), kitchen hands (42.1%), and waiters (54.9%).[24] In other words, the expansion of the service industry during the years of slowdown and restructuring elsewhere (see chapter 6) was very much at the price of those members of the reserve army who were forced to accept the wages and conditions of the bottom slot in the familial hierarchy.

Apart from their reduced wages and access to company welfare and other facilities, the job security of all the different workers in the reserve army is notably less than those outside it. A rough rule of thumb is the notice they receive should lay-offs be required: about a year for non-regulars, a month for regular part-timers, perhaps a week or so for temporary part-timers, and of course no warning at all for day labourers. In the case of unmarried women under 35, whom I have regarded as non-regulars even though they are officially accorded regular status so long as they remain single (or at least do not have children), this period is longer. The nearly four million women in this category are perhaps on the boundary between the reserve army and the other fractions of the working class.

It is now possible to estimate the numbers of workers who fulfil the functions of the Japanese reserve army, which turns out to be a surprisingly large force in view of that country's reputation for 'lifelong employment.' Table 5.20 provides these estimates using mainly previously supplied data. The most important characteristics of the Japanese working class are its sex composition and its large, but mainly floating and latent, reserves. Although only just over half of

Table 5.20. Summary of class membership of all employees and the working class, by main fractions and by sex, 1979 (1,000 persons)

	Non-monopoly			Monopoly			Total		
	Males	Females	Total	Males	Females	Total	Males	Females	Total
Bourgeoisie	5,484	301	5,785	1,346	74	1,420	6,830	375	7,205
Middle class	1,200	690	1,890	1,328	570	1,899	2,527	1,262	3,789
Active working class	10,708	8,630	19,339	6,126	2,971	9,096	16,834	11,601	28,435
Aristocracy	—	—	—	5,410	300	5,710	5,410	300	5,710
Mass workers	6,615	800	7,415	—	—	—	6,615	800	7,415
Floating reserve	4,093	7,829	11,922	716	2,671	3,387	4,809	10,500	15,309
Non-regulars[a]	2,098	5,191	7,289	470	2,011	2,481	2,568	7,202	9,770
Part-timers[b]	1,193	2,048	3,241	147	512	659	1,340	2,560	3,900
Day labourers[b]	802	590	1,392	99	148	247	901	738	1,639
Inactive working class	—	—	—	—	—	—	1,829	8,524	10,353
Latent reserve	—	—	—	—	—	—	1,006	6,705	7,711
Stagnant reserve	—	—	—	—	—	—	823	1,819	2,642
Total working class	—	—	—	—	—	—	18,663	20,125	38,788

[a] The males in this category are the ones over 55 without university education.
[b] For the sex and size of firm they work in, see Shūgyō kōzō chōsa hōkoku, 1979, pp. 56, 60.
Sources: Tables 5.4, 5.5. and 4.12; Shūgyō kōzō chōsa hōkoku, 1979.

Table 5.21. *Total employees, by industry (excluding directors),*
occupation, and sex, 1974–9 (1,000 persons)

	1974		1979	
	Total	Females as a % of total	Total	Females as a % of total
Industry				
Primary	630	34.1	459	24.0
Mining	138	14.5	99	12.1
Construction	3,283	13.0	3,848	13.3
Manufacturing	11,180	32.9	10,707	34.1
Wholesale/retail	6,026	43.4	7,249	44.6
Finance/insurance/real estate	1,496	45.7	1,675	48.4
Transport/communications	3,055	11.8	3,165	11.9
Electricity/gas/water	312	11.9	356	12.9
Services	6,007	48.2	7,407	50.1
Total (excluding government)	32,127	34.0	35,011	35.6
Occupation				
Professional and technical workers	3,171	39.5	3,821	45.3
Managers and officials	1,924	5.3	2,328	5.1
Clerical workers	8,348	45.6	8,818	49.2
Sales workers	3,727	32.0	4,658	31.4
Farmers/woodcutters/fisherpeople	586	35.5	424	22.9
Miners and related	81	6.2	51	3.9
Transport and communications workers	2,292	7.6	2,308	6.2
Craftspeople and production process workers	11,852	24.5	12,116	24.4
Labourers	1,355	34.0	1,530	36.2
'Protective' services (police etc.)	578	2.4	605	2.5
Service workers	2,169	67.1	2,734	66.1
Total (including government)	36,105	32.1	39,442	33.6

Source: *Shūgyō kōzō kihon chōsa hōkoku*, 1974, pp. 30–5, 44–5; 1979, pp. 44–8, 62–3.

the working class as a whole consists of women, the proportion rises to over two-thirds of the reserve army and 87% of the latent reserve. The stagnant reserve has remained comparatively small (6.8%), mainly because the patriarchal family and the petty bourgeois firm have taken over the function of securing the subsistence needs of unemployed workers.

Although having such a huge and submissive reserve army has contributed immeasurably to the survival of Japanese capitalism, the large proportion of women in it is a two-edged sword, since women cannot be relied on so heavily to perform both of the two main functions required of a reserve army. While they might almost entirely carry the burden of working at high rates of exploitation through their low wages, they cannot on their own be used to regulate the numbers of workers to the required degree in times of crisis. This is because women do not do the whole range of jobs which are affected by the crisis to the same degree as men, but are concentrated in certain industries and occupations. Table 5.21 shows that these are largely clerical jobs in the service and retail sectors. But since the industries which were worst hit by the recession in the late 1970s were in manufacturing, large numbers of men were also thrown out of work (see chapter 6). That they have been mainly older men has not helped matters either, because older men are meant to be accorded respect and obedience in Japanese society, not discarded on the scrap heap.

As a means of ensuring the reproduction of capitalist relations, therefore, channelling the members of the working class into its three main fractions on the basis of sex and education is superior to doing so on the basis of age. This is because all workers eventually become old and are sooner or later subjected to the demands placed on retired workers, while men who have once obtained a prestige education need not otherwise experience any of what being in the reserve army implies. The price capital must pay for its ability to make class society take the form of a familial-type stratified society is that the entire working class at some time or other gets a taste of being in the bottom 'strata.' So long as accumulation does not falter too greatly and male members of these 'strata' can at least continue to find jobs, this disadvantage of relying on age to conceal class relations is more than outweighed by its advantages. Until recently, therefore, capital has used age along with sex and educational background to ensure that the forces which divide the working class, like those which separate different classes, take the form of divisions within the traditional family: an aristocracy comprising younger men with the 'best' education; a mass of less-well-educated men, also in their prime; and a reserve of women and elderly men. The correspondence between the working class *positions* in each fraction and the familial attributes of the *agents* who occupy the positions, although never perfect, has been close enough to guarantee the appearance that divisions within the working class result from personal merits and failures rather than from capital's demands. Women and elderly men are thus made to blame their sex and age for the conditions under which they work (or fail to work).

The key to the survival of Japanese capitalism therefore lies not in its alleged provision of lifelong employment but in the fact that over half the economically active members of the working class have been conditioned to accept the antithesis of lifelong employment.

Organisation and ideology

Only when the phenomenal form assumed by class relations visibly becomes the capital–labour relation can the agents of the working class constitute themselves into a revolutionary social force. This relation must not simply be *determinant*, it must also be *dominant*: classes must both exist and appear to exist. In other words, class society must take the form of class society, so that the most important *determining* influence of one's work, one's income, and one's consumption, as well as on the persons with whom one is brought together side by side in engaging in these activities, is at the same time the most *visible* influence.[25] The essence of capitalist society, the creation and extraction of surplus value, must be laid bare so that it can dominate the minds, and not simply determine the lives, of the labouring masses.

Bringing together the substance and the form of class relations is not, however, simply a matter of propaganda, but primarily of understanding the conditions on which their separation is based and striving to alter these. The ideologies workers subscribe to, like those of other class agents, are shaped largely by their experiences and by what they do, and only marginally by what they are told. Whatever dominates these experiences and activities will dominate working-class ideology, and this is the form that their experiences take.

We have seen that the disjunction between the reality and the appearance of Japanese capitalism is based on the functioning of traditional familial relations as relations of production (that is, between classes) and as relations among the members of the working class. As a result of the traditional family's superimposition of its distinctions onto the different material forces which regulate capitalist development, infrastructural realities came to be mediated by familial relations and thus to serve as the basis of the dominance of these relations in everyday life. It is to be expected, therefore, that the organisation and ideology of the Japanese working class will reflect the familial form rather than the substance of class relations in that country.

Organisation

The most striking and notorious feature of trade unions in Japan is their organisation on the basis of enterprises rather than industries. Although the major enterprise unions in any industry might form loose associations, the latter do little more than permit the exchange of information, while all negotiations take place between the employers of particular firms and their respective unions, which are almost entirely autonomous in these matters. The sole external consideration is their tendency to confine what is negotiable to limits set by the top state and non-state organisations of the bourgeoisie, such as Keidanren.

The enterprise union as a form of working-class organisation in Japan is a product of the very forces which give that class its characteristic form: secure employment for males until retirement and the channelling of employees into classes (and fractions of classes) according to personal attributes associated with the traditional family and with their educational background. Since the dominant influences on union membership are identical to the dominant influences on class formation (the process by which classes assume their form), it is hardly surprising that unions function primarily to control workers and to contain class struggles rather than as vehicles of these struggles.

The most important basis of union membership, which is also dominant in the formation of both the labour aristocracy and the mass worker, is the status of regular employee. Union membership is limited not simply to employees in a particular company but to its regular employees. Day labourers, part-timers, and persons hired temporarily after retirement – that is, the entire reserve army apart from young women (who are regulars in name only) – are excluded. Employees destined for managerial positions are included until they reach the rank of section manager, while the jobs of defeated or retired union officials are kept open at the level of seniority they would have attained had they not assumed this position.

Unions are not therefore organisations of the working class, but of certain strata in the familial hierarchy, beneath which class relations are submerged in particular companies. Since regular employees can only retrieve their deferred wages by remaining in the same company, this becomes the only logical level at which to organise a union. But for this very reason, the union functions mainly as a means of integrating workers into the institution from which alone they can ultimately secure living wages. From capital's point of view, the need for a company union stems from the same source which requires the use of deferred wages and other methods of securing workers' loyalty.

It is no accident, therefore, that organised workers are overwhelmingly in the labour aristocracy (the main exception being young women). Since these are potentially the most threatening workers who are in firms too large for employers to create loyalties to themselves as individuals, organisations are needed to personalise the family relations for which material incentives could only lay the foundation. The use of the company song is just one example of monopoly capital's quest for alternatives to non-monopoly capital's personal touch.

There is very little evidence that unions have had much influence on levels of wages, which depend instead on firm size and industry, that is, on variations in rates of accumulation. Rather, company unions have been essential to securing the labour aristocracy's compliance with such requirements of faltering accumulation as characterised the latter half of the 1970s: cuts in real wages, increases in weekly working hours, and rationalisations of staff and equipment. Without company unions, for example, wages in the monopoly sector could not have been brought into line with the rate of accumulation as swiftly as they were, particularly in the years 1972–5. In the non-monopoly sector, where there are very few trade unions, this function is fulfilled by the close personal ties between workers and employers: the former are made to feel grateful for no more than what the latter can afford. Table 5.22 shows how the index of real wages in the manufacturing industry as a whole has closely followed the index of productivity.

The enormous discrepancy between the degree of unionisation in the monopoly and non-monopoly sectors therefore results from very much more than the greater ability of the collective worker in large factories to organise. It also has a lot to do with the fact that unions in the monopoly sector are tolerated by capital because they can be used to control workers. Monopoly capital's response to militant trade unions has rarely been an assault on unionism as such, but has almost always taken the form of encouraging the development of a rival company union, which can be used to bring workers into line. It is extremely difficult for militants to form an effective organisation, because the company is the only realistic level at which this can be

Table 5.22. *Indices of labour productivity, employment, real wages, and working hours in manufacturing 1970–80 (1975 = 100)*

	1970	1972	1974	1975	1976	1978	1980
Labour productivity	76.7	89.0	104.1	100.0	112.3	127.4	156.0
Employment	107.0	105.7	105.5	100.0	98.0	94.9	94.8
Real wages	75.3	89.6	100.3	100.0	102.7	105.3	109.3
Working hours	111.4	109.0	103.1	100.0	103.5	104.6	105.9

Source: Shūkan Tōyō Keizai, *Dēta fuairu: chingin, nenkin, jinji kanri*, pp. 258–9.

Table 5.23. *Numbers of unionised workers and proportions of total employees unionised, by firm size, 1974–9*

Firm size (persons)	No. of unionists		Unionists as % of total employees	
	1974	1979	1974	1979
Government	3,608,966	3,735,859	81.5	77.2
1,000 and over	5,221,502	4,841,050	78.5	75.5
300–999	1,361,254	1,369,999	48.1	47.6
100–299	1,006,159	1,014,758	41.1	27.7
30–99	444,553	465,488	9.1	8.6
Under 30	66,427	69,537	1.0	0.6
Others	752,938	812,065	25.5	23.3
Total	12,461,799	12,308,756	34.5	31.2

Sources: Nihon rōdō nenkan, 1977, pp. 178, 181; 1982, pp. 188, 191; *Shūgyō kōzō kihon chōsa hōkoku*, 1974, p. 36; 1979, p. 52.

done. It therefore seems inevitable that unions should comprise mainly company employees, that their members should always be subject to the control of their employers, and that the unions should only exist on conditions which employers accept. Over 90% of all unions in Japan therefore continue to be enterprise unions, and about one in six business executives is a former union leader. Table 5.23 shows the proportions of employees in firms of different sizes who are organised in this way. Among the members of the working class the proportions are even higher, since quite a substantial number of employees, particularly in large firms, are in either the bourgeoisie or the middle class. Yet in the years 1975–80 the levels of organisation of

Table 5.24. *Trade union members, by industry and sex, 1975–80*

	Total no.		Of which females (%)	
	1975	1980	1975	1980
Primary	114,431	91,412	11.6	11.0
Mining	65,517	47,568	7.0	6.2
Construction	676,366	704,351	15.4	14.0
Manufacturing	4,602,954	4,001,168	23.6	20.9
Wholesale/retail	702,896	865,897	41.0	36.8
Finance/insurance/real estate	961,382	1,027,646	55.2	57.0
Transport/communications	2,083,397	2,018,509	10.4	9.8
Electricity/public utilities	228,356	231,093	9.2	10.0
Service	1,545,389	1,823,080	42.2	44.4
Public administration	1,420,047	1,388,522	32.8	34.7
Total	12,472,974	12,240,652	27.6	27.6

Source: Fujin rōdō no jitsujō, 1976, p. 83; 1981, p. 109.

the working class in trade unions, with all their faults, actually fell. This was particularly the case in large firms in the private sector.

Even more significant is that out of over 13.2 million women employees in 1980 only about 3.4 million were trade unionists, predominantly those of pre-retirement age in the monopoly sector. However, the regular status accorded to young women, which allows them to become members of unions, does not in any way affect their position in the reserve army, since unions have enforced the deferment of their wages and have excluded them when they re-enter the workforce as non-regulars. Far from assisting young female members, unions have subjected them to the political and ideological domination of the male labour aristocracy, without allowing them the material advantages which this fraction of their class has been able to exact. Table 5.24 provides a breakdown of unionised workers by their sex and their major industry of employment in 1975–80.

Not all unions, however, have been equally submissive to the requirements of their organisational form, although the differences must not be exaggerated. The unions affiliated to Sōhyō (Nihon Rōdō Kumiai Sōhyōgikai, or the General Council of Japanese Trade Unions), for example, have in general been more militant than those affiliated to Dōmei (Zen Nihon Rōdō Sōdōmei Kumiai Kaigi, or the Japan Confederation of Labour), the two major national federations

Table 5.25. *Affiliations of trade unionists, by industry and major national federations, 1980*

	Total	Sōhyō	Dōmei	Shinsanbetsu	Chūritsurōren	Other
Total no. (1,000)	12,369	4,551	2,162	62	1,358	4,627
Industry (% each)						
Agriculture	100	26.6	24.0	—	0.5	48.9
Forestry/hunting	100	75.8	14.0	—	—	10.2
Fisheries	100	0.4	14.3	—	20.8	64.4
Mining	100	51.0	17.1	—	3.2	28.7
Construction	100	16.0	5.0	—	38.6	40.9
Manufacturing	100	17.1	29.5	1.3	16.4	41.5
Wholesale/retail	100	6.3	27.3	0.0	3.7	72.1
Finance/insurance	100	1.9	1.3	—	32.6	64.7
Real estate	100	26.2	9.6	—	0.3	86.7
Transport/communications	100	58.0	20.1	0.4	0.0	25.5
Electricity/gas/water	100	25.9	61.2	—	10.7	2.5
Service	100	60.0	4.3	0.0	0.8	35.5
Public administration	100	89.3	2.7	—	—	8.1
Other	100	26.2	8.8	—	4.1	60.9
Total	100	36.9	17.6	0.5	10.9	37.4

Source: Nihon rōdō nenkan, 1982, p. 197.

which loosely bring together associations of mainly company unions in various industries. Since their different leanings are examined in more detail in the next section, we simply note here, in table 5.25, their membership and their relative strengths in the major groups of industries. The only other important federation is Chūritsurōren, or the National Council of Independent Unions, which stands somewhere between the occasional militance of Sōhyō and the rabid anti-communism of Dōmei.

Ideology

There is little reason to doubt the general findings of a number of bourgeois studies that members of the Japanese working class see the world primarily in terms of rank rather than class.[26] That sex, age, education, and the size of firm they are employed in are the uppermost considerations in workers' minds is too widely documented to require either elaboration or scepticism. However, since the most perceptive studies were based on in-depth interviews or participant observation, they do not tell us much about the relative dominance of the different forms which class relations assume. Neither do they examine variations in 'rank consciousness' among different types of workers. Though these gaps result partly from the questions bourgeois scholars pose, they have as much to do with the limitations of in-depth studies of small groups of workers. While this method of probing ideas and feelings produces more accurate information, its advantage turns into a shortcoming when attempts are made to generalise about different types of workers and the dominant influences on them.

Recognising that written questionnaires can end up with either incorrect or irrelevant information, I found that my previously mentioned survey (of 459 employees in fifty-three companies of varying sizes) in the winter of 1976–7 did help fill in some gaps. The sample was, however, too small to allow firm conclusions, but the results suggest some interesting tendencies on questions not raised elsewhere and on which I have been unable to locate more reliable data.[27] Three main aspects of class awareness were probed: how far the existence of classes was recognised, how far class interests were seen as contradictory, and the extent to which struggles between classes were perceived. In each case replies were grouped into two broad categories: minimal awareness and considerable awareness ('None/little' and 'Fair/great' in the tables). I did not contrast consciousness of rank and class, but examined the relationship

Table 5.26. *Class consciousness, by class position, 1976*

	None/little		Fair/great		Total no.[a]
	No.	%	No.	%	
Existence of classes					
Bourgeoisie[b]	121	85.4	18	12.8	141
Middle class[c]	50	71.4	18	25.7	70
Working class[d]	151	64.5	76	32.5	234
Antagonism of class interests					
Bourgeoisie	115	81.6	25	17.7	141
Middle class	41	58.6	25	35.7	70
Working class	124	53.0	92	39.3	234
Existence of class struggles					
Bourgeoisie	60	42.6	74	52.5	141
Middle class	29	41.4	36	51.4	70
Working class	97	41.6	108	46.1	234

[a]Includes the numbers who responded to the question on their rank but not to the questions relating to the table. Of the total of 459 respondents, 14 never stated their rank. Only very small proportions of the remainder did not attempt the questions on class consciousness.
[b]Persons in the managerial hierarchy, that is, from directors to section managers.
[c]*Shunin* only.
[d]Persons below the rank of *shunin*.

between class consciousness and the various personal attributes associated with rank, to see which of these attributes is most dominant in concealing class society and which can be employed in strategies to further an understanding of that society.

Table 5.26 provides a general picture of the degree to which class relations in Japan tend to be concealed. It is interesting that all employees were more prepared to recognise the dynamics of these relations, the existence of class struggle, than to accept them as class relations or to see antagonistic interests as the cause of the struggles. In fact the bourgeois members of the sample, perhaps quite naturally, revealed the strongest tendency to deny that classes either exist or have conflicting interests and at the same time to realise that class struggles were a part of their lives. As far as the workers were concerned, only about a third to two-fifths could be described as having any understanding of the struggles which just under half of them acknowledged to exist.

Table 5.27. Class consciousness, by class position and sex, 1976

| | None/little | | | | Fair/great | | | | Total no. | |
| | Males | | Females | | Males | | Females | | Males | Females |
	No.	%	No.	%	No.	%	No.	%		
Existence of classes										
Bourgeoisie	117	86.7	4	66.7	16	11.9	2	33.3	135	6
Middle class	47	73.4	3	50.0	15	23.4	3	50.0	64	6
Working class	86	64.2	65	65.0	46	34.3	30	30.0	134	100
Antagonism of class interests										
Bourgeoisie	112	83.0	3	50.0	22	16.3	3	50.0	135	6
Middle class	40	62.5	1	16.7	21	32.8	4	66.7	64	6
Working class	82	61.2	42	42.0	44	32.9	48	48.0	134	100
Existence of class struggles										
Bourgeoisie	58	43.0	2	33.3	72	53.3	2	33.3	135	6
Middle class	26	40.6	3	50.0	34	53.1	2	33.3	64	6
Working class	59	44.0	38	38.0	64	47.8	44	44.0	134	100

Since about 90% of the female but only 40% of the male respondents were in the working class, one would expect the different general experiences of the two sexes even within this class to produce different degrees of class awareness. Since working men must see many of their own sex in the upper classes, they might be expected to be less class-conscious than women. However, table 5.27 suggests that this has happened only to a limited degree, possibly because gender relations obscure class relations through men's domination of women in almost every area of social life. Only in their perceptions of contradictory interests do female workers seem to be more class-conscious than male workers, while on the other two dimensions they appear to show less awareness. This might be because of the difficulties imposed on women to express their recognition of contradictions in actual struggles.

The degree to which age (also as a form of class relations and divisions within the working class) either conceals or can be used to heighten class awareness is not immediately clear, because age affects the sexes differently and together with education channels some men into the upper classes but most women into the reserve army. Table 5.28 confirms the likelihood of diminishing class consciousness among male workers as they approach the age of 55. Unfortunately, my sample included too few workers over this age to see how far the trend is reversed after retirement. In the case of women, table 5.28 suggests considerable influence of early retirement and of non-regular employment after that.

To interpret these data requires knowing something about the women in the different age groups. Almost all of those under 25 were unmarried and anticipated leaving their jobs by the time they turned 30, while the same applied to about 60% of the 25–9 age group. Those older than this comprised almost equal proportions of unmarried, married, and no-longer-married women, most of whom could either not say when they might leave (44%) or thought this would be between the ages of 50 and 60 (37%). Although the numbers of persons in the different categories are too small to generalise, a change seems to take place when women are transformed from nominally regular employees into non-regulars. They apparently become more inclined than men to recognise both the existence and the antagonistic interests of classes, but they seem to submit to their inability to engage in effective struggles and increasingly deny that class struggles take place.

Table 5.28. *Workers' class consciousness, by age and sex, 1976*

	None/little				Fair/great				Total no.	
	Males		Females		Males		Females		Males	Females
	No.	%	No.	%	No.	%	No.	%		
Existence of classes										
Under 25	8	50.0	18	39.1	8	50.0	14	30.4	16	46
25–9	36	70.6	20	76.9	15	29.4	5	19.2	51	26
30–54	40	63.5	16	59.3	21	33.3	11	40.7	63	27
Over 54	2		1		2		0		4	1
Antagonism of class interests										
Under 25	5	31.3	23	50.0	11	68.8	18	39.1	16	46
25–9	34	66.7	11	42.3	15	29.4	13	50.0	51	26
30–54	41	65.1	7	25.9	17	27.0	17	63.0	63	27
Over 54	2		1		1		0		4	1
Existence of class struggles										
Under 25	6	37.5	16	34.8	9	56.3	22	47.8	16	46
25–9	25	49.0	11	42.3	24	47.1	13	50.0	51	26
30–54	27	42.9	10	37.0	29	46.1	9	33.3	63	27
Over 54	1		1		2		0		4	1

Should my small sample be representative, one could conclude that the ideological and political domination of male over female workers diminishes with age and experience, and that one way to fight patriarchy among workers is to emphasise the function of age in the reproduction of the agents of the reserve army. Even though they enter the reserve at different ages, the current crisis is bringing home to male and female workers that 'lifelong employment' is a myth. To tackle capital on this question can provide both sexes with positive common ground from which to wage united struggles.

The difficulty in trying to isolate the forms of class relations which can most effectively uncover their substance is that both inter- and intra-class relations assume the almost identical forms. To seize on and emphasise a form in which differences between classes manifest themselves simultaneously gets one into emphasising differences within the working class. We also saw in chapter 4 (table 4.15) that workers' class consciousness diminishes with education, which like sex and age channels agents into different classes as well as into different fractions within the working class. Those workers with the highest education (or the favoured age or sex qualification) are thus likely to have the greatest aspirations for class mobility, and they can exercise powerful ideological influences over less-educated workers (as well as over younger ones and females). Table 5.29 provides some confirmation that the less-educated mass workers in small firms are more class-conscious than the aristocracy in the monopoly sector. The physical separation of these workers in different companies may also reduce the aristocracy's ideological dominance and be a factor behind the wide differences in their class consciousness.

It is impossible to tell how far membership in a company union is an independent factor which suppresses class consciousness, since my sample included very few union members in small firms and very few non-members in large ones. Variations in class consciousness by union membership almost exactly coincided with variations by firm size. The unorganised mass workers in my sample showed a much greater recognition of the existence and antagonistic interests of classes than did the labour aristocracy, though their perception of class struggles was more or less the same. Among the organised workers in the monopoly sector, about 20% of Sōhyō and Chūritsurōren but only 10% of Dōmei affiliates revealed a strong class consciousness when an overall score was computed from all the relevant questions. This suggests that Sōhyō and Chūritsurōren have

Table 5.29. *Workers' class consciousness, by firm size, 1976*

	None/little		Fair/great		Total no.
	No.	%	No.	%	
Existence of classes					
Under 100	33	55.9	24	40.7	59
100–999	50	62.5	29	36.3	80
1,000 and over	68	71.5	23	24.2	95
Antagonism of class interests					
Under 100	21	35.6	30	50.8	59
100–999	40	50.0	36	45.0	80
1,000 and over	63	66.3	26	27.4	95
Existence of class struggles					
Under 100	18	30.5	28	47.5	59
100–999	35	43.8	40	50.0	80
1,000 and over	44	46.4	40	42.1	95

played a less repressive role than Dōmei, but that they have not raised class awareness to levels which certain militant leaders might lead one to expect.

In conclusion, my survey suggests that class awareness among the Japanese working class, particularly mass workers and members of the reserve army, is greater than the bourgeois studies of largely the labour aristocracy have found. Although each of the forms assumed by class relations – sex, age, education, and firm size – to some extent conceals these relations by making differences between classes appear the same as differences within the working class, it also seems that they can be used to heighten class awareness, particularly in times of crisis.

The crisis and the Japanese working class

Since a detailed analysis of the main forms the crisis took during the 1970s is provided in the next two chapters, it is pertinent at this point only to relate the themes of this chapter to the general question of the crisis. A few of the more obvious examples will be used to illustrate the argument.

During the postwar boom and even the first few years of the recession, the attributes of class agents which slot them into the system (their sex, age, and education) seemed so obviously to determine their life chances that the real determinant, *class position*, could hardly have been further from people's minds. However, very slowly at first but more surely as time moved on, the persistence of crisis conditions and the growing numbers of people who were affected forced the question of class and class struggle back onto the political agenda. The main reason for this was that even people with the favoured personal attributes found that Japanese society was quite unable to deliver all it promised to such deserving people as themselves. The immediate effects on workers were fewer jobs and stagnating real wages, but both presented themselves in the form of a crisis of an ageing society.

Problems like these were bound to present themselves in this way, because their impact fell mainly on two groups of workers: school leavers, who found that capital no longer hired its normal quota of new workers (*shūshokusha*), and retired persons, some 30% of whom could no longer find second jobs (*saishūshokusha*). In spite of the pressure to postpone retirement, capital was under an even greater pressure to hire young workers, not least because they were cheaper. Yet the crisis fell more or less equally on the backs of both: the males among them finding it harder to get jobs and the females finding it harder to get paid adequately. One of the four main themes of the 1981 White Paper on Labour was the growth during the recession of female employment, a development which seemed strangely related to a large increase in the difference between male and female wages.

Apart from a propaganda campaign heralding the discovery that the system of lifelong employment was a pre-modern institution which needed to be 'modernised,' capital muddled its way through the crisis years, wherever possible rationalising equipment and workforces. Employment in a number of manufacturing industries in particular was slashed by means of a combination of expedients. Table 5.30 lists the proportions of firms which already in 1975 resorted to these measures to deal with what was called 'overemployment.'

In one year (1974–5), the employment of regulars fell by an average of 2.0%, though this concealed a fall of 7.5% in mining, 5.7% in construction, and 5.4% in manufacturing.[28] In the same period, the proportion of employees who worked fewer than thirty-five hours a week, mainly women, jumped by 16.3%.[29] The next year, 1976, Sony Corporation introduced a new scheme which also foreshadowed a practice that would become more common towards the end of the decade. It recruited for a new plant only older workers between 50 and 60, and offered them a basic salary which was only just over half

Table 5.30. *Forms of redundancy, by firm size, 1975 (% of firms)*

	Firm size (operatives)		
	Under 21	21–300	Over 300
Refrain from recruiting	52	77	82
Regulate overtime	36	47	73
Increase holidays	35	18	18
Lay off part-timers and temporaries	9	34	44
Temporarily lay off regulars	3	33	35
Invite early retirement and lay off			
retired workers	18	31	17

Source: Watanabe Mutsumi *et al.*, *Chūshō kigyō to rōdō kumiai* [Small and Medium Enterprises and Trade Unions] (Tokyo: Rōdō junpōsha, 1977), p. 122.

that paid to its regular employees in other factories.[30]

All these developments pointed in the same direction: jobs had dried up in the monopoly sector and the only workers who would find employment easy to obtain would be the very low-paid. An important change had taken place in the roles required of the reserve army. Since agents of this fraction of the working class are normally conditioned to accept low job security and below-average wages, one might expect them to carry the main burden of both lay-offs and wage reductions during a crisis. However, although they did have to put up with more of both, the emphasis fell increasingly on the latter, while workers outside the reserve army were more and more singled out for redundancies. The reasons why this change took place are not hard to find. Laying off regular workers from monopoly firms, of which there were numerous outstanding cases, only threatens the legitimacy of the system, whereas failure to reduce wage bills can threaten the life of particular businesses. Once the question is one of the survival of particular capitals, among whom competition only intensifies during slumps, members of the capitalist class quite naturally find it much harder to place their common interests above their individual interests. In the next chapter I show how they have to rely on the state to see that such short-sightedness does not land them in too much trouble.

Altering the composition of the workforce is the most natural strategy for a corporation in Japan to pursue in times of crisis. Since the largest variations in wages, by sex and age, have very little to do with abilities to do most jobs (with or without training), Japanese corporations can do something which dumbfounds their Western competitors: increase the numbers of workers but decrease the size of the wage bill! Problems of profitability can thus be attenuated, not by laying off the bottom layers of the working class, but by 'making efficient use of them' (*katsuyō shite*), a phrase which seems to crop up all the time in writings on the subject. And how much wiser to bring in 'inefficiently used' reserve workers (women) than young male school or university graduates, whose deferred wages will one day have to be paid. Since apart from rationalising plant and equipment, cutting wage costs is capital's most pressing need in times of crisis, traditionally low-paid workers are more likely to be the last to lose their jobs as a recession deepens. Unless organised workers can find ways of protecting their jobs, they will also soon find that their wages too will be undercut by the substitution of reserve for regular workers. A survey in 1978 by the Industrial Labour Research Institute noted that many firms were following Sony Corporation and hiring part-time employees as a 'cheap and easily replaceable' labour force. It pointed out that part-time wages had risen by only two-thirds as much as regular wages.[31] Already in the years leading up to the crisis, 1970–3, the wages of day labourers had fallen from 43.7% to 38.6% of regular wages.[32]

Indices of average wages therefore conceal the vital differences in capital's ability to reduce wages and exploit workers, without which it would be impossible to revive sagging business conditions. Moreover, there are so many ways of withholding wages that it is hard to know how far indices of real wages reflect movements in real living standards. In 1974–9, for example, bonuses fell from an average of 4.83 months' pay to 4.17 months' pay, but the reductions were by no means uniform for all the different categories of workers.[33] Uneven bites out of basic pay are also absorbed by taxation: in 1977–80, for example, for every 1% increase in annual income, taxes increased by an average of 2.5% and social security payments by 1.2%. Yet the heaviest burden fell on workers over 55, whose real disposable income fell by 4.9% during the three years.[34]

The crisis has thus affected the working class very unevenly: for some people the main problem has been jobs, one which is not even remotely reflected in the mere 1.22 million registered unemployed in 1982. At least ten times that number were either 'wishing to work' or were eking out some sort of existence in petty enterprises. However,

since most workers still do actually have jobs, the problems of most of
them centre more and more on how to survive on the wages they
receive. Only male workers in the 35–55 age group can be said to have
stable or rising incomes, and even then only those in the monopoly
sector.

Our analysis of the working class and the crisis it has faced suggests
a number of conclusions about the possibilities of revolutionary social
change in Japan. These relate solely to the findings of this chapter and
will be discussed in the context of Japan's class structure as a whole
only in the final chapter. Since the possibility that socialist revolution
might be the outcome of the current crisis in Japan depends more
than anything else on the types of revolutionary organisations that
develop, I concentrate on the conditions that facilitate the growth of
appropriate working-class organisation and ideology. And because
the ideas workers embrace and the organisations they form grow out
of their day-to-day experiences and activities, to identify the
beginnings of a revolutionary process is a matter of discovering those
activities, as well as the conditions of engaging in them, which further
the growth of revolutionary forms of organising and understanding
the world.

We have seen that family ideology and company unions cannot be
wished away, because both are rooted in the way the familial
attributes of class agents function as the concrete forms in which
infrastructural forces are mediated. It is only because sex, age, and
education slot workers into the positions which are created (and
destroyed) by the process of capital accumulation that the ideas
associated with them can serve to legitimate Japanese capitalism.
However, we have also seen that to forestall a prolonged interruption
of the accumulation process, capital has had to alter the boom-time
patterns of channelling agents into jobs. Reserve-army functions are
now required of both men and women of all ages, and positions in the
labour aristocracy, not to mention mobility out of the working class,
cannot be guaranteed for all males with higher education, even when
this is obtained in prestige universities. The breakdown of family
ideology and company unionism is thus a process which is regulated
by the expedients forced on the bourgeoisie to cope with the crisis.

Of the main attributes of class agents which conceal production
relations, it seems that only age might also contribute to uncovering
them. This is because sex and education remain with one for life, and
if they are drawn attention to as the forms which classes assume, the

result could equally be the creation of contradictions among the masses and their fragmentation into antagonistic camps. This does not mean of course that patriarchy is not the greatest enemy the working class faces from within its own camp, but simply that one cannot wage the working-class struggle as if it were an exclusively women's struggle. There are far too many men in it for that. It is also in the growing insecurity of even those male workers with higher education that conditions are emerging which might eliminate educational differences among workers as causes of division. At any rate, to pick on the bourgeoisie as the educated class would play right into its hands, since this would reinforce the ideology that people are themselves responsible for their life chances.

However, neither patriarchy nor educational elitism will disappear from within the working class until the development of appropriate conditions: not until men and women with different levels of education are more equally affected by the crisis will the class forces which place them in similar situations vis-à-vis capital as a whole become at all visible.

Of these two forms of working-class disunity, gender is by far the more difficult to overcome, because the material conditions which lie behind the role of gender in the class system are as fundamental a part of the infrastructure as the capitalist mode of production itself, if not more fundamental. On the other hand, the material factors which are responsible for the role of education in class formation are part and parcel of the functioning of capitalism. Yet precisely because technical skills are part of the forces of production, to wait for a random distribution in each class of persons with different technical skills is to wait for the abolition of classes themselves. Since patriarchy has its ultimate material basis in mechanisms (species reproduction) which are distinct from modes of production, it can exist independently of capitalism, but since meritocracy has its basis in the mode of production, the class struggle is simultaneously a struggle against meritocracy. Is one then back to the problem of seeing the bourgeoisie as both the educated class and wanting to avoid emphasising this?

Not necessarily, because a period of prolonged capitalist crisis can homogenise the different working-class *positions*, so that what their *jobs* demand of them becomes more and more similar for different working-class people, regardless of their different formal educations. Once the large numbers of university-educated workers who do not move out of their class are subjected to the same job insecurities, wage reductions, etc. as other workers, the infrastructural basis for meritocratic divisions within the working class will be undermined. So even though the upper classes will never include anything like equal proportions of well-educated and less-educated persons, the important thing is that the Japanese working class is coming to do just that. Furthermore, the greater the proportion of workers with higher education, the less will education be a dominant form of class relations. Growing numbers of Japanese are finding out that sacrificing their youth for the sake of getting into prestige universities guarantees little these days, and that such guarantees as it does provide are not worth it anyway.

Since I shall try to confront the thorny question of patriarchy within the working class in the final chapter, I conclude this discussion of the working class with a few words on how the role of age in concealing class relations might be reversed. Unlike meritocracy, but somewhat like patriarchy, gerontocracy in Japan is a two-edged sword for the ruling class. Since older men are meant to be the rulers of society in the traditional scheme of things, it is never a good idea to subject them, the system's preferred agents, to the same form of exploitation as the less-favoured types. Insofar as capitalism in Japan has required the exploitation of older men, it has created potentially important contradictions within the ruling class. Not simply because all men, indeed all workers, sooner or later reach retirement age and are affected by capital's treatment of non-regulars (increasingly in its 'modernised' form), but also because one's age has no material relevance to one's ability to perform most jobs, the seeds of the revolutionary process in Japan might well lie in capital's treatment of older people. The growing effects of the crisis on people of all ages have laid bare many of the realities that lie behind the so-called *shūshin kōyōsei* (lifelong employment system). Since even in the traditional ideology, the parent–child relationship is stronger than the husband–wife relationship, there is a much firmer basis for common action between old and young in Japan than in other capitalist societies. However, the real question is whether existing forms of working-class organisation have it in them to forge the sort of unity among the masses that can lead to revolutionary change. The reasons why they are unlikely to be able to take advantage of conditions which are increasingly favouring them are discussed in the final chapter.

6

Crisis and the state: accumulation functions

One of the main problems, if not the central one, which underlie arguments over the possibilities of revolutionary social change in Japan is how to understand the role of the state. Very similar debates to the ones which have been raging in the West have taken place on this question, and they are associated with corresponding political differences. However, in Japan they have not taken the peculiar Althusserian form that has characterised the discussion, at least among academic Marxists, in the West.[1] The reason is simple: few of the people concerned with the debate in Japan have even heard of Louis Althusser.

Since my purpose is the analysis of classes and the forms of their action in Japan, I do not wish to rehearse the debates or explicitly enter the controversies. What is more pertinent is to present the main theoretical conclusions on the functioning of the Japanese state which I drew and which then structured the argument in this and the next chapter. The finer points of theory are developed *pari passu* with the analysis of the empirical material. Moreover, since these general conclusions are more the outcome of various attempts to comprehend concrete realities in Japan than 'pure' (if there is such a thing) theoretical reasoning, it also seems inappropriate to diverge into a discussion of the differences among Japanese and Western Marxists.[2]

Theory

The single most important thing to emphasise about the capitalist state is not that it represents the domain of politics and ideology (as opposed to economics), as if there were no power relations or people with ideas in capitalist enterprises, but that state institutions are the society-wide forms of organisation of the dominant class. What they must be contrasted with are more limited organisations like firms, trade associations, and even employers' federations, which never achieve the same level of organisation the state institutions do, although at times they might come close to it.

Once the Althusserian separation of economics from politics and ideology is made, it becomes almost impossible to piece the parts together without raising further problems. My starting point is therefore to avoid making such a distinction and to recognise that in all the different institutions (private corporations, nationalised industries, schools, government departments, etc.) there are simultaneously power relationships (politics, if you like), ideas held by the agents about what they are doing (call it ideology), and some or other type of labour process (economics ?). In fact, a nationalised industry may be a much more direct manifestation of capitalist production than a private advertising firm, and the employment system in a giant Japanese corporation can more directly manifest the bourgeoisie's social control over the working class than does the Welfare Ministry. So rather than see politics and ideology as something the state is peculiarly concerned with, I follow Godelier in seeing them (if they must for any analytic purpose be separated) as functional requirements of the capitalist infrastructure.[3] In other words, the uninterrupted turnover of the total social capital requires that concrete individuals comply with certain demands the system makes on them. The laws of motion of the capitalist mode of production with all their contradictions tell us what these requirements are: briefly, money must be converted into means of production and labour power; these must be set to work in a production process to produce new commodities, which must then be sold for more money than was originally laid out; and that extra money must be reinvested, and so on. However, none of the tendential laws of capitalist production, exchange, and distribution tells us anything at all about how the members of a concrete society might go about complying with these requirements. If politics and ideology have to be distinguished and seen as belonging to the superstructure, then this is only because what they refer to are the concrete visible forms in which class relations are experienced and conceived.

I therefore use two broad theoretical distinctions to establish the context for the analysis of the Japanese state. The first is between what must be done to secure the uninterrupted turnover of the total social capital and what must be done to secure lower-class compliance with these measures. In other words, the distinction is between the job (functional requirement) of working out what class agents must do and the job (function) of working out how to get them to do it. It is similar to the one between accumulation and legitimation made by some writers.[4] In the concrete world there is a close dialectical relationship between them: for example, failure to secure compliance with something that needs to be done results in a demand for something else to be done, which in turn affects the way compliance is then secured. Nevertheless, the distinction is a real one and is used to separate the subject matter of this chapter, the specific measures through which the state is attempting to maintain uninterrupted capital accumulation, from that of the next: the ways in which lower-class compliance is being secured.

The second broad theoretical distinction that must be clarified is thus between state and non-state institutions. This has nothing whatsoever to do with fragmenting society into economic, political, and ideological levels, but concerns the form of organisation of the bourgeoisie. Since all concrete institutions are forms in which infrastructural forces manifest themselves, what private corporations and government departments have in common is that they are forms of bourgeois predominance. What distinguishes them are the different levels of organisation of this class that are involved: private corporations, although increasingly tied into conglomerates and even wider business associations, do not reveal that society-wide reach that characterises state institutions such as the Ministry of International Trade and Industry.

There is nothing fixed about which functions (accumulation or compliance) are tackled by the state and which ones are left to lesser bourgeois organisations. Whether or not the state assumes a particular job depends entirely on the historical development of class struggles and whether non-state forms of bourgeois organisation could cope. For example, the use of social welfare to secure working-class compliance has historically been something the bourgeoisie has done through private companies rather than the state. Only when these became more and more unable to perform their function adequately did a higher level of bourgeois organisation through the state become necessary.

The term used by almost all shades of left-wing theoretical opinion in Japan, *kokka dokusen shihonshugi* ('state monopoly capitalism'), can be quite confusing if, as it often does, it suggests that there can be such a thing as capitalist society without the state. In one form or another, capitalism has always been state capitalism, since certain functional requirements of the infrastructure have always been maintained by the state. Which ones they happen to be depends on which obstacles to accumulation or compliance can be overcome only by society-wide organisation of the bourgeoisie. The capitalist state cannot therefore be grasped other than historically and dialectically: historically in the sense that accumulation and compliance are continually encountering new obstacles, and dialectically in the sense that a solution to one obstacle lays the seeds for the development of the next.[5]

My concluding theoretical point about the state recalls an argument in the Introduction that state institutions, in the sense of the mechanisms governing what they do, are part (a subordinate part) of the infrastructure. Even though they are the society-wide forms of ruling-class organisation which developed in response to some or other crisis, and even though this development was subject to the laws of the most fundamental mechanisms, nevertheless they have their own internal (hidden) structures and their own tendential forces. These forces can, particularly when they act in combination with other subordinate forces, have a profound impact on the form concrete reality takes. One example in Japan is the bureaucratic method of decision-making known as *ringisei*, which bourgeois scholars have correctly shown to have important effects on state policy.[6] Unfortunately they have not drawn attention to the more fundamental mechanisms which set the limits on the possible effects of the *ringisei* system.

The Japanese state: accumulation functions

From the very beginning, capitalism in Japan has been associated with extensive state involvement in maintaining capital accumulation. The main form this took in the period of transition in the late nineteenth century was a direct result of the vast differences between productive forces in Japan and those in the imperialist countries which sought to open Japan up to free trade. No emerging capitalist enterprise, or even combination of enterprises, could match Western technology, and even many of the more powerful merchant houses of the feudal period were ruined by cheap imports. Since the basic obstacle to capitalist development in Japan was the absence of strong monopoly capitals, the emerging bourgeoisie could not survive unless capital in key sectors was rapidly concentrated and centralised.

The establishment by the state of a whole range of government enterprises and their subsequent sale around 1884 to the most promising private interests had little to do with any control particular bourgeois individuals had over the state apparatus, but was more or less dictated by the requirements of capital accumulation.[7] It was a concrete expression of the needs of the bourgeoisie as a social force rather than a response to the wishes of particular capitalists. By means of direct and indirect state involvement, that is, the highest form of bourgeois organisation, concentration and centralisation were achieved in communications, mining, chemicals, metals, and even textiles. Before the turn of the century, capitalist development in Japan had been assured. As Japanese monopoly capital became increasingly, though very unevenly, able to hold its own against imperialist capital, the state withdrew from its role of pioneering new industries and moved more into providing general assistance to established private enterprises. Direct involvement in the productive process gave way to selective subsidies and the promotion of mergers among the leading firms in key industries, an emphasis which has continued to the present day. The means of ensuring the circulation of capital, primarily through managing aggregate demand, have also remained much the same, although they have been gradually extended.

So even though the main institutions and means by which the Japanese state is attempting to cope with the current crisis have all been used before, the unprecedented form the crisis is taking has also required many innovations. Some expedients are able to fulfil a number of functions simultaneously, but others seem to confront certain problems in ways which sharpen contradictions elsewhere. In fact, the more the production process is socialised through growing concentration and centralisation of capital, the more immediately does production affect circulation and vice versa. Any signs of breakdown in one part of the system therefore quickly spread to others and increase the possibility of a general crisis.

Analysis of a capitalist crisis (whether bourgeois or Marxist-inspired) is always in danger of slipping into what is known as 'economism,' that is, presenting what are essentially social relations among people as if they were natural or purely technical phenomena. This danger is inherent in capitalism itself, since social relations do not present themselves as such but take the form of commodity exchanges. Even when one uses Marxist theory, which through the concept of value can grasp the social realities which lie behind their commodity forms, the danger is ever present: the extensive use by

Marxists of the very word 'economic' shows how they can forget that in essence commodity exchange is the visible form assumed by class relationships. It is therefore crucial constantly to bear in mind and make explicit that the breakdown of commodity exchange is the typical form in which class relations in bourgeois society break down. A general crisis of capitalism, that is, a total breakdown of class relations, is therefore not a very frequent occurrence. Usually the malfunctioning is more irregular and scattered, although even in what are called boom times, somewhere or other there is always a certain degree of failure: a go-slow, a strike, or a bankruptcy.

So rather than attempt a logically watertight theory of the causes of the crisis in Japan, I concentrate on the more acute forms in which class relations have been breaking down since around the first 'oil shock.' How deeply one needs to go into a theoretical reconstruction of basic causes depends very much on how acute these forms of crisis have been. Throughout, the unifying theme is the ruling class's most organised attempts through the state to patch up and extend bourgeois social relations. Although the focus is on forms of the crisis, the argument is ordered according to the relative importance of the different simple mechanisms that together comprise the capitalist mode of production.

The production process

Production of constant capital goods. Although the nationalisation of an industry can serve a number of functions, when a constant capital goods industry (producing means of production) is nationalised this is usually because it had caused bottlenecks in the accumulation process as a whole. Even when nationalisation resolves these, the industry might remain under state control for some time, particularly if it can simultaneously serve other functions. The nationalisation of the trunk railways in 1906 is a case in point. Until its comparatively recent eclipse by road haulage, the National Railways' primary function had been freight, and to a lesser degree passenger, transportation, but it is now being used increasingly to stimulate aggregate demand.

Competition from road transportation and the private railways, the existence of many uneconomic passenger lines (only 5 out of 243 were paying operations in 1977), as well as a tradition of comparatively well-organised radical trade unionism have led to growing deficits, which by 1980 exceeded ¥1 trillion.[8] Attempts to remedy the situation by means of regular fare hikes (50% in November 1976!) have led to declines in freight and passenger volumes, which in some cases have led to reductions in total revenue. In the years 1975 to September 1980, passenger fares increased by a whopping 113.2%, that is, almost three times the general consumer price increase of 40% in the same period. The share of the National Railways had, by 1977, fallen to 11% in freight and 28% in passenger transport.

The diminishing importance of the National Railways in the industry has also led to severe cuts in the numbers of stations which handle freight – 1,524 in 1974 and 276 in 1977 – and the substitution of express trains for regular passenger services. From 1960 to 1975, the proportion of expresses among the total daily trains increased from 0.26% to 11.29%. Since express trains do not stop in the poorest working-class areas, the repercussions, like those of the fare hikes, extend far beyond the railway workers. Other expedients being used in an attempt to solve the crisis include cutting uneconomic local lines (thirty-eight out of a planned forty to be abolished by 1983) and, as is to be expected, laying off workers. From a workforce of 424,000 in 1979, it is planned that only 350,000 will still have jobs in 1985: a grand total of 74,000 workers will be made redundant.[9]

One of the main areas of expansion for the National Railway centres on the role of capital expenditure in stimulating demand in the construction-related industries. This has been one of the chief effects of the massive investment in the Shinkansen (the New Tokkaido Line, or 'Bullet' Train), which is now being extended to the North. Another important development is the growing proportion of expenditure on huge station buildings, which boosts the construction industries and also provides convenient access to the major department stores and hotels in the area. For example, in 1976 some 40% of investment was in this category. It has the dual function of stimulating demand (like other public works programmes) and providing infrastructure for commercial industries.[10]

State provision of infrastructure for the transport industries has recently centred more on roads and highways than on railways. In 1960–76, road investments were over ¥25 trillion, while investments by the National Railways were only ¥7.5 trillion. Table 6.1 shows that over 60% of the total investments by the Construction Ministry in 1962–73 were in roads, and, according to the 1978 White Paper on Construction, road construction would receive top priority over the

Table 6.1. *Public investment by the*
Construction Ministry, 1962–73

	Total amount (¥ bil.)	Share (%)
Roads	15,367.7	60.1
Rivers/coasts/slopes	3,646.5	14.3
Drainage	2,323.6	9.1
Parks	505.9	2.0
Housing	3,703.3	14.5
Total	27,348.0	100.0

Source: Sumita Shōji, 'Jūtaku mondai no konnichiteki seikaku to seisaku kadai' [The Present-Day Character of the Housing Problem and the Subject of Policy], *Keizai*, no. 164 (December 1977), p. 134.

next ten years.[11] The proportion of the total area of Japan given up to roads increased from 1.1% in 1965 to 2.4% in 1973 and to 2.6% in 1977.[12]

Apart from the state's growing involvement in road transportation, another reason for its progressive withdrawal from railways is the need to tackle what has been made to seem the major obstacle to capital accumulation: the energy crisis, which triggered off the recession following the first 'oil shock' in late 1973. Although almost every government statement on the recession refers to this event, the state's actions do not suggest that it sees any energy shortage as the basic problem. Rather, rhetoric on the issue seems largely to serve the function of justifying the activities which are designed to get at the real problem: excessive investment in plant and equipment during the preceding ten to fifteen years. The state's efforts have therefore overwhelmingly centred on restructuring the productive sectors of the country and on maintaining aggregate demand while this is being done. Both have been the core of its energy policy.

Since the energy-related industries are already more concentrated and centralised than all others, restructuring has involved an attempt to diversify energy supplies in order to reduce dependence on OPEC countries. That diversification of supply, rather than an increase in supply or reduction in costs, is the uppermost consideration is clear from the direction in which state policy is moving. There are no plans to nationalise energy-producing firms, and even in the generation of

Table 6.2. *Finance needed to secure energy supplies, 1966–75 and 1976–85 (¥ billion, at 1975 prices)*

	1966–75			1976–85		
	Private	Public	Total	Private	Public	Total
Electricity	10,616	44	10,660	34,140	460	34,600
Nuclear	102	436	539	780	3,040	3,820
Oil	5,881	173	6,055	11,540	1,650	13,190
Liquid petroleum gas	—	—	—	900	20	920
Liquid natural gas	664	—	664	2,910	—	2,910
Coal	676	829	1,505	1,250	1,130	2,380
City gas etc.	1,213	—	1,213	2,330	—	2,330
New types (e.g. solar)	—	6	6	70	670	740
Subtotal	19,152	1,488	20,640	53,570	6,970	60,540
Finance for consumers						
To economise	—	—	—	—	—	6,140
To diversify fuels	—	—	—	—	—	240
To use solar energy etc.	—	—	—	—	—	640
Total	19,152	1,488	20,640	—	—	67,560

Source: Asahi Shinbun, 19 August 1977, in *Shinbun Geppō*, 370 (September 1977), p. 158.

electricity by means of nuclear power the state is assisting private enterprise rather than itself seeking to monopolise production. Although the government-owned Japan Atomic Energy Company pioneered the field in July 1966, when its first Tōkai plant started commercial production, by August 1980 it owned only two more (Tōkai No. 2 and Tsuruga) of the twenty-one reactors which had been opened. The rest were in the hands of the main electric power companies.

Having pioneered atomic energy production, the state's involvement in energy procurement is now largely confined to planning for diversification of supplies through financing expansion in new areas and granting licences. In August 1977, one of MITI's (Ministry of International Trade and Industry) advisory councils on energy reported that ¥67 trillion (at 1975 prices), or an amount equal to about 70% of national expenditure in 1975, would be needed to finance research and equipment investment for the period ending 1985. Table 6.2 summarises the recommendations and the expected sources of finance. The state will continue to provide the bulk of the

Table 6.3. *Planned diversification of total energy supplies (%)*

	1977	1985	1990	1995
Hydro power	4.8	4.7	4.6	4.6
Subterranean	0.0	0.4	1.0	1.8
Domestic oil and natural gas	0.9	1.4	1.4	1.7
Domestic coal	3.2	2.5	2.0	1.8
Nuclear	2.0	6.7	10.9	14.3
Imported Coal	11.6	13.6	15.6	16.5
LNG	2.9	7.2	9.0	8.7
New forms of energy	0.1	0.9	5.5	7.6
Imported oil	74.5	62.9	50.0	43.1

Source: Mainichi Shinbun, 1 September 1979, in *Shinbun Geppō,* 395 (October 1979), p. 116.

finance only for those pioneering sectors which might prove risky for private enterprise. In all, about ¥7 trillion, or 10% of the total, will be met by the state (from the General and Special accounts of the budget).

The degree of diversification and the rate at which it is expected to be achieved are set out in table 6.3. It is not altogether clear what the main reason is behind making nuclear energy the fastest-expanding source of supply. Already by the end of 1978, Japan had become the second largest nuclear power producer in the non-Communist world following the United States.[13] One factor is probably pressure from that country, but there are others which are more specifically related to the state's overall counter-depression measures.

First, there is the ideological effect of government forecasts and reports which set out the plans for diversification: even if the expected targets are not reached, people are taught to look for the cause of the crisis in OPEC countries and problems which are beyond the control of the Japanese state. Those who resist the development of nuclear power can then be seen to frustrate one of the few ways in which the state can claim to bring control of these problems into Japanese hands. The anti-nuclear movement in Japan has come up against this again and again.

Second, whatever the deeper forces which lay behind the current worldwide capitalist crisis, the oil price hikes, no doubt effects of those forces, clearly had a far more destabilising impact on capital accumulation in Japan than in any comparable country. With over

Table 6.4. *Terms of trade of major capitalist powers, 1973–80 (period just before each major oil price rise = 100)*

Year	Quarter	Japan	United States	West Germany
1973	III	100	100	100
	IV	81.8	98.1	95.8
1974	I	77.8	91.3	88.6
	II	80.1	83.1	90.9
	III	79.0	83.0	91.5
	IV	74.4	85.1	93.9
1975	I	74.4	87.4	98.5
	II	74.9	86.1	99.2
	III	72.8	88.6	98.4
1978	IV	100	100	100
1979	I	96.2	102.4	96.8
	II	88.1	100.6	92.4
	III	79.6	96.3	89.6
	IV	71.0	91.5	89.9
1980	I	64.1	85.5	85.8
	II	63.6	82.6	86.1
	III	65.1	84.2	87.0

Source: Kudō Akira, 'Nihon keizai no genkyokumen to futatsu no seisaku rosen, ge' [The Present Economic Situation in Japan and Two Political Lines, part 2], *Keizai*, no. 207 (July 1981), p. 9.

99% of the oil used in Japan coming from imports (of which almost 80% comes from the Middle East) and three-quarters of energy supplies deriving from oil, Japanese capital was bound to be vulnerable to any organised manipulation of oil prices. Table 6.4 shows how much more were its terms of trade, for example, affected than were those of either United States or West German capital.

In times of worldwide capitalist crisis, conflicts among the major powers have always centred on non-reproducible means of production, such as land, raw materials, or fuels, since monopoly ownership of these is a way of appropriating extra profits from what Marx called 'absolute rent.'[14] The unprecedented profits of the oil companies confirm what this can mean in practice, as do the many threats of war over oil and raw material supplies. In this context, the commitment of the Japanese bourgeoisie to nuclear power is simultaneously intended rapidly to reduce dependence on the increasingly organised owners of oil supplies and surreptitiously to create the military capability of dealing with possibly more destabilising uses of their monopoly

Table 6.5. *Capacity utilisation rates of nuclear reactors, 1973–80*

Company	Plant	Approved capacity 10,000kw	Opened (year)	Capacity utilisation (%)			
				1973	1974	1976	Aug. 1980
Tokyo Electric Power Co.	Fukushima 1	46.0	1971	48.4	26.1	24.8	44.6
	Fukushima 2	78.4	1974	—	—	47.7	0.0
	Fukushima 3	78.4	1976	—	—	72.0	94.8
	Fukushima 4	78.4	1978	—	—	—	95.1
	Fukushima 5	78.4	1978	—	—	—	58.5
	Fukushima 6	110.0	1979	—	—	—	98.7
Chūbu Electric Power Co.	Hamaoka 1	54.0	1976	—	—	53.0	84.8
	Hamaoka 2	84.0	1978	—	—	—	95.7
Kansai Electric Power Co.	Mihama 1	34.0	1970	27.4	7.4	0.0	64.4
	Mihama 2	50.0	1972	54.0	63.7	46.7	98.6
	Mihama 3	82.6	1976	—	—	88.7	96.3
	Takahama 1	82.6	1974	—	—	52.1	0.0
	Takahama 2	82.6	1975	—	—	38.3	99.7
	Daihan 1	117.5	1979	—	—	—	100.0
	Daihan 2	117.5	1979	—	—	—	0.0
Chūgoku Electric Power Co.	Shimane 1	46.0	1974	—	75.2	63.3	95.4
Shikoku Electric Power Co.	Ikata 1	56.6	1977	—	—	—	86.6
Kyūshū Electric Power Co.	Genkai 1	55.9	1975	—	—	73.5	100.0
Japan Atomic Energy Co.	Tōkai 1	16.6	1966	70.4	67.9	69.5	82.6
	Tōkai 2	110.0	1978	—	—	—	96.9
	Tsuruga	35.7	1970	78.9	48.8	68.5	91.4
Average		1,495.2 (total)		54.0	48.2	52.8	73.6

Sources: Sasaki, p. 100; *Nihon Keizai Shinbun*, 7 September 1980, in *Shinbun Geppō*, 407 (October 1980), p. 170, and *Yomiuri Shinbun*, 15 April 1979, in *Shinbun Geppō*, 390 (May 1979), p. 77; Genshiryoku Iinkai [Committee on Atomic Power], *Genshiryoku hakusho* [White Paper on Atomic Power], 1978 (Tokyo: Ōkurashō insatsukyoku, 1979), pp. 41–3.

power. The current military build-up in Japan, which is examined in more detail later, is the light in which the rapid expansion of nuclear powered electricity generation must be viewed: conversion of the reactors for military purposes is a comparatively simple task. Hence, the unused capacity and opening of new reactors at a time when the recession reduced demand for electricity is not as surprising as it might first appear (See table 6.5). Neither is the ability of Japanese capital in only one year substantially to reduce the proportion of imported oil from militantly nationalist Iran (from 16.9% to 9.9% in 1978–9) and at the same time to raise by 1.6 percentage points the share from its almost total neo-colony of Indonesia (from 12.8% to 14.4%).[15]

Another depression-related reason for the planned investments in electric power generation concerns the management of aggregate demand. MITI officials have noted that the GNP increase resulting from a given amount of private investment is normally higher than the increase resulting from a similar amount of government expenditure. The electric power industry is one of the most important in this regard, since growth in it directly benefits heavy electrical firms, construction companies, steel producers, and pollution prevention equipment makers. The investments induced in these industries are about 1.2 times, and the addition to GNP is 1.8 times, the investments undertaken by the electric power industry.[16] That stimulation of aggregate demand, rather than increasing power generating capacity (at a time of considerable unused capacity), has been a major factor behind the encouragement of investment programmes in the industry is confirmed by the large proportion of recent investments which have been in such areas as improving distribution systems and pollution prevention. Table 6.6 gives an example from the trough year of 1977.

Apart from encouraging investment programmes and channelling finance to energy-related companies, the state also approves power charges under the electricity and gas laws. Electric lighting rates for households have regularly been much higher than those for bulk industrial use, although because of high profitability in the industry following the rise of the yen, these were temporarily equalised by granting households a discount from October 1978 until March 1979. Nevertheless, from a base of 100 in 1975, household electricity and gas price indices stood at 170.3 and 178 respectively in September 1980, which was twice the increase in the overall consumer price index

Table 6.6. *Distribution of equipment investment in the electric power industry, 1977 (¥ billion and %)*

	Estimated expenditures in 1977		Planned expenditures for 1978	
	Amount	Share	Amount	Share
To expand capacity	851.6	33.8	1,026.0	34.1
Hydro	154.4	—	222.0	—
Subterranean	377.5	—	400.1	—
Nuclear	319.7	—	403.9	—
Unrelated to capacity	1,669.3	66.2	1,980.8	65.9
Total	2,520.9	100.0	3,006.8	100.0

Source: Keizai, no. 167 (March 1978), p. 100.

(140).[17] Far from there being a shortage of energy in Japan, there is in fact plenty of spare capacity, and rising prices have kept the industry profitable. The largely foreign-based oil companies have been registering such large surpluses even in the trough year of 1977 that MITI was forced to lower the prices of naphtha, gasoline, and other oil products, mainly in response to demands from the petrochemical and textile industries. The 1978 budget even included a new oil tax to channel some of the surpluses into state coffers.[18]

The so-called energy crisis was in many ways a golden opportunity for the state to implement other more fundamental measures to counteract the depression. Of the total estimated energy requirements in 1985, imported oil will still make up around 63%, which is a reduction of only ten percentage points from the 1975 proportion. All the fuss over the fuels for electric power generation has more to do with managing the crisis in other ways than with making Japan more independent of OPEC countries, important as this might be to the Japanese ruling class.

Although the most important constant capital goods produced by public corporations are transportation infrastructure and energy, both of which also fulfil functions in the circulation process, there are in all upwards of 110 public or semi-public corporations in Japan. Since many are either finance companies or produce only wage goods, they are not relevant here. Among those which do produce constant capital goods, the most important are the Postal Service, the

Japan National Railways, the Japan Telegraph and Telephone Corporation, the Japan Public Highways Authority, the Japan Railway Construction Corporation, the Japan Oil Development Corporation, and the Japan Atomic Energy Company.

Public corporations are funded from internal revenues and from the annual budget's Fiscal Investment and Loan Programme (FILP), the chief function of which is demand management and which is therefore discussed more fully in the next section. In the case of the seven corporations above, however, the procurement of a secure and a cheap supply of essential constant capital goods is not without importance. Table 6.7 shows their total investment funds for the peak years of the recession, 1977–8, and how much of these funds were granted under the 'second budget,' the FILP.

About one-third of the FILP allocations for purposes other than lending through public finance companies are made to the main seven corporations which produce constant capital goods. Although the investments made by each of the remainder are small by comparison, the goods provided can be quite significant. This is often true of those corporations set up for specific purposes, such as the New Tokyo International Airport Corporation or the Honshu–Shikoku Bridge Corporation. Both projects provide important additions to the infrastructure capital utilises.

However, more important in times of recession than the state's production of any particular constant capital good is its role in restructuring the different industries in order to restore general profitability. The nationalisation of any individual industry merely serves to spread its costs more evenly among the various capitals that depend on it, while restructuring it can make more surplus value available for accumulation and gets closer to the root causes of the recession. The state plays this role in response to, but within the limits of, the workings of the general laws of capital accumulation.

Restructuring. To clarify the different ways in which the state has been helping restructure Japanese industry requires a brief outline of the types of structural problems that can arise under capitalism, as well as the forms they have taken in that country. The problems normally fall into two broad groups: those resulting from the law of the tendency of the average rate of profit to fall and those resulting from uneven developments among the different industries.[19] Usually, neither set of problems is on its own sufficient to cause a severe crisis, though when

Table 6.7. *Investment funds of major public corporations producing constant capital goods, 1977–8* (¥ 100 million)

	1978			1977		
	FILP	Internal	Total	FILP	Internal	Total
Postal Service	387	640	1,027	360	534	894
Japan National Railways	11,855	−1,487	10,368	9,492	−571	8,921
Japan Telegraph and Telephone	480	15,620	16,100	480	15,720	16,200
Japan Public Highways	8,151	6,066	14,217	6,967	4,789	11,756
Japan Railway Construction	2,663	3,250	5,913	2,234	2,693	4,927
Japan Oil Development	809	4,061	4,870	748	1,415	2,163
Japan Atomic Energy	785	471	1,256	605	336	941
Total for the seven	25,130	28,621	53,751	20,886	24,916	45,802
Total FILP allocations	148,876			125,382		
Total FILP allocations to finance companies	75,349			62,193		

Source: Nihon Keizai Shinbun, 30 December 1977, in *Shinbun Geppō*, 374 (January 1978), pp. 62–3.

they occur simultaneously they can lead to prolonged depressions. Although both first manifest themselves in the circulation process and are initially confronted in that form, it soon becomes clear that only a restructuring of the production process can provide anything approaching a permanent solution. In both cases, the state cannot achieve the desired restructuring unless it allows the depression to run at least part of its natural course, that is, to eliminate inefficient production units by allowing them to fall into bankruptcy. The state's role therefore increasingly moves from one of guiding the restructuring to one of justifying it and ensuring working-class compliance. Since this can involve forestalling bankruptcies and lay-offs, it can frustrate the sole way in which the crisis can be overcome.

Since there are many counter-tendencies to the tendency of the rate of profit to fall, there is no necessary reason why this should on its own lead to a crisis. In many such cases, the state might anticipate the causes of the tendency and concentrate on mobilising the counter-tendencies. Had there not also been considerable uneven development of the different industries in Japan and had some catalyst – the oil shocks – not tipped the precarious balance that had previously existed, the different infrastructural problems might not have been unleashed simultaneously and allowed to cause a crisis as general as this one is proving to be.

The main factor behind the tendency of the rate of profit to fall is the growth of the organic composition of capital: an increase in the ratio of the value of constant capital (means of production) to the value of variable capital (labour power). Since the hidden source of profit is ultimately the new value workers produce, and then only that portion which they do not receive in the form of wages, the larger the share of old value (embodied in constant capital) in the value of total output, the smaller is the amount from which profits can be extracted. Although raising the rate of exploitation (increasing that portion of new value which workers do not receive) is one counter-tendency to falling profitability, it has obvious limitations if the organic composition of capital continues to rise. A more important counter-tendency is therefore the cheapening of constant capital goods, which lowers the organic composition of capital.

Though it is almost impossible to get market-price data which directly manifest the value relations above, there are reasons to believe that the organic composition of capital in Japan did rise greatly during the postwar boom. The equipment investment of

Table 6.8. *Major economic indices during the postwar boom, 1955–71*

Year	Real mining and manufacturing production	Real GNP	Equipment investment	State FILP	Wholesale prices	Regular manufacturing employment	Real wages
1955	100	100	100	100	100	38.8	100
1956	122.4	106.8	154.6	109.7	104.4	42.6	108.6
1957	144.4	115.6	209.0	133.2	107.5	47.8	109.3
1958	141.5	122.2	193.5	142.6	100.5	49.4	112.2
1959	170.2	136.6	227.4	188.6	101.6	55.4	119.2
1960	212.5	154.6	327.6	209.7	102.6	64.3	124.2
1961	253.7	176.9	461.9	275.8	103.7	72.2	131.7
1962	275.0	187.0	477.3	319.1	102.0	77.4	134.6
1963	306.3	211.1	501.5	405.0	103.8	80.5	136.9
1964	354.4	233.8	606.8	480.2	104.0	84.3	145.7
1965	367.6	246.8	572.7	596.0	104.8	86.5	148.4
1966	416.2	275.3	657.0	699.7	107.3	87.0	157.7
1967	497.1	312.4	853.0	835.6	109.3	89.9	171.7
1968	585.3	355.2	1,019.1	933.9	110.2	93.6	187.3
1969	683.5	398.9	1,350.8	1,072.1	112.6	96.9	207.0
1970	793.8	436.9	1,626.4	1,280.2	118.8	100.0	226.2
1971	833.1	461.7	1,676.4	1,436.2	115.8	99.9	242.5

Source: Keizai, no. 109 (May 1973), p. 426.

private enterprises grew much more rapidly than either GNP or industrial production, suggesting that it comprised a growing proportion of the value embodied in its final outputs. A major reason for the maintenance of profitability must have been the increasing numbers of workers in manufacturing and their growing exploitation, but this could not have remained sufficient indefinitely. Table 6.8 includes the main indices which explain why this is so.

Even setting aside the build-up of forces outside Japan which were to cause a worldwide capitalist crisis, there were signs in Japan of possible difficulties in the massive investments of 1965–70 and in the approach of a 'full-employment ceiling.' To have prevented a fall in profitability, it would have been necessary to ensure an even more intense exploitation of the working class and a check in the rising organic composition of capital. However, even if the required revolutionary technical developments had been able to cheapen the value of both wage goods and of the large new equipment investments of the early 1970s, two other changes had been taking place which would have intensified the pressure on average profitability: the progressive expansion of the unproductive sector and the rapid rise in land prices. Both resulted from capital's attempts to get a share of boom-time profits without having to engage in the production process, and both therefore resulted in additions to the amounts of constant capital invested but not in the amount of surplus value created. Table 6.9 shows that increasing proportions of the new value created in the productive sector were being absorbed by the unproductive sector.

The large increase in the share of Net Domestic Product of finance, insurance, and real estate in 1972–3 had a great deal to do with the boom in land speculation that peaked the following year. Table 6.10 shows how land prices spiralled as a result.[20]

Once accumulation began to falter (in 1974), the high indebtedness of large Japanese corporations to banks became a serious problem for them, because interest payments had to be made regardless of their profitability.[21] The collapse in February 1978 of Japan's largest plywood supplier and a leading construction firm, Eidai Company, was a direct result of its overinvestment in land speculation. Leaving liabilities of about ¥180 billion, its failure was the second worst in Japan's postwar history (the worst being that of Kōjin Company, a textile firm which left debts of ¥200 billion in 1975), and the event sent a shudder throughout the banking world.

Table 6.9. *Industrial origins of Net Domestic Product, 1961–75 (%)*

	1961	1965	1970	1972	1973	1975
Productive sector	*60.8*	*55.7*	*54.3*	*51.8*	*51.1*	*50.1*
Primary	14.0	11.2	7.7	7.0	6.8	6.6
Secondary	46.8	44.4	46.5	45.1	44.3	43.5
Mining	1.4	0.9	0.6	0.5	0.4	0.4
Manufacturing	30.0	27.9	30.6	28.7	28.3	26.8
Construction	5.9	7.0	7.4	8.0	8.3	8.6
Transport/communications/ public utilities	9.5	8.6	8.0	7.8	7.4	7.3
Unproductive sector	*39.2*	*44.4*	*45.7*	*48.2*	*48.9*	*49.9*
Wholesale/retail	16.1	16.9	18.0	18.1	17.9	19.3
Finance/insurance/real estate	8.9	10.5	11.4	11.9	13.0	11.5
Services	10.3	12.8	12.5	14.0	14.0	14.5
Public administration/defence	3.9	4.1	3.8	4.1	4.0	4.6
Total	100.0	100.0	100.0	100.0	100.0	100.0

Source: Economic and Foreign Affairs Research Association, *Statistical Survey of Japan's Economy* (Tokyo: Keizai gaikō kenkyūkai, 1969, 1974, 1977), p. 71.

Table 6.10. *Indices of land prices, 1955–77*

	Type of land			
	Housing	Factory	Commercial	Total
1955	100	100	100	100
1960	269	293	282	280
1963	542	701	561	594
1965	707	911	712	768
1970	1,412	1,449	1,333	1,395
1973	2,453	2,373	2,047	2,286
1974	3,094	2,921	2,442	2,812
1975	2,969	2,765	2,348	2,691
1976	3,013	2,772	2,361	2,712
1977	3,132	2,794	2,387	2,770

Source: Moriya Fumio, 'Takuchi to takuchi kakaku ni tsuite' [Concerning Housing Land and Housing Land Prices], *Keizai*, no. 174 (October 1978), p. 154.

One worried banker remarked: 'We may have more problem businesses going down the drain this year. It's going to be a hard year for banks too.' In fact eighty-one quoted companies faced bankruptcy because of excessive deficits. Already in September 1976, the twenty-three major banks had bad loans of ¥1.6 trillion, and during the six months preceding September 1977 the questionable loans of the thirteen leading banks increased by nine times.[22]

In 1977–8 banking had become an unprofitable business, partly because the recession had reduced the demand for loans, partly because in an effort to stimulate demand the state had slashed the official discount rate from 9.0% in 1973 to 3.0% in August 1978. In September 1977, half of the thirteen leading banks were paying more for their deposits than they were earning on their loans.[23] The expansion of the unproductive sector during the boom therefore resulted in more than the previously noted new claims on surplus value: it increased the vulnerability of productive enterprises because of their indebtedness to commercial banks whose stability had become questionable. Should a major bank fall victim to the recession, a whole wave of giant corporations could go under. The state's initial attempts to solve the crisis by intervening in the circulation process by such measures as manipulation of the discount rate therefore had to give way to attempts to restructure the unproductive sector as well. In its analysis 'Japan's Ailing Banking System,' the *Japan Times Weekly* concluded:

> In fact, Japanese banks are plagued by 'structural' problems – such as the controlled system of interest rates and the proliferation of banks which leads to 'excessive' competition which in turn impairs the financial health of individual banks.
> As overcapacity and unbridled sales wars in manufacturing industries are prompting moves towards reorganization, so these and other problems in the banking industry may well trigger similar moves towards change.[24]

Once the state gets seriously involved in restructuring, it faces a dilemma, because lowering average organic composition of capital means that some businesses have to disappear altogether, while investment in others has to be curtailed. And since the only way to do this is to allow the recession to run its natural course, the state gets into the contradictory position of simultaneously assisting and preventing restructuring. It helps the process through the encouragement of mergers, the use of selective subsidies, and the announcement of plans for the future structure of industry, but it frustrates reorganisation by keeping ailing businesses going.

In very general terms, the recession process has fallen into three main periods. The first began with the 'oil shock' in 1973 and lasted

Table 6.11. *Main indicators of the recession in manufacturing, 1973–8*

	Operating profits in 1977 (1973 = 100)	Capacity utilisation in 1977 (1973 = 100)	Regular employment in 1978 (1975 = 100)	Labour productivity in 1978 (1975 = 100)
Manufacturing average	87.3	83.9	92.7	127.4
Iron/steel	57.4	73.6	87.0	121.4
Nonferrous metals	56.1	79.2	89.3	148.3
Metal products	109.4	67.7	87.3	141.0
Machines	94.9[a]	87.9	86.2[a]	131.7
Ceramics	60.2	80.8	91.4	131.2
Chemicals	88.5	78.4	91.0	136.9
Petroleum products	60.0	83.6	91.7	105.2
Pulp/paper products	74.2	85.3	89.2	129.8
Textiles	8.8	89.5	81.1	124.2

[a]General.
Sources: Shūkan Tōyō Keizai, *Keizai tōkei nenkan*, 1979, pp. 245, 248, 266; Gary R. Saxonhouse, 'Industrial Restructuring in Japan,' *Journal of Japanese Studies*, 5, 2 (Summer 1979), p. 281.

until around the end of 1977. It was characterised by widespread falls in employment and profitability as well as excess capacity on the one hand, and a frenzy of restructuring activity involving bankruptcies, mergers, lay-offs, rationalisation of production and technical innovation, and wage restraint on the other. The result was a second period comprising a mini-boom, led mainly by the export industries, which lasted until early 1980. The final period saw the continuation of the depression process, which had been only briefly interrupted, and its manifestation mainly in Japan's myriad of small firms which had escaped the restructuring that took place in 1974–8. The following analysis of the state's restructuring activities therefore concentrates on that period. Table 6.11 provides an overview of the problems that were tackled (low profitability and excess capacity) and the solutions that were found (loss of jobs and raising labour productivity through technical innovation).

Since the manner in which this was accomplished was related to those structural problems which arose out of uneven accumulation, the main forms assumed by the latter in Japan must briefly be mentioned. We have already seen (pp. 105–6) why productive forces develop at different rates in different industries, the fundamental reason being variations in capital's opportunities to get ahead of rivals by means of technical improvements. Industries where the greatest such opportunities exist are the ones in which most new capital is invested, and they might come to produce more goods than can be absorbed by the domestic market. If they can also maintain a competitive edge over foreign capital, their expansion can take place in overseas markets. This happened in a major Japanese manufacturing industry which had once been the mainstay of capitalist development in that country: textiles. But when foreign capital began to match or surpass its competitive power, Japanese capital no longer found it as profitable as before, and it had to be run down. I discuss the industry in some detail.

Although once the mainstay of capitalist development in Japan, the textile industry began to decline around the mid-1960s, largely because it offered few opportunities for technical innovation in comparison with the chemical, motor vehicle, and electric appliance industries. Since in a comparatively labour-intensive industry (such as textiles had become) capital's competitive advantage depends on paying lower wages than rivals, monopoly capital moved more and more into neighbouring Asian countries. By 1976, 303 out of 432 overseas textile projects (worth $429 million out of $656 million) were in Asia. However, as a solution to staving off bankruptcies in Japan, foreign investment was a two-edged sword, because Japan became a major market for the exports of the new subsidiaries. The *sōgō shōsha* (the general trading companies) assumed the role of importing cheap textiles, and bankruptcies in Japan proliferated. For example, from 1969 to 1974, Marubeni's exports of textiles from Korea to Japan rose by ten.[25] Table 6.12 shows the major markets of Japanese overseas textile firms at that time.

In order to adapt the Japanese textile industry to cheap imports from subsidiaries in Asia, the state allowed many small textile firms to go bankrupt and struggling large ones to form cartels. Table 6.13 shows that during the worst period of the recession bankruptcies among textile firms rose much more rapidly than did those among other firms. Since this weeding out of small inefficient producers reduces the total capacity of the industry, the amount of old value (constant capital) locked up in textile equipment falls. To the extent that the remaining larger firms can introduce newer and cheaper equipment, the organic composition of capital in the industry can also fall. However, even if this latter is not achieved in the short term, eliminating inefficient firms raises the rate of exploitation and can help restore profitability in that way. This seems to have been the

Table 6.12. *Markets of Japanese overseas textile firms, 1974*

Location of subsidiary	Market					
	Fibres			Clothes and other textiles		
	Local	Japan	Other	Local	Japan	Other
North America	100.0	—	—	86.5	7.5	6.0
Central/South America	75.9	7.2	16.8	53.0	—	47.0
Asia	63.9	11.8	24.2	11.5	57.9	30.5
Middle East	—	—	—	100.0	—	—
Europe	100.0	—	—	42.5	—	57.5
Africa	97.1	—	2.8	97.4	—	2.5
Oceania	50.5	49.5	—	—	—	—
Total	72.0	9.2	18.6	30.5	42.3	27.0

Source: Fujii Mitsuo, 'Sen'i sangyō ni okeru kaigai chokusetsu tōshi' [Direct Overseas Investment in the Textile Industry], *Keizai*, no. 175 (November 1978), p. 107.

Table 6.13. *Bankruptcies of textile firms, 1974–7*

	1974	1975	1976	1977
Textiles				
No.	779	756	908	1,328
% increase	70.5	−3.0	20.1	46.3
Liabilities (¥ bil.)	191.4	287.7	166.0	388.2
% increase	342.8	50.3	−42.3	133.8
All industries				
No.	11,681	12,606	15,641	18,471
% increase	42.4	7.9	24.1	18.1
Liabilities (¥ tril.)	1.6	1.9	2.3	3.0
% increase	133.8	16.1	18.3	31.4

Source: As table 6.12, p. 108.

thinking behind the state's policies towards large textile firms. It assisted in the rehabilitation of Kōjin following its collapse, and allowed the conclusion of an accord among the top three textile firms in 1975: Toyobo, Kanebo, and Unitika, which had been suffering huge losses. Between March 1974 and March 1978, they also slashed their work forces by 7,275, 6,938, and 8,914 respectively. During the same period, the total cuts in personnel by the top thirteen textile

Table 6.14. *Employment indices in manufacturing, by firm size, 1962–74*

Firm size (operatives)	1962	1971	1974
1–4	62	100	114
5–29	79	100	101
30–99	83	100	107
100–299	79	100	102
300–999	75	100	99
1,000 and over	73	100	96
Total	77	100	101

Source: Keizai, no. 169 (May 1978), p. 27.

firms amounted to 54,590 out of a workforce of 166,483.[26] Although on occasion, to ensure working-class compliance with such measures, the state offers capital subsidies to slow down the speed of restructuring, substantial 'progress' has been made in the textile industry.

Yet special loans to small less-efficient businesses actually frustrate the normal profit-restoring function of the recession. This is where the state's policies are the most contradictory, since the rapid growth of employment in small manufacturing firms during the boom was an important contributing factor to the eventual collapse. Though the state's pump-priming which had kept them going served to maintain aggregate demand, it also preserved their below-average rates of exploitation and their backward technologies. Table 6.14 shows that in 1962–71 employment in the smallest manufacturing firms grew the most rapidly of all and that it continued to grow even after the onset of the recession, when substantial rationalisation of large firms took place. In fact the rationalisation of large firms and the expansion of small ones was a general feature of the restructuring that took place in 1974–8 and a factor in the slump that set in again towards the beginning of 1980.

The limits on the state's ability to solve the crisis are brought out strikingly by this contradiction: to let small firms go bankrupt without offering any assistance could lead to a breakdown in the mechanisms of social control and unmanageable social unrest, but to offer such assistance prevents the required degree of restructuring from taking place. The result was that while large firms were rationalising their equipment and labour forces, little structural change was taking place where it was most needed.[27]

The difficulties in other 'structurally depressed industries' (*kōzō fukyō gyōshu*) did not, however, manifest themselves until after the 'oil shock,' even though they had been building up well before this and were directly related to uneven capitalist development and shifts in the international division of labour. In fact, government attempts to restructure them have been explicitly linked to official thinking and forecasts about movements in world trade and in the world division of labour. The exact extent of the desired restructuring is not yet clear, but the state's planning is increasingly being based on quite firm assumptions: Japan will specialise in high-technology and heavy industries, while underdeveloped countries will continue to produce raw materials but also take over the production of light manufactures (with imported plant). Trade must everywhere be liberalised, and among imperialist countries the greatest possible cooperation and equality must be achieved.[28]

This vision of the future has been built up gradually out of the state's sometimes muddled attempts to cope with the recession and appropriately to restructure the depressed industries. Problems resulting from the growing dependence of some of them on imported raw materials, including oil, were sooner or later bound to become apparent. During the decade before 1973, the shares of most domestic raw material supplies fell rapidly, and Japanese capital came to rely predominantly on imported supplies.[29] Table 6.15 shows the main changes that took place.

By 1972, raw materials for factory consumption accounted for 66.2% of total imports, and by 1976 this proportion had risen to 72.9%. In the same period, the share of mineral fuels in total imports rose from 24.4% to 43.7%.[30] This growing external dependence for non-reproducible constant capital goods has made Japanese capital highly vulnerable to crises in other capitalist countries. And so from the second half of 1973 to the first half of 1977, all industries dependent on raw materials excepting electricity went into decline: iron and steel, non-ferrous metals, chemical fertilisers, soda, plastics, oil refining, cardboard, synthetic textiles, ceramics, lumber, and wooden manufactures.[31]

It seemed for a while that the effects of falling production in these industries need not necessarily extend beyond them, because during the same period an export boom in a number of other industries

Table 6.15. *Degree of dependence on imports for major raw materials, 1967–77*

	1967	1977
Energy	71.2	91.8
Coal	27.4	76.6
Crude oil	99.1	99.7
Natural gas	0.0	73.0
Iron ore	91.9	98.8
Copper	80.9	92.8
Lead	61.1	77.7
Zinc	43.1	58.7
Tin	94.3	98.0
Aluminium	100.0	100.0
Nickel	100.0	100.0
Lumber	32.1	61.3
Raw wool	99.8	100.0
Raw cotton	100.0	100.0
Soya beans	91.9	97.0
Corn	98.5	99.9
Wheat	80.6	96.0
Beef	11.0	25.1

Source: Tsūshō sangyōshō tsūshō seisakukyoku [Trade Policy Bureau of the Ministry of International Trade and Industry], *Zusetsu tsūshō hakusho* [White Paper on Trade and Industry in Diagrams], 1979 (Tokyo: Tsūshō sangyō chōsakai, 1979), p. 120.

helped maintain aggregate demand. Production expanded by anything from 30% to 100% in colour TVs, sound equipment, motor cars, watches, telecommunications and electronics parts, office machines, and agricultural machines. Although shipbuilding and iron and steel also managed to increase exports, the amount was insufficient to compensate for falling domestic demand. All the equipment investment industries also suffered from excess capacity after 1973, so that by 1978 very few industries had escaped the effects of the crisis.[32] Table 6.16 shows the main changes in the composition of exports that took place during the export boom.

However, far from representing a solution to the crisis, the export boom was short-lived and highlighted the contradictions of Japanese capitalism: the massive trading surpluses led to a phenomenal rise in

Table 6.16. *Changing composition of Japanese trade, 1971–80 ($ million and %)*

	1971 Value	%	1974 Value	%	1977 Value	%	1980 Value	%
Exports (total)	24,019	100	55,536	100	80,495	100	129,807	100
Foodstuffs	679	2.8	846	1.5	870	1.1	1,588	1.2
Raw fuels	276	1.1	780	1.4	692	0.9	1,270	1.0
Heavy industry	17,930	74.6	45,641	82.2	68,129	84.6	109,567	84.4
Machinery	11,874	49.4	27,891	50.2	49,744	61.8	81,481	62.8
General machines	2,448	10.2	5,948	10.7	10,097	12.5	18,088	13.9
Electrical machines	3,402	14.2	6,721	12.1	12,773	15.9	22,760	17.5
Transportation equipment	5,283	22.0	13,469	24.3	23,409	29.1	34,373	26.5
Passenger cars	1,811	7.5	3,510	6.3	8,004	9.9	16,115	12.4
Metallic products	4,570	19.0	13,691	24.7	14,084	17.5	21,319	16.4
Iron and steel	3,542	14.7	10,758	19.3	10,519	13.1	15,454	11.9
Chemical products	1,486	6.2	4,059	7.3	4,300	5.3	6,767	5.2
Light industry	4,945	20.6	7,459	13.4	10,106	12.6	15,786	12.1
Textiles	2,772	11.5	4,065	7.3	4,700	5.8	6,296	4.9
Imports (total)	19,712	100	62,111	100	70,809	100	140,528	100
Foodstuffs	2,918	14.8	8,122	13.1	10,105	14.3	14,666	10.4
Raw materials	6,400	32.5	14,379	23.2	14,342	20.3	23,760	16.9
Mineral fuels	4,752	24.1	24,895	40.1	31,149	44.0	69,991	49.8
Manufactures	5,499	27.9	14,541	23.4	14,651	20.7	30,568	21.8

Source: Tsūshō sangyōshō [Ministry of International Trade and Industry], *Tsūshō hakusho* [White Paper on Trade and Industry], 1981 (Tokyo: Ōkurashō insatsukyoku, 1981), Summary supplement.

Table 6.17. *Changes in the use of computer equipment in iron and steel, 1971–80*

| | No. in use by type | | | |
Year	Business computers	Process computers	Other types	Total
1971	194	175	—	369
1972	186	223	—	409
1973	201	280	—	481
1974	181	328	—	509
1975	173	377	—	550
1976	178	439	—	617
1977	175	585	—	760
1978	158	625	—	783
1979	152	625	28	853
1980	174	705	24	907

Source: Kimoto Shin'ichirō, 'Seisan katei no saihen to "gōrika": sakushu kyōka' [Reorganisation of the Production Process and 'Rationalisation': Strengthening Exploitation], *Keizai*, no. 202 (February 1981), p. 40.

the value of the yen, which, in combination with measures in other countries to reduce trading deficits, put an end to the ability of overseas markets to take the place of sagging domestic ones. By the end of 1977, therefore, it was clear that the structural problems of Japanese industry, in spite of the extensive restructuring that had taken place, were far from over. After a brief revival of domestic demand in 1978–80, they were to re-emerge in very similar forms.

A clear example was the iron and steel industry. Even though the top forty companies cut their staff by a total of 17,648 in 1973–7, the industry was still operating at only 67% of capacity in 1977. Turnover fell by 8.2% from its 1976 level and business profits by 90.86%. Rationalisations have therefore continued unabated: in 1977–9, 4,961 clerical and technical jobs and 17,704 skilled jobs were lost in the top thirty-eight firms.[33] Table 6.17 shows the increase in the number of computers that accompanied these staff reductions.

The shipbuilding industry, another of the traditional mainstays of Japanese capitalism, was no better off: although twenty companies went bankrupt in 1977, excess capacity in the remainder showed no signs of abating. Table 6.18 shows the increase in unused capacity that took place in 1974–7 and the anticipated increases after that. In

Table 6.18. *Use of capacity in major shipbuilding firms, 1974–7 and estimated use, 1978–9*

	1974	1977	1978	1979
7 class A companies (ships of over 1 mil. tons)	100	67	63	55
17 class B companies (ships of 100,000–1 mil. tons)	100	76	70	66
14 class C companies (10,000–100,000 tons)	100	80	75	70
7 class D companies (5,000–10,000 tons)	100	100	85	80

Source: Sasaki, p. 77.

almost the same period (March 1973 to March 1977), the top six shipbuilding firms cut staff by 19,352, and the top twenty still had plans to lay off a further 30,000 in their main and sub-contracted factories. The first sign of any improvement in the industry was when the yen began to depreciate again and, for the first time in six years, orders from Japanese shipyards picked up substantially in fiscal 1979 (ending March 1980), the very time that recession conditions were returning to other industries.[34] The limits on the state's ability to do much more than let the depression run its natural course were strikingly brought out by the recommendations of the Council for Rationalisation of Shipping (Kaiun Zōsen Gōrika Shingikai) in July 1978: cut capacity by 35% and hasten mergers.[35]

Not dissimilar problems occurred in the electric appliance industries, which in some ways trod a path like that of textiles. In spite of the export boom of the mid-1970s, which also slowed down following the rise of the yen, the top sixty quoted companies cut their workforces by 112,000 in the period 1970–7 (Matsushita Electric Industrial by 12,825 and Hitachi by 10,061). With falling domestic demand for almost all products – video equipment being a notable exception – and difficulties in fully compensating by means of exports, solutions were increasingly sought through foreign investments. By 1976 15.4% of Matsushita's, 28.8% of Nihon Denki's, and 18.9% of Sanyo's production was by overseas subsidiaries. Bankruptcies in the industry in Japan reached record levels (573 firms) in 1977, and because subsidiaries in low-wage countries, like their counterparts in textiles, continue to look to Japan for markets, the crisis in the industry is by no means over.[36]

In chemicals, too, the crisis has taken the form of excess capacity and huge reductions in staff. Employment in the ninety largest firms

Table 6.19. *Production indices of chemicals, 1965–77*

	1965	1970	1976	1977
Average	45	100	121	122
Fertilisers	85	100	81	89
Soda	55	100	108	107
Textile materials	43	100	138	117
Plastics	29	100	113	113
Petrochemicals	23	100	133	125

Source: As table 6.18, p. 81.

fell by 50,000 in 1970–7, and in the latter year the appreciation of the yen interrupted accumulation in the export sector and led to 558 bankruptcies.[37] Table 6.19, which provides the indices of production in the main branches of the industry, shows the extent to which things worsened in 1977.

The main industry which might seem, because of its unprecedented growth throughout the recession, to have escaped restructuring was motor vehicles. New car production, for example, increased by 57.4% in the years 1973–80 – from 4.47 million to 7.04 million – and Japan replaced the United States, where production had fallen by 51.6% and 200,000 workers had lost their jobs, as the world's top automaker. Almost every way in which the production statistics are presented tells a story of only briefly interrupted success. Yet when one asks who has been buying all these motor vehicles, one can detect early signs of problems which by the end of 1981 had become quite serious. Each year the domestic market became more and more saturated, and alternative outlets had to be found overseas, particularly in Europe and America, which by 1980 absorbed 64% of the exported vehicles. Less than a year later, their governments had become quite aggressive in their determination somehow to stem the tide of Japanese cars, although they had not yet found a means of doing so.[38] Table 6.20 shows the growth of production and exports of the Japanese motor industry since 1960.

However, in spite of the growth in motor vehicle production during the recession, the industry was quite radically restructured. But what characterised the restructuring was not the massive loss of jobs that occurred elsewhere,[39] but the 'robotisation' of some 40% of the

Table 6.20. *Production and export of motor vehicles in Japan, 1960–80*

	Production	Exports	% exported
1960	481,551	38,809	8.1
1965	1,875,614	194,168	10.4
1970	5,289,157	1,086,776	20.6
1973	7,082,757	2,067,556	29.2
1974	6,551,840	2,618,087	40.0
1975	6,941,591	2,677,612	38.6
1976	7,841,447	3,709,608	47.3
1977	8,514,522	4,352,817	51.1
1978	9,269,153	4,600,735	49.6
1979	9,635,546	4,562,781	47.4
1980	11,042,884	5,966,961	54.0

Source: Sono Haruo, 'Japanese Automotive Capital and International Competition, part 1,' *Ampo*, 13, 1 (1981), p. 62.

assembly-line work. Along with electric appliances, precision instruments, and metal products, the motor industry has been a major target of the *mekatoronikusu* (electronics combined with machines) revolution that is sweeping through Japanese industry.[40] Table 6.21 shows the numbers of industrial robots produced annually since 1968 along with their average prices in relation to average wage costs in selected years.

These represent only the tip of an iceberg of adaptations of microtechnology which are being used to transform the office and factory in Japan. All kinds of computerised systems are being introduced into the whole range of industries, with remarkable results in terms of increases in productivity. Since most of it has taken place since the mid-1970s, this is when labour productivity in Japan once again soared ahead of that of other advanced capitalist countries. Table 6.22 shows the numbers of independent computerised systems that were in use in 1973 and 1979 in the different industries, and table 6.23 shows how much more rapid and effective was Japanese capital in restructuring its manufacturing industries than were its competitors overseas.

However, the restructuring of manufacturing, both in terms of technological reorganisation and the destruction of jobs, was largely confined to monopoly capital: of the total of 940,000 jobs lost in manufacturing in 1974–9, 920,000 were in firms with over 500

Table 6.21. *Production of industrial robots, robot prices, and average wages, 1968–79*

	Industrial robots			
	Average price (¥1,000)	No. produced	Total no. to date	Average wage costs (¥1,000)
1968	—	200	2,500	—
1970	4,580 (1971)	1,700	3,100	989
1971	—	1,300	4,800	—
1972	—	1,700	6,100	—
1973	—	2,500	7,800	—
1974	—	4,200	12,000	—
1975	4,060	4,400	16,400	2,303
1976	3,860	7,200	23,600	2,584
1977	4,670	8,600	32,200	2,838
1978	5,230	10,200	42,400	3,038
1979	—	14,500	56,900	—

Sources: Kimoto, p. 41; Hayashi Masaki, 'Mekatoronikusuka to Nihonteki keiei' [Mechatronics-isation and Japanese-Style Management], *Keizai*, no. 203 (March 1981), p. 57.

Table 6.22. *Numbers of independent computerised systems in use, by industry, 1973–9*

	1973	1979
Manufacturing/construction	240	1,758
Finance/insurance/real estate	155	541
Government/universities/etc.	130	447
Commerce	43	983
Software/communications industries	42	294
Others	96	575

Source: Arima Jirō, '80 nendai jōhōka to media kōzō no saihensei' [The Transformation of Information in the 1980s and the Reorganisation of the Structure of the Media], *Keizai*, no. 206 (June 1981), p. 54.

workers. In small firms of under 100 workers, manufacturing employment actually increased by 110,000 in the same period (See table 6.24). As a result of the restructuring of large firms and the expansion of employment in small ones during the worst years of the recession, manufacturing production finally surpassed its 1973 levels in 1978.[41]

Table 6.23. *Hourly labour productivity in manufacturing and average hourly wage costs in major capitalist countries, 1960–79 (annual percentage increase)*

	Japan	U.S.A.	United Kingdom	West Germany
1960–5				
Labour productivity	7.1	4.5	3.5	6.5
Wage costs	4.4	− 1.5	2.7	2.8
1965–70				
Labour productivity	12.9	1.2	3.7	6.2
Wage costs	2.1	3.8	4.7	1.4
1970–3				
Labour productivity	9.6	4.4	5.6	7.1
Wage costs	8.3	2.4	7.6	3.1
1973–5				
Labour productivity	− 1.0	− 0.3	0.2	4.7
Wage costs	24.6	8.9	23.9	4.9
1975–8				
Labour productivity	7.4	2.7	1.8	5.5
Wage costs	− 0.1	5.7	9.9	1.0
1979				
Labour productivity	8.2	1.7	1.9	5.1
Wage costs	− 1.7	6.6	14.7	0.4

Source: Umino Hisao, 'Chūshō kigyō no genkyokumen to rōdō undō no shiten' [The Present Situation in Small Firms and the Labour Movement Viewpoint], *Keizai*, no. 202 (February 1981), p. 55.

The depth of the crisis and degree of restructuring in non-manufacturing industries was, by comparison, moderate. Among the worst hit was construction, in which, in spite of public works programmes designed to stimulate aggregate demand, restructuring took place mainly through a flood of bankruptcies in the non-monopoly sector. Table 6.25 shows that the share of bankruptcies of this industry increased steadily during the worst years of the recession. Yet, as table 6.26 shows, in the industry as a whole employment fell only in 1974 and building orders only in 1975. In 1977, however, the yen crisis had a profound impact on large construction firms: the October overseas orders of the top forty-five companies fell by 92.7% from the previous year. Coupled with low private sector demand, the

Table 6.24. *Numbers of employees in manufacturing, by firm size, 1974–9 (1,000 persons)*

	1974	1979	Change in 1974–9
Total	12,010	11,070	−940
Firm size by operatives			
1–29	3,170	3,250	80
30–99	2,120	2,150	30
100–499	2,280	2,150	−130
500 and over	4,420	3,500	−920
Government	20	20	—

Source: Kudō, part 1, p. 104.

Table 6.25. *Bankruptcies in the construction industry, 1968–77*

	Total bankruptcies (A)	Those in construction (B)	B/A = %
1968	10,776	2,447	22.7
1970	9,765	2,247	23.0
1973	8,202	2,512	30.6
1974	11,681	3,669	31.4
1975	12,606	3,443	27.3
1976	15,641	4,989	31.9
1977	15,206	4,748	31.2

Source: Sasaki, p. 124.

yen crisis made the industry precariously dependent on public works projects.[42]

In the unproductive sector, the most important forms of restructuring were the introduction of computerised office equipment and the reorganisation of large-scale retailing: department stores gave way to supermarkets. From 1967 to 1976, the share of supermarkets in the sales of the top one hundred retailers rose from 28.0% to 48.7%, while that of department stores fell from 62.3% to 43.4%.[43] Many provincial department stores were absorbed by leading supermarket chains like Daiei, Nichii, and Jusco, and in February 1981 the first tie-up between a leading supermarket chain and a major national department store was announced: Daiei would transfer to Takashimaya

Table 6.26. *Employment and changes in building orders in construction, 1973–9*

	1973	1974	1975	1976	1977	1978	1979
Employment (1,000 persons)	4,670	4,640	4,790	4,920	4,990	5,200	N.A.
Building orders (% change)	18.3	4.4	−7.5	2.4	12.9	10.9	14.6

Sources: Shūkan Tōyō Keizai, *Keizai tōkei nenkan*, 1979. p. 92; *Shinbun Geppō*, 410 and 361 (January 1981 and December 1976), p. 194.

shares equivalent to 10.5% of the latter's outstanding capital stock.[44]

These tie-ups are particularly significant, because distribution businesses had for many years been outside the state's 'administrative guidance' (*gyōsei shidō*) and because Japan's distribution system had become such a drain on surplus value. Table 6.9 showed how the share of surplus value absorbed by wholesale and retail firms increased in the years leading up to the recession. One example of the problem, taken from a series of articles on distribution by the *Japan Times Weekly*, concerns beef. Imported at ¥350–450 per kilogram in 1978, beef retailed in Tokyo at ¥3,000 per kilogram.[45] The state has never seriously tackled the main source of the drain, which is that a product normally passes through the hands of several wholesalers before it gets to a retailer. In recent years, the total sales of wholesalers have been about four times those of retailers, who are the first to feel the pinch when it comes.

The slowdown in household spending around 1977 and again since mid-1980 raised the burden of squandering such large amounts of surplus value in the circulation process, a burden which falls heavily not simply on small firms but on large department stores in the distribution sector. In 1977, the sales of these department stores rose by only 6%, the smallest on record, while those of the more streamlined supermarkets rose by 18.8%.[46] In addition to mergers, takeovers, and bankruptcies, restructuring was also carried out by introducing new technology and rationalising staff. For example, in 1976 almost all the major department stores reduced staff by about 5%, as did four of the top ten supermarket chains. The latter also enormously expanded the proportions of their part-time workers (mainly women), who already in 1976 made up about 33% of the total. A full 50.3% of Izumiya's 3,691 workers were part-timers.[47]

By the end of 1977, therefore, almost every major sector of Japanese industry was undergoing some or other form of restructuring, which the state more and more tried to bring into line with an overall economic plan. Particularly after 1975, many such plans were drafted by a variety of government departments and advisory councils. The most important of these were the Third National Development Plan (Dai Sanji Zenkoku Sōgō Kaihatsu Keikaku) announced in November 1977, the Seven Year Socio-Economic Plan (Shin Keizai Shakai Nanakanen Keikaku) of January 1979, the Reports of the Industrial Structure Council (Sangyō Kōzō Shingikai), and the annual White Papers on the economy.[48] The thrust of the state's

Classes in contemporary Japan

Table 6.27. *The Seven Year Plan's vision of the industrial structure in 1985*

	1970 (%)	1975 (%)	1978 (%)	1985 (%)	Average growth 1979–85
Primary industry	*4.2*	*·3.7*	*3.1*	*2.3*	*1.4*
Secondary industry	*59.9*	*57.6*	*58.6*	*58.8*	*5.7*
Manufacturing	50.0	48.1	49.4	49.0	5.6
Chemicals etc.[a]	9.6	8.9	8.7	8.4	5.1
Primary Metals[a]	8.1	7.4	7.3	6.5	3.8
Machines[a]	17.5	17.7	19.8	21.5	6.9
Other[a]	14.8	14.0	13.5	12.7	4.7
Construction	9.8	9.4	9.2	9.8	6.6
Tertiary industry	*35.9*	*38.7*	*38.3*	*38.8*	*5.9*
Electricity/gas/water	1.7	1.9	1.9	1.9	5.4
Finance/insurance	2.9	3.6	3.4	3.5	6.2
Transport/communications	4.5	4.7	4.5	4.5	5.6
Services etc.[a]	26.7	28.6	28.5	29.0	5.9
Total	100.0	100.0	100.0	100.0	5.7
Value of production at 1970 prices (¥ tril.)	166.3	207.9	247.0	363.0	—

[a]The plan used a new system of industrial classification, which is as follows:
Chemicals etc.: mining, pulp/paper, chemicals, petroleum products, coal products, ceramics/stone and clay products.
Primary metals: pig iron/unrefined steel, iron/steel primary manufactures, nonferrous metals primary manufactures.
Machines: metallic products, general machines, electric machines, transport machines, precision instruments.
Other: food, textiles, other manufactures.
Services etc.: wholesale/retail, real estate, services.
Source: Keizai kikakuchō [Economic Planning Agency], *Shin keizai shakai nanakanen keikaku* [New Seven Year Socio-Economic Plan] (Tokyo: Ōkurashō insatsukyoku, 1979), p. 161.

emerging vision for the future is to restructure Japanese industry to fit into what it sees as a new international division of labour.

Japanese capital should continue to concentrate on heavy industry for overseas and domestic markets, but it should also specialise more in products with higher value added. To raise productivity through trade and to help balance its international payments, low-priced semi-finished goods should be imported, in many cases from Asian subsidiaries, so that dependence on high-priced domestic ones can be reduced. Industries which cannot compete with these imports, such

Table 6.28. *Growth of real GNP, 1973–80*

Year	% growth
1973	5.3
1974	−0.2
1975	3.6
1976	5.1
1977	5.3
1978	5.2
1979	5.5
1980	3.8

Source: Keizai kikakuchō [Economic Planning Agency], *Keizai hakusho* [White Paper on the Economy], 1981 (Tokyo: Ōkurashō insatsukyoku, 1981), p. 411.

as aluminium smelting and synthetic fibres, will have to be run down. Light industry should as far as possible expand in the same way, but focus on the domestic market. Table 6.27 shows the structure of Japanese industry that is anticipated in 1985 and the growth rates expected in the main sectors.

The anticipated growth rates were, of course, based on a quite unrealistic degree of optimism: a 5.7% average growth rate could not possibly be sustained, since this could not even be achieved in 1979, the year of the mini-boom which soon collapsed. In 1980, GNP expanded by only 3.8%, and this was expected to fall to 3.5% in 1981 (see table 6.28). Already in August that year the Seven Year Plan was being reviewed, its estimates revised, and the fiscal policies which underlay it radically altered.

One might be tempted to think that 1980–1 was very similar to 1974–5 and that with a bit more restructuring here and there the bubble could be reflated. Nothing would be further from the truth: the downturn of the early 1980s was a direct result of the slowdown in personal spending, which was an inevitable result of the clampdown on wages of the preceding years. It most of all affected small businesses, which could only be restructured by having them all go bankrupt. Moreover, the high profitability of the already re-structured large businesses could be upset very easily by conditions in export markets, which were in a constant state of uncertainty. Businesses therefore planned large reductions in equipment invest-ment for 1982, as is revealed by table 6.29.

Table 6.29. Changes in planned equipment investments by industry for 1981-2

	1981		1982
	Amount (¥100 mil.)	Change from 1980	Planned change from 1981
Total	109,394	11.9	10.8
Total excluding electric power	71,529	13.1	−1.7
Manufacturing	*41,395*	*17.0*	*1.1*
Food	1,665	10.6	−12.2
Textiles	1,555	1.9	−18.8
Pulp/paper	882	−34.4	−32.4
Chemicals	5,054	21.2	−6.2
Organic	3,000	26.1	2.6
Other	2,055	14.8	−17.4
Petroleum refining	1,711	11.5	−13.8
Ceramics	1,780	−5.7	−26.5
Iron/steel	8,515	33.0	21.1
Nonferrous metals	1,901	49.1	12.5
Metal products	498	−35.7	−9.4
General machines	1,801	11.4	−19.9
Electric machines	5,812	25.9	0.2
Motor vehicles	7,553	19.6	−39.5
Shipbuilding	1,476	14.7	−14.4
Other manufactures	1,182	6.2	−8.7
Non-manufacturing	*68,000*	*9.0*	*14.1*
(excluding electric power)	*30,135*	*8.2*	*−4.7*
Agriculture/forestry/fishing/mining	777	20.3	−16.5
Construction	1,542	0.7	−23.0
Wholesale/retail	4,420	7.5	−1.3
Department stores/supermarkets	3,218	8.2	−5.7
Real estate	1,457	8.7	−10.1
Transportation	9,750	−0.1	−26.7
Land	3,034	6.4	−47.2
Sea	3,620	22.4	1.0
Other	3,096	−21.6	−39.1
Electric power	37,865	9.7	22.9
Gas	2,912	40.1	16.8
Services	8,384	12.9	16.5
Other non-manufacturing	892	−8.1	24.5

Source: *Nihon Keizai Shinbun*, 21 August 1981, in *Shinbun Geppō*, 418 (September 1981), p. 103.

Table 6.30. *Main cuts in public servants planned for 1982–7*

	No. in 1981	Planned reduction	% reduction
Office of the Prime Minister	3,342	213	6.37
National Public Safety Commission	7,630	279	3.66
Hokkaido Development Agency	9,987	814	8.15
Defence Agency	27,528	1,576	5.73
Justice Ministry	49,943	2,217	4.44
Foreign Ministry	3,560	206	5.79
Finance Ministry	68,188	3,362	4.93
Education Ministry	132,556	4,797	3.62
Welfare Ministry	74,669	2,678	3.59
Agriculture and Forestry Ministry	49,395	4,223	8.55
MITI	12,741	756	5.93
Transport Ministry	38,196	1,883	4.93
Labour Ministry	25,447	1,621	6.37
Construction Ministry	28,388	1,985	6.99
Other administrative	11,997	569	4.74
Subtotal	543,567	27,179	5.00
Post Office	312,702	15,635	5.00
National Forestry	32,074	1,604	5.00
Government Printing	6,787	339	4.99
National Mint	1,704	85	4.99
Alcohol Monopoly	883	44	4.98
Total	897,717	44,886	5.00

Source: Asahi Shinbun, 11 September 1981, in *Shinbun Geppō*, 419 (October 1981), p. 42.

Apart from the rather radical changes in the government's fiscal policies (which are examined in the next section) which the abandonment of its optimism of the late 1970s made necessary, the only new targets for restructuring it could think of were national civil servants. *Gyōsei kaikaku* or *gyōkaku* ('administrative reform') is part of a drive to cut government expenditure in response to the growing fiscal crisis of the state, which is examined in the next section. What is pertinent here is the Cabinet's adoption of proposals from an *ad hoc* commission headed by Toshio Doko, past President of Keidanren, to cut the number of central government employees by 44,886 (5%) in the five years beginning in fiscal 1982. Table 6.30 indicates the planned reductions. Another of the commission's proposals which is relevant here is the one to hand over to private hands certain public corporations, but these have not yet been seriously taken up by the state.

Table 6.31. *Direct overseas investments, 1951–79 (fiscal years, ending March 1980)*

	No. of cases	Value ($ mil.)
1951–62	961	545
1963–7	1,128	906
1968	369	557
1969	544	665
1970	729	904
1971	904	858
1951–71	4,635	4,435
1972	1,774	2,338
1973	3,093	3,494
1974	1,911	2,395
1975	1,591	3,280
1976	1,652	3,462
1977	1,761	2,806
1978	2,395	4,598
1979	2,694	4,995
1972–9	16,873	27,369
Total accumulated investments	21,508	31,804

Source: Shūkan Tōyō Keizai [The Oriental Economist], *Kaigai shinshutsu kigyō sōran* [Japanese Multinationals, Facts and Figures], 1981, Rinji zōkan [Special issue], no. 4261 (Tokyo: Tōyō keizai shinpōsha, 1981), p. 553.

The phenomenon of *gyōkaku* is of course quite familiar in capitalist countries these days. It tends to indicate that the state has run out of ideas on how to restructure industry and restore confidence, and it thus turns on its own employees as a sort of scapegoat.

However, if it is remembered that the state, like individual corporations or even groups of them, is simply a form of organisation of the bourgeoisie which is as subject to the infrastructural demands of the system as any other, it should not come as a surprise to find the state running out of expedients to cope with the crisis. There is nothing miraculous about the tools available to the bourgeoisie in this its most society-wide form of organisation: as far as accumulation functions are concerned, fiscal spending, information sharing, and granting or withholding permissions and subsidies to particular firms are just about all that is available. State restructuring is thus essentially not much more than a matter of speeding up the depression process in some sectors and attempting to initiate the revival and expansion of others. Since the state cannot even employ the limited means available to it to their full potential if it is simultaneously to maintain social control, the restructuring of the non-monopoly sector is unlikely to proceed any more rapidly in the 1980s than it did in the 1970s. As it did in the past, the state will muddle through the contradictions and attempt to pursue all objectives simultaneously. Attempts will increasingly be made to justify rather than eliminate the mounting stagnation (and repression) at home, and solutions will be sought abroad: not just through exports, but through foreign investments, particularly in Asia.

In fact, during the recession of the 1970s Japanese imperialism developed more rapidly than ever before. Each year saw huge increases in direct overseas investments, as is revealed by table 6.31, and giant corporations expanded their overseas workforces while they cut their domestic ones. In the four years from January 1974 to December 1977, only eighteen of the top one hundred firms which scrapped domestic jobs also cut the numbers of their overseas employees. Table 6.32 shows the extent to which those which were responsible for the largest job losses in Japan were also the ones which most expanded their hiring abroad. Only the main forty-eight are explicitly listed: those in which over 1,000 jobs were lost and any others which boosted their overseas employment by more than 1,000.

There are four main types of manufacturing investment which affect domestic employment: investment to secure markets in underdeveloped countries (not yet very important), 'offshore' production aimed at the American and European markets (having a great impact on domestic employment), 'offshore' production for the Japanese market (also having a great impact), and production in Europe and America to avoid problems of import controls (increasing in importance).[49] By the end of the 1970s, most overseas manufacturing was of the second and third types, and was located in underdeveloped countries, particularly in Asia where wages were only 20% of what they were in Japan. Investments in mining and raw-material-related industries were also mainly in underdeveloped countries, while the bulk of those in commerce and services were in Europe and America (See tables 6.33 and 6.34).

One of the characteristics of overseas investments in the 1980s will be an expansion in the first and fourth types of manufacturing: to establish subsidiaries in underdeveloped and developed countries for the local market, what is being called *genchi seisan hanbai kei*. The aim is

Table 6.32. *The top 100 firms' rationalisation of employment at home and expansion of employment abroad, 1974–8*

Firm	Domestic employees		Overseas employees		Change in ratio (%) of overseas to domestic employees
	No. in March 1978	Change since March 1974	No. in Dec. 1977	Change since Jan. 1974	
Over 1,000 jobs lost					
Nippon Steel	76,034	-2,580	1,050	965	0.11 to 1.38
Kawasaki Steel	36,690	-1,367	1,505	1,462	0.11 to 4.10
Kobe Steel	33,541	-1,538	15,459	13,777	4.79 to 46.09
Riccar	3,000	-1,068	80	26	1.33 to 2.67
Hitachi	70,847	-10,061	8,300	2,968	6.58 to 11.72
Tokyo Shibaura Electric	64,048	-7,426	11,600	-2,100	19.17 to 18.11
Mitsubishi Electric	50,809	-4,726	6,800	1,168	10.14 to 13.38
Fuji Electric	14,853	-5,542	1,100	1,083	0.08 to 7.41
Matsushita Electric	33,535	-12,825	21,000	6,711	30.82 to 62.62
Sony	9,682	-1,287	5,500	3,300	20.06 to 56.81
Nippon Electric	31,170	-1,955	9,632	3,906	17.29 to 30.90
Mitsubishi Heavy Industries	68,463	-11,720	4,895	4,841	0.07 to 7.15
Ishikawajima-Harima Heavy Industries	36,688	-1,168	7,850	1,768	16.07 to 21.40
Kawasaki Heavy Industries	31,262	-3,354	2,698	2,638	0.17 to 8.63
Hitachi Shipbuilding	21,562	-2,254	1,303	890	1.73 to 6.04
Sumitomo Heavy Industries	11,145	-1,382	1,105	1,044	0.49 to 9.91
Toyo Kogyo	29,548	-7,343	1,327	-353	4.55 to 4.49
Fuji Heavy Industries	13,467	-1,182	120	116	0.03 to 0.89
Sumitomo Chemical	11,179	-3,054	2,527	572	13.74 to 22.60
Asahi Glass	9,800	-1,633	3,362	226	27.43 to 34.31
Nippon Sheet Glass	3,660	-2,455	2,623	742	30.76 to 71.67
Unitika	7,465	-8,914	5,923	-645	40.10 to 79.34

Company				
Toyobo	17,337	−7,275	10,200	9,000	4.88 to 58.83
Kanebo	13,881	−6,938	10,200	4,600	26.90 to 73.48
Kurabo Industries	6,388	−1,326	2,360	1,104	16.28 to 36.94
Nisshin Spinning	6,176	−3,266	818	318	5.30 to 13.24
Toray	15,880	−7,221	30,300	8,000	96.53 to 190.81
Teijin	12,205	−1,796	16,500	904	111.39 to 135.19
Asahi Chemical	15,113	−2,929	4,500	4,485	0.08 to 29.78
Mitsubishi Rayon	4,373	−4,534	4,977	−2,034	78.71 to 113.81
Kuraray	5,936	−5,271	2,108	1,560	4.89 to 35.51
Gunze	6,871	−1,466	323	183	1.68 to 4.70
Jujo Paper	5,869	−1,044	8	−342	5.06 to 0.13
Dai Nippon Printing	9,674	−3,038	2,318	433	20.96 to 23.96
Showa Denko	6,165	−2,944	1,563	1,559	0.04 to 25.35
Mitsubishi Metal	4,906	−3,939	138	136	0.02 to 2.81

Others which expanded overseas employment by more than 1,000

Company				
Komatsu	17,262	−413	1,607	1,257	1.98 to 9.31
Daikin Kogyo	5,573	−512	10,041	9,808	3.83 to 180.17
Brother Industries	5,552	−532	1,500	1,230	4.43 to 27.02
Sharp	11,038	−269	3,379	2,659	6.37 to 30.61
Oki Electric Industry	14,201	−914	1,615	1,585	0.20 to 11.37
Canon	9,506	−574	4,000	2,588	14.01 to 42.08
Noritake	2,737	−886	2,426	1,531	24.70 to 88.64
Bridgestone Tire	17,883	−260	3,500	2,032	8.09 to 19.57
Renown	3,937	−128	2,239	1,439	19.68 to 56.87
Honshu Paper	4,918	−473	1,804	1,794	0.19 to 36.68
Hitachi Cable	5,097	−45	2,606	2,597	0.18 to 51.13
Sumitomo Metal Mining	3,223	−773	3,553	1,677	46.95 to 110.24
Total for the 100 firms	1,159,244	−170,358	267,666	115,725	11.43 to 23.09

Source: Kudō, part 2, pp. 18–19.

Table 6.33. *Breakdown of Japanese overseas investments, by area and main industries (shares of accumulated total as of March 1980)*

Area	Manufacturing	Mining/agric./ forestry/ fisheries	Others (mainly services)	Total
North America	18.6	9.6	40.2	25.8
Europe	6.3	11.7	17.3	12.2
Oceania	6.1	10.7	4.6	6.5
Subtotal	31.0	32.0	62.0	44.5
South and Central America	23.8	18.5	12.1	17.5
Asia	35.4	41.8	12.7	27.2
Middle East	9.0	0.6	8.0	6.6
Africa	0.8	7.0	5.2	4.1
Subtotal	69.0	68.0	38.0	55.5
Total	100.0	100.0	100.0	100.0

Source: Shūkan Tōyō Keizai, *Kaigai shinshutsu kigyō sōran*, 1981, pp. 554–5.

Table 6.34. *Japanese overseas investments, by area, workers in subsidiaries, and wage rates in subsidiaries, March 1980*

Area	Value of investments ($ mil.)	No. of employees in subsidiaries	Wage index in subsidiaries (Japan = 100)
North America	8,202	69,136	135
Europe	3,893	33,282	98
Oceania	2,078	22,521	62
South and Central America	5,580	99,468	47
Asia	8,643	450,487	20
Middle East	2,101	14,318	32
Africa	1,306	36,540	15
Total	31,804	725,752	38

Source: Tōkei bunseki kenkyūkai, 'Kokusai kyōsōryoku no himitsu' [The Secret of International Competitive Power], *Keizai*, no. 209 (September 1981), p. 166.

to create a system of ultra-imperialism in which a number of fairly autonomous powers cooperate in maintaining and extending their sway. Japanese capital's need for such a system is not simply to obtain stable supplies of low-priced raw materials or even to locate production where workers are cheap and disciplined. The need is more and more to get round the rising tide of protectionism that always builds up in slumps and which has been making Japanese capital so nervous. Yet cooperation with other imperialist powers is not proving at all easy to obtain, particularly from the United States.[50] There is thus a real possibility that further bottlenecks will develop in the circulation process in the 1980s and multiply the effects of any domestic downturn. We must therefore examine the circulation process in Japan as well as the ways the state has tried to keep it functioning.

The circulation process

Because most sales in capitalist societies such as Japan are among businesses, it is easy to see how the failure of even a few to keep up their purchases from others can quickly result in vast numbers being unable to sell their products. If nothing is done to maintain buying power, even a minor bottleneck in the circulation process can lead to a widespread collapse of markets. Hence, should a downturn occur simply because the circulation of capital is interrupted for reasons unrelated to the production process, the state should be able to restore aggregate demand by expanding its own expenditures. However, in cases where the crisis originates in the production process, as it did in Japan, no amount of state expenditure can solve it.

Since bourgeois macro-economic theory concentrates on the market, its prescriptions in times of crisis centre on managing market demand. This is partly why, even though the Japanese state intervenes considerably in the production process, it tends to lack a coherent theory of what it is doing and in an *ad hoc* way to respond to the problems as they manifest themselves. Its intervention in the circulation process, however, is guided by a coherent theory, Keynesian demand management, and until 1973 this had been more or less effective in flattening out fluctuations in the rate of accumulation. Although many of the fiscal and monetary policies were also intended to fulfil functions of social control, such as expenditure on housing, these are not pertinent at the moment. Furthermore, since demand management is fairly thoroughly dealt with by bourgeois scholars,[51] I concentrate here on its limitations: inflation and fiscal crisis.

There are two broad ways in which the state tries to stimulate aggregate demand: directly, through its own expenditures financed

Table 6.35. *Overview of fiscal and monetary policy, 1970–81*

	Budget General Account (% change)	Bond Ratio (%)	FILP (% change)	Money supply (M₂) (% change)	Discount Rate (%)	Bankruptcy liabilities (% change)	Nominal GNP (% change)	CPI (% change)
1970	17.9	5.4	16.3	17.9	6.00	36.2	15.8	7.3
1971	18.4	4.5	19.6	22.5	4.75	−18.6	10.2	5.7
1972	21.8	17.0	31.6	26.8	4.25	−24.0	16.6	5.2
1973	24.6	16.4	22.9	19.6	9.00	88.7	21.0	16.1
1974	19.7	12.6	14.4	11.4	9.00	88.0	18.4	21.8
1975	24.5	9.4	17.5	13.9	6.50	21.9	10.0	10.4
1976	14.1	29.9	14.1	14.4	6.50	15.7	12.2	9.4
1977	17.4	29.7	18.1	10.9	4.25	34.8	10.9	6.7
1978	20.3	32.0	18.7	12.1	3.50	−36.7	9.6	3.4
1979	12.6	39.5	13.1	11.4	6.25	15.2	7.7	4.8
1980	10.3	33.5	8.0	8.4	7.25	21.8	8.0	7.8
1981	9.9	26.2	7.2	8.3[a]	6.25	—	8.0[a]	5.3[a]
1982	6.2	21.0	4.1	—	—	—	—	—

[a]Forecasts.
Sources: Zaisei kin'yū tōkei geppō, no. 355, 1981, supplement; Ōkurashō shukeikyoku chōsaka [Research Section of the Budget Bureau of the Ministry of Finance], *Zaisei tōkei* [Financial Statistics], 1980 (Tokyo: Ōkurashō insatsukyoku, 1980); contemporary newspapers.

by taxation or borrowing, and indirectly, through placing more buying power in private hands in any of a variety of ways, including lending, cutting taxes, and controlling the money supply. Both broad methods can be regulated to increase or decrease demand more in some sectors than in others. Table 6.35 summarises the main tools available to the Japanese state as well as the broad ways in which they have been used.

The first column, the General Account of the Annual Budget, shows the average changes in the expenditures the government allocated to things like social security, public works, defence, and grants to local governments.[52] Since in 1980 these allocations accounted for about 18% of National Expenditure, variations can have important effects. For example, the extremely small increase for 1982, particularly in comparison with the increase in 1978, was bound to contribute to, rather than counteract, the downturn in household expenditure. The Bond Ratio refers to the proportion of the budgeted expenditure that the government intended raising by means of borrowing. Since 1966 was the first year this was done, it might seem that until then standard Keynesian pump-priming was not used. In that period of rigid adherence to balanced budgets, the General Account was expansionary only in the sense that the state's share of National Expenditure increased. Because the increases were financed solely from the growth of taxation, the state's expenditure served mainly to reallocate spending that would have taken place anyway. However, since at least part of the money would have been saved and remained idle had it not been taxed and spent, even the pre-1966 budgets contained elements of Keynesianism.

More important than this, and not explicitly noticed by the advocates of balanced budgets, was the extensive borrowing from the Post Office Savings Banks and the Post Office Insurance funds to sustain what is known as the 'second budget,' the *Zaisei tōyū shi* (Fiscal Investment and Loan Programme, column three in table 6.35). There was actually no difference in principle between the state raising funds by selling bonds and doing so by borrowing from the Post Office Savings Banks, since both involved throwing into circulation money which was being saved.

The fourth column indicates changes in the supply of the money that can be used for making purchases. Although expansion of buying power by this means can be inflationary, it can also stimulate aggregate demand in ways which do not affect the level of prices. The fourth column from the right, the Bank of Japan's official Discount Rate (which determines all interest rates) is a far more important instrument of demand management in Japan than it is in other capitalist societies. This is because the high level of debt financing by large corporations in that country makes them much more sensitive to changes in the rate of interest when making their investment decisions. The final three columns provide a very general view of how successfully the state has used the fiscal and monetary tools at its disposal. An increase in liabilities from bankrupt firms may be evidence of fine restructuring work, but it does not reveal good demand management. The same applies to slowdowns in the increase in nominal GNP, particularly when consumer prices increase by greater or even similar amounts. On the other hand, low consumer price rises combined with large increases in nominal GNP are signs of greater success.

It would be difficult to argue that demand management did much to stem the tide of recession or even to smooth out its unevennesses. More often than not the state used the different instruments at its disposal in contradictory ways, with little net overall effect on aggregate demand. For example, although fiscal policy remained expansionary for some years after the onset of the recession, a tight monetary policy and high discount rate reduced its impact. However, in response to the 21.8% inflation rate in 1974, government spending did eventually become a bit more restrained, though a larger share of it was financed by means of borrowing. The result was a growing fiscal crisis, which clearly laid bare even for government eyes to see that managing demand in the circulation process had definite limits as a means for solving problems in the production process. Almost 40% of the 1979 budget was to be financed by bonds; and considerable tax cuts, which left total tax revenues the same as the year before, were made to stimulate personal spending. By lowering the discount rate, it was also hoped that investment demand would increase, but capital was very wary of spending under conditions of excess capacity.

The failure of fiscal and monetary policy to sustain anything more than a short-lived mini-boom reinforced those who felt that the fiscal crisis had become intolerable and that government expenditure should be reduced. Moreover, with growing shares of the budget going into bond servicing (from 6.9% in 1976 to 10.6% in 1979 and 15.8% in 1982), it became clear that some radical changes in the tax system had to be made. Although the state desperately needed new sources of revenue, it feared the social consequences of introducing a consumption tax or of raising income taxes, not to mention the effects such taxes might have on aggregate demand. It therefore dithered for a year or so, gradually reducing its borrowing and expenditures before it finally took the plunge in its 1982 budget: tax and stamp revenues were substantially raised (13.4%), and both the General Account and the Fiscal Investment and Loan Programme were slashed to their lowest rates of increase in more than two decades. Fiscal crisis finally seemed to force the state into abandoning demand management as a means of solving the crisis. The grandiose Seven Year Plan's expenditures had to be quietly forgotten.

Although still small by international standards, government expenditure in Japan grew very fast in the 1960s and 1970s. However, because of the mounting structural problems in the production system, each successive increase in state expenditure had a diminishing impact on capital accumulation. In spite of deficit financing, tax cuts, and low interest rates, the overall rate of accumulation has been tardy and in the early 1980s threatened to grind once again to a halt.

Since the consequences of this downturn and retrenchment in state expenditure will emerge in the form of new problems in maintaining social control, examination of the composition of government spending is left to the next chapter.

Analysis of the accumulation functions of the state has therefore established the context for looking at the functions of social control: the working masses had to comply with the effects of all the different forms of restructuring (bankruptcy, plant rationalisation, lay-offs, and imperialism) and with cuts in government spending brought on by the fiscal crisis. More concretely, the state's job was to see that people complied with what the system required of them: unemployment, job insecurity, difficulties in making ends meet, and all the accompanying problems. As the most highly developed form of organisation of the bourgeoisie, its task was to ensure that no potentially comparable form of organisation of the working masses could get off the ground.

7

Crisis and the state: functions of social control

The Japanese state's production of certain constant capital goods and its various attempts to restructure mainly ailing sectors and industries, as well as its many forms of demand management, are all results of the inability of non-state forms of bourgeois organisation to maintain uninterrupted capital accumulation. Although state forms of organisation are not necessarily any more effective in carrying out accumulation functions than their more fragmented non-state counterparts, in practice they tend to be so because of the high degree of interdependence of capitalist enterprises as far as accumulation functions are concerned. Yet the limited ability of the state to solve the problems of capital accumulation in Japan was only too clear during the crisis.

Much the same could be said of the state's functions of social control: they are expanded when non-state forms of organisation begin to lose their grip and greater coordination is needed to secure working-class compliance with all the measures needed to restore capital accumulation. However, in contrast to accumulation functions, the maintenance of social control is in practice better performed by fragmented than by centralised forms of organisation. The latter only make bourgeois power more visible and provoke more centralised forms of working-class organisation. The result is that the more the state tries to do what faltering non-state organisations have failed to accomplish, the more does social control break down. The contradictions of the system make it extremely difficult for the state not simply to work out what to do to revive capital accumulation but how to get the working masses to do what it eventually decides on.

Theory

In contrast to its rigorous reconstructions of the functional requirements of capital accumulation, the Marxist tradition has done very

little investigation into the functions of social control, whether or not
these are performed by the state. However, though some of the
confusion of Marxist theory in this area stems from the lack of
attention it has received, much results from the tendency to equate
accumulation with capitalist enterprises (economics) and social
control with the state (politics). A study of Japan can help resolve
some of the confusion, since one of the distinctive characteristics of
Japanese capitalism is that the state has been far more involved in
accumulation functions, and private enterprises in functions of social
control, than anywhere in Europe or America.

It has of course always been recognised in some form or other that
accumulation functions are the more fundamental: the requirements
of capital accumulation come first and tell us what the working
masses must comply with. Only then can we begin to analyse how
they are made to do so. In the language of the Introduction, the
(hidden) infrastructural mechanisms of social control in capitalist
society develop within the limits of the more fundamental mechanisms of capital accumulation. However, although not as basic as the
latter, the functions of social control are performed by real mechanisms which may or may not present themselves directly to observation
and which are therefore part of the infrastructure. Among such
mechanisms examined below are the social welfare, the parliamentary, the educational, and the military systems. The corresponding
concrete institutions, as they are seen and experienced, are but forms
of the infrastructural mechanisms through which the functions of
social control are performed.

Marx provided only a few general pointers to how one might go
about reconstructing the mechanisms of social control in capitalist
society as well as their particular functions. Since the overall functions
of the mechanisms of production, exchange, and distribution are the
extraction and accumulation of surplus value, what is at stake is
whether or not labour power can be made to produce sufficiently
more value than it receives in the form of wages. At times
accumulation will require quite drastic reductions in its exchange
value (which takes the form of wage cuts, etc.), while at others the
emphasis might shift to increasing the new value it creates. Our
analysis of how the mechanisms of accumulation in Japan have been
functioning and malfunctioning has indicated that both are currently
needed in that country. What the mechanisms of social control must
ensure is that labour power always has the skills and preparedness to

meet all the new and old demands that are made on it. It must cooperate with wage cuts or loss of jobs when these are necessary, it must acquire the whole range of skills and knowledges needed in the accumulation process, and the application of these must be kept up so that its full potential use value is continually realised.

Within the overall function of maintaining social control, the specific functions (as well as the infrastructural mechanisms through which they are performed) which I have found to be most important in Japan are: the stabilisation of working-class subsistence; ensuring the acquisition and maintenance of its skills; the conversion of submission into consent; and the function of compelling submission when consent breaks down. Although each of these functions is performed by a distinctive mechanism, the concrete institutional forms in which the workings of the mechanisms are expressed are not confined to any one type of organisation. Both state and non-state institutions are involved. However, I concentrate on the former because of their increased importance in periods of crisis.

The Japanese state: crisis and social control

The prewar Japanese state was known, particularly in the 1930s, for its role not simply in assisting capital accumulation but as a vehicle of widespread repression at home and in its overseas colonies. Among the changes in the functions of the state that took place after the war were reduced involvement in maintaining social control and a greater involvement in furthering capital accumulation. Both developments were in response to changes in the ability of capital to perform the required functions by means of non-state forms of organisation. The long boom and its accompanying 'lifelong employment' reduced the need for the state to regulate even such things as working-class subsistence or education to anything like the degree to which it had done during the more austere 1930s. Hence, the widespread use of overt force and blatant ideological indoctrination gave way to more liberal means of persuasion and the encouragement of the bourgeoisie to perform the required functions of social control through less-visible forms of organisation. I examine each of the four main functions in some detail.

Subsistence stabilisation

Of all the functions of social control, stabilising working-class subsistence is the most important. This is because if people's material livelihood becomes too insecure, no amount of propaganda or force will be able to keep them in line for very long. It is not just or even mainly that workers must be healthy and rested if they are to be of any use to an employer, but that if their discontent is to be kept within limits, the fundamental reasons for discontent must be minimised. Historically, it has always been instabilities in people's material circumstances which have been the most intolerable rather than any particular level of material well-being. So long as changes are not too sudden, people can be conditioned into putting up with living standards that barely keep body and soul together.

Since under capitalism the working class gets its subsistence requirements mainly from the commodities which it must buy with its wages, the general level of working-class subsistence, as well as fluctuations in that level, is dependent on the process of accumulation, which sets an upper and a lower limit on wages. The upper limit is set by the general conditions which determine profitability. For example, the more labour productivity can be raised the less do wage increases affect profitability, and vice versa. So if the upper limit on wages is set by what capital can afford to pay and still remain profitable, the lower limit is set by what capital must pay if it is to find adequate markets. This is of course dependent on the structure of industry and markets (themselves the results of class struggles): if large shares of the total social capital are in wage-goods industries and a large propor- tion of the market for them is domestic rather than export, then a growth in working- class buying power is an important condition of uninterrupted accumulation. For example, the wage squeeze in Japan would have had an even greater effect on accumulation if such a large proportion of the motor vehicle industry's output had not been exported.

However, what is relevant here is not the absolute level of working- class subsistence which capital accumulation in Japan has required, but the types of fluctuations in that level which all the irregularities and interruptions in the accumulation process bring on. Since major capitalist crises cause great fluctuations in what capital can afford and in what it would like the working class to spend, the main problem the mechanisms of social control confront is to ensure that the working class accepts that level of subsistence appropriate to each stage of capital accumulation. Sometimes this means getting workers to adjust to less than they have become accustomed to; at others, encouragement to expect more. In either case, the mechanisms must adjust actual working-class consumption to the needs of uneven development. But because the process of capital accumulation is fraught with unevennesses (within industries between monopoly and non-monopoly capital, among industries between expanding ones and declining ones, and less frequently industry-wide booms and recessions), one of the most important mechanisms is the one through which counter-cyclical interventions attempt to stabilise working-class subsistence so that the fluctuations are less frequent and less violent.

In comparison with other capitalist societies, the state in Japan has been relatively uninvolved in carrying out this function. In the prewar period, force and propaganda were more-favoured expedients to compel workers (and peasants) to adjust to uneven accumulation, while during the postwar boom measures to regulate working-class subsistence have been implemented by the bourgeoisie mainly at the company level. Although state intervention has increased, particularly since the onset of the current crisis, companies have themselves carried the main responsibility for each of the three main ways in which standards of living can be stabilised: direct provision of free or subsidised wage goods, as far as possible separating changes in wage payments from changes in the rate of accumulation, and some provision for subsistence when no wages are paid, that is, when workers are unemployed. The functioning of each of these very simple mechanisms can take a variety of concrete forms.

In Japan, granting or subsidising basic wage goods as a means of stabilising working-class subsistence is highly developed only in large firms. We have already seen (pp. 166–7 above) that the welfare system in the monopoly sector is sufficiently all-embracing to cushion the labour aristocracy (so long as regular status is retained) from excessive fluctuations in living standards. In comparison with this and with the development of the welfare state in other advanced capitalist societies, the Japanese state's involvement in this area is still in its infancy.[1] Table 7.1, which shows the shares of total taxation and social security contributions in the national income of major capitalist powers, provides a general indication of the differences.

Particularly in times of crisis, increases in taxes and social security contributions do not, and are not intended to, counteract income inequalities between classes, but function rather to even out some of the irregularities within the working class's subsistence. Table 7.2 shows that the taxes of low-income recipients increase much more rapidly than do those of high-income recipients, and table 7.3 shows

Table 7.1. *Taxation and social security contributions as shares of national income in major capitalist countries, 1977 (Japan also 1980)*

	Taxation	Social security contributions	Total
United States	28.8	9.3	38.1
United Kingdom	37.4	10.4	47.8
West Germany	32.2	19.9	52.1
France	29.8	23.8	53.6
Sweden	52.7	20.1	72.8
Japan, 1977	19.3	8.6	27.9
1980	21.8	9.7	31.5

Source: Miyajima Ryōhei, 'Fukushi no futan o dō kaiketsu suru ka' [How Shall We Solve the Social Welfare Burden?], *Keizai*, no. 200 (December 1980), p. 46.

how tax increases and their equivalents (for example, public utility charges) conceal falls in real disposable income.

Because so many people in Japan have been outside the large companies' welfare systems, the crisis has forced the state to take over for the bourgeoisie as a whole the function of evening out the variations in working-class livelihood. The Seven Year Socio-Economic Plan therefore called for taxation to increase from 19.9% of National Income in 1978 to 26.5% in 1985, and social security contributions from 9.0% to 11.0% in the same period.[2] During a general industry-wide downswing, such as the present crisis, the state cannot do much to cushion the decline in living standards even for those members of the working class who do have secure jobs. On the contrary, in order to pay for or subsidise basic wage goods for the class as a whole and even out differences within it, the incomes of earning members must fall substantially. Wage increases which do not keep up with price increases is one way to conceal the decline, while another is for the state to take growing proportions of money wages in taxes.

But because Japanese workers still pay less in taxes (and their equivalents) than Western workers, most of them (the labour aristocracy being the exception) must directly purchase a larger proportion of their subsistence requirements, and they therefore face larger fluctuations in living standards in times of crisis. This applies both to the variations over time and to the discrepancies that occur among the different fractions of their class. In 1976, social security

Table 7.2. *Estimates of the rising tax burden, by income group, 1977–84 (¥1,000 and %)*

	1977	1981	1982	1984	Increase in 1977–82 (%)	Increase in 1977–84 (%)
Assumed increase in annual income	—	5.5%	5.5%	5.0%		
Annual income	2,500.0	3,063.2	3,216.3	3,546.0	28.6	41.8
Taxation	16.8	71.4	85.8	117.0	410.7	596.4
Annual income	5,000.0	6,126.4	6,432.7	7,092.0	28.6	41.8
Taxation	266.6	445.8	503.7	628.3	88.9	135.7
Annual income	10,000.0	12,252.7	12,865.4	14,184.1	28.6	41.8
Taxation	1,308.0	2,065.0	2,286.1	2,785.2	74.8	112.9

Source: Washimi Tomoyoshi, 'Kyōki no Rēgan gunkaku to Nihon daigunkaku' [The Insane Reagan Military Expansion and the Huge Japanese Military Expansion], *Keizai*, no. 211 (November 1981), p. 128.

Table 7.3. *Changes in the structure of monthly average household*
expenditure of employees, 1974–80

	1974 Amount	%	1980 Amount	%
Actual income (A)	205,792	100.00	349,686	100.00
Non-consumption expenditures (B)	17,967	8.73	44,137	12.62
Taxes	9,717	4.72	24,209	6.92
Social security contributions	7,979	3.88	19,593	5.60
Other	271	0.13	335	0.10
Actual disposable income (A − B = C)	187,825	91.27	305,549	87.38
Actual disposable income (C)	187,825	100.00	305,549	100.00
Public utility expenses (D)	19,798	10.54	40,324	13.20
Water supply	576	0.31	1,555	0.51
Heat/lighting	4,961	2.64	11,138	3.65
Health/medicine	3,379	1.80	5,771	1.89
Transport/communications	4,222	2.25	9,061	3.00
Education	3,089	1.64	6,876	2.25
Barber/sanitation	3,571	1.90	5,923	1.94
Committed expenses (E)	24,984	13.30	50,731	16.60
Insurance	7,192	3.83	17,051	5.58
Damages insurance	508	0.27	1,394	0.46
Land and house loan repayments	3,549	1.89	11,930	3.90
Other loan repayments	2,187	1.16	2,606	0.85
Hire purchase payments	5,379	2.86	7,947	2.60
Monthly accounts	2,045	1.09	2,921	0.95
House and land rent	4,124	2.20	6,882	2.25
Motor-car-related expenses (F)	4,553	2.42	11,175	3.66
Remaining expenses, C − (D + E + F)	138,490	73.73	203,319	66.54

Source: Kudō, part 2, p. 35.

expenditures (on health and benefit payments) were only 10.12% of
National Income in Japan, but 25.18% in West Germany, 16.10% in
the U.K., and 21.78% in France. Despite all the fanfare in Japan
about increases in the welfare state in recent years, the share had risen
only to 12.31% by 1979.[3]

The main reason behind the smaller scale of the welfare state in
Japan is not that the function of subsistence stabilisation has fallen by
the wayside, but that the institutional forms through which it is
carried out are different from their Western counterparts. Company
policies (e.g. payment by length of service, company welfare, etc.)
originally designed to prevent the desertion of skilled workers (see pp.

159ff above) have come to perform the additional function of stabilising the subsistence of the most-organised and therefore most-threatening fraction of the working-class. State forms of organisation of the bourgeoisie were thus less necessary in Japan than they were in other advanced capitalist societies.

Nevertheless, particularly since the 'oil shock' and the resulting insecurities of mass workers and the reserve army, new forms of working-class organisation and struggle have developed which have demanded more state welfare. One indication of this was the gradual decline in the electoral fortunes of the ruling Liberal Democratic Party, which, although it did not result from an anti-capitalist movement, at least reflected a growing tide of reformist demands which the party had ignored. Since an important element in that reformism was widespread support for an expanded welfare state, the LDP found it necessary, particularly after 1973, to move in this direction in order to retain its support among the insecure and unprotected masses (the bulk of the working class, the peasantry, and the petty bourgeoisie). The result is that a great deal of what is currently regarded as the welfare state in Japan was built up in the years immediately after 1973. In 1973 to 1976 social security expenditures as a proportion of National Income increased from 6.7%, which was similar to what had existed since the mid-1960s, to 10.12%.[4]

Evaluations of the importance of the welfare state can easily fall between two stools. One is the tendency to focus purely on infrastructural functions such as subsistence stabilisation, and to see in the welfare state one form in which their functioning is manifested and nothing else. The political danger of this exclusive preoccupation lies in its failure to recognise that the more the working class's subsistence is socialised (e.g. the greater the proportion of wage goods obtained via taxation), the more can it wage its struggles as a class rather than as isolated individuals. By evening out differences in workers' material circumstances, the welfare state helps overcome some of the divisions which weaken the working class. The other extreme position sees the welfare state as an unambiguous victory for the working class and as the solution to all its problems. The political dangers of this view, which has in varying degrees dominated the trade union leadership in Japan, stems from its blindness to the infrastructural mechanisms behind the rise of the welfare state, a blindness which results in a naive reformism.

Table 7.4. *Social security expenditures, 1966–79*

	1966	1970	1973	1975	1977	1979
Total expenditures (¥ tril.)	1.87	3.52	6.12	11.67	16.85	21.91
Share of national income (%)	6.00	5.79	6.40	9.48	11.03	12.31
Breakdown of total (%)	100.0	100.0	100.0	100.0	100.0	100.0
Medical insurance	48.4	50.5	46.4	42.2	39.1	38.6
Retirement insurance	10.6	13.5	17.6	24.9	30.3	32.4
Unemployment and accident compensation insurance	10.3	8.2	7.4	8.7	7.1	6.5
Child benefit	—		1.2	1.2	1.0	0.8
Livelihood protection	8.5	7.8	7.3	5.8	5.3	5.1
Social welfare	3.1	3.8	7.0	6.5	6.6	6.6
Health/sanitation	6.2	5.1	3.8	2.8	2.4	2.1
Old age pensions	12.0	9.7	8.7	7.5	7.8	7.6
Adjustment	0.8	1.3	0.5	0.4	0.4	0.2

Source: Kōseishō [Welfare Ministry], *Kōsei hakusho* [White Paper on Welfare], 1981 (Tokyo: Ōkurashō insatsukyoku, 1981), pp. 550–r.

Because the state must raise taxes on earning members of the working class if it is to increase its welfare expenditures, the growth of the welfare state in the mid-1970s came to almost as sudden a halt a few years later with the growing fiscal crisis it helped bring about. Even the substantial tax increases of the period could not meet the proliferation of demands for government expenditure. The result was that the rate of increase in the budget's social-security-related expenditures fell from 31.2% and 39.7% in 1973 and 1974 to 12.9% in 1979 and to 2.8% in 1982.[5]

All the shortcomings and lop-sided emphasis on health insurance of the system therefore showed little change. Of all the free or subsidised wage goods received by the employees of large firms, the only comparable state-provided good has been medical insurance. However, although this makes up nearly half of all social security payments, it has not eliminated (but only reduced) the need for low-income families to set aside money for medical expenses.[6] Table 7.4 shows the total social security payments in 1966–79 as well as the proportions the different parts of the system absorbed. A significant extension of benefits beyond medical insurance did take place in 1973–6, mainly in the area of retirement insurance, but this falls outside the present category of state-provided wage goods.

Neither of the two remaining wage goods which are of major significance in the value of labour power, education and housing, is adequately provided by the Japanese state, even though it is heavily involved in both. However, since education simultaneously fulfils a number of functions of social control, it is examined in more detail later on. The inadequacy of state housing as a means of stabilising working-class subsistence stems from the dominance of the construction and real estate industries by the more fundamental mechanisms of capital accumulation.

The emphasis of the state's housing policy throughout the postwar period has been on financing the purchase of new houses rather than on building low-rent houses for workers. This is because the construction industry has been a major means of Keynesian demand management, and by providing housing finance the state could stimulate demand in all the industries which somehow depended on a sustained building boom. The predominance of private capital in housing finance dates from the rise in land prices in the late 1960s and the resulting tie-ups between real estate companies and private financial institutions, which together cashed in on the rising urban

Table 7.5. *Housing finance, 1965–78* (¥ *billion and* %)

	1965	1970	1973	1975	1978
Total amount	708	3,571	10,265	18,107	34,458
Share	100.0	100.0	100.0	100.0	100.0
Public institutions (amount)	616	1,677	3,004	5,321	10,181
(share)	87.0	47.0	29.3	29.4	29.6
Housing Finance Corporation (amount)	466	1,133	2,178	4,124	8,308
(share)	65.8	31.7	21.2	22.8	24.1
Private institutions (amount)	92	1,893	7,260	12,786	24,277
(share)	13.0	53.0	70.7	70.6	70.5

Source: Okuchi Masashi, 'Keizai seisaku no tenkai to jūtaku mondai' [The Development of Economic Policy and Housing Problems], *Keizai*, no. 208 (August 1981), p. 63.

Table 7.6. *Housing and national finances, 1960–80*

	1960	1970	1975	1980
Nominal Gross National Expenditure (¥ 10 bil.)	*1,621*	*7,509*	*15,180*	*22,270*
Household expenditure (%)	54.8	51.9	56.7	58.0
Dwellings (%)	8.9	11.7	12.0	13.3
Domestic gross fixed capital formation (%)	31.1	35.6	32.5	32.1
Private (%)	23.6	27.4	23.3	22.3
Equipment (%)	19.5	20.9	16.0	15.3
Housing (%)	4.1	6.5	7.3	7.0
Public (%)	7.5	8.2	9.2	9.8
Equipment (%)	7.2	7.7	8.6	9.4
Housing (%)	0.3	0.5	0.6	0.4
Budget General Account (¥ 10 bil.)	*177*	*821*	*2,084*	*4,259*
Public Works (%)	18.2	17.2	15.9	15.6
Housing policy (%)	0.7	1.2	1.5	1.8
Fiscal Investment and Loan Programme (¥ 10 bil.)	*63*	*358*	*931*	*1,818*
Housing (%)	12.6	19.3	21.4	26.2

Source: Okuchi, p. 55.

rent.[7] Table 7.5 shows how the real estate boom led to a declining state share in housing finance, and table 7.6 locates housing in the overall national finances.

The only real form of low-rent public housing in Japan is built and administered by local bodies out of the housing allocation in the budget General Account, which has been a mere pittance. In sharp contrast to these homes (known as *kōei jūtaku*), those built by the Japan Housing Corporation (known as *kōdan jūtaku*) and the Housing Finance Corporation (known as *kōko jūtaku*) out of the FILP allocations cater for the income groups who can afford their own homes, and who use these public houses as stepping stones. So even where the state has played a part in building houses, the emphasis has shifted from using them as cheap rented dwellings to selling them at market prices or renting them at market rates.[8] Table 7.7 shows the numbers of houses built by the different public corporations as well as the ones built privately without state involvement.

Between the people who can obtain the *kōei jūtaku* and those who can afford their own homes lie the great mass of workers. Table 7.8, which shows the distribution of the population by the type of housing inhabited and the results of surveys on housing satisfaction in 1973 and 1978, suggests they make up over 25% of the population. Unable to afford their own homes or benefit from any form of subsidised housing, they must rent private apartments largely without adequate space.[9]

Even the people who apparently own their homes have not, however, escaped the housing crisis. In greater Tokyo, for example, though 49.9% of the 8.4 million homes were 'owned' by their occupants, 5.9% were apartments and 9.1% were on rented land, leaving only 34.9% which seemed to be genuine privately owned homes.[10] However, housing land prices have skyrocketed so much in recent years (between 20% and 30% a year in some parts of metropolitan Japan) that it is becoming quite common for people to take out mortgages which they will never pay off but which are so arranged that their children take them over when the parents die. Table 7.9 shows that the state's policy of mainly assisting the purchase of homes rather than providing cheap rented housing has enabled only upper-income and older people to better their chances of buying a home. For the struggling masses, particularly in urban areas, there is a mounting housing crisis which the state has been quite unable to reverse. Rent for totally inadequate living space is gobbling up a full fifth of family income.

Table 7.7. *Houses built during Five Year Plans, by type of company,*
1966–80 (1,000)

	1966–70		1971–5		1976–80	
	No.	%	No.	%	No.	%
Total	6,739	100.0	8,280	100.0	7,642	100.0
Completely private	4,174	61.9	5,172	62.5	3,810	49.9
Dependent on public finance	2,565	38.1	3,108	37.5	3,832	50.1
Local body (*kōei jūtaku*)	479	7.1	494	6.0	386	5.1
Japan Housing Corporation	335	5.0	284	3.4	189	2.5
Housing Finance Corporation	1,087	16.1	1,664	20.1	2,519	33.0
Other	664	9.9	666	8.0	738	9.7

Source: Okuchi, p. 62.

Table 7.8. *Housing, by type and degree of satisfaction, 1973–8 (1,000)*

	No.	Composition (%)	Average area (m²)	Satisfied (%)	In distress (%)
1973					
Total	28,730	100	77.1	20.5	35.1
Own homes	17,010	59	103.1	27.4	25.9
Rented homes	11,720	41	39.5	7.6	52.7
Private (private facilities)	6,350	22	40.4	7.1	55.3
(common facilities)	1,540	5	17.8		
Public	2,000	7	40.0	6.5	53.5
Company	1,840	6	53.9	10.9	39.7
1978					
Total	32,190	100	80.3	18.6	38.9
Own homes	19,430	60	106.2	24.4	30.8
Rented homes	12,690	39	40.6	6.9	55.3
Private (private facilities)	7,160	22	40.7	6.5	57.7
(common facilities)	1,250	4	16.2		
Public	2,440	8	42.1	6.0	56.7
Company	1,840	6	55.3	9.8	44.0

Source: Okuchi, p. 49.

Table 7.9. *Home ownership in metropolitan Japan, by age and income class, 1973–8*

	Average		25–9 years		30–9 years		40–9 years		Over 60 years	
	1973	1978	1973	1978	1973	1978	1973	1978	1973	1978
Total	47.1	49.5	17.4	17.6	40.6	43.8	61.6	63.1	75.5	73.4
Bottom quintile	29.3	27.4	10.9	9.6	27.4	25.0	43.9	39.4	63.1	58.1
Second quintile	34.5	35.6	14.2	13.7	32.0	32.0	50.5	48.8	71.4	70.8
Third quintile	42.4	45.9	17.4	18.2	37.6	39.7	56.6	58.2	76.2	78.4
Fourth quintile	56.3	63.0	25.3	32.4	46.5	54.8	64.9	69.1	82.1	84.0
Top quintile	74.1	78.6	39.0	44.9	59.9	65.9	75.0	79.5	89.2	90.9
Difference between bottom and top	44.8	51.2	28.1	35.3	32.5	40.9	31.1	40.1	26.1	32.8

Source: Miyake Tōru, 'Dai toshien no jūtaku jijō' [The Metropolitan Housing Situation], *Keizai*, no. 208 (August 1981), p. 76.

It was largely because of the growing shortage of land in Japan that urban rent became a major form in which surplus value was appropriated and housing became a focus of working-class discontent. However, for this very reason it was extremely difficult for the different sections of the bourgeoisie to cooperate and, through their common organisation, the state, to subsidise the housing of mass workers much above what was done. Apart from the difficulty of raising government expenditure without intolerable tax increases, further subsidisation of housing for mass workers would simply alter the form in which the urban rent was extracted and distributed. Instead of going directly from mass workers to finance companies, real estate companies, and construction firms, it would go indirectly to the same capitals via the state but from the whole range of classes which could be sufficiently taxed. It seemed far safer to leave the crisis on the backs of people who were isolated and disorganised, and to dangle the carrot of 'my home' in front of the rest.

On the whole, therefore, none of the basic wage goods is sufficiently subsidised by the state to function as a significant stabiliser of working-class subsistence. Each of medical care, education, and housing remain major burdens on the disposable income of huge sections of the labouring masses and other low-income recipients, and cuts in disposable income meant severe deterioration in the quality of the goods received.

But subsidisation of wage goods is not the only mechanism through which working-class subsistence can be stabilised. A much more important one in Japan has been through a wage system which partly separates changes in wage rates from changes in the rate of accumulation, so that at some times (or for some workers) wages are lower than what profitability allows, while at others (or for other workers) they are higher. Capital accumulation does not necessarily require a uniform rate of exploitation of all workers, but can compensate for a reduced exploitation of some by a higher rate in the case of others. Apart from evening out fluctuations in living standards, such systems help preserve the appearance that workers are paid for what they do or have achieved rather than what they require to reproduce themselves (within the limits of profitability).

The wage system which developed in postwar Japan (with many prewar elements too) tended to function so close to the ideal through non-state institutions that state intervention in the area was confined mainly to propaganda. Payment by age, sex, and education ensured that some workers were always paid less and others more than what an average rate of exploitation required. Wage costs and the overall rate of exploitation could be adjusted to fluctuations in the rate of accumulation simply by altering the relative numbers of workers in each group. However, since shunting persons around had obvious limitations, some adjustments in basic scales (as opposed to movements up the scale) also had to be made, and these were made during the annual spring 'offensive.'

In times of rapid inflation, demands for compensating wage increases make it seem that the working class is actually on the 'offensive,' whereas in fact it is normally on the defensive. Each spring, the main participating federations of unions, Sōhyo and Chūritsurōren, in response to what employers have said they can afford and what the government has emphasised must not be exceeded, present demands for slightly more. It is then up to individual unions to negotiate what they can, and the amounts vary with company profitability. These variations increased during the recession, and in 1979 they were obviously so wide that even the nominal demand for a standard wage increase was abandoned. The year before, the *Japan Times Weekly* had commented:

> Japanese unions now face a choice between job security and higher income. Given that they are organized on a company-to-company basis, the former always takes precedence over the latter in hard times . . .
>
> Given the wide gap – and the gap is likely to widen – in business performance between competitive and less competitive companies or industries, the natural course of the shunto [spring offensive] would be for individual employers (and unions) to go their own way, each according to their paying ability . . .
>
> In fact, this is what is now happening.[11]

Since the only way to protect living standards once the scales themselves began to freeze in this way was by movements up a scale with length of service, subsistence stabilisation depended heavily on the *nenkō* system. However, reductions in the numbers of new (low-paid) recruits have meant rising wage bills as workforces age, and many struggling capitals tried to replace regular workers with non-regulars. To the extent that accumulation functions continue to require a phasing out of payment by age, this system's ability to stabilise working-class subsistence will also decrease. Payment by age at least also allowed workers to save in later life for all sorts of contingencies, and these savings functioned as a form of stabilisation resulting from the *nenkō* system. In Japan a full 21% of individual income was saved in 1979, which when added to the 12% which went to taxation and social security contributions, was about the same as the 35.2% of income saved in West Germany mainly through taxation and social security contributions (26%). The *nenkō* system has therefore forced individuals to save what the state has not taxed in one way or another: 42% of individual savings in Japan are intended for medical costs, 18% for old age, 12% for housing, and 23% for children's education and marriage.[12]

When capital can no longer afford to provide either secure jobs or living wages, not even for workers with long employment records, the function of stabilising working-class subsistence has to fall more heavily on the final expedient: some form of unemployment insurance. However, this is another area in which non-state institutions have traditionally borne the burden in Japan. Rural areas have always functioned as a temporary source of subsistence for non-earning members of the reserve army, as has the family for its female members. The petty bourgeoisie, we saw in chapter 2, is also a form of subsistence stabilisation for the unemployed working class in Japan. Yet in spite of the flexibility of non-state institutions in Japan to mop up the unemployed and enable them to contribute to their subsistence outside the capitalist sector, the sudden increase in state retirement pensions and unemployment insurance since 1973 resulted from the need for a society-wide approach to the problem. What became the most important mechanism of social control had been the most underdeveloped by the state. This was because the real guarantor of working-class subsistence was the boom itself, which resulted in a continual expansion of employment and little need for unemployment benefits. Even the relatively substantial retirement payments made by large companies were not intended for living on, but were to encourage the move from high-paid regular jobs to low-paid temporary ones. However, since the latter had been plentiful and could normally be retained for as long as desired, they were in practice simply low-paid regular jobs, compensated by varying amounts of retirement pay. However, now that even non-regular jobs have become scarce, the inadequacy of retirement pay as a source of subsistence has called for drastic state intervention to deal with the social consequences of rising unemployment, in all its concealed and unconcealed forms.

This intervention itself took two main forms: measures to create or preserve jobs and measures to improve unemployment insurance. They were explicitly brought together for the first time in 1974 under the Employment Insurance Law.[13] Henceforth, the insurance system would pay for unemployment benefits as well as contribute towards the costs of creating or preserving jobs, such as grants to enterprises to extend the retirement age beyond 55 or to keep on workers for a bit longer when the scale of operations is being reduced. The state has gone to great lengths to encourage the use of these grants, and in September 1978 their terms were extended to lengthen the period during which the subsidy was paid and to relax the conditions of receiving it. However, this Rōdō Antei Shikin Seido (Financial System to Stabilise Employment) has not been particularly success-ful, since so pressing was the need to reduce staff, mainly the numbers of older, higher-paid workers, that employers did not find the subsidies sufficiently attractive. In 1978, only ¥20 billion out of a budgeted ¥60 billion was actually used. In November that year, a Labour Ministry survey revealed that the proportion of over-55-year-olds on the payrolls of large firms was only 3.9%, which was well below the state's target of 6%.[14]

Unable substantially to prevent or even delay growing unemploy-ment, the state was forced to focus more exclusively on providing pension insurance. However, the publication towards the end of 1978 of the White Paper on Welfare already made it clear that the ability to finance the growing burden of social security expenditure had been exhausted, and that taxes and insurance contributions would have to rise considerably if even existing benefits were to be maintained.[15] We know that the fiscal crisis of the state which had been building up finally led to a mere 2.8% increase in social security allocations in 1982. A year before, in December 1980, the Labour Ministry published the results of a survey which showed that pensions and retirement pay were so inadequate that almost 90% of men aged 55–9, 75% aged 60–4, and 61% aged 65–9 were gainfully occupied, many in petty establishments, mainly because pensions (state and private schemes) were insufficient to support them.[16] And so, in spite of the reluctance of employers to keep on high-paid older workers, the state's policy has moved more and more towards attempts to extend the retirement age to 65. Two weeks before the Labour Ministry published this survey, it had announced the termination of the long-used scheme to provide jobs for the unemployed: Shitsugyō Taisaku Jigyō (Public Works for Combating Unemployment). Although

100,000 people at the time were engaged in them (for an average of 20.5 years), it was felt that extending the retirement age to 65 would have a greater impact on unemployment. The average age of the workers was 63.5 years.[17]

It therefore gradually became necessary for the Japanese bourgeoisie to abandon the goal of adequately stabilising the working class's subsistence, since the mechanisms through which this might be done, however well they functioned during the boom, had broken down during the slump. Neither state nor non-state forms of organisation could get them going. With the very basis of working-class compliance being thus eroded, problems of social control were bound to increase: strikes, faltering work discipline, demonstrations, suicides, divorce, and many other forms in which deteriorating bourgeois social relations are manifested. Unable to prevent reductions in workers' livelihood, the state had to turn to other mechanisms of social control in order to win or compel cooperation with what had become unavoidable. It undertook this task in two stages: first, ideologies were mobilised in order to justify and explain the cuts as somehow necessary, and then, failing acceptance of this reasoning, violence had to be used to force what could not be made acceptable.

It is important to remember that the use value of labour power is always greatest when workers cooperate willingly and enthusiastically in capitalist production, but that this willingness is itself ultimately dependent on the material benefits workers receive in return. Since cooperation rests on the security of material subsistence, something is always amiss when ideology or violence is used to enforce declines in material circumstances. In the case of Japan, the familial ideology and harmony characteristic of industrial relations during the boom resulted overwhelmingly from the job security and wage increases workers received and could not be expected to survive the erosion of those benefits, no matter how loudly harmony was preached or how uncompromisingly cooperation was enforced. Nevertheless, this is exactly what the bourgeoisie tried to do, at the very time when the material conditions for its success had been eroded.

What must therefore now be examined are the mechanisms through which submission is converted into consent, or the processes by which people somehow self-consciously declare their support for bourgeois society, in spite of the numerous forms in which their actions indicate an unconscious rejection of it. Since among the main institutions through which this is done are schools and universities, which simultaneously fulfil a number of functions of social control, the argument in the following section does not rigidly focus on only one function at a time, but shows how educational institutions function to maintain social control.

Education in Japan: wage goods, skills, and misrepresentations

Education, at least up to middle school (which is compulsory in Japan), is at one and the same time a particular type of wage good – it provides the skills workers must have to sell their labour power – and a process of indoctrination. From the point of view of the agents who pass through them (as opposed to the middle class which works in them), the importance of educational institutions lies in their function of reproducing labour power with both the skills and preparedness to fill all the positions needed to ensure uninterrupted capital accumulation. They provide the average (compulsory) and above-average (higher education) skills demanded by capital accumulation and the misrepresentations of capitalist society necessary for social control. Since the 'knowledge' one acquires is for use in a specifically capitalist society, education is simultaneously a process of acquiring skills and of becoming misinformed about what one is doing. The one-dimensional Althusserian approach to education as simply a process of imbibing wrong ideas fails to grasp that the skills learnt are real and are used in real work situations.[18] In learning and using skills in capitalist society, workers therefore engage in one of those many daily practices which reinforce bourgeois ideology because they do actually correspond to the concrete ways in which the world is experienced.

Direct state involvement in education in Japan is at its greatest up to the compulsory level of middle school. After that, the proportion and quality of private institutions increase and in many cases surpass that of state institutions. However, although the largely state-managed compulsory education might be sufficient to provide the average skills needed in the labouring jobs most workers perform, it is increasingly insufficient if those jobs are to be obtained in large corporations. It does not indicate to monopoly capital a sufficient commitment to self-betterment and individual ambition and therefore potential usefulness from cooperation and willingness to go the extra mile. We have already seen that even while children are at middle school sizeable outlays must be made on private education (for example, private tutors) by households wanting more than

Table 7.10. *Annual education costs for households, by type of institution,* *1979* (¥)

	Total	School expenses	Expenses at home	(1978 total)
Public kindergartens	138,134	69,904	68,230	133,752
Private kindergartens	310,802	186,922	123,880	296,325
Elementary schools (public)	115,071	43,122	71,949	107,354
Public middle schools	126,842	75,226	51,616	118,663
Public high schools	187,083	153,225	33,858	174,904
Private high schools	490,043	425,683	64,360	387,278

Source: Tōkei bunseki kenkyūkai, [Research Association for Analysing Statistics], 'Bukka to kakei' [Prices and Household Finances], *Keizai*, no. 202 (February 1981), p. 189.

compulsory education for their children, that is, by over 90% of the population. Table 7.10 shows the total costs of schooling by the type of institution attended in 1979. Although many of these expenditures are not related to the skills workers need on the job, they are related to the types of employers they can find and therefore have important functions in the mechanisms of social control. If low-paid workers, or low-income recipients in other classes, were to abandon their attempts to use high school and university as a means of upward mobility for their children – something being forced on them by the crisis – the role of the educational rat-race in concealing more fundamental determinants of life chances would become more visible. The bourgeoisie cannot urge belt-tightening in education expenditure without undermining one of the main forms in which its legitimacy is established: the ability of education to make class membership appear to depend on individual merit.

In Japan, there has been a far greater awareness by both the ruling class and the working-class movement than in other capitalist societies that education fulfils a number of functions simultaneously. The ruling class in particular has always recognised that workers must be willing and equipped to meet all the demands of the positions in society which they occupy, and the technical and ideological functions of education have never been separated or allowed to lag behind such ideals as education of the whole person. This relatively sophisticated understanding of the role of education in capitalist society has its origins in certain problems the state faced in the period of transition from feudalism to capitalism. There was from the beginning an enormous gap between the numbers of available skilled jobs, which were boosted by the rapid concentration and centralis- ation of capital, and the numbers of persons with the training to fill them. Because the state telescoped the transitional period by establishing monopoly capitals from the beginning, there was a continual tendency for the demands of the jobs to exceed the capabilities of the class agents in them. To have left the training of the required numbers and types of agents to the feudal and family education systems would have meant intolerable delays in bridging the gap. Therefore as deliberate and self-conscious a form of state intervention was needed to create a suitable education system as was required to concentrate and centralise capital.

There are at least three areas in which the new education system fulfilled important functions in the reproduction of suitably skilled and controlled labour power: direct ideological manipulation through the teaching of ethics, legitimation of class society through intense competition, and the fusion of bourgeois ideology with the acquisition of technical skills.

Although the first of these is only part of what education does, it has not been unimportant in Japan. Since in the prewar period crucial state functions were to complete what isolated capitals could not (concentration and centralisation of capital), it is not surprising that bourgeois ideology took one or other form of statism and that this ideology was explicitly incorporated into the school curricula.[19] Loyalty and obedience to the Emperor, who himself wielded no power but in whose name all state power was exercised, were taught in specially constituted ethics courses, so that the disruption of people's lives during the transition, of which the state seemed to be the direct cause, would be willingly accepted as a patriotic duty. From 1890 to the end of the Second World War, all ethical and civic instruction was based on this idea, which was set out in the Imperial Rescript on Education in 1890 and distributed to all schools throughout the country.[20] Prewar schooling, both inside and outside the classroom, played a vital role in extending the ideas of harmony and filial piety to all authority relations, whether they involved the family, employers, or the latter's highest forms of organisation in the state. It was thus a major process through which traditional family ideology was preserved and transmitted, even though, as has been repeatedly emphasised, its success depended on the existence of important material conditions.

In the postwar period, such explicit and self-conscious ideological indoctrination in schools has been more difficult and also less necessary. It has been more difficult because of the reconstruction during the Occupation period of the school curricula, made possible partly by American policy and partly by the struggles of organis-ations, such as the Japan Teachers' Union, which were opposed to ethics courses. However, although postwar education was not anything like as deliberate a means of propagating specific forms of bourgeois ideology as was prewar education, it would be wrong to think that schools suddenly ceased to indoctrinate students. Ethics courses were simply replaced by social studies courses, which provided equal opportunities for teaching ethics. The way the state ensured that these were of the appropriate kind was through the Ministry of Education's screening of textbooks. It was therefore hardly coincidental that the top thirteen textbook publishing com-panies in 1981 were also the top thirteen donors to the ruling LDP,[21] or that a fall in the number of textbook publishing companies has accompanied a fall in the range of available school texts (See table 7.11). Nevertheless, in spite of the recent interest in restoring ethics courses to the importance they had in the prewar period, there is much less blatant indoctrination today than there was then. Current practice in Japan has many parallels elsewhere, including the distribution to schools of a leaflet by the top one hundred power and electric appliance companies on the virtues of atomic power (one million copies have been printed each year since 1974).[22]

A more important reason for the break with the past, temporary though it might prove to be, was the boom of the 1950s and 1960s. Throughout this period and even for some time into the recession, the improving material conditions of the masses (in contrast to their deterioration in the prewar years when 'statism' was most vigorously propagated) made resort to extreme methods of indoctrination less necessary. Even in the current crisis the state has not been able to reverse this policy as rapidly as many might have liked, and the textbooks accepted by the Ministry of Education for the years 1977–9 were found by the Japan Teachers' Union to have been less biased than their predecessors.[23] Although this tells us something about what had been happening to the Teachers' Union, it also suggests that there might be subtler and more powerful ways in which the education system 'prepares' people for capitalist society.

One of the greatest accomplishments of Japanese education lies in how it makes the roles people play in society look like and be accepted

Table 7.11. *Numbers of school textbook publishing companies and the range of texts published, 1959–80*

	1959	1961	1967	1980
Elementary school				
No. of companies	29	25	19	10
Types of textbook	174	101	81	43
Middle school				
No. of companies	47	44	32	22
Types of textbook	336	174	114	68
	1960	1963	1967	1978
High school				
No. of companies	77	75	70	57
Types of textbook	166	121	161	115
	1957	1963	1973	1978
Total no. of textbook publishing companies	104	87	64	62
	1971	1973	1977	1981
Share of the top 3 companies (%)	32.5	34.1	38.2	40.0

Source: Tokutake Toshio, 'Kyōkasho no kiki: jisshitsuteki kokuteika no kiken' [The Crisis of School Textbooks: The Danger of Virtual State Texts], *Keizai*, no. 207 (July 1981), p. 85.

as results of individual merits and failures. What people do at work and what they receive in return seem to be shaped by what they are or have made themselves through their education. Upper-class life has been made to look like a reward for educational success and working-class life a punishment for laziness and a lack of ability.

Not all education systems are equally able to present the attributes of people as if they were the determinants of their working conditions. The relative success of the Japanese system has depended considerably on two conditions, which are beginning to show signs of breakdown. The first is the high degree and intensity of competition among applicants to prestige schools and universities, while the second is the sexual division of labour which separates applicants into two groups, women and men, who compete largely among themselves for entry into mainly single-sex institutions.

The degree and intensity of competition among applicants to an educational institution can be very roughly measured by the ratio of their number to the number of vacancies. It is therefore very much a product of expectations of success in entrance examinations and the consequences of not even applying. Applicants are both attracted by the prospect of upward social mobility and propelled by the costs of a life in the lower classes.

Expectations of success are of course ultimately shaped by reality, and the reality facing young Japanese has comprised three distinct but merging phases. The first covered the period leading up to the boom and including its early stages, when class positions above that of the mass worker could be secured by a high school education, which at that time provided above-average skills. The second phase grew out of the rapidly rising proportion of middle school graduates who proceeded to high school, which gradually came to provide no more than average skills. Thereafter, to legitimate the separation of agents into classes, it became necessary to create a new educational hurdle for persons who aspired to upper-class membership, namely a university degree or its equivalent. From 1950 to 1961, the proportion of middle school graduates who proceeded to high school grew from 42.5% to 60.0%, and by 1975 when it reached 91.9% high schools no longer fulfilled their function of separating the upper from the lower classes. Aspirants to upper-class positions were therefore required to proceed from high school to university, and the ratio of university entrance increased from 10.3% in 1960 to 38.4% in 1975.[24]

Just as the mass influx into high schools two decades earlier ultimately destroyed the discriminatory function of schools, the rush into the universities that followed opened up a third phase in the process by which agents were channelled into classes. When almost four out of ten Japanese began to enter universities, the chief form of competition among agents became the type of university attended. Increasingly, therefore, the crucial point in young people's lives which determined future class membership was when they competed for entry into prestige universities. All previous schooling became concerned in one way or another with assisting this final stage of the sorting process.

For example, although the overwhelming majority of the over half a million first-year students in the country each year would like to go to Tokyo University, most are informed in a variety of subtle and less subtle ways that they would have no chance of doing so. In about 80% of prefectures, the same proportion of third-year middle school pupils are given intelligence–achievement tests prepared by busi-

Table 7.12. *Ratios of applicants to vacancies in academic universities, by type of department and type of university, 1969–74, and the total numbers of applicants to academic universities, 1974–80*

Ratios of applicants to vacancies

	State universities		Private universities	
	1969	1974	1969	1974
Humanities	9.7	8.3	5.9	5.9
Social sciences	7.9	6.8	6.7	6.1
Physics/engineering	6.7	5.3	6.1	6.5
Agriculture	7.0	5.6	3.4	3.9
Pharmacology	9.9	7.4	7.6	6.9
Medicine/dentistry	13.5	11.6	12.3	7.4
Education	5.2	4.8	4.1	4.2

Total applicants

Year	1974	1975	1976	1977	1978	1979	1980
No.	433,080	457,363	459,491	476,571	455,924	451,784	452,515

Source: Wagakuni no kyōiku suijun, 1975, p. 218; 1980, fuzoku shiryō, p. 56.

nesses, and the results are used by teachers in advising pupils on which high schools to apply for. By the time they leave high school, young people have a fairly good idea of the 'rank' of university they would stand some chance of entering.[25] The ratio of applicants to the number of vacancies therefore underestimates the competition to enter university.

Nevertheless, in the case of the prestige state-run universities, this ratio has been consistently high. In March 1976, a record 221,203 applicants vied for 40,028 positions in these institutions; that is, a ratio of 5:1.[26] However, table 7.12 shows that ratios have fallen in recent years, partly because the less-formal tests at school are becoming institutionalised ways of easing the formal competition later on, partly because the reality of a low success rate was bound to affect expectations and so the rate of application.

Another measure of the level and intensity of competition for entry into the upper classes is the proportion of university applicants who have spent a year or more of full-time study, either privately or in a cram school (*juku*) specifically geared to preparing candidates for university entrance examinations. These *rōnin*, as they are called,

Table 7.13. Rōnin *as proportions of applicants and entrants to academic universities, by type of department and type of university, 1969–74, and composition of university entrants in 1980, by sex and years spent as* rōnin

Proportions of rōnin

	Applicants				Entrants			
	State		Private		State		Private	
Department	1969	1974	1969	1974	1969	1974	1969	1974
Humanities	45.0	39.5	38.0	33.0	43.6	34.6	30.0	23.0
Social sciences	48.5	42.5	44.5	40.9	52.2	42.5	38.0	31.0
Physics/engineering	43.0	40.0	40.6	42.7	45.3	39.0	35.9	33.5
Agriculture	46.7	43.5	28.8	34.1	51.5	41.5	23.1	26.4
Pharmacology	45.8	37.7	30.9	30.1	41.7	31.0	32.3	27.5
Medicine/dentistry	62.3	65.9	58.3	58.4	65.0	70.0	59.1	52.7
Education	31.0	26.4	36.7	33.5	31.7	24.8	19.3	14.4

1980 entrants		Years spent as *rōnin*					
		0	1	2	3	4	Other
Total and % in each	412,437	65.7	26.1	5.6	1.3	1.0	0.3
Males	317,358	61.4	28.8	6.8	1.6	1.1	0.3
Females	95,079	80.1	17.0	1.7	0.4	0.6	0.4

Source: Wagakuni no kyōiku suijun, 1975, p. 219; 1980, fuzoku shiryō, p. 61.

have comprised very high but now falling proportions (particularly in state universities) of both applicants and entrants to academic universities. Table 7.13 shows the proportions in state and private universities in 1969–74, as well as the numbers of years those who entered university in 1980 had spent as *rōnin*.

The greatest change in the 1970s has been the decline in the proportion of *rōnin* among university entrants, suggesting that private study after high school became less able to compensate for failure to attend the right schools earlier on. Possibly in response to a recognition of this, fewer *rōnin* bothered to apply, although the rising costs of university education towards the end of the 1970s in particular also acted as a deterrent. The *ad hoc* commission on administrative reform headed by Toshio Doko in mid-1981 called for cuts in government subsidies to private universities, which increased from 7.2% of running expenses in 1970 to 29.5% in 1980 and therefore to some extent eased the fee increases that were made.[27] If the cuts are made, private university fees will further reduce the *rōnin* who seek university entrance.

This process of reduction seems to have taken place in two main stages. First, those students who realise the hopelessness of applying to state universities try one of the private colleges. They then find out not simply that competition for the more costly private universities is equally stiff, at least in the better ones, but that even a good higher education does not guarantee upper-class membership to the extent that it used to. The sacrifice of their youth for no more than the possibility of a secure job has ceased, in the minds of many young people, to be worth while. In 1977, for the first time since the perennial increases, the percentage of college-bound high school graduates declined, and by 1979 it had fallen to 37.4%.[28] Competition had been shifting back more and more into the schools – increasingly even pre-schools – and a rigid system of ranking among these institutions became the means of allocating people into universities, where the sorting process was formalised.

However, the pre-selection that takes place through the ranking of schools has not eliminated the problems of administering the final stage of the sorting process, the university entrance examinations. By the late 1970s, approximately 700,000 students sat about three million tests annually for public and private universities. In 1979, therefore, a uniform public university examination was introduced, and in January 1981, its third year of operation, 357,633 students took part.[29] One advantage of this more streamlined system is that it speeds up the sorting process by eliminating the repetition of tests. In the past, students would apply to and write entrance examinations for two or more colleges, and much time and effort would be wasted.

Although the institutional forms through which competitive mechanisms functioned kept breaking down, there always seemed to be new avenues for them to work through. The visible focus of competition shifted from schools to universities and then to different types of universities. It finally came back to schools and even kindergartens as the places which ultimately determined university selection. The only real sign of breakdown of the mechanisms themselves was the tendency for some people to opt out of the education rat-race altogether, either because they came to prefer less-well-paid jobs in the countryside or because they came to believe that even a 'good' education could leave them unemployed or in a job they could get without going to university. Where people could not be

Table 7.14. *Distribution of persons at junior colleges, by sex, jobs after graduation, and regular courses, 1980–1*

Total no. of graduates, 1980	169,930
Females	155,200
Males	14,730
Occupations of graduates who entered jobs in 1981	
Primary industry	526
Production/transportation	2,623
Sales/services	5,537
Clerical/technical/managerial	93,949
Regular courses of students enrolled in 1980	
Humanities	21.6%
Social sciences	9.1%
Technical/industrial	5.5%
Household management	26.7%
Education	24.4%
Other	12.7%

Source: Wagakuni no kyōiku suijun, 1980, pp. 31, fuzoku shiryō, 138, 140.

induced to compete for the acquisition, if not of special skills, at least of 'brand names' favoured by employers, the system's ability to make them blame themselves for their difficulties did begin to break down.

This is precisely why the sexual division of labour has always been a two-edged sword in Japan. Women have not competed with men in large numbers for entrance to prestige universities, but mainly among themselves for an education which does not put them in the running for bourgeois positions in Japanese society. The main professional positions open to them after graduation from women's colleges are in teaching. Table 7.14 shows that junior colleges are mainly places where women go to prepare for their roles as wives and mothers or as clerical and factory workers.

The educational system's legitimating powers are therefore mainly confined to men, among whom competition is most intense because the ultimate prizes include top positions in the corporate hierarchy. Since these jobs are not open to women anyway, at least not to mothers, there is little point in women trying to get the above-average skills and university 'brand names' which sort males into different classes. Mothers are destined, when they enter paid jobs, to remain in the bottom layers of the working class, so that the patriarchal component in Japanese education, at least as far as they are concerned, comes before its class component. Examination of these patriarchal mechanisms is, unfortunately, beyond the scope of this study.

However, although patriarchal mechanisms are what ultimately lie behind the sexual division of labour which sends women and men to mainly single-sex educational institutions, where they compete among themselves, women's schools and colleges do help legitimate the class positions women in Japan occupy. They can always be made to blame the lower-class jobs on their lack of appropriate education, even or especially when the sexual division of labour breaks down at the fringes and allows a small number of women to enter prestige universities and even the corporate hierarchy. Mothers who might have felt it was their sex that kept them from acquiring the relevant skills would be confronted with factual evidence to the contrary.

The processes by which skills, and especially above-average skills, are acquired therefore legitimate class relations in Japan in a whole variety of ways which overlap and sometimes contradict one another. Since what propertyless people sell are their skills and capacities, the value they can obtain for their labour power depends on the level and types of skills they have or can acquire. At the highest level are the knowledges and 'brand names' that put people into the running for bourgeois jobs, whereas at the lowest level is compulsory education up to middle school, specifically girls' schools. Since the particular levels people reach overlap closely with their sex, the function of education in channelling people into classes is simultaneously a form in which patriarchy is maintained.

The main job of the state in the exercise of these functions is neither partial socialisation of the costs of compulsory education in order to stabilise working-class subsistence, nor ensuring that all workers possess the minimum required skills, nor even indoctrination of the young into the virtues of social harmony and filial piety. Although each of these functions is in part carried out by the state, the major task it faces is to regulate the types and degrees of competition for the higher levels of skills. Optimal functioning of this legitimating mechanism would see that changes in the numbers of different types of jobs requiring different types of skills exactly match changes in the numbers of agents with the appropriate qualifications. This crucial function, which falls mainly on the state, involves maintaining

equality between the demand and the supply of the various skills and
capacities required by capital accumulation. It is an extremely
complicated job, because uneven and often erratic accumulation
results in lags in the ability of the state to ensure that just the right
numbers of people are trained for the available jobs. There are thus
always some people who struggled hard for their qualifications but for
whom no jobs are available. They are the ones whom the bourgeoisie
has most reason to fear, because it is hard to make them blame
themselves rather than the system for their situation. In times of crisis,
when the supply of job opportunities shrinks, the numbers of such
people can reach dangerous proportions.

Parliamentarism and the extraction of 'consent'

How adequately mechanisms of social control which function mainly
through education can paper over cracks in bourgeois society
depends partly on the available alternatives. Among these are
mechanisms whose specific function is to extract consent, that is, to
present bourgeois social relations as the products of individual
choice. Although there are many concrete daily activities through
which the functioning of these mechanisms is manifested (such as the
selection of a basket of groceries in a supermarket), one of the most
important activities organised by the state is parliamentary politics.

Marxist writing on parliamentarism in both Japan and the West is
probably more superficial than it is on any other area of social life.
The institutions of liberal democracy tend either to be dismissed
outright as a 'sham' and therefore unworthy of serious study, or they
are welcomed as major means of possible working-class power and
socialist transformation. What both of these approaches have in
common is their failure to attempt an analysis of the real mechanisms
behind the parliamentary forms and the tendency to make purely
moralistic judgements. What is required therefore is middle-level
theory to reconstruct the infrastructural mechanisms which lie
between the capitalist mode of production and the concrete parliamentary forms as they are experienced.[30] Rather than go into the
details of Japanese parliamentarism, which are more than adequately
described by bourgeois scholars,[31] I concentrate on reconstructing
these mechanisms and showing in broad outline how their functioning is manifested in Japan.

Since the relationships among classes in capitalist society are
fundamentally unequal in power, one should never say that workers

Table 7.15. *Voter turnout in*
Lower House elections, 1946–80

Date of election	% vote
10 April 1946	72.08
25 April 1947	67.95
23 January 1949	74.04
1 October 1952	76.43
19 April 1953	74.22
27 February 1955	76.99
22 May 1958	75.84
20 November 1960	73.51
21 November 1963	71.14
29 January 1967	73.99
27 December 1969	68.51
10 December 1972	71.76
5 December 1976	73.45
7 October 1979	68.01
22 June 1980	74.57

Source: *Asahi   Nenkan*   [Asahi
Yearbook], 1981 (Tokyo: Asahi shinbunsha, 1981), p. 233.

'consent' to the proposals of their employers unless this word is put
into inverted commas. People in inferior power situations do not
agree to but submit to proposals which work to their disadvantage,
although submission to those in commanding positions can be
transformed into an apparent willingness to cooperate with them. All
social mechanisms which generate unequal power relations, such as
the capitalist mode of production, require for their legitimation
additional mechanisms of social control through which the submission of the weaker party is somehow transformed into 'consent.' Some
of the most important of these in capitalist society are the ones which
make it seem that the different classes actually have equal power.

Universal franchise, which gives every individual, whether the
poorest worker or the most wealthy capitalist, one vote and only one
vote, is therefore a practical activity in which people from totally
different classes are in fact perfectly equal. Universal franchise
establishes practices in which there are no inequalities of power
whatsoever, and to the extent that these practices can dominate day-
to-day political life and working-class political organisations, the

Table 7.16. *Election turnout in
selected prefectures, 1979–80*

	1980	1979
Average	74.57	68.01
Osaka	67.40	60.82
Tokyo	67.49	53.19
Kyoto	67.89	61.03
Chiba	69.49	60.18
Kanagawa	69.96	54.71
Saga	85.02	83.29
Fukui	85.39	75.40
Oita	86.24	82.75
Shimane	87.61	85.24

Source: *Nihon Keizai Shinbun*, 24 June 1980,
in *Shinbun Geppō*, 404 (July 1980), p. 48.

fundamental differences in power between classes can be obscured.
Frequent elections and widespread working-class participation in
them are likely to assist this function of universal suffrage.

In postwar Japan, when universal suffrage for adults finally
became a reality, there have been an unusually large number of
elections to the National Diet. Every three years, the Constitution
requires half the members of the House of Councillors (an upper
chamber with a veto power somewhere between that of the British
House of Lords and the American Senate) to be elected, and although
the House of Representatives has a four-year term, there were fifteen
elections in the years from 1946 to 1980, that is, an average of one
every 1.6 years. The rate of participation in these activities was not
very high, though as table 7.15 shows it varied somewhat. The large
difference in turnout between the 1979 and 1980 elections probably
had a lot to do with the rare coincidence that in 1980 there was an
election to both houses. A far greater fanfare was made of the occasion
than most people could remember. It also had something to do with
the fact that Prime Minister Ōhira had died; many people seemed to
have turned out in sympathy. However, as on previous occasions, in
the urban areas where the working class is concentrated, people were
far less enthusiastic about voting than they were in rural areas. Table
7.16 shows the prefectures with the highest and lowest turnouts in
1979 and 1980.

In addition to national elections, there are a mass of locally elected positions with four-year terms in Japan which arouse varying degrees of excitement. Most important is the prefectural level, where the governorships (in all, 47) and assembly seats (2,846 in all) are fairly keenly contested and voters turn out in numbers comparable with those in national elections. However, below that level, interest can vary from almost nothing to the opposite extreme in the executive (3,278 city, ward, town, and village mayors) and legislative (a total of 69,793) positions that come up almost mechanically for re-election. In recent years, even the Ministry of Local Government has been complaining of a fall-off in interest in these affairs. For example, it noted that out of 3,740 positions which came up for re-election in 1979, a full 842 were filled unopposed, including 78 city and ward mayoralties, and 591 town and village mayoralties.[32]

It is extremely difficult to assess accurately how far the lower classes in Japan are dominated by electoral politics. The organisation of almost all political parties predominantly for the purpose of winning elections undoubtedly draws masses of people into this type of activity and shapes their understanding of what politics is all about. There is also little uncertainty that when people self-consciously discuss the degree of their involvement in politics, that word connotes to them, as it does to people in other liberal democracies, involvement in elections and electioneering. Yet how far these experiences and conceptions constrain people and prevent them from engaging in extra-parliamentary forms of organised struggle is very hard to determine. There is some evidence from public opinion surveys that however strong its grip on the masses in the past, electoral politics is being understood for what it is by more and more people. For example, in pre-election surveys in the period 1967 to 1980, the proportion of respondents who said there was no party that they liked grew from just under 10% to 19.8%. It had been even higher the year before, 20.7%. A much more constant proportion (just under 20% in 1967 and 15.7% in 1980) offered no answer to the question.[33] Between 35% and 40% of people have thus in varying degrees managed to extricate themselves from the world of electioneering. Growing numbers of them have been developing forms of organisation which provide real alternatives to the ideology that politics is a separate world from daily life where the rules put everyone in an equal position.

The second way in which parliamentarism functions to extract consent results from the competitive nature of elections. Just as when they make selections from among competing commodities as con- sumers (where everyone is equal and pays the same prices), the labouring masses get from elections an opportunity to engage in a real, concrete practice which nurtures the ideology of free and equal choice in bourgeois society. Regularly going through the act of choosing from a limited range of loudly competing alternatives can blind one to the fundamental similarities among them, so that being able to pick out one of them can also look like being able to choose what the alternatives will be. That the hidden rules of the entire infrastructure determine the latter can be obscured by the constant activity of selecting particular alternatives. Thus a vote even for an opposition political party's candidate can be transformed into an act of 'consent' to the outcome of the election. Insofar as elections do offer choices and people do make selections, they can seem to have agreed to almost anything: from all that might happen during the elected person's term of office to the whole system of social relations that existed before it and during it. Once again, the more frequently people can exercise some or other electoral choice, the keener the competition among the candidates, and the greater the variety of 'goods' offered, the more fully will 'consent' be extracted.

A few special characteristics of elections in Japan have ensured an unusual degree of effectiveness in the functioning of this mechanism. The frequency of elections in that country has already been mentioned, or at least one aspect of it. Another derives from a unique electoral system. In elections to the House of Councillors, people get two votes each which they cast in two entirely different constituencies. One is the single nationwide national constituency, in which everyone takes part in a sort of national popularity poll and the top fifty candidates (every three years) win. The other is the local consistuency in each voter's area, and although it may contain more than one seat, nobody has more than one vote in it. Seventy-six members are elected every three years in this way. The 511 Lower House members are all elected in local districts (in all, 129), one of which has only one seat but all the rest having from three to five seats. Again, even in multi-member constituencies, no more than one vote can be cast.

One consequence of this system is that the intensity of the competition is much greater than in other liberal democracies, because it occurs both within and among parties. The reason is that parties which aim for anything like overall majorities must forward more than one candidate in most of the multi-member constituencies. For example, in 1980 the Liberal Democratic Party forwarded 310 and the Japan Socialist Party 149 out of the total of 835 candidates in the 129 Lower House constituencies (in which the competition was for 511 seats). In the Upper House's 47 local constituencies (which elect 76 members) these parties entered only 54 and 39 candidates respectively out of a total of 192, but in the national constituency (with its 50 members) they fielded 23 and 10 respectively out of a total of 93.[34] Whenever there is more than one candidate from the same party in a constituency, they must not simply compete for the single vote of each elector with opposition party candidates, but with those from their own party as well. The results, of course, are often quite chaotic, as candidates (particularly from the ruling party) attack one another regardless of their affiliation.

However, as a means of drawing voters into making choices from among intensely competing but narrow alternatives, the system has on balance been quite successful. It is true that many people have lost interest in elections, but some of these seem to be bewildered and possibly even intimidated by the available choices: at least two conservative parties (the LDP and the New Liberal Club, an offshoot from it) plus alternatives within one of them; at least five social democratic parties covering the whole range of what this term embraces (from right to left: Democratic Socialist Party, Clean Government Party, Social Democratic Federation, Japan Socialist Party, and Japan Communist Party); here and there a local faction or minute sect; and a host of 'independents.' Small wonder many cannot say which party they support. Until they recognise that none probably attracts them, they can be made to believe that the choices are there and that the 'citizens' have only themselves to blame for their failure to choose suitable governments.

The third aspect of the legitimating mechanisms which function through parliamentarism is how they depoliticise power relations by presenting them as conflicts among individual personalities. Because votes are cast not for policies or systems of social relations but for individuals (who may or may not have any understanding of whether the claims they make are realistic), the substance of politics is transformed into personal differences among candidates and groups of candidates in political parties. Considering this in the light of the two points previously discussed, the following is what broadly happens in parliamentary elections: all voters have equal power, which they use to select the candidates of their choice, who in turn concentrate in themselves a collective power equal to the numbers of votes received. When a majority of like-minded successful candidates come together in a political party, they concentrate among themselves enough power to rule society, that is, to do to it what they choose. The way the infrastructural reality behind these experiences is concealed by the forms they assume is ingenious. First, of course the majority party does really have enough votes to pass through the parliament what it likes, but this is very different from the resulting ideology that it has the power to transform society through parliament. Second, it is true that the individuals in government office are really chosen by universal franchise in what are on the whole fair elections,[35] but it is quite another thing for the appearance to be created that the electors 'choose' the policies that the system imposes on the individuals in the majority party.

In Japan, the degree to which the substance of politics has been transformed into personality conflicts by parliamentary mechanisms is also quite unique. It occurs in two main arenas: the elections of Diet members and the election by the majority party of its leaders for Cabinet office. Both result mainly from the unique electoral system which pits even members of the same party against one another, thereby counteracting the degree to which parties might depersonalise political conflicts. They also result, though not to anything like the extent which bourgeois scholars have made out, from certain cultural traditions in Japan which have placed a greater emphasis on personal relationships than has occurred in the West.

Because the electoral system forces such a great degree of competition among candidates from the ruling party, they find it harder to distinguish themselves from one another in voters' minds than does a single candidate from an entirely different party. Candidates from the ruling party have thus had to declare themselves allied to intra-party factions based on top-ranking party leaders. However, these are not ordinary factions as might be found in Western political parties. They are disciplined, loyal, and have separate meetings and separate finances, which can amount to as much as a third or more of what the party collectively commands. Faction monies, which are donated by big businesses, are distributed by their leaders to help allied candidates 'distinguish themselves in voters' minds' from their party colleagues in other factions.

Table 7.17. *Numbers of seats and share of vote of main parliamentary parties in Lower House elections, 1960–80*

	LDP	NLC	DSP	CGP	SDF[a]	JSP	JCP	Others	Total
1960: seats	296	—	17	—	—	145	3	6	467
% vote	57.6	—	8.8	—	—	27.6	2.9	3.1	100
1963: seats	283	—	23	—	—	144	5	12	467
% vote	54.7	—	7.4	—	—	29.0	4.0	4.9	100
1967: seats	277	—	30	25	—	140	5	9	486
% vote	48.8	—	7.4	5.4	—	27.9	4.8	5.7	100
1969: seats	288	—	31	47	—	90	14	16	486
% vote	47.6	—	7.7	10.9	—	21.4	6.8	5.6	100
1972: seats	271	—	19	29	—	118	38	16	491
% vote	46.9	—	7.0	8.5	—	21.9	10.5	5.2	100
1976: seats	249	17	29	55	—	123	17	21	511
% vote	41.8	4.2	6.3	10.9	—	20.7	10.4	5.7	100
1979: seats	248	4	35	57	2	107	39	19	511
% vote	44.6	3.0	6.8	9.8	0.7	19.7	10.4	5.0	100
1980: seats	284	12	32	33	3	107	29	11	511
% vote	47.9	3.0	6.6	9.0	0.7	19.3	9.8	3.7	100

[a]The Social Democratic Federation. For the other abbreviations, see table 2.23.
Sources: Nihon Keizai Shinbun, 9 October 1979, in *Shinbun Geppō*, 396 (November 1979), p. 44; and *Asahi Shinbun*, 24 June 1980, and *Yomiuri Shinbun*, 24 June 1980, in *Shinbun Geppō*, 404 (July 1980), pp. 28, 38–9.

The massive electoral expenditures LDP candidates make to draw attention to themselves in this way are on anything from free souvenirs (e.g. umbrellas) to subsidised visits to hot springs. The actual amounts of money collected and spent during elections are shrouded in mystery beneath the amounts officially declared.[36] They are believed to be so substantial that the scandals which keep occurring over them are seen as brief glimpses of the iceberg whose tip is the officially declared amount. This 'money power politics' was most openly and successfully practised by former Prime Minister Tanaka Kakuei, whose faction continues as one of the strongest in the party in spite of his leading role in the Lockheed pay-off scandal.[37] However, 'money power politics' is not confined to this one faction, but is used by all of them and has in fact played an important part in the party's overall ability to remain in office ever since its formation in 1955. Table 7.17 summarises the electoral fortunes of all the main parliamentary parties since 1972, and table 7.18 indicates the strength of the different LDP factions following the 1979 and 1980 elections.

Table 7.18. *Liberal Democratic Party factional strength in the Lower House, 1979 and 1980*

	1979	1980
Ōhira (Suzuki after his death)	49	55
Tanaka	50	55
Fukuda	47	46
Nakasone	38	43
Miki (subsequently Komoto)	27	32
Nakagawa group	9	12
Others and non-aligned	37	43
Total[a]	257	286

[a]The totals refer to the situation after independents had aligned themselves.
Source: Mainichi Shinbun, 24 June 1980, in *Shinbun Geppo*, 404 (July 1980), pp. 37–8.

In spite of the reluctance of some of them, all the opposition parliamentary parties have been compelled to emulate at least in part the political style of the highly successful LDP. Even though none can match the handouts its candidates can make to highlight their suitability, almost all act out the requirements of the system by emphasising the personal qualities of their candidates far more than the distinctiveness of their policies. The result is that such differences among them as they might possess before they enter the electoral arena tend to be concealed by (and to disappear eventually as a result of) the common ways in which they must approach the masses at election time. Considerable public dissatisfaction with them is hardly surprising, neither is the fact that such large numbers of people get caught up in the personality-centred election campaigns. Both are natural reactions to a typical statement once made by an LDP Diet member to a group of his supporters: 'My friends, politics is not a matter for the head. Let us put aside difficult things like policy debate. Let's be friendly! Let's sing and dance! Let's enjoy ourselves!'[38]

The depoliticisation of class relations in Japan through their personalisation by parliamentarism is not only manifested at election times. Almost equally important has been the way the ruling party elects its top leaders for Cabinet office, in particular its president, who becomes prime minister. The details of how this is done are not relevant, though the central role of the factions cannot be overemphasised.

Table 7.19. *Leadership changes, leadership popularity, and LDP fortunes, 1960–80*

Date of election	Date and name of new Cabinet	Popular support for new Cabinet (party support in brackets)	Popular support for Cabinet when it fell (party support in brackets)
November 1960	Aug. 1960, Ikeda	51 (49)	39 (45)
November 1963	Nov. 1964, Sato	47 (51)	37 (45)
January 1967	—	—	—
December 1969	—	—	—
December 1972	Aug. 1972, Tanaka	62 (51)	27 (44)
December 1976	Dec. 1974, Miki	45 (45)	34 (45)
	Feb. 1977, Fukuda	28 (37)	30 (41)
October 1979	Dec. 1978, Ōhira	42 (51)	31 (49)
June 1980	Jul. 1980, Suzuki	52 (52)	36 (50)[a]

[a]After one year in office.
Sources: *Asahi Shinbun*, 28 July 1980 and 25 October 1980, in *Shinbun Geppō*, 405 (August 1980), p. 171, and 408 (November 1980), p. 164; and *Asahi Shinbun*, 16 June 1981, pp. 1, 2.

Japanese prime ministers have, since the formation of the LDP, been major faction leaders who came to office following often very bitter conflicts (and money exchanges) among the factions. Normally, when a prime minister begins to lose his popular appeal after a few years in office, faction leaders in the running to replace him begin to convey, sometimes quite openly, their own dissatisfaction with him. Gradually they ally themselves more openly with the growing public mood against him, so that by the time he is at the nadir of his popularity, there is within the LDP a champion of the public discontent who is ready to step into his office. When the party can time things properly, it tries to ensure that the leadership changes immediately before elections, so that the party can benefit electorally from the honeymoon period of the new Cabinet and its prime minister.

On each of the three occasions in its history when the LDP managed to do this (deliberately with the rise of the Ikeda and Tanaka Cabinets, accidentally with the fall of the Ōhira Cabinet on the death of the prime minister), its electoral fortunes were above the level expected from the trend at the time. On the other hand, each time it went into an election with an unpopular prime minister (particularly in 1976 when Miki was at the helm) he seemed to drag it down. Table 7.19 shows that the party's fortunes were significantly related to the popularity of its leader and its leadership changes, which therefore became an important form in which Japanese parliamentarism functioned to extract 'consent.'

However, lest one exaggerate the legitimating impact of even newly elected Cabinets with high levels of popular support, it is sobering to examine people's reasons for expressing support. In the case of the Suzuki Cabinet, the *Asahi* poll which tested public opinion just after its formation came up with the following reasons:[39]

Because Suzuki is the prime minister	14%
Because it is an LDP Cabinet	24%
Because of its policies	8%
Others/no reply	6%
Total which supported	52%

The part played by the prime minister was impressive, as was the submergence of policy considerations, but there is strong loyalty to the party regardless of either of these.

The final way in which parliamentarism helps extract consent in Japan is also very important: its ability to make capitalism itself appear unalterable and permanent. This results from the power the government seems to have to do whatever it chooses and the fact that parliamentary institutions cannot transform bourgeois social relations, which then appear unalterable.

The inability of parliamentary institutions fundamentally to change capitalist society stems from the fact that they do not even play an important part in keeping it together. All the important functions of capital accumulation, such as information gathering and working out what to do to ensure uninterrupted accumulation, are, when society-wide organisation is required, carried out by the civil bureaucracy. The essence of parliamentarism has little to do with these functions, but centres on the legitimating functions of extracting consent. Ways have to be found to ensure that everything that is worked out by the fragmented (trade associations, etc.) and centralised (government departments) forms of bourgeois organisation to maintain capital accumulation is complied with, preferably 'consented' to, by the labouring masses. Everything must therefore go through the parliamentary procedures, which to function as effective legitimators must assume the appearance of possessing the ultimate power in society. That they do not possess this power has been confirmed by experience, but the form the experience took led to the drawing of different conclusions: every socialist party that has tried to transform bourgeois society anywhere in the world by means of parliament has failed, and in the process was constrained to decide that capitalism was unalterable.

The Japan Socialist Party has been a bit slower than most parties of its type in coming to this conclusion. The main reason for this is that when it was briefly in office in 1947–8 it could blame its failure even to put some dents into capitalist society on its short term and on the absence of an absolute majority, which made it dependent on other parties. Nevertheless, slowly but surely over the years, parliamentary experience (even in opposition) has swelled those of its numbers who had come to accept the 'inevitable.' In 1960 a major faction deserted to form the Democratic Socialist Party, and in 1979 the Social Democratic Federation, a similar grouping, contested the general election as a separate party. The rump that remained contains a small but dogmatic socialist left, the Shakaishugi Kyōkai (Socialist Association), which still insists on the classical Marxist–Leninist path to socialism, while the bulk of the party is thoroughly social democratic and committed to parliamentarism.

These latter characteristics have always tended to go together: welfare capitalism and liberal democracy. Even the Japan Communist Party has managed, without ever even holding government office, to be so involved in parliamentary electioneering that socialist reconstruction has slipped more and more into the distance as a goal, perhaps in theory attainable, but so far away that for purposes of practical discussion and activity it is not.

There is little doubt that the overall impact of the legitimating mechanisms which function through parliamentarism in Japan have reinforced the effectiveness of other mechanisms: the provision of material security, training for specifically capitalist labour processes, and formally extracting 'consent' combine to form a powerful structure of social control. As far as the overwhelming majority of the population is concerned, their joint impact has so far been sufficient. Any one's failure to keep people in line here or there has usually been compensated for by the ability of another to fill the gap. People have either been materially secure, or have accepted the jobs for which they were trained, or think nothing can be done until the people themselves 'choose' a new government. But there are some people who have been outside even the combined grip of all these mechanisms of social control, people who in every possible way refuse to knuckle under. They are the ones who are said to understand no language other than force.

Violence and compelling submission

The use of violence as the final means of holding bourgeois society together can and does take a large variety of forms. Some of these are more able than others to conceal the fact that violence is being used, while there are also some which can make it seem that force in bourgeois society is always exercised with complete impartiality towards people of different classes. For example, most of the violence against women takes place within the family and is therefore largely concealed from public view, as is the violence which is wielded within the company against militant workers, either by the union hierarchy or by hired thugs.[40] On the other hand, the (perfectly visible) violence that imprisons the unemployed worker for theft does not appear to be any more partially used than when the offender is an employer.

In each case, the organisational form through which force is used or threatened depends mainly on the form of breakdown of bourgeois social relations. In most cases, isolated forms of insubordination, such as indiscipline on the job by one or two militants, can easily be dealt with by employers themselves, either by means of dismissal or by having someone use or threaten more forceful means.[41] The extreme case of using the police or military against organised workers is much more rare, because of the difficulty of workers in organising sufficiently to require it, but it is by no means unknown.

To analyse all the different organisational forms of ruling-class violence in Japan, as well as the infrastructural mechanisms behind them, is well beyond the scope of this discussion. I have excluded patriarchal violence against women, even though it is fundamental to the relationship between male employers and female workers. Also excluded are all the non-state forms of violence which are used against the working class, such as the gangster brotherhoods (the *yakuza*) and the private armies of right-wing patriotic organisations. The focus is thus on what Althusser called the repressive state apparatuses, the police and the military, but there is no suggestion that the ruling class uses only these society-wide organisations. The emphasis is on them because of their increasing importance in times of crisis, when working-class struggles are harder to control by mainly non-state forms of organisation.

The main areas in which the police force bears the final responsibility for preserving bourgeois social relations correspond to the two broad areas of their breakdown: insubordination on the job and 'crime' in the world of consumption. The functions performed by the police in these two worlds are intimately related, with the appearance of neutrality which characterises police activity deriving from their extensive involvement in the world of 'crime.' I therefore begin with this world.

When workers leave the office or factory with their wages in their pockets, they suddenly become free from all the discipline and inequality of power they endured during the day. They are free to make choices and even to own property – not means of production, to be sure, but articles of consumption ranging from a glass of beer to a home. And since their wages set narrow limits on what they are actually able to buy, there is not much to stop them from taking what they might not quite have the money to purchase. There is perhaps more to stop them than in other capitalist societies, since the *yakuza* (the gangsters) take a dim view of small-scale crime and try to keep it under their control. There are also a much more intimate family system and cohesive neighbourhood community in Japan than in the West, which also reduce the 'freedom' of workers simply to take from people like themselves what they cannot afford. Nevertheless, the contrast between their lack of power and regimentation at work and their relative freedom and equality after work means that poverty will inevitably breed 'crime' among the working class. Table 7.20 shows that a very high (and increasing) proportion of criminal offences in Japan fall into the category of simple thefts. The result is that a major part of police work is in this area.

Herein lies the basis of the ideology that the police are impartial towards people of different classes. After all, workers have property too, and when this gets stolen or damaged the police try to recover it just as they do when employers' property is stolen. In cases of other more serious crimes too, the police are equally impartial in protecting the personal safety of workers and employers alike. What lies behind the ideology of police fairness is that in the world of consumption the police really do protect the persons and property of both workers and capitalists. True, the latter have more to protect, but this does not mean the working class has no stake in police protection. Just try telling a woman who has been raped that she should not call in the police against a 'fellow worker'!

However, in almost total contrast to this world of comparative

Table 7.20. *Reported criminal offences, 1969–78*

	1969		1978	
	No.	%	No.	%
Brutal crimes	*11,808*	*0.9*	*8,695*	*0.7*
Murder	2,098		1,862	
Robbery with violence	2,724		1,932	
Arson	1,304		2,004	
Rape	5,682		2,897	
Violent crimes	*110,022*	*8.8*	*59,055*	*4.4*
Assault	33,134		18,135	
Bodily harm	54,392		28,938	
Intimidation	3,967		1,937	
Blackmail	18,204		9,895	
Thefts	*1,008,013*	*80.4*	*1,136,648*	*85.0*
Breaking and entering	350,481		315,138	
On public transport	191,957		354,638	
Other	465,575		466,872	
'White collar' crimes	*75,373*	*6.0*	*91,579*	*6.9*
Fraud	58,662		64,866	
Embezzlement	9,001		15,781	
Forgery	5,560		9,802	
Bribery	1,817		908	
Misappropriation	333		222	
Public indecency	*12,468*	*1.0*	*8,265*	*0.6*
Gambling	3,447		2,574	
Obscenity	9,021		5,691	
Other	*36,266*	*2.9*	*32,680*	*2.4*
Obstructing police	2,754		2,037	
Trespass	10,351		11,002	
Kidnapping	917		738	
Wilful damage	6,165		8,457	
Total	1,253,950	100	1,336,922	100

Source: *Keisatsu hakusho*, 1979, pp. 332–5.

freedom and equality, the situation at work is completely different: since people have unequal power and are under rigid discipline, bringing in the police to restore a breakdown of order can mean only one thing. Because most struggles never reach such a stage, few people have direct experience of police action against them during a labour dispute. Table 7.21 shows that even during the years of vigorous restructuring and rationalisation of workforces, their numbers were not large. The ideology of an impartial police force is thus very widespread.

Table 7.21. *Persons arrested and illegal incidents accompanying labour disputes, plus total working days lost through strikes, 1974–80*

	Illegal incidents	Persons arrested	Total days lost through strikes
1973	—	—	4,603,821
1974	622	1,223	9,662,945
1975	546	1,016	8,015,772
1976	704	1,285	3,253,715
1977	304	588	1,518,476
1978	352	572	1,357,502
1979	372	780	930,304
1980	237	444	1,001,224

Sources: Keisatsu hakusho, 1979, p. 268; 1981, p. 235; *Rōdō hakusho,* 1981, fuzoku tōkeihyō [appended statistical tables], p. 88.

Since most labour disputes like these which involve the police take place at work, only those most directly involved get to see what really happens. However, there are occasionally confrontations outside working hours which involve large numbers of people and which are clearly visible to even more. When the police enter these conflicts, they are quickly stripped of their veneer of impartiality. For example, their removal of JSP Diet members from the chamber at a time when millions of people were expressing their opposition to the Security treaty with the U.S.A.,[42] their use of riot gear against unarmed student demonstrations in the 1960s,[43] and their clearing of Narita Airport of its legal (till the law was changed) occupants and their allies by means of cranes, bulldozers, and thousands of riot police[44] have each in its own way laid bare the reality that ultimately governs what the police are for. The 100,000 riot police who can be mobilised on forty-eight hours' notice cannot, by any twist of daily experience, be presented as protecting the persons and property of workers. Neither could the 422,000-person security system which was mobilised for the Tokyo Summit in June 1979 and which put the city virtually under martial law. Steadily throughout the 1970s, the police built up this massive security system, continually harassing 'radicals' and protest leaders as they did so. It would not therefore be an exaggeration to say that the present-day Japanese police force, with its quarter of a million regulars, has reached a level of repressive capability that is equal to what existed in the prewar period. Many people today are speaking of the re-emergence of the police state.[45]

However, the most important police work is not to assemble a 100,000-member riot squad, impressive as this is, since the military could surpass even that level of organised might if this were required. It is in their day-to-day work of surveillance and security among the people in local areas that the police perform their main repressive function. Sheer brute force on the largest possible scale is really a matter for the military.

In most respects, the military is in a similar situation to the police. Although it is really the ultimate weapon of Japanese capital against the labouring masses of Japan and nearby Asia, in particular South Korea,[46] the use of this ultimate weapon has not been required in the postwar period.

The time spent by Self Defence Forces, as they are called, in disaster relief work and the like thus has an effect similar to the involvement in crime of the police force. Among a people devasted by the ravages of war and nuclear destruction, whose constitution even outlaws the maintenance of military forces and who are organised more massively in peace struggles than any other, the high degree of support for the, strictly speaking, illegal Self Defence Forces seems strange at first sight. However, the basis of this support is the innocuous but ideologically important role played in disaster relief work. So worried has the state been about the strength of the peace movement in Japan that in its 1981 White Paper on Defence, for the first time in the postwar period, it devoted a special section to the need for greater patriotism and preparedness among the people to fight. It had felt constrained to say: 'True patriotism is not only to love peace and to love one's country. It should come out in the form of one's zeal to defend the nation in cooperation with other citizens in case of a national crisis.'[47]

What national crisis? Why the massive planned five-year military build-up for 1980–5?[48] Already before the plan began to be implemented, Japanese military expenditure was ninth largest in the world. Yet defence appropriations have continued their steady rates of increase, despite the fiscal crisis and cuts that had to be made to such areas as social security and education, as revealed by table 7.22. The 1981 White Paper on Defence which argued the case for the build-up presented the existing strength of the military as follows:

Table 7.22. *Budgetary allocations on military expenditure, 1970–82*

	Amount (¥ bil.)	Increase over previous year	Military expenditure as % of GNP
1970	569.5	17.7	0.79
1971	670.9	17.8	0.80
1972	800.2	19.3	0.88
1973	935.5	16.9	0.85
1974	1,093.0	16.8	0.83
1975	1,327.3	21.4	0.84
1976	1,512.4	13.9	0.90
1977	1,690.6	11.8	0.88
1978	1,901.0	12.4	0.90
1979	2,094.5	10.2	0.90
1980	2,230.2	6.5	0.90
1981	2,400.0	7.6	0.91
1982	2,586.1	7.8	0.93

Sources: Bōei hakusho, 1981, p. 256; *Japan Times Weekly*, 2 January 1982, p. 2.

155,000 ground forces, a 207,000-ton navy, and an air force of 390 aircraft (plus 24,000 U.S. military personnel and 180 aircraft).[49] Yet it did not emphasise the high quality of the Japanese conventional weaponry which made it the top conventional force in Asia. Neither did it mention the ease with which a nuclear infrastructure (transport, generation, and delivery systems) has been built up for easy conversion to nuclear preparedness.

The five-year build-up is mainly for battle tanks, anti-aircraft missiles, combat aircraft, and warships armed with missiles. A full 40% of the money in the first year was to be spent on the navy (euphemistically called Maritime Self Defence Forces), whose job has become to 'guard' the sea over a distance of 1,000 nautical miles off the coast of Japan. The focal point has been to strengthen the U.S.–South Korean–Japanese axis in the Far East. More recently, to this overwhelming preoccupation with maintaining stability in and around South Korea has been added a willingness to cooperate with other imperialist powers in protecting Japanese interests much further afield. The historic participation of Japanese destroyers with units from Australia, New Zealand, Canada, and the U.S. in manoeuvres in the Central Pacific in spring 1980 (code-named RimPac, or Rim of the Pacific) was the first major indicator of this. At about the same time, a government study group called for the conclusion of bilateral 'investment protection agreements' with underdeveloped countries where Japanese investments might be at political risk. The U.S. at the time had 114 such agreements, while Japan had only one (with Egypt).[50]

Although it is unlikely that in the immediate future Japanese troops will find themselves defending overseas investments in Asia, partly because the peoples of these countries could not be compelled even by their reactionary regimes into tolerating that, other forms of military cooperation, such as the deep involvement in South Korea, could easily be extended to include more Japanese satellites. One of the surest signs of a crisis of accumulation is always the increased attention the ruling class gives to the means by which social control is maintained at home and to expanding imperialism abroad. And one of the surest signs that the more subtle mechanisms of social control (such as subsistence stabilisation or the extraction of consent) and imperialism abroad have also begun to break down is the extra attention the bourgeoisie gives to its 'final solutions': the repressive state apparatuses. However, precisely because their use is so much of a last resort, the remilitarisation of Japan is a sign of the ruling class's weakness. Force is something much more safely applied by the bourgeoisie in less visible forms than by the police or the army. Paradoxically, therefore, the more the state steps in to maintain social control through force, the more rapid is the breakdown of the subtler mechanisms of social control whose functioning depends on the concealment of the role of force.

8
Conclusion

That a system of social relations is in a state of crisis, as we have seen class relations are in Japan, in no way implies that they are in a process of transformation. A capitalist crisis is no more than a breakdown of certain functional requirements of the capitalist system, and they could just as easily be replaced by new ways of achieving the same end as by a transition to a new system of social relations. In fact, the latter would occur only under certain quite exceptional circumstances. To assess the possibilities of revolutionary social change in Japan requires a brief examination of what these circumstances are.

One way to understand the problem of revolutionary social change is to recall the argument in the Introduction that the visible world is a product of a variety of forces of unequal strengths, frequently working in opposite directions and emanating from a series of hidden mechanisms, some of which are more fundamental than others. Although the malfunctioning of any of these mechanisms can lead to some degree of social dislocation, a capitalist crisis has its origin in the malfunctioning of the capitalist mode of production, which is one of the most fundamental of all infrastructural mechanisms. So whenever one talks about social change, it is important to specify which mechanism one thinks might undergo a transformation: of course the more fundamental the mechanism, the more far-reaching the resulting social change. Since the type of revolutionary change we are contemplating stems from a transformation of the capitalist mode of production, it is of considerable importance, even though it is not the only important change which one might contemplate in modern society. A bit later we will consider the transformation of patriarchy.

However, if the capitalist mode of production is to undergo a qualitative change, then this can only happen if its weaker force, labour, somehow gains sufficient strength to predominate over its stronger force, capital. But surely this can only happen after the mode of production has become one in which labour is the principal force? If labour is the weaker force under capitalism, how can it possibly become stronger than capital so long as capitalism exists, let alone strong enough to transform capitalism? In most cases it cannot, no matter how severe the crisis, and capital simply reasserts its predominance, perhaps through some new mechanisms of social control.

The weaker forces of the more fundamental mechanisms of the infrastructure, such as the capitalist mode of production, can predominate over their stronger forces only when they can be brought into combinations with other subordinate forces. So long as these combinations hold together and a force can be created which is stronger even than the predominant one of the infrastructural mechanism concerned, in this case a combination which is of greater strength than capital itself, then a transformation of this mechanism is a possibility.

As far as Japan is concerned, what this means is that socialist revolution requires a sufficient combination of subordinate forces to outweigh the power of capital. What are the possible sources of such a combination, and what are the possibilities of it actually coming about? Table 8.1 draws together our analysis of the agents of the major class forces (that is, it excludes fractional forces) in present-day Japan, although their sex composition, to which we will return, has its basis not in the capitalist mode of production but in what we might call the patriarchal mode of reproduction. If one takes the numbers of agents who mediate each class force as a rough indicator of its potential strength, that is, the strength it would have if the mechanism of production which generates it allowed its agents to act in concert, then one can get a broad idea of the potential strength of the different possible combinations of class forces in Japan. Clearly, the working class would need to be in any effective alliance, and only the petty bourgeoisie would be in any real position to hold the balance of power.

If the agents of a particular class are fully to mediate its potential strength, and combinations of agents are fully to mediate the potential strength of class alliances, then it is essential that they act in concert in united organisations. It is precisely through the way a mechanism brings together the agents of its predominant force that they (even though numerically inferior to the agents of the weaker force, whom the functioning of the mechanism scatters) can maintain

Table 8.1. *Total population over the age of 15, by economically active class, non-active class, and sex, 1979 (1,000 persons)*

	Males		Females		Total	
	No.	%	No.	%	No.	%
Total population over 15 years	42,825	—	45,472	—	88,297	—
Economically active (adjusted)	34,017	100	20,720	100	54,736	100
Bourgeoisie[a]	7,389	21.7	423	2.1	7,812	14.3
Petty bourgeoisie[b]	4,827	14.1	4,629	22.5	9,456	17.3
Peasantry[c]	2,552	7.5	2,661	12.9	5,213	9.5
Middle class	2,527	7.4	1,262	6.1	3,789	6.9
Working class	16,834	49.3	11,601	56.4	28,435	51.2
Total	34,129	100	20,576	100	54,705	100
Adjustment[d]	−112		+144		+32	
Not economically active	8,808	100	24,751	100	33,559	100
Bourgeoisie (owners)[e]	1,133	12.9	60	0.2	1,193	3.6
Middle class (students)[f]	3,994	45.3	3,325	13.4	7,319	21.8
Peasantry (on farms)[g]	(940)		(1,938)		(2,878)	
Working class (latent and stagnant)	1,829	20.8	8,524	34.4	10,353	30.9
Keeping house[h]	119	1.4	9,478	38.3	9,597	28.6
Others[i]	1,733	19.7	3,364	13.6	5,097	15.2

[a]In addition to the employees in the bourgeoisie, this number includes the 608,000 proprietors mentioned in table 1.22. Their composition by sex comes from *Shūgyō kōzō kihon chōsa hōkoku*, 1979, pp. 53, 58.

[b]Their composition by sex comes from *ibid*.

[c]These numbers are fewer than the ones indicated in table 3.7 as the persons mainly engaged in agriculture. Since the discrepancy results from double counting in my sources, I have avoided this here by including only the numbers of self-employed and family workers in agriculture listed in *Shūgyō kōzō kihon chōsa hōkoku*, 1979, pp. 50, 53, 58.

[d]The adjustment is needed to bring my estimates into line with the totals in *ibid*. The differences result from certain categories which were unreported, and a possibly slight underestimation on my part of the numbers of women in the bourgeoisie and middle class.

[e]To estimate the proportion of women among these owners 'without occupation,' it does not matter whether one takes the 5.2% average so far used for women in the bourgeoisie or the fact that only 5.0% of two-or-more-person households have women as household heads.

[f]I have included all students, apart from those 'wishing to work,' in the middle class because of the contradictory forces they face at school and university. When they leave school or university, most of the contradictions will be resolved, and most will enter particular classes.

their hegemony. Their highest form of organisation is of course the state. But unity among the agents of even the same subordinate class forces, let alone between the agents of different subordinate forces, is extremely rare, precisely because the system functions to fragment and divide them. For example, the agents of the petty bourgeoisie are kept apart by both the dispersal of their minute enterprises throughout all corners of the country and by the intense competition which exists among them for survival. The main sources of division among workers which stem from the functioning of capitalism are the fractional forces we have analysed. A typical example of the form in which the divisions present themselves is when a company needs to lay off a small number of workers so that it may remain profitable enough to keep on the rest. In only the most exceptional of such cases do we find those whose jobs are not threatened offering sustained support for those who have been singled out for dismissal. It is much more common to find a Dōmei-affiliated union actually cooperating with management in the selection of capital's victims.

The reason why revolutionary social change is a possible outcome of a capitalist crisis lies mainly in the way a crisis might unleash new unifying forces among the agents of subordinate classes which outweigh the ones which fragment them. For example, workers learn from their experience that so long as they rely on the agents of capital for their welfare none of them is secure, and that the only thing that can protect them is solidarity among themselves. This is not the sort of lesson workers pick up in boom times, because as a matter of fact they can do quite well in such times even without much sticking together. We have seen that the current crisis in Japan is beginning to school the members of the different fractions of the working class in this lesson. However, even this process of forging unity within the working class has a long way to go and is by no means proceeding without considerable setbacks.

Notes to table 8.1 *(cont.)*

*g*The persons on farms who are not economically active. See *Nōrinsuisanshō tōkeihyō*, 1979–80, pp. 24–5. Since most would be at school or keeping house, the numbers are in brackets to avoid double counting.
*h*All the people keeping house apart from those 'willing to work,' who are included in the latent and stagnant reserves of the working class.
*i*Most of these are elderly people over 65 or disabled people who are not looking for paid jobs.
Sources: Tables 1.5, 1.22, 2.2, 4.12, and 5.20; sources mentioned in the notes above.

One of the main setbacks is the current drive within the trade union movement to form a united organisation around Dōmei and all that it stands for: militarism, imperialism, anti-communism, and cooperation with management. This *tōitsu sensen* (united front), as it is known, is intended first to incorporate the main private-sector unions and then the public-sector ones with a view to either isolating or submerging such genuine working-class organisational tendencies in the movement as there are. Even the Sōhyō leadership is going along with the idea and is desperately trying to sell it to rank-and-file unionists. There is little doubt that the labour movement will have to experience for itself much more of what unity on this basis means before it begins to unite on a socialist basis. Workers will also have to experience much more fully for themselves some of the consequences of what lies behind the success that the 'united labour front' movement is having: bureaucratic enterprise unionism which grows out of the very forces through which capital binds workers to itself. In fact the limits of any form of trade unionism as a vehicle of working-class organisation for socialist change have yet to be brought home to the socialist movement in Japan. Although there are some democratic unions which do fairly adequately represent their members rather than capital, it is extremely difficult for a trade union, which is organised to help workers get the best possible price and conditions for the sale of their labour power, to transcend this function in an organisation whose task it is to transform the whole system of selling labour power.

Yet in pockets of industrial Japan, certain trade unions have been completely revolutionised into organisations of workers' control and independence from capital, particularly those which had waged struggles against the closure of their factories and ended up taking them over (*jishu seisan*). One such company which is famous in Tokyo, at least among the working-class people in the area, is Petri Camera, which has been run by the union and its approximately 150 members ever since they took the place over following management's withdrawal in 1977, after a twenty-year period of almost continuous struggle.[1] However, the centre of the workers' control movement in present-day Japan is in the Minato ward of Osaka, where the local branch of the same union that was involved in Petri, Zenkin (The National Metal Workers' Union), has brought together some 1,000 workers from a number of bankrupted companies in the area, the most famous of which is Tanaka Machinery. This company is a sort of stronghold and centre of the community's life, and it serves as a meeting place for militant workers from other parts of Osaka and even other cities.[2]

Many workers are gaining similar experiences all over the country, mainly through on-the-job struggles over such issues as redundancies, the replacement of regular with part-time workers, factory closures, and other manifestations of the recession. Japan Communist Party members have generally played important roles in these struggles, helping workers to organise and taking on union thugs and management in whatever forms they have tried to keep workers divided. One example of a style of work of which mass revolutionary movements are made was the grass-roots organising done by Communists along with other progressive workers in the long dispute over the lay-offs at Ōki Electric Company. The struggle group (*sōgidan*) remained in existence for some time after the dismissals, and functioned from a headquarters where other workers could go to learn from the experiences of those who had been involved.[3]

Developments like these are all important seeds of the form of working-class organisation that will ultimately be required to muster the full potential of this class. Yet they are no more than seeds, since they are confined to a small proportion of working-class people, most of whom are manipulated by both management and the unions for ends which have little to do with workers' needs. Moreover, even these promising beginnings of a mass-based revolutionary movement have problems which, even if nothing else did, would sooner or later throw up barriers in front of further development. The main ones stem from their patriarchal ways of doing things, which continually result in men occupying the main leadership positions and which reflect the fact that children tie down their mothers but not their fathers. Instead of adapting their methods of work to mothers and learning to share among men the function of mothering the young, even these more militant workers have organised themselves according to principles that suit men.

Of course patriarchy need not necessarily interfere with the development of the working class into an organised force with the power to initiate a socialist revolution. It did not prevent the Russian revolution or any of the other broadly similar ones that have occurred since. Why should it then be a problem in Japan? Patriarchy is a real barrier in the way of a socialist Japan for the same reason that it is a barrier in the United States but not in South Africa. The reason is that the more advanced the productive forces in a country are, the larger the proportion of its people who can move into either upper-class positions or at least into ones which avoid the high levels of insecurity and exploitation characteristic of the bottom two fractions of the working class. What patriarchy ensures is that where the development of productive forces allows growing numbers of people to move out of these positions the great bulk of those who manage to do so are men.

The result of this movement of men out of the bottom layers of the class structure and their replacement by women is that the forces of the gender infrastructure and the class infrastructure, instead of cross-cutting one another as they do in technically backward societies, increasingly work in concert. In sharp contrast to the early capitalist society where the great mass of men were concentrated in insecure working-class jobs, in the advanced capitalist society most of these men (so long as they are not Black) have been replaced by women. The working class is therefore feminised with the development of productive forces, while the bourgeoisie, which was a predominantly male class from the beginning, grows in absolute and relative size, but mainly out of men. The two main infrastructural mechanisms of course continue to generate cross-cutting forces, but nothing like to the same degree as in the past: a lot of men remain in the working class, some even in its reserve army, and some women manage to avoid sinking into that and other lower-class positions. Yet slowly but surely over time, class and gender forces come to work more and more in the same direction.

By the time a stage such as exists in present-day Japan is reached, the overlap is so great that patriarchal forces lend their weight to those of capital in opposing socialism: men have become sufficiently bourgeois and the working class sufficiently feminised for the gender struggle in part to take the form of the class struggle and vice versa. For example, tables 8.1 and 5.20 show that in Japan only 14.1% of economically active men but 50.7% of economically active women are in the floating reserve of the working class, while 21% of men but only 2.1% of women who are economically active are in the bourgeoisie. If one takes the entire population over the age of 15, the overlap between capitalist and patriarchal forces is about the same: 64% of women are either in the bottom two fractions of the working class or doing housework for men, while only 31% of men are in a comparable position. Moreover, within the classes not explicitly mentioned in this context so far, the situation is broadly similar. Within the petty bourgeoisie, for example, the persons of self-employed status are normally men, while the unpaid family workers or people engaged in home handicrafts are normally women. Within the middle class, those who are close to the bourgeoisie such as doctors and high-ranking teachers are men, while those who are bordering on the working class, nurses and the mass of younger teachers in public schools and in kindergartens, are women. The evidence presented so far is too telling to be denied or explained away. The members of the bourgeoisie are therefore not simply the agents of capital, but also of the patriarchy, while members of the working class are increasingly subordinate to both of these forces simultaneously.

Neither can it be claimed that this conclusion is built into the way I classified the members of the different sexes, since all the various sources I relied on – from the Marxist works of Ōhashi and Horie to the government's Employment Status Survey – provide similar evidence for that conclusion. They also support quite unambiguously the historical tendency that was identified: the proletariat gets feminised over time and the bourgeoisie grows in both absolute and relative size, its members coming as in the past mainly out of men.

If one is to provide a scientific explanation for the sex composition of the different classes in Japan as well as for the direction in which it has changed over time, and if one is to assess the effect of both of these on class struggles and their possible outcomes, then the infrastructural realities behind all of these things must be reconstructed in much the same manner as Marx reconstructed the reality behind the visible forms of class. Although this is not the place to attempt a detailed reconstruction of the mechanisms which lie behind the visible forms of gender in Japan, it is pertinent to present here the bare bones of such a reconstruction if any sense is to be made of the findings of this study.

The infrastructural mechanism which channels men into the bourgeoisie and women into the reserve army must be at least as fundamental as the mode of production itself, because otherwise the functioning of the capitalist mode of production should be able to account, in broad terms at least, for the phenomena we have noted. However, the attempts of Marxists to use traditional materialist explanations to do so have been extremely weak, although it has only been comparatively recently that a sufficient body of feminist augmentation and evidence has been built up to lay these attempts to rest once and for all. There are thus very good grounds for postulating the existence of a mechanism which might be called the patriarchal mode of reproduction.

Since this is the mechanism through which human beings are made, it involves a work process, in which hitherto only one gender, males, have been the non-labourers, while the other, females, have been the labourers. Although there is no necessary connection between the biological sex group men and the socially constituted gender group males on the one hand, or between the sex group women and the gender group females on the other, there are material reasons why they have been generally associated. In other words, while it is possible for women to be 'males' (the non-labourers in the work of reproduction) and for men to be 'females' (the labourers in this work), it is unusual. Why is this?

The mechanism behind the process by which sexes are transformed into genders might be called the patriarchal mode of reproduction, which is held together by a combination of biological and social conditions. The main biological ones centre on the fact that the first stage in the work of species reproduction – call it foetus formation – is under present technical conditions necessarily one which women do. Thus far, therefore, females are necessarily women. However, in human reproduction this is only a small proportion of the total work which must be done, since many years of feeding and nurturing are required before the infant is able to care for itself.

Why is it that women are also the labourers in the work of child care and all that accompanies it? The short answer is that women's exclusive role in foetus formation has consequences which, unless they are counteracted by effective political organisations, further subordinate women to the role of labourers in all the remaining reproductive work of society as well. Pregnancy, particularly its later stages, confines women to locations not too far from home, whereas men can be highly mobile and can gain access to all the various resources, material and organisational, that are needed to establish themselves in the political role of non-labourer in the entire reproductive work process. It is because women bear babies that men can get into the positions which then force women also to look after and raise children. That, in a nutshell, is how the patriarchal mode of reproduction functions.

However, the functioning of this mechanism has consequences beyond itself. The most important are the limits the requirement to do reproductive work sets on the possible roles people can play in the world of production. Males and females enter this world with vastly unequal social power, and females face demands which preclude their participation in the race for upper-class positions. They cannot promise uninterrupted service, nor to go to whatever remote corner of the country (even the world) capital might require, sometimes without the slightest notice. All the major demands made by the system on members of the bourgeoisie are ones which exclude females from membership of this class: constant mobility, uninterrupted service, and freedom in the evenings to plan business strategies with people in related and competing enterprises. The Japanese nightclubs that bustle with businessmen every evening are not just there for the 'pleasure' of the men who frequent them: they function to bring class agents together who could not meet during the day but among whom communication is essential if there is to be any coordination among the different parts of the system.

Persons tied down in child-care work are automatically excluded from all these activities, and the only jobs the system offers which they are 'free' to accept are ones in the reserve army. Although one might find women in other jobs, one does not find active mothers in them. Even nominal mothers have to make arrangements (that is, have someone else tied down) for the care of their children if they are to accept jobs requiring uninterrupted (during the day and over time) service. It is hardly an accident that the largest expansion in women's employment during the recession was among married women in part-time jobs; that is, among mothers.

The capitalist who takes on a woman worker, particularly one who is or might soon become a mother, hires someone who is already in a politically subordinate position in another work process. Such people are easier to discipline and to use as one pleases, and because they come to the factory gates with some of their subsistence requirements already met, they are immeasurably cheaper than men. Small wonder their employment in Japan has increased so rapidly during the recession.

If some such mechanism as we have described is what lies behind the changes in the sex composition of the main classes in Japan, then there is something very important about women members of the working class which distinguishes them from the men. Male leaders who have no involvement in mothering will simply be out of touch with the real forces which shape the lives of the bulk of the working class. They will plan activities and employ strategies that exclude people who must get children fed and to sleep. In other words, the militant male leadership in unions like Zenkin cater for that relatively small group of men whom the system treats almost like women but who are not as politically subordinated as women and therefore not as easy to force into submission.

Nothing in the argument above is meant to imply that a socialist movement in Japan will have to be exclusively female if it is to get anywhere. It means rather that a movement which continues to exclude females will founder in ways that are now very familiar in Japan. New principles of organisation, methods of political work, and strategies as well as tactics will have to become institutionalised in the socialist movement before there will be any need to modify the conclusion that socialist change in Japan is extremely unlikely in the foreseeable future. Yet the required principles and methods of work are not really new, since they have been part of most of the many highly developed women's organisations in Japan for a long time. What would be new would be their incorporation into the socialist movement.

In some senses the successes of feminism in Japan have been far greater than in the West. For example, one of the most remarkable traditions in Japan is the way women have always come together in formal and informal ways to assist one another. A large number of mass organisations of women (with millions of members) have been in existence for some time, and even ones which might on the surface appear to be conservative reveal an understanding of the women's struggle in Japan which one seldom has the opportunity to hear. Take, for example, the White Paper on Women put out by Fudanren (Nihon Fujin Dantai Rengōkai, or the Federation of Japanese Women's Organisations) and try to find a comparable document in the West, among any circles at all.[4] Or consider the mature combination of day-to-day practical work and theory that one finds in Shinfujin (Shin Fujin no Kai, or New Women's Association), the organisation most closely related to the Communist Party.

In certain concrete struggles which have involved men as well there have been further seeds of the communist–feminist combination without which no real social change in Japan is likely. The Narita struggle was important in this respect as well as in many others, and the people who write for *Ampo* provide an English-language window into a part of this world. A perhaps much less well known and also less dramatic case of men and women working out some sort of socialist

feminist programme would be in the Union of Japan Airline Workers
(Nihon Kōkū Rōdō Kumiai), though few of them would say that this
was what they were doing. For some time the victims of wage and
other forms of discrimination by the company in favour of the workers
in the rival Dōmei union, the men in Nikō Rōkumi gradually began
to understand why the women were so upset about the discrimination
they suffered. Although the union still faces many internal as well as
external problems, there are not many cases of similarly advanced
organisations involving women and men anywhere in Japan.

Situations like the one which moulded Nikō Rōkumi into a fairly
solid fighting force in opposition to both capitalism and patriarchy
have been springing up everywhere, as capital has had to find male
victims of its rationalisations and other cost-reducing policies.
Inevitably, the process of building united organisations which do not
subordinate the needs of women and which include men is slow and
extremely uneven. Yet it is in this process that the most important
developments in present-day Japan are almost invisibly occurring: in
the job struggles where male and female workers are thrown together
in ways that were rare during boom times, and in the many so-called
citizens' struggles over such issues as land use, pollution, atomic
power, and so on. The latter are important too for the opportunities
they provide to build alliances among members of different classes,
since job struggles can seldom even involve large numbers of workers,
let alone bring in other people as well.

In sharp contrast to the student movement of the 1960s and all the
bravado that accompanied its rise and internal strife that helped
bring about its fall, the revolutionary movement that is building up in
Japan today is much more silent because it is so much more secure.
One of the many lessons of the 1960s was that sustained mass action is
possible only if it is based on a solid foundation of mass organisation,
and that mass organisation builds up from the bottom, growing out of
the strategies working people are forced into just in order to cope with
day-to-day problems. Building pockets of resistance such as the one in
South Osaka or a really democratic trade union such as Nikō Rōkumi
is the most important part of this organisational effort. Yet society-
wide coordination among the various groups that grow out of
particular struggles is as vital to the ultimate success of the movement
as is its need to have a mass base. However, traditional methods of
forging such society-wide organisations through some or other
political party are likely to give way to new ones which leave the

centre of gravity where it belongs, among the masses and not in a male bureaucracy. One of the seeds of what might emerge is *Rōdō Jōhō* [Labour News], a twice-monthly publication which conveys to the different groups of militant workers all over the country something of one another's experiences and the lessons which grew out of them.

However, the internal struggles within the different groups, against patriarchy, against sectarianism, and against bureaucratic forms of organisation, will all have to continue if any national organisation that emerges out of them is to retain its mass base. This applies especially to existing political parties, such as the Japan Communist Party and the Japan Socialist Party, which have each in its own way done much to advance the development of socialist organisations in Japan but neither of which is likely to be at the centre of any successful communist–feminist revolutionary change in Japan.

Notes

Introduction

1. My statistical information comes mainly from government publications and a survey of 459 persons in 53 companies which I conducted in winter 1976–7. Of the 69 companies approached in that survey, 53 agreed to cooperate, and of the 619 questionnaires distributed, 459 (74.2%) were returned. Wherever possible I have used the most recently published statistics, although in some cases I could not obtain these.

2. Among the signs that even non-Marxist scholars are beginning to do this is a monograph by Sugimoto Yoshio and Ross Mouer which critically examines the work of mainly English-speaking scholars on Japan. See Sugimoto Yoshio and Ross Mouer, *Japanese Society: Stereotypes and Realities*, Papers of the Japanese Studies Centre, no. 1 (Melbourne: Monash University, 1981).

3. Since the relevant Japanese studies are too numerous to mention here, and since the most important are listed in the bibliography, a quotation from Sugimoto and Mouer will illustrate the point (see p. 8): 'We also feel that the absence of the conflict tradition in the writings on Japanese society is more pronounced in the English-language literature than in the Japanese-language literature. Ōhashi's *Nihon no Kaikyū Kōsei* (1971) and Horie's *Nihon no Rōdōsha Kaikyū* (1971) have no counterpart in English, although the work by Halliday (1975) and Steven (1979) represents a move in that direction. There is a solid Marxist/socialist tradition in Japanese scholarship on Japanese society, but the small dribble which comes out in English through *Ampo, Ronin*, or the *Bulletin of Concerned Asian Scholars* does not match it either in volume or in creative diversity.'

4. Since I wanted to avoid overlap with his work, I selected themes he was either not in a position to cover (such as the current crisis) or to which he could give only limited space.

5. Ōhashi Ryūken, *Nihon no kaikyū kōsei* [Japan's Class Composition] (Tokyo: Iwanami shoten, 1971).

6. See in particular his *For Marx* (Penguin Books, 1969); his essays with Etienne Balibar, *Reading 'Capital'* (London: New Left Books, 1970); his *Lenin and Philosophy and Other Essays* (London: New Left Books, 1971); and his *Essays in Self-Criticism* (London: New Left Books, 1976).

7. It was translated in 1975 and published by New Left Books that year. Other studies influenced by the Althusserian orthodoxy include a collection of essays by Guglielmo Carchedi, *On the Economic Identification of Social Classes* (London: Routledge and Kegan Paul, 1977); Alan Hunt ed., *Class and Class Structure* (London: Lawrence and Wishart, 1977); Erik Olin Wright, *Class, Crisis and the State* (London: New Left Books, 1978); and Rosemary Crompton and Jon

Gubbay, *Economy and Class Structure* (London: Macmillan, 1977). The last two works are more a blending of Althusserian and Weberian influences.

8. Maurice Godelier, 'Infrastructures, Societies and History,' *New Left Review*, no. 112 (November–December 1978); and Derek Sayer, *Marx's Method: Ideology, Science and Critique in 'Capital'* (Hassocks, Sussex: Harvester Press, 1979).

9. Gabriel A. Almond and G. Bingham Powell, Jr, *Comparative Politics: A Developmental Approach* (Boston: Little, Brown and Company, 1966).

10. See in particular Althusser's 'Ideology and Ideological State Apparatuses,' in his *Lenin and Philosophy and Other Essays*.

11. See his *Class, Crisis and the State*.

12. Maurice Godelier first drew my attention to the original German. I am also indebted to his 'Structure and Contradiction in *Capital*,' in Robin Blackburn comp., *Ideology in Social Science: Readings in Critical Social Theory* (London: Fontana/Collins, 1972).

13. In the following pages I am reconstructing what in my view is the method Marx actually used, particularly in *Capital*. The interpretation is, however, greatly influenced by Godelier, Sayer, and Mao (mainly *On Contradiction*).

14. My interpretation owes much to Althusser, particularly his 'On the Materialist Dialectic,' in *For Marx*; Ben Fine and Lawrence Harris, *Rereading 'Capital'* (London: Macmillan, 1979); and Sayer, *Marx's Method*.

15. The better interpretations and critiques of Althusser's epistemology include John Mepham and D.-H. Ruben eds., *Issues in Marxist Philosophy*, vol. 3, *Epistemology, Science, Ideology* (Hassocks, Sussex: Harvester Press, 1979); Sayer, *Marx's Method*; Simon Clarke *et al.*, *One Dimensional Marxism: Althusser and the Politics of Culture* (London: Allison and Busby, 1980); and Simon Mohun, 'Ideology, Knowledge and Neoclassical Economics: Some Elements of a Marxist Account,' in Francis Green and Petter Nore, *Issues in Political Economy: A Critical Approach* (London: Macmillan, 1979).

16. Since this is the view of class which is elaborated in the text, it is only briefly stated here. Although original in many respects, it follows naturally from the discussion on method above, for which I have already acknowledged my debts.

17. The list is far too long to mention here, although most are included in the bibliography. Yet I should draw attention to the journal *Feminist Review* and one or two of the most important works: Shulamith Firestone, *The Dialectic of Sex* (London: Paladin, 1972); Zillah Eisenstein ed., *Capitalist Patriarchy and the Case for Socialist Feminism* (New York: Monthly Review Press, 1979); Annette Kuhn and AnnMarie Wolpe, *Feminism and Materialism* (London: Routledge and Kegan Paul, 1978); Michèle Barrett, *Women's Oppression Today* (London: Verso, 1980); and Sheila Rowbotham, Lynne Segal, and Hilary Wainwright, *Beyond the Fragments: Feminism and the Making of Socialism* (London: Merlin Press, 1979).

18. Rob Steven, 'Japanese Society and Theories of Capitalist Patriarchy,' paper presented to the International Colloquium on the Comparative Study of Japanese Society, February 1982.

1. The bourgeoisie

1. Yamamura Kozo, *Economic Policy in Postwar Japan: Growth Versus Economic Democracy* (Berkeley: University of California Press, 1967), pp. 123ff.

2. Zenkoku shōken torihikijo [Japan Stock Exchange], *Kabushiki bunpu jōkyō chōsa* [Survey on the Distribution of Shares], 1980 (Tokyo: Zenkoku shōken torihikijo, 1981), p. 9.

3. Shūkan Tōyō Keizai [The Oriental Economist], *Kigyō keiretsu sōran* [A General View of Linked Companies], 1982, Rinji zōkan [Special issue], no. 4333 (Tokyo: Tōyō keizai shinpōsha, 1981), p. 366. In this most recent issue of the publication, the shares owned by directors were not listed. The proportion of 3.46% is therefore taken from the issue published in 1976 (no. 3974), p. 200.

4. *Kabushiki bunpu jōkyō chōsa*, 1975, p. 24; 1980, p. 30.

5. Keizai kikakuchō keizai kenkyūjo [Institute of Economic Research of the Economic Planning Agency], *Kokumin keizai keisan nenpō* [Annual Report on National Economic Accounts], 1981 (Tokyo: Ōkurashō insatsukyoku, 1981), p. 143.

6. The amounts of unearned income are based on an assumed average return of 7%. The implication that people who receive under ¥210,000 in unearned income have no interest in capitalism may seem strange, since this is a large amount of money. However, savings of under ¥3 million in 1980 were considered moderate in Japan, since they are undertaken primarily in order to compensate for the country's poor systems of social security. All a 7% return on these amounts could do was preserve the savings – which get used to pay for old-age expenses like children's education and pension supplements – from inflation.

7. Kokuzeichō [National Taxation Agency], *Kokuzeichō tōkei nenpōsho* [Annual Statistical Report of the National Taxation Agency], no. 105, 1979 (Tokyo: Kokuzeichō, 1981), p. 38.

8. *Kokumin keizai keisan nenpō*, 1981, p. 143.

9. Ōhashi, pp. 138ff.

10. Unproductive labourers are hired to help convert capital from one form to another without increasing its value in the process, for example, from commodity capital into money capital or from money capital into productive capital. Unproductive members of the working class neither own nor control capital in any of these processes.

11. Fujii Tokuzō, 'Kanrishoku no chingin wa dō kimeru beki ka?' [How Should Managerial Salaries Be Determined?], in *Gendai no kanrishoku mondai*, p. 211.

12. *Chūshō kigyō hakusho*, 1980, p. 118.

13. *Asahi Shinbun* [Asahi Newspaper], 9 December 1977, in *Shinbun Geppō* [Documentary News of the Month], vol. 374 (January 1978), p. 150.

14. *Chūshō kigyō hakusho*, 1980, p. 14.

15. *Ibid.*, 1975, p. 60.

16. *Kigyō keiretsu sōran*, 1982, p. 256.

17. *Ibid.*, p. 98.

18. Dodwell Marketing Consultants, *Industrial Groupings in Japan*, rev. ed. (Tokyo: Dodwell Marketing Consultants, 1978), p. 451.

19. *Kigyō keiretsu sōran*, 1982, pp. 30–51.

20. *Industrial Groupings in Japan*, 1973, revised in 1978 and 1980–1.

21. *Kigyō keiretsu sōran*, 1982, pp. 54–63.

22. *Ibid.*, p. 243.

23. *Ibid.*, p. 337.

24. For a useful bourgeois study in English, see Yanaga Chitoshi, *Big Business in Japanese Politics* (New Haven: Yale University Press, 1968), esp. pp. 42–6, 52–6.

2. The petty bourgeoisie

1. See *Shūgyō kōzō kihon chōsa hōkoku*, 1974 and 1979.
2. *Chūshō kigyō hakusho*, 1980, pp. 103, 105.
3. *Ibid.*, p. 102.
4. See Sōrifu tōkeikyoku [Bureau of Statistics, Office of the Prime Minister], *Jigyōsho tōkei chōsa hōkoku* [Establishment Census of Japan], vol. 4, *Sabisugyō* [Services], 1972 and 1978 (Tokyo: Nihon tōkei kyōkai, 1974 and 1980), pp. 128–9 and p. 2.
5. *Shūgyō kōzō kihon chōsa hōkoku*, 1979, pp. 50–2.
6. *Jigyōsho tōkei chōsa hōkoku*, 1978, p. 2.
7. *Kojin kigyō keizai chōsa nenpō*, 1980, pp. 38–41.
8. *Shūgyō kōzō kihon chōsa hōkoku*, 1979, p. 148.

3. The peasantry

1. A great deal of theoretical analysis of peasants in pre-capitalist and emerging capitalist societies has been done in recent years. However, most of it is not directly relevant to understanding 'simple commodity producers in agriculture' in advanced capitalist societies such as Japan. One useful article is by Judith Ennew, Paul Hirst, and Keith Tribe, '"Peasants" as an Economic Category,' *Journal of Peasant Studies*, 4, 4 (July 1977). A superb analysis of the Japanese peasantry is by Bernard Bernier, 'The Japanese Peasantry and Economic Growth since the Land Reform of 1946–47,' *Bulletin of Concerned Asian Scholars*, 12, 1 (January–March 1980).
2. See ch. 6 n. 14 below for references to the theory of rent and its wider implications.
3. *Zenkoku shōhi jittai chōsa hōkoku*, 1979, vol. 3, *Chochikuhen*, pp. 148–53.
4. The data in this table come from the five-yearly agricultural census taken in 1975. It provides the most detailed information on Japanese agriculture. The 1980 census results will not be published until March 1982, too late to use in this book.
5. The 1975 census, which broke them down by the size of holding cultivated, revealed that the persons solely or mainly engaged in their own farming made up 35.4% of household members on the smallest holdings (under 0.5 hectares) and 83.7% on the largest ones (above 3 hectares). See *Nōka chōsa hōkokusho*, 1975, *Nōka jinkō hen*, pp. 418–19.
6. See also the study by Hoshi Makoto, 'Nōgyō: tochi shoyū no saihensei to nōgyō kiki' [Agriculture: The Reorganisation of Land Ownership and the Crisis in Agriculture], in *Shin Marukusu keizai kōza* [Lectures on New Marxist Economics], ed. Shima Yasuhiko, Udaka Motosuke, Ōhashi Ryūken, and Usami Seijirō, vol. 5, *Sengo Nihon shihonshugi no kōzō* [The Structure of Postwar Japanese Capitalism] (Tokyo: Yūhikaku, 1976), p. 163.
7. *Ibid.*, p. 141.
8. OECD Agricultural Policy Reports, *Agricultural Policy in Japan* (Paris: OECD, 1974), p. 8; *Nōrinsuisanshō tōkeihyō*, 1979–80, p. 428.
9. Tsūshō sangyōshō [Ministry of International Trade and Industry], *Tsūshō hakusho* [White Paper on Trade and Industry], 1981, *Kakuron* [Detailed

Exposition] (Tokyo: Ōkurashō insatsukyoku, 1981), '1980 no wagakuni no bōeki tōkei' [Our Country's Trade Statistics in 1980], p. 111.

10. *Ibid.*, main volume (not statistical appendix), p. 60.
11. *Nōrinshō tōkeihyō*, 1974–5, p. 192; *Nōrinsuisanshō tōkeihyō*, 1979–80, pp. 212–13.
12. *Nōrinsuisanshō tōkeihyō*, 1979–80, p. 429; *Zaisei kin'yū tōkei geppō*, no. 295, 1976, p. 51, and no. 355, 1981, pp. 50–1.
13. *Shūgyō kōzō kihon chōsa hōkoku*, 1979, p. 50.
14. OECD, *Agricultural Policy in Japan*, p. 23.
15. Fukutake Tadashi, *Japanese Rural Society*, trans. R. P. Dore (Tokyo: Oxford University Press, 1967), p. 59.
16. Fukutake Tadashi, *Japanese Society Today* (Tokyo: University of Tokyo Press, 1974), p. 57.
17. Fukutake, *Japanese Rural Society*, pp. 193–4.
18. *Japan Times Weekly*, 23 February 1974, p. 6.
19. Uehara Nobuhiro, 'Sengo nōson no kaikyū kōsei to nōmin soshiki, nōmin undō' [Class Composition of the Postwar Rural Community and Farmers' Organisations: The Farmers' Movement], in Shima *et al.* eds., *Shin Marukusu keizai kōza*, vol. 6, *Sengo Nihon shihonshugi no kaikyū kōsei* [The Composition of Classes in Postwar Japanese Capitalism], p. 329.
20. *Ibid.*, pp. 331–2.
21. For these and similar struggles, see Hōsei Daigaku, Ōhara shakai mondai kenkyūjo [Ōhara Institute for Social Research, Hōsei University], *Nihon rōdō nenkan* [The Labour Yearbook of Japan], 1977 (Tokyo: Rōdō junpōsha, 1976), pp. 412–32. Each year this excellent source lists and updates developments in popular struggles. For a history of the Narita struggle, the best source is the journal *Ampo*, which published articles regularly as the struggle proceeded.

4. The middle class

1. Henri Lefebvre, *The Survival of Capitalism: Reproduction of the Relations of Production* (London: Allison and Busby, 1976), p. 25.
2. See, for example, Wright, pp. 61ff, and Carchedi, pp. 43ff. Though they express themselves differently, their arguments are similar.
3. *Shūgyō kōzō kihon chōsa hōkoku*, 1979, p. 62.
4. *Ibid.*, p. 44.
5. *Wagakuni no kyōiku suijun*, 1980, fuzoku shiryō, pp. 96–7, 99.
6. *Ibid.*, p. 83.
7. This was roughly the proportion in those firms with over one hundred operatives which were surveyed in *Minkan kyūyo no jittai*, 1981, p. 24.
8. See, for example, the three-part article in the *Japan Times Weekly*, which began on 14 January 1978, p. 11.
9. The position of supervisor is not one the same people occupy for most of their lives, and in that sense supervisors are not a stable group.
10. Mannari Hiroshi, *The Japanese Business Leaders* (Tokyo: University of Tokyo Press, 1974), p. 73.
11. Thomas P. Rohlen, 'Is Japanese Education Becoming Less Egalitarian? Notes on High School Stratification and Reform,' *Journal of Japanese Studies*, 3, 1 (Winter 1977), p. 41.
12. *Wagakuni no kyōiku suijun*, 1980, fuzoku shiryō, pp. 48–59, shows that the proportion going on to high school had increased to 93.1% for boys and 95.4%

for girls by 1980. The proportion of high school graduates going on to university actually fell to 34% in 1977 and to 32% in 1980.

13. Herbert Passin, *Society and Education in Japan* (New York: Teachers' College, Columbia University, 1965), p. 115.

14. Rohlen, 'Is Japanese Education Becoming Less Egalitarian?' p. 41.

15. *Ibid.*, p. 65.

16. *Japan Times Weekly*, 17 December 1977, p. 3.

17. Tōkei bunseki kenkyūkai [Research Association for Analysing Statistics], 'Konnichi no gakusei seikatsu' [Living Conditions of Today's Students], *Keizai*, no. 205 (May 1981), p. 216.

18. Nakane Chie, *Japanese Society* (Berkeley: University of California Press, 1972).

19. For useful discussions in English of the JTU, see Donald R. Thurston, *Teachers and Politics in Japan* (Princeton: Princeton University Press, 1973) and Benjamin C. Duke, *Japan's Militant Teachers: A History of the Left-Wing Teachers' Movement* (Honolulu: University Press of Hawaii, 1973).

20. Thurston, p. 164.

21. *Ibid.*, p. 283.

22. *Nihon rōdō nenkan*, 1982, p. 557.

23. For a detailed discussion of the JMA, see William E. Steslike, *Doctors in Politics: The Political Life of the Japan Medical Association* (New York: Praeger, 1973).

24. For a useful discussion in English of Zengakuren, see Halliday, ch. 9.

25. Hijikata Bunichirō, 'Keiei soshikijō no ichizuke to kanrishokutai no tokushitsu' [The Location of Managerial Problems and the Special Characteristics of Management], in *Gendai no kanrishoku mondai*, p. 13.

26. Kōnenreisha kōyō kaihatsu kyōkai [Association for the Development of Elderly People's Employment], *Teinen hakusho* [White Paper on Retirement] (Tokyo: Kōnenreisha kōyō kaihatsu kyōkai, 1980), p. 184.

27. *Wagakuni no kyōiku suijun*, 1980, fuzoku shiryō, p. 56.

28. *Rikurūto chōsa geppō*, April 1976, p. 35.

29. *Japan Times Weekly*, 14 December 1974, p. 10.

5. The working class

1. See Ezra Vogel, *Japan as Number One: Lessons for America* (Cambridge, Mass.: Harvard University Press, 1979).

2. For detailed historical studies, see Taira Koji, *Economic Development and the Labor Market in Japan* (New York: Columbia University Press, 1970), Ronald Dore, *British Factory – Japanese Factory* (London: George Allen and Unwin, 1973), and Sydney Crawcour, 'The Japanese Employment System,' *Journal of Japanese Studies*, 4, 2 (Summer 1978).

3. Shūkan Tōyō Keizai [The Oriental Economist], *Chingin sōran* [A General View of Wages], Rinji zōkan [Special issue], 1977, no. 3980 (Tokyo: Tōyō keizai shinpōsha, 1976), p. 89.

4. *Zaisei kin'yū tōkei geppō*, no. 355, 1981, pp. 46–7.

5. For a discussion of industrial conflict in medium-sized firms, see Robert E. Cole, *Japanese Blue Collar: The Changing Tradition* (Berkeley: University of California Press, 1971).

6. Tokyo Metropolitan Government, *Minor Industries and Workers in Tokyo* (Tokyo: Tokyo Metropolitan Government, 1972), p. 30.

7. *Shūgyō kōzō kihon chōsa hōkoku*, 1974, pp. 141, 151.
8. Rōdōshō [Ministry of Labour], *Rōdō hakusho* [Labour White Paper] (Tokyo: Nihon rōdō kyōkai, 1976), p. 286.
9. In the short term it might seem that micro-technology would merely destroy jobs, since it is hard to see the development of new industries which grow out of it. Yet this is exactly what has been happening in Japan.
10. *Fujin rōdō no jitsujō*, 1981, p. 100.
11. *Ibid.*, p. 112.
12. *Ibid.*, p. 92.
13. *Shūgyō kōzō kihon chōsa hōkoku*, 1974, pp. 84–5; 1979, pp. 112, 114.
14. *Fujin rōdō no jitsujō*, 1981, p. 108.
15. *Shūgyō kōzō kihon chōsa hōkoku*, 1979, pp. 64, 72.
16. *Ibid.*, p. 294.
17. Same source as table 5.17, pp. 5, 7, 13.
18. *Teinen hakusho*, 1980, p. 8.
19. *Ibid.*, p. 26.
20. *Burakumin* are people traditionally discriminated against in Japan allegedly because of their long association with work involving animals, such as leather work, etc. They have been forced into particular hamlets, *buraku*, so that when employers ask them where they come from they are easily identifiable. Discussion of these approximately 2 million people falls beyond the scope of this study. The subject is a can of worms on its own, and a useful introduction to it is George A. De Vos and Wagatsuma Hiroshi, *Japan's Invisible Race: Caste in Culture and Personality* (Berkeley: University of California Press, 1972).
21. For the study of day labourers, see Nishioka Yukiyasu *et al.*, 'Hiyatoi rōdōsha: Sanya no seikatsu to rōdō' [Day Labouring Workers: Life and Work in Sanya], *Shakai kagaku nenpō* [Social Science Yearbook], no. 8, 1974, p. 36. For the pay and conditions of the various categories of non-regular workers in 1980, see Shūkan Tōyō Keizai, *Dēta fuairu: chingin, nenkin, jinji kanri*, 1982, pp. 324–7.
22. *Rōdō hakusho*, 1981, pp. 184–206, provides a general overview.
23. Tōkei bunseki kenkyūkai [Research Association for Analysing Statistics], 'Koyō to shitsugyō' [Employment and Unemployment], *Keizai*, no. 204 (April 1981), p. 148.
24. Shūkan Tōyō Keizai, *Dēta fuairu: chingin, nenkin, jinji kanri*, 1982, p. 325.
25. I am indebted to Maurice Godelier for this distinction between what is determinant and what is dominant. See his 'Infrastructures, Societies and History.'
26. See, for example, Dore, *British Factory – Japanese Factory*; Cole, *Japanese Blue Collar*; Thomas P. Rohlen, *For Harmony and Strength: Japanese White Collar Organization in Anthropological Perspective* (Berkeley: University of California Press, 1974).
27. One study which contrasted 'company' consciousness with 'union' consciousness is by Motojima Kunio, 'Daikigyō no naka de yureru kyōsōteki jinsei' [Competitive Life Trembling Inside Large Companies], *Keizai*, no. 210 (October 1981), pp. 85ff.
28. Rōdō daijin kanbō tōkei jōhōbu [The Statistical Information Department of the Secretariat of the Minister of Labour], *Maitsuki kinrō chōsa sōgō hōkokusho* [General Report on the Survey of Monthly Employment], 1975 (Tokyo: Rōdō daijin kanbō tōkei jōhōbu, 1976), pp. 6–7.

29. *Fujin rōdō no jitsujō*, 1976, p. 51.
30. *Japan Times Weekly*, 19 June 1976, p. 4.
31. *Ibid.*, 18 November 1978, p. 10.
32. Nihon Kyōsantō chūō iinkai kikanshi keieikyoku [Management Bureau of the Organs of the Central Committee of the Japan Communist Party], *Seiji nenkan* [Politics Yearbook], 1974 (Tokyo, 1974), p. 264.
33. Furukawa ed., *Chingin kentō shiryō*, 1982, p. 6.
34. *Japan Times Weekly*, 19 December 1981, p. 4.

6. Crisis and the state: accumulation functions

1. The most typical is Nicos Poulantzas, *Political Power and Social Classes* (London: New Left Books, 1973).
2. For brief discussions and references to further reading on the debates in Japan, see, for example, Ono Yoshihiko, *Gendai Nihon shihonshugi no kiki: kokka dokusen shihonshugi no tenkai* [The Present Crisis of Japanese Capitalism: The Development of State Monopoly Capitalism] (Tokyo: Shinsensha, 1976); Enomoto Masatoshi, 'Gendai shihonshugiron no hōhō' [On the Method of Present-Day Theory of Capitalism], *Keizaigaku Hihan*, no. 2 (1977); Katō Ei'ichi, 'Gendai shihonshugiron no shikaku' [A View of Present-Day Theory of Capitalism], *Keizaigaku Hihan*, no. 1 (1976). *Keizaigaku Hihan* is a comparatively recent theoretical journal associated with the Japan Socialist Party. It is more heavily theoretical than, but not as rich in empirical analysis as, the Japan Communist Party's equivalent, *Keizai*. As a source of accurate information on the crisis, I have found the latter extremely useful. The May issues of 1973, 1977, and 1978 provide examples of theoretical thinking on 'state monopoly capitalism,' as do the July and October issues of 1978. My own theoretical position is most indebted to John Holloway and Sol Picciotto eds., *State and Capital: A Marxist Debate* (London: Edward Arnold, 1978); Harry Cleaver, *Reading 'Capital' Politically* (Brighton: Harvester Press, 1979); and above all Philip Corrigan ed., *Capitalism, State Formation and Marxist Theory* (London: Quartet Books, 1980).
3. Godelier, 'Infrastructures, Societies and history.'
4. See for example, James O'Connor, *The Fiscal Crisis of the State* (New York: St Martin's Press, 1973).
5. See Wright.
6. See, for example, Tsuji Kiyoaki, 'Decision-Making in the Japanese Government: A Study of Ringisei,' in *Political Development in Modern Japan*, ed. Robert E. Ward (Princeton: Princeton University Press, 1970).
7. See Thomas C. Smith, *Political Change and Industrial Development in Japan: Government Enterprise, 1868–1880* (Stanford: Stanford University Press, 1955) and E. Herbert Norman, *Japan's Emergence as a Modern State: Political and Economic Problems of the Meiji Period* (New York: Institute of Pacific Relations, 1940).
8. The cumulative deficit rose to ¥10.2629 trillion. See *Japan Times Weekly*, 5 September 1981, p. 2; *Asahi Shinbun*, 28 August 1981, in *Shinbun Geppō*, 418 (September 1981), p. 40.
9. For an overview of this and other industries, see Sasaki Noriaki, 'Enerugī sangyō no shindōkō to tenbō' [New Directions and Outlook for the Energy Industries], *Keizai*, no. 167 (March 1978), pp. 115ff; *Asahi Shinbun*, 19 August 1977, in *Shinbun Geppō*, 370 (September 1977), p. 110; *Yomiuri Shinbun*, 26 September 1981, in

Shinbun Geppō, 419 (October 1981), p. 43; *Mainichi Shinbun*, 22 September 1981, in *ibid.*; *Asahi Shinbun*, 29 August 1981, in *Shinbun Geppō*, 418 (September 1981), p. 41; Tōkei bunseki kenkyūkai [Research Association for Analysing Statistics], 'Bukka to kakei' [Prices and Household Finances], *Keizai*, no. 201 (January 1981), p. 247.

10. Sasaki, p. 118.
11. *Asahi Shinbun*, 11 July 1978, in *Shinbun Geppō*, 381 (August 1978), pp. 158–61.
12. Moritaka Ken'ichirō, 'Kokudo kaihatsu no tenkai to minshuteki tenkan no tenbō, ge' [The Unfolding of Territorial Development and the View of Democratic Change, part 2], *Keizai*, no. 161 (September 1977), p. 100; *Mainichi Shinbun*, 15 May 1979, in *Shinbun Geppō*, 391 (June 1979), p. 186.
13. She was overtaken by France some time after that. However, plans are for expansion to continue and for full independence to be achieved: a prototype uranium enrichment plant has already proven successful, and negotiations were in progress in early 1982 to secure fast-breeder reactors.
14. For a useful discussion of Marx's theory of rent, see Ben Fine, 'On Marx's Theory of Agricultural Rent,' *Economy and Society*, 8, 3 (August 1979); for an application, see Petter Nore, 'Oil and Contemporary Capitalism,' in Green and Nore, *Issues in Political Economy*.
15. The share from Indonesia in 1980 rose to 15%. See *Nihon Keizai Shinbun*, 25 January 1980, in *Shinbun Geppō*, 399 (February 1980), p. 153, and *Asahi Shinbun*, 23 April 1981, in *Shinbun Geppō*, 414 (May 1981), pp. 133–4.
16. *Japan Times Weekly*, 30 October 1976, p. 9.
17. *Nihon Keizai Shinbun*, 26 August 1978, in *Shinbun Geppō*, 382 (September 1978), p. 142; *Keizai*, no. 169 (May 1978), p. 33, and no. 201 (January 1981), p. 247.
18. Sasaki, pp. 93–6; *Japan Times Weekly*, 7 January 1978, p. 2.
19. There is a massive literature on the causes of capitalist crises. I therefore simply note the theoretical work which comes closest to capturing the way things seem to have happened in Japan: Fine and Harris, *Rereading 'Capital*,' chs. 3–5.
20. Although there was an easing of the rise in land prices after 1977, in 1979 and 1980 the average increases were 9.0% and 8.3% (11.5% and 10.9% for housing land) respectively. In the metropolitan areas the increases were even higher; for example, 16.4% for housing land in Tokyo in 1979. See *Mainichi Shinbun*, 12 February 1981, in *Shinbun Geppō*, 412 (March 1981), p. 170.
21. One of the main consequences of the land boom was to raise corporate indebtedness to commercial banks, which supplied large proportions of the funds: ¥6.1 trillion out of ¥9.8 trillion invested in land in 1973. See *Japan Times Weekly*, 10 April 1976, p. 3. The average percentage of owned capital in Japanese enterprises fell from 19% in 1965 to 16.1% in 1970 and to 13.9% in 1975. See Shūkan Tōyō Keizai, *Keizai tōkei nenkan*, 1979, p. 350.
22. *Japan Times Weekly*, 10 April 1976, p. 3, 25 February 1978, p. 1, and 11 March 1978, p. 8.
23. *Nihon Keizai Shinbun*, 4 September 1977, in *Shinbun Geppō*, 371 (October 1977), p. 101; *Nihon Keizai Shinbun*, 10 August 1978, in *Shinbun Geppō*, 382 (September 1978), p. 117; *Japan Times Weekly*, 11 March 1978, p. 8.
24. *Ibid.*
25. Same as table 6.12 source.
26. See table 6.32 below and *Japan Times Weekly*, 11 October 1975, p. 9, 11 September 1976, p. 9, and 20 December 1975, p. 2; *Nihon Keizai Shinbun*, 6 September 1978, in *Shinbun Geppō*, 383 (October 1978), p. 152.

27. The state actually intervened in a variety of ways to prop up small enterprises. For example, under the law on temporary measures against the depression in the countryside, preferential tax and financial treatment as well as public works projects have been given to small firms in specified parts of the country. See *Asahi Shinbun*, 29 August 1978, in *Shinbun Geppō*, 382 (September 1978), p. 122; and *Mainichi Shinbun*, 21 October 1978, in *Shinbun Geppō*, 384 (November 1978), p. 55. A law was also passed limiting competition from large enterprises in certain industries. However, in spite of such attempts to restrict monopolies and cartels, another bill, in typically contradictory fashion, guaranteed that the state would not prevent further concentration and centralisation of capital. For a detailed discussion of the attempts to put teeth into the anti-monopoly legislation, see Kurono Munemitsu, 'Dokushihō kaisei mondai to Fukuda naikaku: Nihon dokusen shihon' [The Fukuda Cabinet and the Problems of Reforming the Anti-Monopoly Law: Japanese Monopoly Capital], *Keizai*, no. 158 (June 1977), esp. p. 73. It seems that the state hoped to solve the contradiction by helping small firms to move into new labour-intensive industries requiring high levels of technical skill. Such a division of labour would prevent the different fractions of capital from competing against one another and help to restore profitability in general. However, since it is a long-term 'solution,' actual restructuring centred on improving overall efficiency through promoting greater concentration and centralisation of capital and helping new industries take the place of declining ones.

28. *Asahi Shinbun*, 1 September 1978, in *Shinbun Geppō*, 383 (October 1978), pp. 119–20; Yamashiro Gorō, 'Zaikai no sangyō kōzō "kaikaku" no nerai' [Zaikai's Aim of a 'Reformed' Industrial Structure], *Keizai*, no. 167 (March 1978), pp. 30–1.

29. Akiba Masashi, 'Sengo Nihon shihonshugi to shigen mondai' [Postwar Japanese Capitalism and Problems of Raw Materials], *Keizai*, no. 125 (September 1974), pp. 49ff.

30. The share of crude oil rose from 9.0% in 1955 to 33.9% in 1975. See *Keizai*, no. 169 (May 1978), p. 22.

31. Giga Sō'ichirō, 'Kōzō fukyō gyōshu o meguru shomujun' [Concerning All the Contradictions of the Structurally Depressed Industries], *Keizai*, no. 167 (March 1978), p. 55.

32. *Ibid.*

33. Sasaki, pp. 71–5. See also the source for table 6.17.

34. Sasaki, pp. 76–9; *Nihon Keizai Shinbun*, 6 September 1978, in *Shinbun Geppō*, 383 (October 1978), p. 152; *Japan Times Weekly*, 6 May 1978, p. 9, 26 March 1977, p. 9, and 10 May 1980, p. 8.

35. *Asahi Shinbun*, 15 July 1978, in *Shinbun Geppō*, 381 (August 1978), pp. 130–1.

36. See table 6.32 below and Sasaki, pp. 106–10; *Nihon Keizai Shinbun*, 6 September 1978, in *Shinbun Geppō*, 383 (October 1978), p. 152; and *Japan Times Weekly*, 14 May 1977, p. 9.

37. Sasaki, pp. 80–3.

38. See source for table 6.20 and Sasaki, pp. 101–5. On the state's role in promoting cooperation among automakers, see *Japan Times Weekly*, 14 February 1976, p. 9.

39. The myth that no jobs were lost is simply false. See table 6.32 for the cuts by Toyo Kogyo, maker of Mazda.

40. See source for table 6.21.

41. *Shinbun Geppō*, 385 (December 1978), p. 194.

42. Sasaki, pp. 123–6. See also the summary of the 1978 White Paper on Construction in *Asahi Shinbun*, 11 July 1978, in *Shinbun Geppō*, 381 (August 1978), pp. 158–61.
43. Sasaki, pp. 154–8.
44. *Japan Times Weekly*, 7 February 1981, p. 8.
45. *Ibid.*, 22 April 1978, p. 6. The articles were run from 15 April to 13 May. See also the two-part article on supermarket chains run by the same paper on 16 and 23 April 1977.
46. *Ibid.*, 4 February 1978, p. 8.
47. Sasaki, p. 157. In the period between the first 'oil shock' and October 1977, investment in the wholesale and retail trades dropped by 20%. See *Japan Times Weekly*, 7 January 1978, p. 9.
48. For summaries of these, see Shūkan Tōyō Keizai, *Keizei tōkei nenkan*, 1979, pp. 59–72. For brief discussions of them, see Yoneda Yasuhiko, 'Sutagufurēshon to Nihon keizai no minshuteki saiken' [Stagflation and the Democratic Reconstruction of the Japanese Economy], *Keizai*, no. 168 (April 1978), pp. 115–16; Ōno Takao, 'Nihon keizai no kiki to sanzensō' [The Crisis in the Japanese Economy and the Third National Development Plan], *Keizai*, no. 167 (March 1978), pp. 214–23; *Nihon Keizai Shinbun*, 29 July 1978, in *Shinbun Geppō*, 381 (August 1978), pp. 131–3; and *Japan Times Weekly*, 26 August 1978, p. 9.
49. For a discussion of these, see source for table 6.32.
50. Japan is still a very junior partner in any ultra-imperialist system. In 1979 its overseas investments still comprised only 7.7% of the world total, in comparison to the U.S. share of 49.1%. In comparison to a net income of $93.6 billion in 1970–9 for the American investments, Japanese capital only got $1.6 billion. However, since it is only since 1974 that the returns have been pouring in for the Japanese companies, future income is likely to increase substantially. See Akita Hiroshi, 'Nihon dokusen shihon no taigai shinshutsu to sono mujun' [Japanese Monopoly Capital's Overseas Advance and Its Contradictions], *Keizai*, no. 211 (November 1981), p. 79
51. See for example, John Creighton Campbell, *Contemporary Japanese Budget Politics* (Berkeley: University of California Press, 1977), T. F. M. Adams and Iwao Hoshii, *A Financial History of the New Japan* (Tokyo: Kodansha International, 1972), and the Bank of Japan Economic Research Department, *Money and Banking in Japan*, trans. S. Nishimura, ed. L. S. Pressnell (London: Macmillan, 1973).
52. Since the total spending of local governments can be as much as the central government's General Account, this is not unimportant. Normally, about half the local governments' spending is received from the central government and half is raised locally by means of taxation and local borrowing. When one therefore considers the national budget's General Account, the FILP, and the local government budgets, the overall effect of the state on demand can be considerable.

7. Crisis and the state: functions of social control

1. For a discussion in English of state and non-state welfare in Japan, see Yakabe Katsumi ed., *Labour Relations in Japan: Fundamental Characteristics* (Tokyo: Ministry of Foreign Affairs, 1977), ch. IV.

2. *Shin keizai shakai nanakanen keikaku*, p. 117.
3. Miyajima Ryōhei, 'Kōreika shakai to shakai hoshō' [Social Security and an Ageing Society], *Keizai*, no. 176 (December 1978), pp. 16–17; *Yomiuri Shinbun*, 20 June 1981, in *Shinbun Geppō*, 416 (July 1981), p. 53.
4. Miyajima, 'Kōreika shakai to shakai hoshō,' p. 17.
5. *Zaisei tōkei*, 1979, pp. 228–9; *Japan Times Weekly*, 2 January 1982, p. 2.
6. It would not be unfair to say that the comparatively highly developed medical side of the system owes a lot to the racketeering that surrounds so much of medicine in Japan: the huge amounts of money doctors get away with, the bribery involved in getting children into medical schools, or the profits of the pharmaceutical companies could all become substantial topics of investigation. For example, in 1980 one student was reported to have 'donated' ¥40 million. See *Japan Times Weekly*, 19 September 1981, p. 10. For a discussion of the production and profitability of pharmaceuticals, see Hino Hideitsu, 'Jūdaika suru iryō mondai' [The Growing Weight of Medical Problems], *Keizai*, no. 200 (December 1980), esp. pp. 100–1.
7. See Moriya, p. 161.
8. In 1971 to 1976 alone, the proportion of Japan Housing Corporation houses that were rented rather than sold fell from 69.0% to 58.5%. During the same period, rents kept up fully with inflation and absorbed a good 17% of household income. However, in 1976 to 1981, the rents of these houses rose by a massive 86%. See Dokusen bunseki kenkyūkai [Research Association for the Analysis of Monopoly], 'Nihon jūtaku kōdan: yachin, kōdan minshuka mondai' [The Japan Housing Corporation: Rents and the Problems of Democratising the Corporation], *Keizai*, no. 164 (December 1977), pp. 190–9; Okuchi, p. 65.
9. Sumita, pp. 134ff.
10. Same as source for table 7.9, p. 74.
11. *Japan Times Weekly*, 20 January 1979, p. 11; 29 April 1978, p. 8.
12. Kyōgoku Takanori, 'Nihon gata fukushi shakai ron o hihan suru' [A Criticism of the Japanese-Style Welfare Theory], *Keizai*, no. 200 (December 1980), p. 73.
13. See Ehud Harari, 'Unemployment in Japan: Policy and Politics,' *Asian Survey*, 18, 10 (October 1978).
14. *Asahi Shinbun*, 19 September 1978, and *Mainichi Shinbun*, 4 November 1978, in *Shinbun Geppō*, 383 (October 1978), p. 155, and 385 (December 1978), p. 103.
15. See *Asahi Shinbun*, 29 November 1978, in *Shinbun Geppō*, 385 (December 1978), pp. 169–71.
16. *Mainichi Shinbun*, 22 December 1980, in *Shinbun Geppō*, 410 (January 1981), pp. 149–50.
17. *Asahi Shinbun*, 7 December 1980, in *ibid.*, p. 148.
18. For a reasonable Althusserian analysis, see Kevin Harris, *Education and Knowledge: The Structured Misrepresentation of Reality* (London: Routledge and Kegan Paul, 1979).
19. Among the bourgeois studies in English which provide a fairly comprehensive account of this theme are: Robert King Hall, *Education for a New Japan* (New Haven: Yale University Press, 1949) and Passin.
20. See Tsunoda Ryusaku *et al.*, *Sources of Japanese Tradition*, vol. 2 (New York: Columbia University Press, 1964), pp. 139–40.
21. Same as source for table 7.11, p. 85, and *Asahi Shinbun*, 4 August 1981, in *Shinbun Geppō*, 418 (September 1981), p. 54.

22. *Japan Times Weekly*, 25 July 1981, p. 10.
23. See *Japan Times Weekly*, 17 July 1976, p. 10.
24. *Wagakuni no kyōiku suijun*, 1975, pp. 17, 30.
25. *Japan Times Weekly*, 21 August 1976, p. 11.
26. *Ibid.*, 13 March 1976, p. 11.
27. Kakuta Noboru, 'Kōtō kyōiku saihen to shigaku' [The Reorganisation of Higher Education and Private Institutions], *Keizai*, no. 209 (September 1981), p. 56; *Japan Times Weekly*, 29 August 1981, p. 11.
28. *Japan Times Weekly*, 20 October 1979, p. 7.
29. *Ibid.*, 17 January 1981, p. 10.
30. One of the few serious works in this regard is Alan Hunt ed., *Marxism and Democracy* (London: Lawrence and Wishart, 1980).
31. See, for example, Nathaniel B. Thayer, *How the Conservatives Rule Japan* (Princeton: Princeton University Press, 1969); Gerald L. Curtis, *Election Campaigning Japanese Style* (New York: Columbia University Press, 1971); Hans Baerwald, *Japan's Parliament: An Introduction* (Cambridge: Cambridge University Press, 1974).
32. *Asahi Shinbun*, 26 February 1980, in *Shinbun Geppō*, 400 (March 1980), p. 74.
33. *Asahi Shinbun*, 20 June 1980, in *Shinbun Geppō*, 404 (July 1980), p. 171.
34. *Asahi Shinbun*, 21 June 1980, p. 1.
35. In spite of the high level of electoral corruption in Japan, the LDP does not really step outside the normal rules of parliamentarism.
36. For the amounts officially declared, see *Asahi Shinbun*, 4 August 1981, in *Shinbun Geppō*, 418 (September 1981), pp. 50–4.
37. This was one of the biggest and most far-reaching of the scandals to have occurred in postwar Japan. Tanaka was forced to resign because of his role in it, and it also was too much for his successor, Miki, to cope with. It involved receiving bribes from Lockheed in return for ordering aircraft.
38. Quoted in Thayer, p. 104.
39. *Asahi Shinbun*, 28 July 1980, in *Shinbun Geppō*, 405 (August 1980), p. 173.
40. See, for example, Azuma Yoshiji, 'Nissan Worker's Diary: The Kangaroo Courts,' *Ampo*, 13, 2 (1981).
41. Sometimes when the state is itself the employer, such threats of dismissal can be effective for a large number of workers. In spring 1979 and 1980, National Railways workers went on a go-slow, and 100,000 of them were disciplined for taking part. See *Japan Times Weekly*, 7 June 1980, p. 10.
42. See George R. Packard, III, *Protest in Tokyo: The Security Treaty Crisis of 1960* (Princeton: Princeton University Press, 1966).
43. For a brief discussion, see Sunada Ichiro, 'Thought and Behaviour of Zengakuren: Trends in the Japanese Student Movement,' *Asian Survey*, 9, 6 (June 1969).
44. The coverage of the Narita struggle by *Ampo* has been excellent over the years. See in particular vol. 9, no. 4 (1977).
45. For an analysis of the growing police state in Japan, see Coalition Committee to Fight Repression and State Power, 'Re-Emergence of the Police State: The Strengthening of Japan's Domestic Security System,' *Ampo*, 12, 1 (1980).
46. See Yamakawa Akio, 'Japan–U.S.–Korea Military Alliance,' *Ampo*, 13, 2 (1981).
47. Quoted in *Japan Times Weekly*, 22 August 1981, p. 2.

48. Once again the writers for *Ampo* have documented developments in this area very well. See Fujii Haruo, 'The Rise of the SDF: Rushing Towards Remilitarization,' *Ampo*, 13, 4 (1981).
49. *Bōei hakusho*, 1981, p. 243.
50. *Japan Times Weekly*, 2 February 1980, p. 8; 1 March 1980, p. 8; 22 March 1980, p. 11.

8. Conclusion

1. For an analysis of this and similar struggles, see Kenmochi Kazumi, *Tōsan no naka no rōdō undō* [The Workers' Movement in the Midst of Bankruptcies] (Tokyo: Shakai hyōronsha, 1978).
2. For a discussion of the movement in South Osaka, see *Ampo* Editors, 'An Interview with Higuchi Tokuzō: Workers' Production Control and the New Militancy,' *Ampo*, 10, 4 (1978); Sasahara Kyoko, 'Labour Unity and Militancy in South Osaka,' *Ampo*, 13, 4 (1981).
3. By some strange coincidence, my apartment was round the corner from their headquarters. Most of the judgements made in this chapter are based on extensive interviews with workers, including many women workers, in the winter of 1979–80.
4. Nihon fujin dantai rengōkai, *Fujin hakusho* [White Paper on Women], 1979 (Tokyo: Sōdo bunka, 1979).

Select bibliography

ENGLISH SOURCES

Adams, T. F. M. and Iwao Hoshii. *A Financial History of the New Japan.* Tokyo: Kodansha International, 1972.

Almond, Gabriel A. and Powell, G. Bingham, Jr. *Comparative Politics: A Developmental Approach.* Boston: Little, Brown and Company, 1966.

Althusser, Louis. *Essays in Self-Criticism.* London: New Left Books, 1976.
For Marx. Penguin Books, 1969.
Lenin and Philosophy and Other Essays. London: New Left Books, 1971.

Althusser, Louis and Balibar, Etienne. *Reading 'Capital'.* London: New Left Books, 1970.

Ampo Editors. 'An Interview with Higuchi Tokuzō: Workers' Production Control and the New Militancy.' *Ampo*, 10, 4 (1978), 28–33.

Azuma Yoshiji. 'Nissan Worker's Diary: The Kangaroo Courts.' *Ampo*, 13, 2 (1981), 52–5.

Baerwald, Hans. *Japan's Parliament: An Introduction.* London: Cambridge University Press, 1974.

Bank of Japan Economic Research Department. *Money and Banking in Japan.* Trans. S. Nishimura. Ed. L. S. Pressnell. London: Macmillan, 1973.

Barrett, Michele. *Women's Oppression Today.* London: Verso, 1980.

Bernier, Bernard. 'The Japanese Peasantry and Economic Growth since the Land Reform of 1946–7.' *Bulletin of Concerned Asian Scholars*, 12, 1 (January–March 1980), 40–52.

Campbell, John Creighton. *Contemporary Japanese Budget Politics.* Berkeley: University of California Press, 1977.

Carchedi, Guglielmo. *On the Economic Identification of Social Classes.* London: Routledge and Kegan Paul, 1977.

Clarke, Simon *et al. One Dimensional Marxism: Althusser and the Politics of Culture.* London: Allison and Busby, 1980.

Cleaver, Harry. *Reading 'Capital' Politically.* Brighton: Harvester Press, 1979.

Coalition Committee to Fight Repression and State Power. 'Re-Emergence of the Police State: The Strengthening of Japan's Domestic Security System.' *Ampo*, 12, 1 (1980), 12–15.

Cole, Robert E. *Japanese Blue Collar: The Changing Tradition.* Berkeley: University of California Press, 1971.

Corrigan, Philip, ed. *Capitalism, State Formation and Marxist Theory.* London: Quartet Books, 1980.

Crawcour, Sydney. 'The Japanese Employment System.' *Journal of Japanese Studies*, 4, 2 (Summer 1978), 225–45.

Crompton, Rosemary and Gubbay, Jon. *Economy and Class Structure.* London: Macmillan, 1977.

Curtis, Gerald L. *Election Campaigning Japanese Style*. New York: Columbia University Press, 1971.

De Vos, George A. and Wagatsuma Hiroshi. *Japan's Invisible Race: Caste in Culture and Personality*. Berkeley: University of California Press, 1972.

Dodwell Marketing Consultants. *Industrial Groupings in Japan*, rev. ed. Tokyo: Dodwell Marketing Consultants, 1978.

Dore, Ronald. *British Factory – Japanese Factory: The Origins of National Diversity in Industrial Relations*. London: George Allen and Unwin, 1973.

Duke, Benjamin C. *Japan's Militant Teachers: A History of the Left-Wing Teachers' Movement*. Honolulu: The University Press of Hawaii, 1973.

Economic and Foreign Affairs Research Association. *Statistical Survey of Japan's Economy*. Tokyo: Keizai gaikō kenkyūkai, 1969, 1974, and 1977.

Eisenstein, Zillah, ed. *Capitalist Patriarchy and the Case for Socialist Feminism*. New York: Monthly Review Press, 1979.

Ennew, Judith, Hirst, Paul, and Tribe, Keith. '"Peasants" as an Economic Category.' *Journal of Peasant Studies*, 4, 4 (July 1977), 245–322.

Fine, Ben. 'On Marx's Theory of Agricultural Rent.' *Economy and Society*, 8, 3 (August 1979), 241–78.

Fine, Ben and Harris, Lawrence. *Rereading 'Capital'*. London: Macmillan, 1979.

Firestone, Shulamith. *The Dialectic of Sex*. London: Paladin, 1972.

Fujii Haruo. 'The Rise of the SDF: Rushing Towards Remilitarization.' *Ampo*, 13, 4 (1981), 34–9.

Fukutake Tadashi. *Japanese Rural Society*. Trans. R. P. Dore. Tokyo: Oxford University Press, 1967.

Japanese Society Today. Tokyo: University of Tokyo Press, 1974.

Godelier, Maurice. 'Infrastructures, Societies and History.' *New Left Review*, no. 112 (November–December 1978), 84–96.

'Structure and Contradiction in *Capital*.' In *Ideology in Social Science: Readings in Critical Social Theory*. Comp. Robin Blackburn. London: Fontana/Collins, 1972.

Gough, Ian. *The Political Economy of the Welfare State*. London: Macmillan, 1979.

Green, Francis and Nore, Petter. *Issues in Political Economy: A Critical Approach*. London: Macmillan, 1979.

Hall, Robert King. *Education for a New Japan*. New Haven: Yale University Press, 1949.

Halliday, Jon. *A Political History of Japanese Capitalism*. New York: Pantheon, 1975.

Harari, Ehud. 'Unemployment in Japan: Policy and Politics.' *Asian Survey*, 18, 10 (October 1978), 1013–28.

Harris, Kevin. *Education and Knowledge: The Structured Misrepresentation of Reality*. London: Routledge and Kegan Paul, 1979.

Holloway, John and Picciotto, Sol, eds. *State and Capital: A Marxist Debate*. London: Edward Arnold, 1978.

Hunt, Alan, ed. *Class and Class Structure*. London: Lawrence and Wishart, 1977.

Marxism and Democracy. London: Lawrence and Wishart, 1980.

Kuhn, Annette and Wolpe, Ann Marie. *Feminism and Materialism*. London: Routledge and Kegan Paul, 1978.

Lefebvre, Henri. *The Survival of Capitalism: Reproduction of the Relations of Production*. London: Allison and Busby, 1976.

Mannari Hiroshi. *The Japanese Business Leaders*. Tokyo: University of Tokyo Press, 1974.

Mepham, John and Ruben, D.-H., eds. *Issues in Marxist Philosophy*, vol. 3, *Epistemology, Science, Ideology*. Hassocks, Sussex: Harvester Press, 1979.

Nakane Chie. *Japanese Society*. Berkeley: University of California Press, 1972.

Norman, E. Herbert. *Japan's Emergence as a Modern State: Political and Economic*

Problems of the Meiji Period. New York: Institute of Pacific Relations, 1940.

O'Connor, James. *The Fiscal Crisis of the State.* New York: St Martin's Press, 1973.

Organisation for Economic Cooperation and Development Agricultural Policy Reports. *Agricultural Policy in Japan.* Paris: OECD, 1974.

Packard, George R., III. *Protest in Tokyo: The Security Treaty Crisis of 1960.* Princeton: Princeton University Press, 1966.

Passin, Herbert. *Society and Education in Japan.* New York: Teachers' College, Columbia University, 1965.

Poulantzas, Nicos. *Political Power and Social Classes.* London: New Left Books, 1973. *Classes in Contemporary Capitalism.* London: New Left Books, 1975.

Rohlen, Thomas P. *For Harmony and Strength: Japanese White Collar Organization in Anthropological Perspective.* Berkeley: University of California Press, 1974.

'Is Japanese Education Becoming Less Egalitarian? Notes on High School Stratification and Reform.' *Journal of Japanese Studies*, 3, 1 (Winter 1977), 37–70.

Rowbotham, Sheila, Segal, Lynne, and Wainwright, Hilary. *Beyond the Fragments: Feminism and the Making of Socialism.* London: Merlin Press, 1979.

Sasahara Kyoko. 'Labour Unity and Militancy in South Osaka.' *Ampo*, 13, 4 (1981), 2–8.

Saxonhouse, Gary R. 'Industrial Restructuring in Japan.' *Journal of Japanese Studies*, 5, 2 (Summer 1979), 273–320.

Sayer, Derek. *Marx's Method: Ideology, Science and Critique in 'Capital'.* Hassocks, Sussex: Harvester Press, 1979.

Smith, Thomas C. *Political Change and Industrial Development in Japan: Government Enterprise, 1868–1880.* Stanford: Stanford University Press, 1955.

Sono Haruo. 'Japanese Automotive Capital and International Competition, part I.' *Ampo*, 13, 1 (1981), 60–9.

Steslike, William E. *Doctors in Politics: The Political Life of the Japan Medical Association.* New York: Praeger Publishers, 1973.

Steven, Rob. 'The Japanese Bourgeoisie.' *Bulletin of Concerned Asian Scholars*, 11, 2 (April–June 1979), 2–24.

'The Japanese Working Class.' *Bulletin of Concerned Asian Scholars*, 12, 3 (July–September 1980), 38–58.

Sugimoto Yoshio and Mouer, Ross. *Japanese Society: Stereotypes and Realities.* Papers of the Japanese Studies Centre, no. 1. Melbourne: Monash University, 1981.

Sunada Ichiro. 'Thought and Behaviour of Zengakuren: Trends in the Japanese Student Movement.' *Asian Survey*, 9, 6 (June 1969), 457–74.

Taira Koji. *Economic Development and the Labor Market in Japan.* New York: Columbia University Press, 1970.

Thayer, Nathaniel B. *How the Conservatives Rule Japan.* Princeton: Princeton University Press, 1969.

Thurston, Donald R. *Teachers and Politics in Japan.* Princeton: Princeton University Press, 1973.

Tokyo Metropolitan Government. *Minor Industries and Workers in Tokyo.* Tokyo: Tokyo Metropolitan Government, 1972.

Tsuji Kiyoaki. 'Decision-Making in the Japanese Government: A Study of Ringisei.' In *Political Development in Modern Japan.* Ed. Robert E. Ward. Princeton: Princeton University Press, 1970.

Tsunoda Ryusaku *et al. Sources of Japanese Tradition*, vol. 2. New York: Columbia University Press, 1964.

Vogel, Ezra. *Japan as Number One: Lessons for America.* Cambridge, Mass.: Harvard University Press, 1979.

Wright, Erik Olin. *Class, Crisis and the State.* London: New Left Books, 1978.

Yakabe Katsumi, ed. *Labour Relations in Japan: Fundamental Characteristics*. Tokyo: International Society for Educational Information, Inc. Japan, 1974 and Ministry of Foreign Affairs, 1977.

Yamakawa Akio. 'Japan–U.S.–Korea Military Alliance.' *Ampo*, 13, 2 (1981), 2–7.

Yamamura Kozo. *Economic Policy in Postwar Japan: Growth Versus Economic Democracy*. Berkeley: University of California Press, 1967.

Yanaga Chitoshi. *Big Business in Japanese Politics*. New Haven: Yale University Press, 1968.

JAPANESE SOURCES

Akiba Masashi. 'Sengo Nihon shihonshugi to shigen mondai' [Postwar Japanese Capitalism and Problems of Raw Materials]. *Keizai*, no. 125 (September 1974), 46–61.

Akita Hiroshi. 'Nihon dokusen shihon no taigai shinshutsu to sono mujun' (Japanese Monopoly Capital's Overseas Advance and Its Contradictions]. *Keizai*, no. 211 (November 1981), 73–91.

Aonuma Yoshimatsu. 'Chūkan kaikyū no jittai wa kō da!' [The Reality of the Middle Class Is Thus!]. *Jitsugyō no Nihon* [Industrial Japan], no. 6, 1 (1967), 46–65.

Arima Jirō. '80 nendai jōhōka to media kōzō no saihensei' [The Transformation of Information in the 1980s and the Reorganisation of the Structure of the Media]. *Keizai*, no. 206 (June 1981), 52–67.

Arita Kyōsuke. *Sōgō shōsha: mirai no kōzu o saguru* [General Trading Companies: In Search of a Future Plan]. Tokyo: Nihon keizai shinbunsha, 1970.

Asahi Nenkan [Asahi Yearbook], 1981. Tokyo: Asahi shinbunsha, 1981.

Bōei hakusho. See Bōeichō.

Bōeichō [Defence Agency]. *Bōei hakusho* [White Paper on Defence], 1976 and 1981. Tokyo: Ōkurashō insatsukyoku, 1976 and 1981.

Chingin seido kenkyūkai to rōdoshō chingin fukushibu [Wage Systems Research Society and the Wages and Welfare Department of the Ministry of Labour]. *Teinen enchō to kore kara no chingin seido* [Extending the Retirement Age and the Wage System from Now On]. Tokyo: Sangyō rōdō chōsajo, 1977.

Chūshō kigyō hakusho. See under Chūshō kigyōchō.

Chūshō kigyōchō [Small and Medium Enterprise Agency]. *Chūshō kigyō hakusho* [White Paper on Small and Medium Enterprises], 1975 and 1980. Tokyo: Ōkurashō insatsukyoku, 1976 and 1981.

Dai 4 kai kōgyō jittai kihon chōsa hōkokusho [Report on the Fourth Basic Survey of Factory Conditions]. *Sōkatsuhen* [Summary volume]. Tokyo: Tsūshō sangyō chōsakai, 1974.

Dai 4 kai kōgyō jittai kihon chōsa hōkokusho. See under Chūshō kigyōchō.

Dokusen bunseki kenkyūkai [Research Association for the Analysis of Monopoly]. 'Nihon jūtaku kōdan: yachin, kōdan minshuka mondai' [The Japan Housing Corporation: Rents and the Problems of Democratising the Corporation]. *Keizai*, no. 164 (December 1977), 186–209.

Enomoto Masatoshi. 'Gendai shihonshugiron no hōhō' [On the Method of Present-Day Theory of Capitalism]. *Keizaigaku Hihan*, no. 2 (1977), 13–35.

Fujii Mitsuo. 'Sen'i sangyō ni okeru kaigai chokusetsu tōshi' [Direct Overseas Investment in the Textile Industry]. *Keizai*, no. 175 (November 1978), 85–108.

Fujii Mitsuo *et al*. *Nihon takokuseki kigyō no shiteki tenkai* [The Historical Development of Japanese Multi-National Enterprises], vols. 1 and 2. Gendai shihonshugi sōsho [Modern Capitalism Series], nos. 12 and 13. Tokyo: Ōtsuki shoten, 1979.

Fujimoto Takeshi. *Saitei chinginsei* [Minimum Wage System]. Iwanami shinsho, no. 629. Tokyo: Iwanami shoten, 1967.

Fujin rōdō no jitsujō. See Rōdōshō fujin–shōnen kyoku.

Furukawa Noboru, ed. *Chingin kentō shiryō* [Materials for Investigating Wages], 1982. Tokyo: Nihon hōrei, 1981.

Gendai no kanrishoku mondai. See Rōmu gyōsei kenkyūjo.

Genshiryoku Iinkai [Committee on Atomic Power]. *Genshiryoku hakusho* [White Paper on Atomic Power], 1978. Tokyo: Ōkurashō insatsukyoku, 1979.

Giga Sō'ichirō. 'Kōzō fukyō gyōshu o meguru shomujun' [Concerning All the Contradictions of the Structurally Depressed Industries]. *Keizai*, no. 167 (March 1978), 54–9.

Hayashi Masaki. 'Mekatoronikusuka to Nihonteki keiei' [Mechatronics-isation and Japanese-Style Management]. *Keizai*, no. 203 (March 1981), 49–62.

Hino Hideitsu. 'Jūdaika suru iryō mondai' [The Growing Weight of Medical Problems]. *Keizai*, no. 200 (December 1980), 95–109.

Hirano Yoshitarō. *Nihon shihonshugi shakai no kikō: shiteki katei yori no kyūmei* [The Structure of Capitalist Society in Japan: An Investigation of the Historical Process], 3rd edn. Tokyo: Iwanami shoten, 1967.

Hironaka Toshio. *Sengo Nihon no keisatsu* [The Police in Postwar Japan]. Iwanami shinsho, no. 684. Tokyo: Iwanami shoten, 1968.

Hōchikei santankumi kyōtō gikai [The Joint Struggle Committee of the Three Hōchi-Related Unions]. *Hayaku takaku shōri o* [For a Quick and Gainful Victory]. Tokyo: Rōdō junpōsha, 1976.

Horie Masanori. *Nihon no rōdōsha kaikyū* [The Japanese Working Class]. Tokyo: Iwanami shoten, 1962.

Hōsei Daigaku, Ōhara shakai mondai kenkyūjo [Ōhara Institute for Social Research, Hōsei University]. *Nihon rōdō nenkan* [The Labour Yearbook of Japan], 1977 and 1982. Tokyo: Rōdō junpōsha, 1976 and 1981.

Imazaki Akemi. *Mitsubishi teikoku no shinwa: kyodai kigyō no genba: rōdōsha gun* [The Myth of the Mitsubishi Empire: The Shop Floor in Giant Corporations: The Work Group]. Tokyo: Rōdō junpōsha, 1977.

Iwata Yukimoto. *Gendai no chūryū kaikyū* [The Present-Day Middle Class]. Tokyo: Nihon keizai shinbunsha, 1971.

Jigyōsho tōkei chōsa hōkoku. See *under* Sōrifu tōkeikyoku.

Jinjiin [National Personnel Authority]. *Kōmuin hakusho* [White Paper on National Civil Servants], 1981. Tokyo: Ōkurashō insatsukyoku, 1981.

Jinjiin kyūyokyoku [Salaries Bureau of the National Personnel Authority]. *Minkan kyūyo no jittai* [The Realities of Private Salaries], 1981. Tokyo: Ōkurashō insatsukyoku, 1981.

Kabushiki bunpu jōkyō chōsa. See Zenkoku shōken torihikijo.

Kajinishi Mitsuhaya *et al. Nihon shihonshugi no botsuraku* [The Downfall of Japanese Capitalism]. Nihon ni okeru shihonshugi no hattatsu [The Development of Japanese Capitalism], vol. 7. Tokyo: Tokyo Daigaku shuppankai, 1975.

Kakuta Noboru. 'Kōtō kyōiku saihen to shigaku' [The Reorganisation of Higher Education and Private Institutions]. *Keizai*, no. 209 (September 1981), 55–65.

Kamata Satoshi. *Shitsugyō: fukyō to gōrika no saizensen kara* [Unemployment: Right from the Front Line of the Recession and Rationalisation]. Tokyo: Chikuma shobō, 1979.

Tōsan [Bankruptcy]. Tokyo: San'ichi shobō, 1979.

Katō Ei'ichi. 'Gendai shihonshugiron no shikaku' [A View of Present-Day Theory of Capitalism]. *Keizaigaku Hihan*, no. 1 (1976), 9–33.

Keisatsu hakusho. See Keisatsuchō.

Keisatsuchō [Police Agency]. *Keisatsu hakusho* [White Paper on the Police], 1979 and 1981. Tokyo: Ōkurashō insatsukyoku, 1979 and 1981.

Keizai kikakuchō [Economic Planning Agency]. *Keizai hakusho* [White Paper on the Economy], 1979 and 1981. Tokyo: Ōkurashō insatsukyoku, 1979 and 1981.
Shin keizai shakai nanakanen keikaku [New Seven Year Socio-Economic Plan]. Tokyo: Ōkurashō insatsukyoku, 1979.
Keizai kikakuchō keizai kenkyūjo [Institute of Economic Research of the Economic Planning Agency]. *Kokumin keizai keisan nenpō* [Annual Report on National Economic Accounts], 1981. Tokyo: Ōkurashō insatsukyoku, 1981.
Kenmochi Kazumi. *Soshite, shitsugyōsha wa nakotta* [And the Unemployed Were Left Behind]. Tokyo: Tabata shoten, 1979.
Tōsan no naka no rōdō undō [The Workers' Movement in the Midst of Bankruptcies]. Tokyo: Shakai hyōronsha, 1978.
Kigyō keiretsu sōran. See under Shūkan Tōyō Keizai.
Kimoto Shin'ichirō. 'Seisan katei no saihen to "gōrika": sakushu kyōka' [Reorganisation of the Production Process and 'Rationalisation': Strengthening Exploitation]. *Keizai*, no. 202 (February 1981), 35–49.
Kogane Yoshihiro. *Nihonteki sangyō shakai no kōzō* [The Structure of the Japanese Industrial Society]. Tokyo: Sangyō nōritsu tanki daigaku shuppanbu, 1975.
Kojima Kenji. *Nihon no chingin* [Wages in Japan], 2nd edn. Iwanami shinsho, no. 716. Tokyo: Iwanami shoten, 1975.
Kojin kigyō keizai chōsa nenpō. See under Sōrifu tōkeikyoku.
Kokuzeichō [National Taxation Agency]. *Kokuzeichō tōkei nenpōsho* [Annual Statistical Report of the National Taxation Agency]. No. 100, 1974 and no. 105, 1979. Tokyo: Kokuzeichō, 1976 and 1981.
Kokuzeichō chōkan kanbō sōmuka [Administrative Division of the Secretariat of the Director of the National Taxation Agency]. *Zeimu tōkei kara mita minkan kyūyo no jittai* [The Real Situation of Private Incomes from the View of Taxation Statistics], 1980. Tokyo: Ōkurashō insatsukyoku, 1981.
Kokuzeichō tōkei nenpōsho. See Kokuzeichō.
Komatsu Ryūji. *Kigyōbetsu kumiai no seisei* [The Formation of Enterprise Unions]. Tokyo: Ocha no mizu shōbo, 1971.
Kōnenreisha koyō kaihatsu kyōkai [Association for the Development of Elderly People's Employment]. *Teinen hakusho* [White Paper on Retirement]. Tokyo: Kōnenreisha koyō kaihatsu kyōkai, 1980.
Kōsei tōkei kyōkai [Health and Welfare Statistics Association]. *Kokumin eisei no dōkō: kōsei no shihyō* [The Direction of the People's Health: Indices of Welfare]. Tokushū [Special issue], 26, 9 (1979). Tokyo: Kōsei tōkei kyōkai, 1979.
Kōseishō [Welfare Ministry]. *Kōsei hakusho* [White Paper on Welfare], 1981. Tokyo: Ōkurashō insatsukyoku, 1981.
Kudō Akira. 'Nihon keizai no genkyokumen to futatsu no seisaku rosen, jōge' [The Present Economic Situation in Japan and Two Political Lines, parts 1 and 2]. *Keizei*, no. 201 (January 1981), 94–124; no. 207 (July 1981), 8–51.
Kurokawa Toshio. *Gendai no chingin riron* [Modern Theory of Wages]. Tokyo: Rōdō junpōsha, 1976.
Kurono Munemitsu. 'Dokushihō kaisei mondai to Fukuda naikaku: Nihon dokusen shihon' [The Fukuda Cabinet and the Problems of Reforming the Anti-Monopoly Law: Japanese Monopoly Capital]. *Keizai*, no. 158 (June 1977), 69–81.
Kyōgoku Takanori. 'Nihon gata fukushi shakai ron o hihan suru' [A Criticism of the Japanese-Style Welfare Theory]. *Keizai*, no. 200 (December 1980), 65–79.
Maeda Toshimitsu. *Nihon shihonshugi to tochi mondai* [Japanese Capitalism and Problems of Land]. Tokyo: Shinhyōron, 1972.
Minkan kyūyo no kittai. See Jinjiin kyūyokyuku.

Miyajima Ryōhei. 'Fukushi no futan o dō kaiketsu sura ka' [How Shall We Solve the Social Welfare Burden?]. *Keizai*, no. 200 (December 1980), 42–52.

'Kōreika shakai to shakai hoshō' [Social Security and an Ageing Society]. *Keizai*, no. 176 (December 1978), 16–29.

Miyake Tōru. 'Dai toshien no jūtaku jijō' [The Metropolitan Housing Situation]. *Keizai*, no. 208 (August 1981), 68–80.

Miyazaki Yoshikazu. *Gendai no Nihon kigyō o kangaeru* [Considering Modern Japanese Enterprises]. Iwanami shinsho, no. 883. Tokyo: Iwanami shoten, 1974.

Monbushō [Ministry of Education]. *Wagakuni no kyōiku suijun* [The Level of Our Country's Education], 1975 and 1980. Tokyo: Ōkurashō insatsukyoku, 1976 and 1981.

Moritaka Ken'ichirō. 'Kokudo kaihatsu no tenkai to minshuteki tenkan no tenbō, ge' [The Unfolding of Territorial Development and the View of Democratic Change, part 2]. *Keizai*, no. 161 (September 1977), 98–108.

Moriya Fumio. 'Takuchi to takuchi kakaku ni tsuite' [Concerning Housing Land and Housing Land Prices]. *Keizai*, no. 174 (October 1978), 151–69.

Motojima Kunio. 'Daikigyō no naka de yureru kyōsōteki jinsei' [Competitive Life Trembling Inside Large Companies]. *Keizai*, no. 210 (October 1981), 75–87.

Nakabaya Shikenjirō. *Rōdō undō to tōitsu sensen* [The Labour Movement and the United Front]. Tokyo: Rōdō junpōsha, 1969.

Nihon fujin dantai renkōkai [Federation of Japanese Women's Organisations]. *Fujin hakusho* [White Paper on Women], 1979. Tokyo: Sōdō bunka, 1979.

Nihon kagakusha kaigi [Japan Conference of Scientists]. *Gendai no shihonshugi* [Modern Capitalism]. Nihon keizai no kōzōteki kiki [The Structural Crisis of the Japanese Economy], vol. 1. Tokyo: Ōtsuki shoten, 1976.

Nihon Kyōsantō chūō iinkai kikanshi keieikyoku [Management Bureau of the Organs of the Central Committee of the Japan Communist Party]. *Seiji nenkan* [Politics Yearbook], 1974. Tokyo, 1974.

Nihon Kyōsantō chūō iinkai keizai seisaku iinkai [Economic Policy Committee of the Central Committee of the Japan Communist Party]. *Nihon keizai e no teigen: kiki ni chōsen suru saiken keikaku* [A Proposal for the Japanese Economy: A Plan for Reconstruction That Challenges the Crisis], 2nd edn. Tokyo: Nihon Kyōsantō chūō iinkai shuppankyoku, 1979.

Nihon rikurūto sentā [Japan Recruit Centre], *Rikurūto chōsa geppō* [Monthly Report on Recruit Surveys], April 1976.

Nihon rōdō nenkan. See Hōsei Daigaku.

Nihon seisansei honbu [Japan Productivity Centre]. *Teinen enchō to koyō shogū seido no kaikaku* [Extending the Retirement Age and Reforming Systems of Employment and Conditions]. Tokyo: Nihon seisansei honbu, 1981.

Nishioka Yukiyasu *et al.* 'Hiyatoi rōdōsha: San'ya no seikatsu to rōdō' [Day-Labouring Workers: Life and Work in Sanya]. *Shakai kagaku nenpō* [Social Science Yearbook], no. 8 (1974).

Nōka chōsa hōkokusho. See under Nōrinshō nōrin keizaikyoku tōkei jōhōbu.

Nōrinshō nōrin keizaikyoku tōkei jōhōbu [Statistics and Information Department of the Ministry of Agriculture and Forestry]. *Nōka chōsa hōkokusho* [Report on the Census of Agricultural Households], 1975. *Nōka jinkō hen* [Volume on Agricultural Households and Population]. Tokyo: Nōrin tōkei kyōkai, 1977.

Nōrinshō tōkeihyō [Statistical Yearbook of the Ministry of Agriculture and Forestry], 1974–5 (Tokyo: Nōrin tōkei kyōkai, 1976).

Nōrinsuisanshō keizaikyoku tōkei jōhōbu [Statistics and Information Department of the Ministry of Agriculture, Forestry, and Fisheries]. *Nōrinsuisanshō tōkeihyō* [Statistical Yearbook of the Ministry of Agriculture, Forestry, and Fisheries], 1979–80. Tokyo: Nōrin tōkei kyōkai, 1981.

Nōrinsuisanshō tōkeihyō. See Norinsuisanshō keizaikyoku tōkei jōhōbu.

Ōhashi Ryūken. *Nihon no kaikyū kōsei* [Japan's Class Composition]. Tokyo: Iwanami shoten, 1971.

Ōki Kazukuni *et al. Gendai koyō mondai to rōdō kumiai* [Trade Unions and the Present-Day Problems of Employment]. Tokyo: Rōdō junpōsha, 1978.

Okuchi Masashi. 'Keizai seisaku no tenkai to jūtaku mondai' [The Development of Economic Policy and Housing Problems]. *Keizai*, no. 208 (August 1981), 48–67.

Ōkurashō [Ministry of Finance]. *Zaisei kin'yū tōkei geppō* [Monthly Bulletin on Monetary and Financial Statistics]. Hōnin kigyō tōkei nenpō tokushū [Special Yearly Issue on Statistics in Incorporated Enterprises], nos. 295 and 355 (November 1976 and 1981). Tokyo: Ōkurashō insatsukyoku, 1976 and 1981.

Ōkurashō shukeikyoku chōsaka [Research Section of the Budget Bureau of the Ministry of Finance]. *Zaisei tōkei* [Financial Statistics], 1979 and 1980. Tokyo: Ōkurashō insatsukyoku, 1979 and 1980.

Ōno Akio. *Zengakuren: sono kōdō to riron* [Zengakuren: Its Theory and Action]. Tokyo: Kōdansha, 1968.

Ōno Takao. 'Nihon keizai no kiki to sanzensō' [The Crisis in the Japanese Economy and the Third National Development Plan]. *Keizai*, no. 167 (March 1978), 214–23.

Ono Yoshihiko. *Gendai Nihon shihonshugi no kiki: kokka dokusen shihonshugi no tenkai* [The Present Crisis of Japanese Capitalism: The Development of State Monopoly Capitalism]. Tokyo: Shinsensha, 1976.

Ōuchi Hideaki, Kamakura Takao, and Nitta Shunzō. *Gendai shihonshugi: sengo taisei no hōkai to saihen* [Modern Capitalism: The Collapse and Reorganisation of the Postwar System]. Sengo Nihon no kihon kōzō [The Basic Structure of Postwar Japan], vols. 4 and 5. Tokyo: Nihon hyōronsha, 1975.

Rōdō daijin kanbō tōkei jōhōbu [The Statistical Information Department of the Secretariat of the Minister of Labour]. *Maitsuki kinrō chōsa sōgō hōkokusho* [General Report on the Survey of Monthly Employment], 1975. Tokyo: Rōdō daijin kanbō tōkei jōhōbu, 1976.

Teinensei no jittai to teinen enchōgo no rōdō jōken [The Realities of the Retirement System and the Conditions of Labour After the Extension of the Retirement Age]. Tokyo: Rōdō hōrei kyōkai, 1980.

Rōdō hakusho. See Rōdōshō.

Rōdōshō [Ministry of Labour]. *Rōdō hakusho* [White Paper on Labour], 1976 and 1981. Tokyo: Nihon rōdō kyōkai, 1976 and 1981.

Rōdōshō fujin–shōnen kyoku [The Women and Young People's Bureau of the Ministry of Labour]. *Fujin rōdō no jitsujō* [The Real Situation of Women Workers], 1976 and 1981. Tokyo: Ōkurashō insatsukyoku, 1976 and 1981.

Rōdōshō rōdō kijunkyoku [Labour Standards Bureau of the Ministry of Labour]. *Teinen tōtatsusha chōsa no kekka* [Results of the Survey of People Who Reach Retirement Age], 1975. Tokyo: Rōdōshō, 1975.

Rōdōshō tōkei jōhōbu [Information Department of the Ministry of Labour]. *Maitsuki kinrō tōkei yōran* [Summary Tables of Monthly Employment Statistics]. Tokyo: Rōdō hōrei kyōkai, 1980.

Rōmu gyōsei kenkyūjo [Research Institute of Labour Administration]. *Gendai no kanrishoku mondai: sono tamenteki kentō to kaiketsu e no michi* [Problems of Contemporary Management: Towards a Thorough Investigation and Solution]. Tokyo: Rōmu gyōsei kenkyūjo, 1976.

Sakisaka Itsurō. *Rōdōsha to tomo ni* [Together with Workers]. Tokyo: Rōdō daigaku, 1976.

Sasaki Noriaki. 'Enerugi sangyō no shindōkō to tenbō' [New Directions and Outlook for the Energy Industries]. *Keizai*, no. 167 (March 1978), 66–175.

Shima Yasuhiko, Udaka Motosuke, Ōhashi Ryūken, and Usami Seijirō, eds. *Shin Marukusu keizai kōza* [Lectures on New Marxist Economics], 6 vols. Tokyo: Yūhikaku, 1976.

Shin keizai shakai nanakanen keikaku. See under Keizai kikakuchō.

Shiozawa Miyoko. *Kekkon taishokugo no watashitachi* [Our Lives After Retirement due to Marriage]. Iwanami shinsho, no. 797. Tokyo: Iwanami shoten, 1971.

Shōji Hikaru and Miyamoto Ken'ichi. *Nihon no kōgai* [Pollution in Japan]. Iwanami shinsho, no. 941. Tokyo: Iwanami shoten, 1975.

Shūgyō kōzō kihon chōsa hōkoku. See under Sōrifu tōkeikyoku.

Shūkan Tōyō Keizai [The Oriental Economist]. *Chingin sōran* [A General View of Wages], 1977. Rinji zōkan [Special issue], no. 3980. Tokyo: Tōyō keizai shinpōsha, 1976.

Dēta fuairu: chingin, nenkin, jinji kanri [Data File: Wages, Pensions, and Personnel Management], 1982. Rinji zōkan, no. 4342. Tokyo: Tōyō keizai shinpōsha, 1981.

Keizai tōkei nenkan [Yearbook of Economic Statistics], 1979. Rinji zōkan, no. 4153. Tokyo: Tōyō keizai shinpōsha, 1979.

Kigyō keiretsu sōran [A General View of Linked Companies], 1982. Rinji zōkan, no. 4333. Tokyo: Tōyō keizai shinpōsha, 1981.

Kaigai shinshutsu kigyō sōran [Japanese Multinationals, Facts and Figures], 1981. Rinji zōkan, no. 4261. Tokyo: Tōyō keizai shinpōsha, 1980.

Sōrifu tōkeikyoku [Bureau of Statistics, Office of the Prime Minister]. *Jigyōsho tōkei chōsa hōkoku* [Establishment Census of Japan], 1972 and 1978. Vol. 4, *Sabisugyō* [Services]. Tokyo: Nihon tōkei kyōkai, 1974 and 1980.

Kojin kigyō keizai chōsa nenpō [Annual Report on the Unincorporated Enterprise Survey], 1980. Tokyo: Nihon tōkei kyōkai, 1981.

Kokufu chōsa [National Wealth Survey], 1970. Vol 6, *Kakei shisan chōsa hōkoku* [Report on the Survey of Household Assets]. Tokyo: Ōkurashō insatsukyoku, 1973.

Shūgyō kōzō kihon chōsa hōkoku [Employment Status Survey], 1974 and 1979. *Zenkokuhen* [All Japan]. Tokyo: Nihon tōkei kyōkai, 1975 and 1980.

Zenkoku shōhi jittai chōsa hōkoku [National Survey of Family Income and Expenditure], 1974 and 1979. *Chochikuhen* [Savings]. Tokyo: Nihon tōkei kyōkai, 1975 and 1980.

Sumita Shōji. 'Jūtaku mondai no konnichiteki seikaku to seisaku kadai' [The Present-Day Character of the Housing Problem and the Subject of Policy]. *Keizai*, no. 164 (December 1977), 125–45.

Sumiya Mikio, Kobayashi Ken'ichi, and Hiyōdō Tsutomu. *Nihon shihonshugi to rōdō mondai* [Japanese Capitalism and Problems of Labour]. Tokyo: Tokyo Diagaku shuppansha, 1967.

Takenaka Emiko. *Fujin no chingin to fukushi* [The Wages and Welfare of Women]. Osaka: Sōgensha, 1977.

Gendai no fujin mondai [The Modern Problems of Women]. Osaka: Sōgensha, 1972.

Teinen hakusho. See Kōnenreisha kōyō kaihatsu kyōkai.

Teinen tōtatsusha chōsa no kekka. See Rōdōshō rōdō kijunkyoku.

Tōbata Sei'ichi. *Nihon shihonshugi no keiseisha* [The Makers of Japanese Capitalism]. Iwanami shinsho, no. 513. Tokyo: Iwanami shoten, 1964.

Tōkei bunseki kenkyūkai [Research Association for Analysing Statistics]. 'Bukka to kakei' [Prices and Household Finances]. *Keizai*, no. 202 (February 1981), 187–91.

'Kokusai kyōsōryoku no himitsu' [The Secret of International Competitive Power]. *Keizai*, no. 209 (September 1981), 162–6.

'Konnichi no gakusei seikatsu' [Living Conditions of Today's Students]. *Keizai*, no. 205 (May 1981), 211–16.

'Koyō to shitsugyō' [Employment and Unemployment]. *Keizai*, no. 204 (April 1981), 148–53.

Tokutake Toshio. 'Kyōkasho no kiki: jisshitsuteki kokuteika no kiken' [The Crisis of School Textbooks: The Danger of Virtual State Texts]. *Keizai*, no. 207 (July 1981), 79–87.

Tsūshō sangyōshō [Ministry of International Trade and Industry]. *Tsūshō hakusho* [White Paper on Trade and Industry], 1981. Tokyo: Ōkurashō insatsukyoku, 1981.

Tsūshō sangyōshō tsūshō seisakukyoku [Trade Policy Bureau of the Ministry of International Trade and Industry]. *Zusetsu tsūshō hakusho* [White Paper on Trade and Industry in Diagrams], 1979. Tokyo: Tsūshō sangyō chōsakai, 1979.

Umino Hisao. 'Chūshō kigyō no genkyokumen to rōdō undō no shiten' [The Present Situation in Small Firms and the Labour Movement Viewpoint]. *Keizai*, no. 202 (February 1981), 50–60.

Wagakuni no kyōiku suijun. See Monbushō.

Washimi Tomoyoshi. 'Kyōki no Rēgan gunkaku to Nihon daigunkaku' [The Insane Reagan Military Expansion and the Huge Japanese Military Expansion]. *Keizai*, no. 211 (November 1981), 120–9.

Watanabe Mutsumi *et al. Chūshō kigyō to rōdō kumiai* [Small and Medium Enterprises and Trade Unions]. Tokyo: Rōdō junpōsha, 1977.

Yamashiro Gorō. 'Zaikai no sangyō kōzō "kaikaku" no nerai' [Zaikai's Aim of a 'Reformed' Industrial Structure]. *Keizai*, no. 167 (March 1978), 28–38.

Yasuda Sabirō. *Gendai Nihon no kaikyū ishiki* [Class Consciousness in Modern Japan]. Tokyo: Yūhikaku, 1973.

Yoneda Yasuhiko. 'Sutagufurēshon to Nihon keizai no minshuteki saiken' [Stagflation and the Democratic Reconstruction of the Japanese Economy]. *Keizai*, no. 168 (April 1978), pp. 110–18.

Zaisei kin'yū tōkei geppō. See Ōkurashō.

Zaisei tōkei. See Ōkurashō shukeikyoku chōsaka.

Zeimu tōkei kara mita minkan kyūyo no jittai. See Kokuzeichō chōkan kanbō sōmuka.

Zenkoku shōhi jittai chōsa hōkoku. See under Sōrifu tōkeikyoku.

Zenkoku shōken torihikijo [Japan Stock Exchange]. *Kabushiki bunpu jōkyō chōsa* [Survey on the Distribution of Shares], 1975 and 1980. Tokyo: Zenkoku shōken torihikijo, 1976 and 1981.

Index

agriculture, *see* peasantry
Almond, Gabriel, 3
Althusser, Louis, 2, 8, 215, 216, 287, 310

bankruptcies, 44, 81–2, 233, 237–8, 243,
    245, 248, 262
banks, *see* finance
bonuses, 163–5
bourgeoisie, 12–61; theory, 12–14, 22–4,
    33–5; corporation directors, 24–5;
    corporation managers, 26–31;
    estimated size, 33; fractions, 33ff, 46ff,
    57ff; interlocking directorships, 51–2;
    organisations of, 47ff; property
    ownership, 15–23
budget, 229, 262, 315; *see also* state:
    accumulation functions: demand
    management
burakumin, 191

capital: control, 23, 124ff; functions of,
    22–3, 27–8, 124ff; ownership, 15–23,
    122–3
chemical industry, 244–5
Chūritsurōren, 201–2, 207
class: theory, 9–10, 22, 24, *and see*
    infrastructure–superstructure *and theory
    of each class*; class membership of
    employees, 171, 193; consciousness, *see*
    ideology; mobility, 142, 292ff;
    summary of Japanese class structure,
    319
computers, 243, 246–7, 249; *see also* robots
construction, 221–2, 248–50; *see also*
    housing
control: of labour power, 26–8, 126; of
    means of production, 23ff, 124ff
crime, 305, 311–13
crisis, 47, 219–20, 317–18; of Japanese
    capitalism, 47, 219–20, 229, 231–6,
    254; and middle class, 152–4; of
    'structurally depressed industries,'
    240–1; of 'underconsumption,' 261ff;
    and working class, 208–14; *see also*

bankruptcies; profitability;
    rationalisations

day labourers, *see* working class: reserve
    army
defence, *see* military
depression cartels, 237–8
Diet, *see* parliamentary system
Dōmei, 200–1, 207–8, 320–1, 328

economism, 219–20
education system, 142–5, 154, 287–98; *see
    also* university
elections, *see* parliamentary system; political
    parties
electrical/electronics industry, 241, 244
employment, 199, 209, 236, 239;
    employment system, 159ff, 214, *and see*
    retirement; *see also* rationalisations;
    unemployment
energy, 222, 228; nuclear, 223–7, 290; *see
    also* state: accumulation functions:
    energy supply
epistemology, 8–9
excess capacity, 227, 236, 241, 243–4

family labour, unpaid, 67, 69, 72, 77–9,
    85–6, 184–5
family system, 114–17, 119, 137, 155, 160,
    163, 173–4, 180, 311
farmers, *see* peasantry
feminism: theory, 11, 324–6; in Japan,
    327–9; *see also* patriarchy; women
finance, 47, 50–1, 233–5

GDP, growth of real, 253, 265
Godelier, Maurice, 2, 216
government, *see* state
government expenditure, *see* state:
    accumulation functions: demand
    management

Halliday, Jon, 1–2
hours, 69–70, 77–9, 176–7, 199

housing: home ownership, 92–5, 279–82; state housing, 276ff

idealism, 8
ideology, 62–3, 87, 93–4, 112–19, 137, 145–9, 155, 196, 202–8, 287, 289, 299–300, 302, 311; *see also* education; parliamentary system
ie, *see* family system
imperialism, 237–8, 240, 244, 252, 256–61, 314–16
income: of middle class, 131–2, 134–5, 138; of peasants, 98, 104, 110; for performing functions of capital, 23–4, 28–9; of petty bourgeoisie, 71–2, 76, 79, 84; from property, 17–21; of working class, *see* wages
inflation, 227–8, 262, 271; *see also* land: prices
infrastructure–superstructure, 2–5, 12, 114, 216–18, 324–6

Japan Communist Party, 39, 46, 59–61, 87–8, 309, 322, 327, 329
Japan Socialist Party, 119, 303, 309, 313, 329

Keidanren, 55
keiretsu, 47–56, 118

labour productivity, 199, 236, 248
land: agricultural holdings, 93, 96–7; prices, 92–9, 233–4, 279
liberal democracy, *see* parliamentary system
Liberal Democratic Party, 89–90, 112, 117, 119–20, 274, 290, 303–9
living standards, *see* state: functions of social control: welfare state
Lockheed scandal, 305

Mao Tse-tung, 7
Marx, Karl, 2–6
middle class: theory, 122–7; composition, 127–8, 140; crisis and struggle, 152–4; educationists, 127–33; ideology, 145–9; income, 131–5, 138; medical practitioners, 127–9, 134–5; nurses, 127–30, 132, 134; organisation, 149–51; reproduction of, 141–5; supervisors, 136–9
military, 139–40, 227, 314–16; *see also* repressive apparatuses
MITI (Ministry of International Trade and Industry), 87, 223
money supply, 262–3
monopoly: theory, 33–5, 37; in Japan, 37–41; monopoly capital, 47

motor vehicles, 241, 245–6

Nakane Chie, 149
nenkō system, *see* wages: by length of service
Nihon Ishikai, 149, 151
Nikkyōso, 149–51, 290
Nōkyō, 118–20

Ōhashi Ryūken, 2, 24, 324
ownership: land, 21; money wealth, 18–21, 122–3; shares, 15–17, 21–3, 51–2

parliamentary system: theory, 298–300, 302, 303–4; Cabinets, 307–8; elections, 299–305; 'money power politics,' 305; personality politics, 303–9
part timers, *see* working class: reserve army
patriarchy, 11, 213–14, 297, 318, 322–7; *see also* family system; feminism; women
peasantry: theory, 91–4; composition, 99–101; decline of Japanese agriculture, 104–11; incomes, 98, 104, 110; organisation and ideology, 111–19; owned and cultivated land, 96–7; part and full time, 97–103; peasant struggles, 119–21; proletarianisation, 102–4
pensions, *see* retirement
Petri Camera, 321
petty bourgeoisie: theory, 59, 62–6; composition, 66–8, 85; incomes, 71–2, 76, 79, 84; in manufacturing, 69–74; organisation and ideology, 87–90; reproduction of, 80–6; in services, 74–7; in wholesale/retail, 77–80; women in, 80, 85–6
police, 139, 311, 313–14; *see also* repressive apparatuses
political parties: factions, 304–6; popular support of, 89–90, 112; right to left, 303; *see also* parliamentary system
pollution, 106, 108, 120–1
Poulantzas, Nicos, 2–3
prime ministers, *see* parliamentary system: Cabinets
productive forces: uneven development of, 64, 77, 95, 104–6
profitability, 36–7, 71, 72–3, 76, 79, 236

rationalisations, 221, 238–9, 243–7, 251, 255, 257; *see also* employment; state: accumulation functions: restructuring; unemployment
raw materials, 225, 227; *see also* trade
rent, 37, 91–2, 225
repressive apparatuses, 139–41, 286, 310–16
reserve army: peasantry as, 86, 92–3, 97,

116, 284; petty bourgeoisie as, 81–6, 90; women as, 184–5, 194, 284, *and see* women; *see also* unemployment; working class
retirement, 83–6, 182, 187–91, 285; pay, 174–6, 275, 285
revolutionary strategy, 39, 46, 58, 59–61, 88–9, 119–21, 152–4, 212–14, 317–29
right-wing organisations, 310
ringisei, 218
robots, 245–7; *see also* computers
Rōdō Jōhō, 329
rōnin, 293–4; *see also* education system

savings, 18–19, 284
Sayer, Derek, 2
Self Defence Forces, *see* military
shipbuilding, 243–4
sōgō shōsha, 53
Sōhyō, 200–1, 207, 321
spring offensive, 283
state: theory, 2, 5, 215–18, 266–8; *see also* infrastructure–superstructure
accumulation functions: contradictions of state management, 239, 257, 264–5; demand management, 221, 227, 261–5, 276; discount rate, 235, 262, 264; energy supply, 223–7; fiscal crisis, 264–5, 285; history of, 218–19; national railways, 220–1; planning, 251–3, 265; public borrowing, 262–5; public corporations, 220ff, 228–9; public utility charges, 221, 227, 271, 273; restructuring, 222, 229ff; transport, 221–2; *see also* budget; taxation
functions of social control: contradictions of state involvement, 285; education, 287–98; health service, 275–6; parliamentarism, 298–310; public housing, 276–82; repression, 310–16; unemployment measures, 284–6; welfare state, 268–87, financing, 270–6
steel industry, 243
strikes, 312–13; *see also* spring offensive
sub-contracts, 42–5, 57, 59, 68, 72–3, 77

Tanaka Machinery Co., 321–2
taxation, 264–5, 270–4, 276, 285
textiles, 237–9

trade: export industries, 241–6; import of raw materials, 225, 227, 240–3; terms of trade, 225
trade unions, 148–9, 197–202

unemployment: concealed in family, 184–5, 194; concealed in peasantry, 116; concealed in petty bourgeoisie, 81–6, 90, 284; registered, 211; after retirement, 188–9, 191; state policy, 284–6; *see also* reserve army; retirement
university: employment of graduates, 70; prestige universities, 142–3, 293, 295; rate of attendance, 143, 153, 292, 295; *see also* education system
unproductive labour, 24–7
unproductive sectors, 233–5, 249, 251

wages: by education, 136, 160–2; by length of service, 82, 84–5, 160–5, 282–4; of part-time and temporary workers, 188, 192, 211; real wage index, 199, 211, 273; by sex, 160–6, 181; wage costs, 248; *see also* income
welfare: company, 166–7; state, 268–87
women: class consciousness, 204–6; class membership, 319, 323–4; in education system, 291, 296–7; employment, 42, 192, 194, 209; in middle class, 128, 140; in peasantry, 101; in petty bourgeoisie, 80, 85–6; in police and military, 139–40; retirement, 174–6, 189; skills, 77; in unions, 200; violence against, 310–11; in working class, 160, 169–72, 180–5, 192, 194; *see also* feminism; patriarchy; wages
working class: theory, 13–14, 58, 156; crisis, 208–14; ideology, 202–8; labour aristocracy, 158–72; mass worker, 172–8; organisation, 197–202; in peasant households, 97, 101–2, 113–14; reserve army, 178–96, 209–11, 251; *see also* reserve army
Wright, Erik, 3, 122

yakuza, 310–11

Zengakuren, 151
Zenkin, 321, 327